Anonymous

A new Collection of Voyages, Discoveries and Travels

Vol. VII.: Containing whatever is worthy of Notice, in Europe, Asia, Africa...

Anonymous

A new Collection of Voyages, Discoveries and Travels
Vol. VII.: Containing whatever is worthy of Notice, in Europe, Asia, Africa...

ISBN/EAN: 9783744793551

Printed in Europe, USA, Canada, Australia, Japan

Cover: Foto ©Andreas Hilbeck / pixelio.de

More available books at **www.hansebooks.com**

A NEW
COLLECTION
OF
VOYAGES,
DISCOVERIES and TRAVELS:

CONTAINING

Whatever is worthy of Notice, in

EUROPE, ASIA,

AFRICA and AMERICA:

IN RESPECT TO

The Situation and Extent of Empires, Kingdoms, and Provinces; their Climates, Soil, Produce, &c.

WITH

The Manners and Cuftoms of the feveral Inhabitants; their Government, Religion, Arts, Sciences, Manufactures, and Commerce.

The whole confifting of fuch ENGLISH and FOREIGN Authors as are in moft Efteem; including the Defcriptions and Remarks of fome celebrated late Travellers, not to be found in any other Collection.

Illuftrated with a Variety of accurate

MAPS, PLANS, and elegant ENGRAVINGS.

VOL. VII.

LONDON:
Printed for J. KNOX, near Southampton-Street, in the Strand. MDCCLXVII.

CONTENTS

OF THE

SEVENTH VOLUME.

AN Account of the Country and Conſtitution of Great Britain in general; and of England in particular, Page 1

A ſhort general Deſcription of the City of London, the Metropolis of the Britiſh empire; the ſeveral Curioſities in the Tower, and the general Contents of the Britiſh Muſeum, 80

An Account of the Kingdom and Laws of Scotland; with the general Articles of its Union with that of England. 99

A Short View of the Naval Tranſactions of Britain; beginning with the reign of queen Elizabeth, and ending with the Peace of Verſailles in 1763,- 193

A Liſt of the Royal Navy of Great Britain, as it ſtood at the cloſe of the year 1762, 527

A

COLLECTION

OF

VOYAGES AND TRAVELS.

Of GREAT BRITAIN in general.

GREAT BRITAIN, the largeſt iſland' in Europe, comprehends the two kingdoms of England and Scotland, with the principality of Wales. Its latitude, at the Lizard Point in Cornwall, according to Moll, is 50° north, and at the head-land at Caithneſs in Scotland, 58° 30'; ſo that, according to the geometrical meaſure of Engliſh ſtatute miles, which is 69 miles and 864 feet to a degree, the length of the iſland, meaſured in a direct line, without attending to the hills and winding of the roads, is 587 miles. Its longitude, Teneriffe being the firſt meridian, is 9° 45' at the Land's-End in Cornwall, and at the South Foreland in Kent, 17° 15'. Now every degree of longitude in this latitude being about 38 ſtatute miles, the breadth therefore between theſe two extremities will be 285 miles.

As an iſland, this country has ſome peculiar natural advantages and diſadvantages: it is ſubject to perpetual varieties of heat and cold, wet and dry; but the heats in ſummer, and the colds in winter, are more temperate than in any part of the Continent that lies in the ſame latitude: the harbours in Holland, Germany, and Denmark, are blocked up with

with ice, while ours, which lie in the fame latitude, are open. To this moderation of the climate is attributed the long lives of many of the inhabitants; and to the fame caufe is owing that almoft perpetual verdure, in a manner peculiar to this country; which in the fummer is frequently refrefhed by feafonable fhowers, and by the warm vapours of the fea, in winter, is generally fecured from any long continuance of froft and fnow.

This happy fituation of our ifland can never be fufficiently valued, as it renders Great Britain a world, as it were, within itfelf, intirely independent of other nations; and furnifhes her with all the neceffaries of life, in fuch abundance, as enables her to fupply other nations.

That part of Great Britain which lies toward the Weftern Ocean, is mountainous, as Cornwall, Wales, and Cumberland; likewife fome of the interior counties, as part of Derbyfhire, Yorkfhire, Weftmorland, Northumberland, and near one half of Scotland. The eaftern and fouthern parts of the country, chiefly confift of little fruitful hills and vallies, champaign fields, inclofed grounds of arable, pafture, and meadow lands; agreeably intermixed with wood and water; and being much inclofed and cultivated, it abounds with profpects that in beauty can fcarcely be exceeded, even by the fictions of imagination.

It has on all fides very convenient harbours, and many extenfive navigable rivers, that convey the riches of all the nations of the known world into the very centre of the kingdom. The moft confiderable rivers in England are the Thames, Severn, and Humber; in Scotland, the Forth, Clyde, and Tay.

Various are the names by which this ifland hath been known, and as different are the reafons affigned for them. It was called Albion by the Greeks, Bretanica by the Phœnicians, and Brittannia by the Romans,

STONE HENGE, a celebrated Monument of the Druids on Salisbury Plain.

mans, who diftinguifhed that part, now the Highlands of Scotland, by the name of Caledonia.

The inhabitants of Great Britain and Ireland, according to fome calculations, fo late as the year 1758, allowing fix perfons to each houfe, are computed at eight millions; viz. in England and Wales 5,700,000; in Scotland 1,300,000; and in Ireland 1,000,000; to thefe may be added near 2,000,000 fuppofed to be in the Britifh fettlements in Afia, Africa, and America.

With refpect to the perfons and character of the Englifh, they are generally of a ftrong active make, well fhaped, and of good ftature. They are induftrious, lovers of the liberal arts, and capable of carrying them to the greateft perfection. They are neither fo heavy as the Germans, nor fo exceedingly mercurial as the French; but are obferved to be generally open and blunt in their behaviour, and particularly averfe to fervility and cringing. Their good nature, generofity and humanity, have been frequently fhewn to their enemies, in fuch a manner as to do honour even to human nature. The lenity of their laws in capital cafes; their compaffion for convicted criminals; even the general humanity of highwaymen and robbers of this nation, compared with thofe of other countries; are all convincing proofs that the fpirit of humanity is natural to them. The many noble foundations for the relief of the miferable and the friendlefs; the large annual fupplies from voluntary charities to thefe foundations, and on every other occafion where their benevolence is folicited, are alfo ftriking proofs of true goodnefs of heart and greatnefs of foul, for which this nation has been always diftinguifhed.

In point of courage no people exceed, and very few equal the Englifh; who are remarkable for this particular, that no people fhew a more refolute obftinacy in battle, though under the greateft difadvantages. Their valour and bravery, both by fea and land,

land, hath been so frequently exerted in many parts of the world, that the most formidable kingdoms have been constrained to yield to the superior force of their arms: so that Great Britain, at this time, by their courage and prudence, gives liberty to Europe, and has acquired an extent of territory equal to the Roman empire when in its meridian of power, and infinitely more useful to the mother country.

The women, beside their natural beauty, which is such as not to need the assistance of paint, so common in other countries, are still more to be valued for their prudent behaviour, thorough cleanliness, and a tender affection for their husbands and children. As to the faults of the English; foreigners have remarked that they are somewhat passionate, melancholy, fickle and unsteady; one moment applauding, what they detest in the next; and that the lower sort of people have too contemptible an idea of other nations; and are thence apt to treat strangers with rudeness. But this latter accusation seems rather to have been founded on particular instances, which a great relish for, and propensity to humour, so observable among the common people, may sometimes betray them into; than to belong to them as a national character.

Of the GOVERNMENT and CIVIL POLICY of BRITAIN.

In all states there is an absolute supreme power; to which the right of legislation belongs; and which, by the singular constitution of these kingdoms, is vested in the king, lords, and commons.

Of the King.

The supreme executive power of Great Britain, and Ireland, is vested by our constitution in a single person, king or queen; for it is indifferent to which

which sex the crown descends: the person entitled to it, whether male or female, is immediately invested with all the ensigns, rights, and prerogatives of sovereign power.

The grand fundamental maxim upon which the right of succession to the throne of these kingdoms depends, is: " that the crown, by common law and constitutional custom, is hereditary; and this in a manner peculiar to itself: but that the right of inheritance may from time to time be changed or limited by act of parliament: under which limitations the crown still continues hereditary."

King Egbert, king Canute, and king William I. have been successively constituted the common stocks, or ancestors, of this descent.

On the death of queen Elizabeth, without issue, the line of Henry VIII. became extinct. It therefore became necessary to recur to the other issue of Henry VII. by Elizabeth of York his queen: whose eldest daughter Margaret having married James IV. king of Scotland, king James the Sixth of Scotland, and of England the First, was the lineal descendant from that alliance. So that in his person, as clearly as in Henry VIII. centered all the claims of the different competitors from the conquest downward; he being indisputably the lineal heir of the conqueror. And, what is still more remarkable, in his person also centered the right of the Saxon monarchs, which had been suspended from the conquest till his accession. For, Margaret the sister of Edgar Atheling, the daughter of Edward the Outlaw, and granddaughter of king Edmund Ironside, was the person in whom the hereditary right of the Saxon kings, supposing it not abolished by the conquest, resided. She married Malcolm king of Scotland; and Henry II. by a descent from Matilda their daughter, is generally called the restorer of the Saxon line. But it must be remembered, that Malcolm by his Saxon queen had sons as well as daughters; and that the royal

royal family of Scotland, from that time downward, were the offspring of Malcolm and Margaret. Of this royal family king James I. was the direct lineal defcendant; and therefore united in his perfon every poffible claim, by hereditary right, to the Englifh as well as Scottifh throne, being the heir both of Egbert and William the Conqueror.

At the revolution, the convention of eftates, or reprefentative body of the nation, declared, that the mifconduct of king James II. amounted to an abdication of the government, and that the throne was thereby vacant.

In confequence of this vacancy, and from a regard to the ancient line, the convention appointed the next Proteftant heirs of the blood royal of king Charles I. to fill the vacant throne, in the old order of fucceffion; with a temporary exception, or preference, to the perfon of king William III.

On the impending failure of the Proteftant line of King Charles I. (whereby the throne might again have become vacant) the king and parliament extended the fettlement of the crown to the Proteftant line of King James I. viz. to the princefs Sophia of Hanover, and the heirs of her body, being Proteftants: and fhe is now the common ftock, from whom the heirs of the crown muft defcend.

The true ground and principle, upon which the revolution proceeded, was an entirely new cafe in politics, which had never before happened in our hiftory; the abdication of the reigning monarch, and the vacancy of the throne thereupon. It was not a defeazance of the right of fucceffion, and a new limitation of the crown, by the king and both houfes of parliament: it was the act of the nation alone, upon a conviction that there was no king in being. For in a full affembly of the lords and commons, met in convention upon the fuppofition of this vacancy, both houfes came to this refolution;

"that

" that king James II. having endeavoured to subvert the constitution of the kingdom, by breaking the original contract between king and people; and, by the advice of jesuits and other wicked persons, having violated the fundamental laws; and having withdrawn himself out of this kingdom; has abdicated the government, and that the throne is thereby vacant." Thus ended at once, by this sudden and unexpected vacancy of the throne, the old line of succession; which from the conquest had lasted above 600 years, and from the union of the heptarchy in king Egbert, almost 900.

Though in some points (owing to the peculiar circumstances of things and persons) the revolution was not altogether so perfect as might have been wished; yet from thence a new æra commenced, in which the bounds of prerogative and liberty have been better defined, the principles of government more thoroughly examined and understood, and the rights of the subject more explicitly guarded by legal provisions, than in any other period of the English history. In particular, it is worthy observation, that the convention, in this their judgment, avoided with great wisdom the wild extreams into which the visionary theories of some zealous republicans would have led them. They held that this misconduct of king James amounted to an endeavour to subvert the constitution, and not to an actual subversion, or total dissolution of the government. They therefore very prudently voted it to amount to no more than an abdication of the government, and a consequent vacancy of the throne; whereby the government was allowed to subsist, though the executive magistrate was gone; and the kingly office to remain, though king James was no longer king. And thus the constitution was kept intire; which upon every sound principle of government must otherwise have fallen to pieces, had so principal and constituent a part

part as the royal authority been abolished, or even suspended *.

Hence it is easy to collect, that the title to the crown is at present hereditary, though not quite so absolutely hereditary as formerly; and the common stock or ancestor, from whom the descent must be derived, is also different. Formerly the common stock was king Egbert's; then William the Conqueror; afterward in James the First's time the two common stocks united, and so continued till the vacancy of the throne in 1688: now it is the princess Sophia, in whom the inheritance was vested by the new king and parliament. Formerly the descent was absolute, and the crown went to the next heir without any re-

* The constitution of England, says Dr. Smollet, had now assumed a new aspect. The maxim of hereditary, indefeasible right, was at length renounced by a free parliament. The power of the crown was acknowledged to flow from no other fountain than that of a contract with the people. Allegiance and protection were declared reciprocal ties depending upon each other. The representatives of the nation made a regular claim of rights in behalf of their constituents; and William III. ascended the throne in consequence of an express capitulation with the people. Yet, on this occasion, the parliament, toward their deliverer, seems to have overshot their attachment to their own liberty and privileges: or, at least, they neglected the fairest opportunity that ever occurred, to retrench those prerogatives of the crown to which they imputed all the late and former calamities of the kingdom. Their new monarch retained the old regal power over parliaments, in its full extent: he was at liberty to convoke, adjourn, prorogue, and dissolve them at his pleasure: he was enabled to influence elections, and oppress corporations: he possessed the right of chusing his own council; of nominating all the great officers of the state, and of the household, of the army, the navy, and the church. He reserved the absolute command of the militia: so that he remained master of all the instruments and engines of corruption and violence, without any other restraint than his own moderation, and prudent regard to the claim of rights and principle of resistance on which the revolution was founded. In a word, the settlement was finished with some precipitation, before the plan had been properly digested and matured; and this will be the case in every establishment, formed upon a sudden emergency in the face of opposition.

striction:

striction: but now, upon the new settlement, the inheritance is conditional; being limited to such heirs only, of the body of the princess Sophia, as are Protestant members of the church of England, and are married to none but Protestants.

And in this due medium consists the true constitutional notion of the right of succession to the imperial crown of these kingdoms. The extreams, between which it steers, are each of them equally destructive of those ends for which societies were formed and are kept on foot. Where the magistrate, upon every succession, is elected by the people, and may by the express provision of the laws be deposed (if not punished) by his subjects, this may found like the perfection of liberty, and look well enough when delineated on paper; but in practice will be ever productive of tumult, contention, and anarchy. And, on the other hand, divine indefeasible hereditary right, when coupled with the doctrine of unlimited passive obedience, is surely of all constitutions the most thoroughly slavish and dreadful. But when such an hereditary right, as our laws have created and vested in the royal stock, is closely interwoven with those liberties, which are equally the inheritance of the subject; this union will form a constitution, in theory the most beautiful of any, in practice the most approved, and, in all probability, will prove in duration the most permanent. This constitution, it is the duty of every good Englishman to understand, to revere, and to defend.

The principal duties of the king are expressed in his oath at the coronation, which is administered by one of the archbishops, or bishops of the realm, in the presence of all the people; who on their parts do reciprocally take the oath of allegiance to the crown. This coronation oath is conceived in the following terms:

" *The archbishop or bishop shall say*, Will you so-
" lemnly promise and swear to govern the people
" of

"of this kingdom of England, and the dominions thereunto belonging, according to the statutes in parliament agreed on, and the laws and customs of the same?——*The king or queen shall say*, I solemnly promise so to do.

"*Archbishop or bishop*. Will you to your power cause law and justice, in mercy, to be executed in all your judgments?——*King or queen.* I will.

"*Archbishop or bishop.* Will you to the utmost of your power maintain the laws of God, the true profession of the gospel, and the Protestant reformed religion established by the law? And will you preserve unto the bishops and clergy of this realm, and to the churches committed to their charge, all such rights and privileges as by law do or shall appertain unto them, or any of them? ——*King or queen.* All this I promise to do.

"*After this the king or queen, laying his or her hand upon the holy gospels, shall say,*. The things which I have here before promised I will perform and keep: so help me God. *And then shall kiss the book.*"

This is the form of the coronation oath, as it is now prescribed by our laws: and we may observe, that in the king's part in this original contract, are expressed all the duties that a monarch can owe to his people; viz. to govern according to law: to execute judgment in mercy: and to maintain the established religion. With respect to the latter of these three branches, we may farther remark, that by the act of union, 5 Ann. c. 8. two preceding statutes are recited and confirmed; the one of the parliament of Scotland, the other of the parliament of England: which enact; the former, that every king at his accession shall take and subscribe an oath, to preserve the Protestant religion and Presbyterian church government in Scotland; the latter, that at his coronation he shall take and subscribe a similar oath, to preserve the settlement of the church of England

England within England, Ireland, Wales, and Berwick, and the territories thereunto belonging.

The king of Great Britain, notwithstanding the limitations or the power of the crown, already mentioned, is one of the greatest monarchs reigning over a free people. His person is sacred in the eye of the law, which makes it high treason so much as to imagine or intend his death; neither can he, in himself, be deemed guilty of any crime, the law taking no cognizance of his actions, but only in the persons of his ministers, if they infringe the laws of the land. As to his power, it has no bounds, (except where it breaks in upon the liberty and property of his subjects, as in making new laws, or raising new taxes) for he can make war or peace; send and receive ambassadors; make treaties of league and commerce; levy armies, fit out fleets, employ them as he thinks proper; grant commissions to his officers both by sea and land, or revoke them at pleasure; dispose of all magazines, castles, &c. summon the parliament to meet, and, when met, adjourn, prorogue, or dissolve it at pleasure; refuse his assent to any bill, though it hath passed both houses; which, consequently, by such a refusal, has no more force than if it had never been moved. He possesseth the right of chusing his own council; of nominating all the great officers of state, of the houshold, and the church; and, in fine, is the fountain of honour, from whom all degrees of nobility and knighthood are derived. Such is the dignity and power of a king of Great Britain.

Of the Parliament.

Parliaments, in some shape, are of as high antiquity as the Saxon government in this island; and have subsisted, in their present form, at least five hundred years.

The parliament is assembled by the king's writs, and it's sitting must not be intermitted above three years.

years. Its conſtituent parts are, the king ſitting there in his royal political capacity, and the three eſtates of the realm; the lords ſpiritual, the lords temporal, (who ſit, together with the king, in one houſe) and the commons, who ſit by themſelves in another. The king and theſe three eſtates, together, form the great corporation or body politic of the kingdom, of which the king is ſaid to be *caput*, *principium*, *et finis*. For upon their coming together the king meets them, either in perſon or by repreſentation; without which there can be no beginning of a parliament; and he alſo has alone the power of diſſolving them.

It is highly neceſſary for preſerving the balance of the conſtitution, that the executive power ſhould be a branch, though not the whole, of the legiſlature. The crown cannot begin of itſelf any alterations in the preſent eſtabliſhed law; but it may approve or diſapprove of the alterations ſuggeſted and conſented to by the two houſes. The legiſlative therefore cannot abridge the executive power of any rights which it now has by law, without it's own conſent: ſince the law muſt perpetually ſtand as it now does, unleſs all the powers will agree to alter it. And herein indeed conſiſts the true excellence of the Engliſh government, that all the parts of it form a mutual check upon each other. In the legiſlature, the people are a check upon the nobility, and the nobility a check upon the people; by the mutual privilege of rejecting what the other has reſolved: while the king is a check upon both, which preſerves the executive power from encroachments.

The lords ſpiritual conſiſt of two archbiſhops and twenty-four biſhops. The lords temporal conſiſt of all the peers of the realm, the biſhops not being in ſtrictneſs held to be ſuch, but meerly lords of parliament. Some of theſe ſit by deſcent, as do all antient peers; ſome by creation, as do all the new-made ones; others, ſince the union with Scotland, by election, which is the caſe of the ſixteen peers, who

repreſent

represent the body of the Scots nobility. Their number is indefinite, and may be encreased at will by the power of the crown.

A body of nobility is more peculiarly necessary in our mixed and compounded constitution, in order to support the rights of both the crown and the people; by forming a barrier to withstand the encroachments of both. It creates and preserves that gradual scale of dignity, which proceeds from the peasant to the prince; rising like a pyramid from a broad foundation, and diminishing to a point as it rises. The nobility therefore are the pillars, which are reared from among the people, more immediately to support the throne; and if that falls, they must also be buried under it's ruins. Accordingly, when in the last century the commons had determined to extirpate monarchy, they also voted the house of lords to be useless and dangerous.

The commons consist of all such men of any property in the kingdom, as have not seats in the house of lords; every one of which has a voice in parliament, either personally, or by his representatives. In a free state, every man, who is supposed a free agent, ought to be, in some measure, his own governor; and therefore a branch at least of the legislative power should reside in the whole body of the people. In so large a state as ours, it is very wisely contrived, that the people should do that by their representatives, which it is impracticable to perform in person: representatives, chosen by a number of minute and separate districts, wherein all the voters are, or easily may be, distinguished. The counties are therefore represented by knights, elected by the proprietors of lands; the cities and boroughs are represented by citizens and burgesses, chosen by the mercantile part or supposed trading interest of the nation. The number of English representatives is 513, and of Scots 45; in all 558. And every member, though chosen by one particular district, when elected and returned,

returned, serves for the whole realm. For the end of his coming thither is not particular, but general; not barely to advantage his conftituents, but the common wealth, and to advife his majefty, as appears from the writ of fummons.

These are the conftituent parts of a parliament, the king, the lords fpiritual and temporal, and the commons. Parts, of which each is fo neceffary, that the confent of all three is required to make any new law that fhould bind the fubject. Whatever is enacted for law by one, or by two only, of the three, is no ftatute; and to it no regard is due, unlefs in matters relating to their own privileges.

The power and jurifdiction of parliament, fays Sir Edward Coke, is fo tranfcendent and abfolute, that it cannot be confined, either for caufes or perfons, within any bounds. It hath fovereign and uncontrolable authority in making, confirming, enlarging, reftraining, abrogating, repealing, reviving, and expounding of laws, concerning matters of all poffible denominations, ecclefiaftical, or temporal, civil, military, maritime, or criminal: this being the place where that abfolute defpotic power, which muft in all governments refide fomewhere, is entrufted by the conftitution of thefe kingdoms. All mifchiefs and grievances, operations and remedies, that tranfcend the ordinary courfe of the laws, are within the reach of this extraordinary tribunal. It can regulate or new model the fucceffion to the crown; as was done in the reign of Henry VIII. and William III. It can alter the eftablifhed religion of the land; as was done in a variety of inftances, in the reigns of king Henry VIII. and his three children. It can change and create afrefh even the conftitution of the kingdom and of parliaments themfelves; as was done by the act of union, and the feveral ftatutes for triennial and feptennial elections. It can, in fhort, do every thing that is not naturally impoffible; and therefore fome have not fcrupled to call it's power, by a figure

rather

rather too bold, the omnipotence of parliament. True it is, that what the parliament doth, no authority upon earth can undo. So that it is a matter moſt eſſential to the liberties of this kingdom, that ſuch members be delegated to this important truſt, as are moſt eminent for their probity, their fortitude, and their knowlege; for it was a known apothegm of the great lord treaſurer Burleigh, " that England " could never be ruined but by a parliament:" and, as Sir Matthew Hale obſerves, this being the higheſt and greateſt court, over which none other can have juriſdiction in the kingdom, if by any means a miſgovernment ſhould any way fall upon it, the ſubjects of this kingdom are left without all manner of remedy.

In order to prevent the miſchiefs that might ariſe, by placing this extenſive authority in hands that are either incapable, or elſe improper, to manage it, it is provided that no one ſhall ſit or vote in either houſe of parliament; unleſs he be twenty-one years of age. To prevent innovations in religion and government, it is enacted, that no member ſhall vote or ſit in either houſe, till he hath in the preſence of the houſe taken the oaths of allegiance, ſupremacy, and abjuration; and ſubſcribed and repeated the declaration againſt tranſubſtantiation, the invocation of ſaints, and the ſacrifice of the maſs. To prevent dangers that may ariſe to the kingdom from foreign attachments, connexions, or dependencies, it is enacted, that no alien, born out of the dominions of the crown of Great Britain, even though he be naturalized, ſhall be capable of being a member of either houſe of parliament.

Some of the more notorious privileges of the members of either houſe are, privilege of ſpeech, of perſon, of their domeſtics, and of their lands and goods. As to the firſt, privilege of ſpeech, it is declared by the ſtatute of 1 W. & M. ſt. 2. c. 2. as one of the liberties of the people, " that the freedom of
" ſpeech,

"speech, and debates, and proceedings in parliament, ought not to be impeached or questioned in any court or place out of parliament." And this freedom of speech is particularly demanded of the king in person, by the speaker of the house of commons, at the opening of every new parliament. So likewise are the other privileges, of person, servants, lands and goods. This includes not only privilege from illegal violence, but also from legal arrests, and seisures by process from the courts of law. To assault by violence a member of either house, or his menial servants, is a high contempt of parliament, and there punished with the utmost severity. Neither can any member of either house be arrested and taken into custody, nor served with any process of the courts of law; nor can his menial servants be arrested; nor can any entry be made on his lands; nor can his goods be distrained or seized; without a breach of the privilege of parliament.

These privileges however, which derogate from the common law, being only indulged to prevent the members being diverted from the public business, endure no longer than the session of parliament, save only as to the freedom of his person: which in a peer is for ever sacred and inviolable; and in a commoner for forty days after every prorogation, and forty days before the next appointed meeting; which is now in effect as long as the parliament subsists, it seldom being prorogued for more than fourscore days at a time. As to all other privileges which obstruct the ordinary course of justice, they cease immediately after the dissolution or prorogation of the parliament, or adjournment of the houses for above a fortnight: and during these recesses a peer, or member of the house of commons, may be sued like an ordinary subject, and in consequence of such suits may be dispossessed of his lands and goods. Likewise, for the benefit of commerce, it is provided, that any trader, having privilege of parliament, may be served with

legal

legal procefs for any juft debt, to the amount of 100 l. and unlefs he makes fatisfaction within two months, it fhall be deemed an act of bankruptcy; and that commiffions of bankrupt may be iffued againft fuch privileged traders, in like manner as againft any other.

The houfe of lords have a right to be attended, and confequently are, by the judges of the court of king's bench and common-pleas, and fuch of the barons of the exchequer as are of the degree of the coif, or have been made ferjeants at law; as likewife by the mafters of the court of chancery; for their advice in point of law, and for the greater dignity of their proceedings.

The fpeaker of the houfe of lords is generally the lord chancellor, or lord-keeper of the great feal, which dignities are commonly vefted in the fame perfon.

Each peer has a right, by leave of the houfe, when a vote paffes contrary to his fentiments, to enter his diffent on the journals of the houfe, with the reafons for fuch diffent; which is ufually ftiled his proteft.

The houfe of commons may be properly ftiled the grand inqueft of Great Britain, impowered to enquire into all national grievances, in order to fee them redreffed.

The peculiar laws and cuftoms of the houfe of commons relate principally to the raifing of taxes, and the elections of members to ferve in parliament.

With regard to taxes: it is the antient indifputable privilege and right of the houfe of commons, that all grants of fubfidies or parliamentary aids do begin in their houfe, and are firft beftowed by them; altho' their grants are not effectual to all intents and purpofes, until they have the affent of the other two branches of the legiflature. The general reafon, given for this exclufive privilege of the houfe of commons, is, that the fupplies are raifed upon the body of the people, and therefore it is proper that they alone

alone should have the right of taxing themselves. And so reasonably jealous are the commons of this privilege, that herein they will not suffer the other house to exert any power but that of rejecting; they will not permit the least alteration or amendment to be made by the lords to the mode of taxing the people by a money bill. Under this appellation are included all bills, by which money is directed to be raised upon the subject, for any purpose or in any shape whatsoever; either for the exigencies of government, and collected from the kingdom in general, as the land tax; or for private benefit, and collected in any particular district, as by turnpikes, parish rates, and the like.

The method of making laws is much the same in both houses. In each house the act of the majority binds the whole: and this majority is declared by votes openly and publicly given: not as at Venice, and many other senatorial assemblies, privately or by ballot. This latter method may be serviceable, to prevent intrigues and unconstitutional combinations: but is impossible to be practised with us; at least in the house of commons, where every member's conduct is subject to the future censure of his constituents, and therefore should be openly submitted to their inspection.

To bring a bill into the house of commons, if the relief sought by it is of a private nature, it is first necessary to prefer a petition; which must be presented by a member, and usually sets forth the grievance desired to be remedied. This petition (when founded on facts that may be in their nature disputed) is referred to a committee of members, who examine the matter alleged, and accordingly report it to the house; and then (or, otherwise, upon the meer petition) leave is given to bring in the bill. In public matters the bill is brought in upon motion made to the house, without any petition. (In the house of lords, if the bill begins there, it is, when of a private nature, referred

to

to two of the judges, to examine and report the state of the facts alleged, to see that all necessary parties consent, and to settle all points of technical propriety.) This is read a first time, and at a convenient distance a second time; and after each reading the speaker opens to the house the substance of the bill, and puts the question, whether it shall proceed any farther. The introduction of the bill may be originally opposed, as the bill itself may at either of the readings; and, if the opposition succeeds, the bill must be dropt for that sessions; as it must also, if opposed with success in any of the subsequent stages.

After the second reading it is committed, that is, referred to a committee; which is either selected by the house in matters of small importance, or else, upon a bill of consequence, the house resolves itself into a committee of the whole house. A committee of the whole house is composed of every member; and, to form it, the speaker quits the chair, (another member being appointed chairman) and may sit and debate as a private member. In these committees the bill is debated clause by clause, amendments made, the blanks filled up, and sometimes the bill entirely new modelled. After it has gone through the committee, the chairman reports it to the house with such amendments as the committee have made; and then the house reconsider the whole bill again, and the question is repeatedly put upon every clause and amendment. When the house have agreed or disagreed to the amendments of the committee, and sometimes added new amendments of their own, the bill is then ordered to be engrossed, or written in a strong gross hand, on one or more long rolls of parchments sewed together. When this is finished, it is read a third time, and amendments are sometimes then made to it; and, if a new clause be added, it is done by tacking a separate piece of parchment on the bill, which is called a ryder. The speaker then again opens the contents; and, holding it up in in his hands, puts the queſtion, whether the bill ſhall paſs. If this is agreed to, the title to it is then ſettled. After this, one of the members is directed to carry it to the lords, and deſire their concurrence; who attended by ſeveral more, carries it to the bar of the houſe of peers, and there delivers it to their ſpeaker, who comes down from his woolſack to receive it. It there paſſes through the forms as in the other houſe, (except engroſſing, which is already done) and, if rejected, no more notice is taken, but it paſſes *ſub ſilentio*, to prevent unbecoming altercations. But if it is agreed to, the lords ſend a meſſage by two maſters in chancery (or ſometimes two of the judges) that they have agreed to the ſame: and the bill remains with the lords, if they have made no amendment to it. But if any amendments are made, ſuch amendments are ſent down with the bill to receive the concurrence of the commons. If the commons diſagree to the amendments, a conference uſually follows between members deputed from each houſe; who for the moſt part ſettle and adjuſt the difference: but, if both houſes remain inflexible, the bill is dropped. If the commons agree to the amendments, the bill is ſent back to the lords by one of the members, with a meſſage to acquaint them therewith. The ſame forms are obſerved, *mutatis mutandis*, when the bill begins in the houſe of lords. But, when an act of grace or pardon is paſſed, it is firſt ſigned by his majeſty, and then read once only in each of the houſes, without any new engroſſing or amendment. And when both houſes have done with any bill, it always is depoſited in the houſe of peers, to wait the royal aſſent; except in the caſe of a money-bill, which after receiving the concurrence of the lords is ſent back to the houſe of commons.

The royal aſſent may be given two ways: 1. In perſon: when the king comes to the houſe of peers, in his crown and royal robes, and ſending for the commons to the bar, the titles of all the bills that
have

have paſſed both houſes are read; and the king's anſwer is declared by the clerk of the parliament in
Norman-French: a badge, it muſt be owned, (now
the only one remaining) of conqueſt; and which one
could wiſh to ſee fall into total oblivion; unleſs it be
reſerved as a ſolemn *memento* to remind us that our
liberties are mortal, having once been deſtroyed by
a foreign force. If the king conſents to a public bill,
the clerk uſually declares, *le roy le veut*, "the king
wills it ſo to be;" if to a private bill, *ſoit fait come il
eſt deſiré*, "be it as it is deſired." If the king refuſes
his aſſent, it is in the gentle language of *le roy ſ' avi-
ſera*. "the king will adviſe upon it." When a money-
bill is paſſed, it is carried up and preſented to the king
by the ſpeaker of the houſe of commons, and the
royal aſſent is thus expreſſed, *le roy remercie ſes loyal
ſubjects, accepte lour benevolence, et auſſi le veut*, "the
king thanks his loyal ſubjects, accepts their benevolence, and wills it ſo to be." In caſe of an act of
grace, which originally proceeds from the crown, and
has the royal aſſent in the firſt ſtage of it, the clerk of
the parliament thus pronounces the gratitude of the
ſubject; *les prelats, ſeigneurs, et commons, en ce preſent
parliament aſſemblees, au nom de touts vous autres ſubjects, remercient tres humblement votre majeſte, et prient
a Dieu vous donner en ſante bone vie et longue*; "the
prelates, lords, and commons, in this preſent parliament aſſembled, in the name of all your other ſubjects, moſt humbly thank your majeſty, and pray to God
to grant you in health and wealth long to live."
2. By the ſtatute 33 Hen. VIII. c. 21. the king may
give his aſſent by letters patent under his great ſeal,
ſigned with his hand, and notified, in his abſence, to
both houſes aſſembled together in the high houſe.
And, when the bill has received the royal aſſent in
either of theſe ways, it is then, and not before, a
ſtatute or act of parliament.

This ſtatute or act is placed among the records of
the kingdom; there needing no formal promulgation

to give it the force of a law, as was neceſſary by the civil law with regard to the emperors edicts: becauſe every man in England is, in judgment of law, party to the making of an act of parliament, being preſent thereat by his repreſentatives. However, a copy thereof is uſually printed at the king's preſs, for the information of the whole land.

An act of parliament, thus made, is the exerciſe of the higheſt authority that this kingdom acknowleges upon earth. It hath power to bind every ſubject in the land, and the dominions thereunto belonging; nay, even the king himſelf, if particularly named therein. And it cannot be altered, amended, diſpenſed with, ſuſpended, or repealed, but in the ſame forms and by the ſame authority of parliament: for it is a maxim in law, that it requires the ſame ſtrength to diſſolve, as to create an obligation.

Such is the parliament of Great Britain; the ſource and guardian of our liberties and properties, the ſtrong cement which binds the foundation and ſuperſtructure of our government, and the wiſely concerted balance maintaining an equal poiſe, that no one part of the three eſtates overpower or diſtreſs either of the other.

Privy counſellors are made by the king's nomination, without either patent or grant; and, on taking the neceſſary oaths, they become immediately privy counſellors during the life of the king that chooſes them, but ſubject to removal at his diſcretion.

The duty of a privy counſellor appears from the oath of office, which conſiſts of ſeven articles: 1. To adviſe the king according to the beſt of his cunning and diſcretion. 2. To adviſe for the king's honour and good of the public, without partiality through affection, love, meed, doubt, or dread. 3. To keep the king's counſel ſecret. 4. To avoid corruption. 5. To help and ſtrengthen the execution of what ſhall be there reſolved. 6. To withſtand all perſons who would attempt the contrary. And, laſtly, in general, 7. To obferve, keep, and do all that a good and true counfellor ought to do to his foyereign lord.

The two principal fecretaries of ftate (one of whom is generally prefent whenever the council is held) are entrufted with the cuftody of the king's fignet. They jointly tranfact the king's affairs relating to Great Britain; but as to thofe concerning foreign nations, they are divided between them; the eldeft fecretary having the fouthern province, containing Flanders, France, &c. affigned to his management; and the younger fecretary manages the northern province, containing fuch nations as lie north of thofe already mentioned.

Of the Courts of Law, &c.

The court of Chancery, which is a court of equity, is next in dignity to the high court of parliament, and is defigned to relieve the fubject againft frauds, breaches of truft, and other oppreffions; and to mitigate the rigour of the law. The lord high chancellor fits as fole judge, and in his abfence the mafter of the Rolls. The form of proceeding is by bills, anfwers, and decrees, the witneffes being examined in private: however, the decrees of this court are only binding to the perfons of thofe concerned in them, for they do not affect their lands and goods; and confequently, if a man refufes to comply with the terms, they can do nothing more than fend him to the prifon of the Fleet. This court is always open; and if a man be fent to prifon, the lord chancellor, in any vacation, can, if he fees reafon for it, grant a *habeas corpus*.

The clerk of the crown likewife belongs to this court, being obliged, or by his deputy, always to attend on the lord chancellor as often as he fits for the difpatch of bufinefs; through his hands pafs all writs for fummoning the parliament or chufing of members; commiffions of the peace, pardons, &c.

The King's Bench, fo called either from the kings of England fometimes fitting there in perfon, or because

cause all matters determinable at common law between the king and the subject, are here tried; except such affairs as properly belong to the court of Exchequer. This court is, likewise, a kind of cheque upon all the inferior courts, their judges and justices of the peace. Here preside four judges, the first of whom is stiled lord chief justice of the king's bench, or by way of eminence, lord chief justice of England, to express the great extent of his jurisdiction over the kingdom: for this court can grant prohibitions in any cause depending either in spiritual or temporal courts; and the house of peers does often direct the lord chief justice to issue out his warrant for apprehending persons under the suspicion of high crimes. The other three judges are called justices, or judges, of the king's bench.

The court of Common Pleas takes cognizance of all pleas debateable between subject and subject; and in it, beside all real actions, fines and recoveries are transacted, and prohibitions are likewise issued out of it, as well as from the King's Bench. The first judge of this court is stiled lord chief justice of the common pleas, or common bench; beside whom there are likewise three other judges, or justices, of this court. None but serjeants at law are allowed to plead here.

The court of Exchequer was instituted for managing the revenues of the crown, and has a power of judging both according to law and according to equity. In the proceedings according to law, the lord chief baron of the Exchequer, and three other barons, preside as judges. They are stiled barons, because formerly none but barons of the realm were allowed to be judges in this court. Beside these, there is a fifth called cursitor baron, who has not a judicial capacity, but is only employed in administring the oath to sheriffs and their officers, and also to several of the officers of the Custom-house.—But when this court proceeds according to equity, then the lord treasurer and the chancellor of the Exchequer preside, assisted by the other barons. All matters touching the king's

trea-

treasury, revenue, customs, and fines, are here tried and determined.——Beside the officers already mentioned, there belong to the Exchequer, the king's remembrancer, who takes and states all accounts of the revenue, customs, excise, parliamentary aids and subsidies, &c. except the accounts of the sheriffs and their officers. The lord treasurer's remembrancer, whose business it is to make out processes against sheriffs, receivers of the revenue, &c.

For putting the laws effectually in execution, an high sheriff is annually appointed for every county (except Westmorland and Cumberland) by the king; whose office is both ministerial and judicial. He is to execute the king's mandates, and all writs directed to him out of the king's courts of justice; to impannel juries, to bring causes and malefactors to trial, to see the sentences both in civil and criminal affairs, executed. And at the assize to attend on the judges, and guard them all the time they are in his county. It is also part of his office to collect all public fines, distresses, and amerciaments, into the Exchequer, or where the king shall appoint, and to make such payments out of them as his majesty shall think proper.

As his office is judicial, he keeps a court, called the county court, which is held by the sheriff, or his under-sheriffs, to hear and determine all civil causes in the county under forty shillings; this however is no court of record; but the court, formerly called the sheriff's turn, was one; and the king's leet, thro' all the county: for in this court, enquiry was made into all criminal offences against the common law, where by the statute law there was no restraint. This court, however, has been long since abolished.

Under the sheriff are various officers, as the under-sheriff, clerks, stewards of courts, bailiffs, (in London called serjeants) constables, gaolers, beadles, &c.

The next officer to the sheriff, is the justice of peace, several of whom are commissioned for each county: and to them is intrusted the power of putting great part of the statute law in execution in relation

tion to the highways, the poor, vagrants, treasons, felonies, riots, the preservation of the game, &c. &c. and they examine and commit to prison all who break or disturb the peace, and disquiet the king's subjects. In order to punish the offenders, they meet every quarter at the county-town, when a jury of 2 men, called the grand inqueſt of the county, is summoned to appear. This jury, upon oath, is to enquire into the cafes of all delinquents, and to prefent them by bill guilty of the indictment, or not guilty: the juſtices commit the former to gaol for their trial at the next affizes, and the latter are acquitted. This is called the quarter-feffions for the county. The juſtice of peace ought to be a perfon of great good fenfe, fagacity, and integrity, and to be not without fome knowlege of the law; for as much power is lodged in his hands, and as nothing is fo intoxicating, without thefe qualifications he will be apt to make miſtakes, and to ſtep beyond his authority, for which he is liable to be called to an account at the court of king's bench.

There are alfo in each county two coroners, who are to enquire by a jury of neighbours, how and by whom any perfon came by a violent death, and to enter it on record as a plea of the crown.

The civil government of cities is a kind of fmall independent policy of itfelf; for every city hath, by charter from the king, a jurifdiction within itfelf to judge in all matters civil and criminal; with this reſtraint only, that all civil caufes may be removed from their courts to the higher courts at Weſtminſter; and all offences that are capital, are committed to the judge of the affize. They are conftituted with a mayor, aldermen, and burgeffes, who together make the corporation of the city, and hold a court of judicature, where the mayor prefides as judge. They likewife, when affembled in council, can make laws, called bye-laws, for the government of the city. And here the mayor, aldermen, and common-council refemble the king, lords and commons in parliament.

The

The government of incorporated boroughs is much after the same manner; in some there is a mayor, and in others two bailiffs. All which, during their mayoralty or magistracy, are justices of the peace within their liberties, and consequently esquires.

For the better government of villages, the lords of the soil or manor (who were formerly called barons) have generally a power to hold courts, called courts-leet, and courts baron, where their tenants are obliged to attend and receive justice. The business of courts-leet is chiefly to present and punish nuisances; and at courts baron, the conveyances and alienations of the copyhold tenants are enrolled, and they are admitted to their estates on a descent or purchase.

There are also high constables appointed for the divisions called hundreds, and petty constables in every parish; whose business it is to keep the peace, and in case of quarrels to search for and take up all rioters, felons, &c. and to keep them in the prison or in safe custody, till they can be brought before a justice of the peace; and in this he is assisted by another officer, called the tithing-man. It is likewise the business of these officers to put in execution within their district, all warrants that are brought them from the justice of the peace.

Beside these, there are courts of conscience settled in many parts of England for the relief of the poor, in the recovery or payment of small debts, not exceeding forty shillings.

The rights of individuals are so attentively considered under the British government, that the subject may, without the least danger, sue his sovereign, or those who act in his name, and under his authority; he may do this in open court, where the king may be cast, and be obliged to pay damages to his subject. He cannot take away the liberty of the least individual, unless he has by some illegal act forfeited his right to liberty, or except when the state is in danger, and the representatives of the people think the public
safety

safety makes it necessary that he should have the power of confining persons, on a suspicion of guilt: but this power is always given him only for a limited time. The king has a right to pardon, but neither he nor the judges, to whom he delegates his authority, can condemn a man as a criminal, except he be first found guilty, by twelve men, who must be his peers or his equals. That the judges may not be influenced by the king, or his ministers, to misrepresent the case to the jury, they have their salaries for life, and not during the pleasure of their sovereign. Neither can the king take away, or endanger the life of any subject, without trial, and the persons being first chargeable with a capital crime, as treasons, murder, felony, or some other act injurious to society: nor can any subject be deprived of his liberty for the highest crime, till some proof of his guilt be given upon oath before a magistrate; and he has then a right to insist upon his being brought, the first opportunity, to a fair trial, or to be restored to liberty on giving bail for his appearance. If a man is charged with a capital offence, he must not undergo the ignominy of being tried for his life, till the evidences of his guilt are laid before the grand jury of the town or county in which the fact is alleged to be committed, and not without twelve of them agreeing to a bill of indictment against him. If they do this, he is to stand a second trial before twelve other men, whose opinion is definitive. In some cases, the man (who is always supposed innocent till there is sufficient proof of his guilt) is allowed a copy of his indictment, in order to help him to make his defence. He is also furnished with the pannel, or list of the jury, who are his true and proper judges, that he may learn their characters, and discover whether they want abilities, or whether they are prejudiced against him. He may in open court peremptorily object to twenty of the number[*], and to as many more as he can give

[*] The party may challenge thirty-five in case of treason.

reason

reason for their not being admitted as his judges; till at last twelve unexceptionable men, the neighbours of the party accused, or living near the place where the supposed fact was committed, are sworn, to give a true verdict according to the evidence produced in court. By challenging the jury, the prisoner prevents all possibility of bribery, or the influence of any superior power: by their living near the place where the fact was committed, they are supposed to be men who know the prisoner's course of life, and the credit of the evidence. These only are the judges, from whose sentence the prisoner is to expect life or death, and upon their integrity and understanding, the lives of all that are brought in danger ultimately depend; and from their judgment there lies no appeal: they are therefore to be all of one mind, and after they have fully heard the evidence, are to be confined without meat, drink, or candle, till they are unanimous in acquitting or condemning the prisoner. Every juryman is therefore invested with a solemn and awful trust: if he without evidence submits his opinion to that of any of the other jury, or yields in complaisance to the opinion of the judge; if he neglects to examine with the utmost care; if he questions the veracity of the witnesses, who may be of an infamous character; or after the most impartial hearing has the least doubt upon his mind, and yet joins in condemning the person accused; he will wound his own conscience, and bring upon himself the complicated guilt of perjury and murder. The freedom of Englishmen consists in its being out of the power of the judge * on the bench to injure them, for declaring

---

* " Some jurymen, says Mr. Clare, in his English Liberties,
" may be apt to say, that if we could not find as the judge directs,
" we may come into trouble, the judge may fine us, &c. I an-
" swer, no judge dares offer any such thing; you are the proper
" judges of the matters before you, and your souls are at stake;
" you ought to act freely, and are not bound, though the court ce-
" mand

ing a man innocent, whom he wishes to be brought in guilty. Was not this the case, juries would be useless; so far from being judges themselves, they would only be the tools of another, whose province it is not to guide, but to give a sanction to their determination. Tyranny might triumph over the lives and liberties of the subject, and the judge on the bench be the minister of the prince's vengeance.

These are the glorious privileges which we enjoy above any other nation upon earth. Juries have always been considered as giving the most effectual check to tyranny; for in a nation like this, where a king can do nothing against law, they are a security that he shall never make the laws, by a bad administration, the instruments of cruelty and oppression. Was it not for juries, the advice given by father Paul, in his maxims of the republic of Venice, might take effect in its fullest latitude. "When the offence
" is committed by a nobleman against a subject, says
" he, let all ways be tried to justify him ; and if that
" is not possible to be done, let him be chastised with
" greater noise than damage. If it be a subject that
" has affronted a nobleman, let him be punished with
" the utmost severity, that the subject may not get
" too great a custom of laying their hands on the
" patrician order." In short, was it not for juries,

" mand it, to give the reason why you bring it in thus or thus; for
" you of the grand jury are sworn to the contrary, viz. to keep
" secret your fellows counsel and your own; and you of the petty
" jury are no way obliged to declare your motives, for it may not
" be convenient. In queen Elizabeth's days, a man was arraigned
" for murder before justice Anderson ; the evidence was so strong,
" that eleven of the twelve were presently for finding him guilty,
" the twelfth man refused, and kept them so long that they were
" ready to starve, and at last made them comply with him, and
" bring in the prisoner not guilty. The judge, who had seve-
" ral times admonished him to join with his fellows, being surpris-
" ed, sent for him, and discoursed him privately; to whom, upon
" promise of indemnity, he at last owned, that he himself was the
" man that did the murder, and the prisoner was innocent, and
" that he was resolved not to add perjury, and a second murder to
" the first."

of GREAT BRITAIN. 31

a corrupt nobleman might, whenever he pleafed, act the tyrant, while the judge would have that power which is now denied to our kings. But by our happy conftitution, which breathes nothing but liberty and equity, all imaginary indulgence is allowed to the meaneft, as well as the greateft. When a prifoner is brought to take his trial, he is freed from all bonds; and though the judges are fuppofed to be counfel for the prifoner, yet, as he may be incapable of vindicating his own caufe, other counfel are allowed him; he may try the validity and legality of the indictment, and may fet it afide, if it be contrary to law. Nothing is wanting to clear up the caufe of innocence, and to prevent the fufferer from finking under the power of corrupt judges, and the oppreffion of the great. The racks and tortures that are cruelly made ufe of in other parts of Europe, to make a man accufe himfelf, are here unknown, and none punifhed without conviction, but he who refufes to plead in his own defence.

As the trial of malefactors in England is very different from that of other nations, the following account thereof may be ufeful to foreigners and others, who have not feen thofe proceedings.

The court being met, and the prifoner called to the bar, the clerk commands him to hold up his hand, then charges him with the crime of which he is accufed, and afks him whether he is *guilty* or *not guilty*. If the prifoner anfwers *guilty*, his trial is at an end; but if he anfwers *not guilty*, the court proceeds on the trial, even tho' he may before have confeffed the fact: for the law of England takes no notice of fuch confeffion; and unlefs the witneffes, who are upon oath, prove him guilty of the crime, the jury muft acquit him, for they are directed to bring in their verdict according to the evidence given in court. If the prifoner refufes to plead, that is, if he will not fay in court, whether he is *guilty* or *not guilty*, he is by the law of England to be preffed to death.

When

When the witnesses have given in their evidence, and the prisoner has, by himself or his counsel, cross examined them, the judge recites to the jury the substance of the evidence given against the prisoner, and bids them discharge their conscience; when, if the matter be very clear, they commonly give their verdict without going out of court; and the foreman, for himself and the rest, declares the prisoner *guilty*, or *not guilty*, as it may happen to be. But if any doubt arises among the jury, and the matter requires debate, they all withdraw into a room with a copy of the indictment, where they are locked up, till they are unanimously agreed on the verdict; and if any one of the jury should die during this their confinement, the prisoner will be acquitted.

When the jury have agreed on the verdict, they inform the court thereof by an officer who waits without, and the prisoner is again set to the bar, to hear his verdict. This is unalterable, except in some doubtful cases, when the verdict is brought in special, and is therefore to be determined by the twelve judges of England.

If the prisoner is found guilty, he is then asked what reason he can give why sentence of death should not be passed upon him? If it be the first fault, and his offence be within the statute made for that purpose, he may demand the benefit of the clergy, which saves his life, and he will be only burnt in the hand. But where the benefit of the clergy is not admitted, the sentence of death, after a summary account of the trial, is pronounced on the prisoner, in these words: *The law is, That thou shalt return to the place from whence thou camest, and from thence be carried to the place of execution, where thou shalt hang by the neck, till thy body be dead, and the Lord have mercy on thy soul:* whereupon the sheriff is charged with the execution.

All prisoners found *not guilty* by the jury, are immediately acquitted and discharged, and in some cases obtain a copy of their indictment from the court to proceed at law against their prosecutors.

Of

Of Punishments.

Though the laws of England are esteemed more merciful, with respect to offenders, than those which at present subsist in any other part of the known world; yet the punishment of such who at their trial refuse to plead guilty or not guilty, is here very cruel. In this case the prisoner is laid upon his back, and his arms and legs being stretched out with cords, and a considerable weight laid upon his breast, he is allowed only three morsels of barley bread, which is given him the next day without drink, after which he is allowed nothing but foul water till he expires. This, however, is a punishment which is scarcely inflicted once in an age; but some offenders have chose it to preserve their estates for their children. Those guilty of this crime are not now suffered to undergo such a length of torture, but have so great a weight placed upon them, that they soon expire. In case of high treason, though the criminal stands mute, judgment is given against him as if he had been convicted, and his estate is confiscated.

The law of England includes all capital crimes under high treason, petty treason, and felony. The first consists in plotting, conspiring, or rising up in arms against the sovereign, or in counterfeiting the coin. The traitor is punished by being drawn on a sledge to the place of execution, when, after being hanged upon a gallows for some minutes, the body is cut down alive, the heart taken out and exposed to public view, and the entrails burnt: the head is then cut off, and the body quartered, after which the head is usually fixed on some conspicuous place. All the criminal's lands and goods are forfeited, his wife loses her dowry, and his children both their estates and nobility.

But though coining of money is adjudged high treason, the criminal is only drawn upon a sledge to the place of execution, and there hanged.

Though the sentence passed upon all traitors is the same, yet with respect to persons of quality, the punishment is generally altered to beheading: a scaffold is erected for that purpose, on which the criminal placing his head upon a block, it is struck off with an axe*.

The punishment for misprision of high treason, that is, for neglecting or concealing it, is imprisonment for life, the forfeiture of all the offender's goods, and of the profits arising from his lands.

Petty treason is when a child kills his father, a wife her husband, a clergyman his bishop, or a servant his master or mistress. This crime is punished by being drawn in a sledge to the place of execution, and there hanged upon a gallows till the criminal is dead. Women guilty both of this crime, and of high treason, are sentenced to be burnt alive, but instead of suffering the full rigour of the law, they are strangled at the stake before the fire takes hold of them.

Felony includes murders, robberies, forging notes, bonds, deeds, &c. These are all punished by hanging, only murderers are to be executed soon after the sentence is passed; and then delivered to the surgeons in order to be publicly dissected. Persons guilty of robbery, when there are some alleviating circumstances, are sometimes transported for a term of years to his majesty's plantations. And in all such felonies where the benefit of the clergy is allowed, as it is in many, the criminal is burnt in the hand with a hot iron.

Other crimes punished by the laws are,

Manslaughter, which is the unlawful killing of a person without premeditated malice, but with a present intent to kill; as when two who formerly meant no harm to each other, quarrel, and the one kills the

---

* This is not to be considered as a different punishment; but as a remission of all the parts of the sentence mentioned before, excepting the article of beheading.

ether; in this cafe, the criminal is allowed the benefit of his clergy for the firſt time, and only burnt in the hand.

Chance-medley, is the accidental killing of a man without an evil intent, for which the offender is alſo to be burnt in the hand; unleſs the offender was doing an unlawful act, which laſt circumſtance makes the puniſhment death.

Shop-lifting, and receiving goods knowing them to be ſtolen, are puniſhed with tranſportation to his majeſty's colonies, or burning in the hand.

Perjury, or keeping diſorderly houſes, are puniſhed with the pillory and impriſonment.

Petty-larceny, or ſmall theft, under the value of twelve-pence, is puniſhed by whipping.

Libelling, uſing falſe weights and meaſures, and foreſtalling the market, are commonly puniſhed with ſtanding on the pillory, or whipping.

For ſtriking, ſo as to draw blood, in the king's court, the criminal is puniſhed with loſing his right-hand.

For ſtriking in Weſtminſter-hall while the courts of juſtice are ſitting, is impriſonment for life, and forfeiture of all the offender's eſtate.

Drunkards, vagabonds, and looſe, idle, diſorderly perſons, are puniſhed by being ſet in the ſtocks, or by paying a fine.

Of the Religion of England.

Chriſtianity was very early planted in England, but when, or by whom, is very uncertain; probably in the latter end of the firſt, or the beginning of the ſecond century. The reformation in England, begun in the reign of Henry VIII. was greatly promoted under his ſon Edward VI. It was, however, checked by queen Mary, but compleated by queen Elizabeth. This reformation being conducted by the biſhops, the eſtabliſhed church of England became Epiſcopal. Calvin

Calvin indeed used many endeavours to obtain a share in the advancement and direction of this ecclesiastical reformation; but being desirous of depriving the bishops of their temporal grandeur, of banishing all external ornaments and pomp from divine worship, and introducing the Genevan constitution; the bishops declined his offers of assistance. Many, however, approving of Calvin's doctrine, formed an ecclesiastical government on his plan. These were afterward termed Puritans, from their avowed desire of freeing the church from the impurities still retained in it, and Nonconformists, from their not conforming to the rules of the established church. Agreeably to Calvin's model, they instituted presbyters without bishops, from whence they obtained the name of Presbyterians; instituting also church-laws among themselves, and being governed by synods composed of the ministers of several different churches. Others maintaining, that every Christian congregation ought to be free, and subject neither to bishops nor synods, these were termed Independents.

The Episcopalians and Presbyterians are the two principal parties, and differ the least from each other; the first form the established religion of England and Ireland, and the latter of Scotland. The most numerous of the other religious sects are the Baptists, who do not believe that infants are the proper subjects of baptism, and in the baptism of adults practise immersion. It is here proper to observe, that the English Presbyterians differ almost as much from the church of Scotland, as from the church of England; synods growing gradually out of use, each separate congregation is become, in a manner, independent of the rest: they have most of them forsaken the opinions of Calvin, and believing universal redemption, maintain that the universal Parent has excluded none of his offspring from a possibility of salvation; while the Independents, and many congregations of the Baptists, agree with the church of
Scotland

Scotland in the doctrines of particular election and reprobation. It muft alfo be added, that the prefbyterians, with the church of England, receive the facrament of the Lord's fupper at noon, while the Independents and Baptifts receive it after the conclufion of the afternoon fervice.

One of the principal of the other fects is the Quakers, who profefs to be guided by an internal revelation dictated by the Spirit of God: they have no regular minifters, and neither practife baptifm, nor commemorate the death of Chrift in the Lord's Supper.

The Methodifts have lately arifen, and now form a very numerous body; moft of them are alfo members of the church of England, and profefs to adhere more clofely than the other members of that church to the thirty-nine articles; and the greateft part of them are rigid Calvinifts.

The number of Papifts here is alfo very confiderable, particularly in Lancafhire, Staffordfhire, and Suffex.

Many authors have exclaimed, with great heat, of the many fects in England; but let it be confidered, that civil and religious liberty are clofely connected; and that it does not become any church, who makes no pretenfions to infallibility, to fet up the ftandard of perfecution.

But to return: the church of England is under the government of two archbifhops and twenty-five bifhops, who are fubject to the king as fupream temporal head of the church. The archbifhop of Canterbury is ftiled the firft peer and metropolitan of the kingdom; he takes place immediately after the royal family, and confequently precedes not only all dukes, but likewife the great officers of ftate. In addreffes to him he enjoys the title of Your grace, in common with dukes, and alfo that of moft reverend father in God. He has the power of holding juridical courts in church affairs, with many other privileges relating to the granting of licenfes and difpenfations, in all cafes formerly fued for at the court of Rome, where they are not repugnant to the law of God, or the king's prerogative. He has alfo within his province, by common law, the probate of all wills, where the party dying is worth upward of five pounds. He has under him twenty-one bifhops, befide his own particular diocefe; thefe are the bifhops of London, Winchefter, Ely, Lincoln, Rochefter, Litchfield and Coventry, Hereford, Worcefter, Bath and Wells, Salifbury, Exeter, Chichefter, Norwich, Gloucefter, Oxford, Peterborough, Briftol; and in Wales, St. David's, Landaff, St. Afaph, and Bangor.

The archbifhop of York likewife takes the precedence of all dukes who are not of the blood royal; as alfo of all the great officers of ftate, excepting the lord chancellor, who is immediately next in rank to the archbifhop of Canterbury. In his diocefe he is ftiled primate of England and metropolitan; he alfo enjoys the title of his grace, and moft reverend father in God. Exclufive of his own diocefe, in his province are Durham, Carlifle, Chefter, and Sodor and Man. In Northumberland he has the power of a palatine, and jurifdiction in all criminal proceedings.

The twenty-five bifhops are ftiled right reverend, and your lordfhip; all thefe walk next after the vifcounts, and precede the barons. In parliament they fit in a double capacity, as bifhops and barons; they alfo enjoy many other privileges, as freedom from arrefts, outlawries, &c. They live in great ftate; their revenues are alfo confiderable; but where the income is not very large, fome other lucrative preferment, as a deanry, is generally annexed to it.

The bufinefs of a bifhop is to examine and ordain priefts and deacons, to confecrate churches and burying-places, and to adminifter the rite of confecration. The jurifdiction of a bifhop relates to the probation of wills; he is to grant adminiftration of goods to fuch as die inteftate; to take care of perifhable

able goods, when no one will administer; to collate to benefices; to grant institutions to livings; to defend the liberties of the church; and to visit his own diocese once in three years.

Next to the bishops are the deans and prebends of cathedrals, out of whom the bishops are chosen. After these are the archdeacons, of which every diocese has one or more, the whole number in the kingdom of England amounting to sixty. Their office is to visit the churches twice or thrice every year. The archdeacons are followed by the rural deans, who were formerly stiled archi-presbyters, and signify the bishop's pleasure to his clergy, the lower class of which consists of priests and deacons.

With respect to the ecclesiastical government and courts, it is proper to observe, that the principal part of the ecclesiastical government was formerly lodged in the convocation, which is a national synod of the clergy, assembled to consider of the state of the church, and to call those to an account who have advanced new opinions, inconsistent with the doctrines of the church of England: but in the reign of his late majesty, they being thought to proceed with too much heat and severity against some learned divines, and to be too great a check upon free inquiry, they have not been permitted to sit for any long time since. However, they are assembled at the same time with the parliament, by the authority of the king, who directs his writs to the archbishop of each province to summon all bishops, deans, archdeacons, &c. to meet at a certain time and place.

The court of arches is the most ancient consistory of the province of Canterbury, and all appeals in church matters, from the judgment of the inferior courts, are directed to this. The processes run in the name of the judge, who is called dean of the arches; and the advocates who plead in this court must be doctors of the civil law. The court of audience has the same authority with this, to which the archbishop's archbishop's chancery was formerly joined. The prerogative court is that wherein wills are proved, and administrations taken out. The court of peculiars, relating to certain parishes, have a jurisdiction among themselves for the probate of wills, and are therefore exempt from the bishop's courts. The see of Canterbury has no less than fifteen of these peculiars. The court of delegates receives its name from its consisting of commoners, delegated or appointed by the royal commission; but it is no standing court. Every bishop has also a court of his own, called the consistory court. Every archdeacon has likewise his court, as well as the dean and chapter of every cathedral.

Of the Revenues of the British Government.

The king's ecclesiastical revenue consists in, 1. The custody of the temporalities of vacant bishoprics. 2. Corodies and pensions. 3. Extra-parochial tithes. 4. The first fruits and tenths of benefices.

The king's ordinary temporal revenue consists in, 1. The demesne lands of the crown. 2. The hereditary excise; being part of the consideration for the purchase of his feodal profits, and the prerogatives of purveyance and pre-emption. 3. An annual sum issuing from the duty on wine licences; being the residue of the same consideration. 4. His forests. 5. His courts of justice, &c.

The extraordinary grants are usually called by the synonimous names of aids, subsidies, and supplies; and are granted, as has been before hinted, by the commons of Great Britain, in parliament assembled: who, when they have voted a supply to his majesty, and settled the *quantum* of that supply, usually resolve themselves into what is called a committee of ways and means, to consider of the ways and means of raising the supply so voted. And in this committee every member (though it is looked upon as the peculiar

culiar province of the chancellor of the exchequer) may propose such scheme of taxation as he thinks will be least detrimental to the public. The resolutions of this committee (when approved by a vote of the house) are in general esteemed to be (as it were) final and conclusive. For, though the supply cannot be actually raised upon the subject till directed by an act of the whole parliament, yet no monied man will scruple to advance to the government any quantity of ready cash, on the credit of a bare vote of the house of commons, though no law be yet passed to establish it.

The annual taxes are, 1. The land tax, or the antient subsidy raised upon a new assessment. 2. The malt tax, being an annual excise on malt, mum, cyder, and perry.

The perpetual taxes are, 1. The customs, or tonnage and poundage of all merchandize exported or imported. 2. The excise duty, or inland imposition, on a great variety of commodities. 3. The salt duty. 4. The * post office, or duty for the carriage of letters. 5. The stamp duty on paper, parchment, &c. 6. The duty on houses and windows. 7. The duty on licences for hackney coaches and chairs. 8. The duty on offices and pensions.

The clear neat produce of these several branches of the revenue, after all charges of collecting and management paid, amounts annually to about seven millions and three quarters sterling; beside two millions and a quarter raised annually, at an average, by the land and malt tax. How these immense sums are appropriated, is next to be considered. And this is, first and principally, to the payment of the interest of the national debt.

In order to take a clear and comprehensive view of the nature of this national debt, it must first be

* From the years 1715 to 1763, the annual amount of franked letters gradually increased from 23,000 l. to 170,700 l.

premised,

premised, that after the revolution, when our new connections with Europe introduced a new syftem of foreign politics; the expences of the nation, not only in settling the new eftablifhment, but in maintaining long wars, as principals, on the continent, for the fecurity of the Dutch barrier, reducing the French monarchy, settling the Spanifh fucceffion, fupporting the houfe of Auftria, maintaining the liberties of the Germanic body, and other purpofes, increafed to an unufual degree: infomuch that it was not thought advifeable to raife all the expences of any one year by taxes to be levied within that year, left the unaccuftomed weight of them fhould create murmurs among the people. It was therefore the policy of the times, to anticipate the revenues of their pofterity, by borrowing immenfe fums for the current fervice of the ftate, and to lay no more taxes upon the fubject than would fuffice to pay the annual intereft of the fums fo borrowed: by this means converting the principal debt into a new fpecies of property, transferable from one man to another at any time and in any quantity. A fyftem which feems to have had its original in the ftate of Florence, *A. D.* 1344: which government then owed about 60,000 l. fterling: and, being unable to pay it, formed the principal into an aggregate fum, called metaphorically a mount or bank; the fhares whereof were transferable like our ftocks. This laid the foundation of what is called the national debt: for a few long annuities created in the reign of Charles II. will hardly deferve that name. And the example then fet has been fo clofely followed, during the long wars in the reign of queen Anne, and fince; that the capital of the national debt (funded and unfunded) amounted in January 1765, to upward of 145,000,000 l. to pay the intereft of which, and the charges for management, amounting annually to about four millions and three quarters, the extraordinary revenues juft now enumerated (excepting only

only the land-tax and annual malt-tax) are in the firſt place mortgaged, and made perpetual by parliament; but ſtill redeemable by the ſame authority that impoſed them: which, if it at any time can pay off the capital, will aboliſh thoſe taxes which are raiſed to diſcharge the intereſt.

It is indiſputably certain, that the preſent magnitude of our national incumbrances very far exceeds all calculations of commercial benefit, and is productive of the greateſt inconveniencies. For, firſt, the enormous taxes that are raiſed upon the neceſſaries of life for the payment of the intereſt of this debt, are a hurt both to trade and manufactures; by raiſing the price, as well of the artificer's ſubſiſtence, as of the raw material, and of courſe, in a much greater proportion, the price of the commodity itſelf. Secondly, if part of this debt be owing to foreigners, either they draw out of the kingdom annually a conſiderable quantity of ſpecie for the intereſt; or elſe it is made an argument to grant them unreaſonable privileges, in order to induce them to reſide here. Thirdly, if the whole be owing to ſubjects only, it is then charging the active and induſtrious ſubject, who pays his ſhare of the taxes, to maintain the indolent and idle creditor who receives them. Laſtly, and principally, it weakens the internal ſtrength of a ſtate, by anticipating thoſe reſources which ſhould be reſerved to defend it in caſe of neceſſity. The intereſt we now pay for our debts would be nearly ſufficient to maintain any war, that any national motives could require. And if our anceſtors in king William's time had annually paid, ſo long as their exigencies laſted, even a leſs ſum than we now annually raiſe upon their accounts, they would, in time of war, have borne no greater burdens than they have bequeathed to, and ſettled upon, their poſterity in time of peace; and might have been eaſed the inſtant the exigence was over.

The

The produce of the several taxes before-mentioned were originally separate and distinct funds; being securities for the sums advanced on each several tax, and for them only. But at last it became necessary, in order to avoid confusion, as they multiplied yearly, to reduce the number of these separate funds, by uniting and blending them together; superadding the faith of parliament for the general security of the whole. So that there are now only three capital funds of any account: the aggregate fund, and the general fund, so called from such union and addition; and the South Sea fund, being the produce of the taxes appropriated to pay the interest of such part of the national debt as was advanced by that company and its annuitants. Whereby the separate funds, which were thus united, are become mutual securities for each other; and the whole produce of them, thus aggregated, liable to pay such interest or annuities as were formerly charged upon each distinct fund; the faith of the legislature being moreover engaged to supply any casual deficiencies.

The customs, excises, and other taxes, which are to support these funds, depending on contingencies, upon exports, imports, and consumptions, must necessarily be of a very uncertain amount: but they have always been considerably more than was sufficient to answer the charge upon them. The surplusses therefore of the three great national funds, the aggregate, general, and South Sea funds, over and above the interest and annuities charged upon them, are directed by statute 3 Geo. I. c. 7. to be carried together, and to attend the disposition of parliament; and are usually denominated the sinking fund, because originally destined to sink and lower the national debt. To this have been since added many other intire duties, granted in subsequent years; and the annual interest of the sums borrowed on their respective credits, is charged on, and payable out of the produce of the sinking fund. However the neat surplusses

surplusses and savings, after all deductions paid, amount annually to a very confiderable sum; particularly in the year ending at Christmas 1764, to about two millions and a quarter. For, as the interest on the national debt has been at several times reduced, (by the consent of the proprietors, who had their option either to lower their interest, or be paid their principal) the savings from the appropriated revenues must needs be extreamly large. This sinking fund is the last resort of the nation; its only domestic resource, on which must chiefly depend all the hopes we can entertain of ever discharging or moderating our incumbrances. And therefore the prudent application of the large sums, now arising from this fund, is a point of the utmost importance, and well worthy the serious attention of parliament; which was thereby enabled, in the year 1765, to reduce above two millions sterling of the public debt.

But, before any part of the aggregate fund (the surplusses whereof are one of the chief ingredients that form the sinking fund) can be applied to diminish the principal of the public debt, it stands mortgaged by parliament to raise an annual sum for the maintenance of the king's houshold and the civil list. For this purpose, in the late reigns, the produce of certain branches of the excise and customs, the post-office, the duty on wine licences, the revenues of the remaining crown lands, the profits arising from courts of justice, (which articles include all the hereditary revenues of the crown) and also a clear annuity of 120,000 l. in money, were settled on the king for life, for the support of his majesty's houshold, and the honour and dignity of the crown. And, as the amount of these several branches was uncertain, (though in the last reign they were computed to have sometimes raised almost a million) if they did not arise annually to 800,000 l. the parliament engaged to make up the deficiency. But his present majesty having, soon after his accession, spontaneously taneoufly fignified his confent, that his own hereditary revenues might be fo difpofed of, as might beft conduce to the utility and fatisfaction of the public; and having gracioufly accepted the limited fum of 800,000 l. *per annum*, for the fupport of his civil lift, (and that alfo charged with three life annuities, to the princefs of Wales, the duke of Cumberland, and princefs Amelia, to the amount of 77,000 l.) the faid hereditary, and other revenues, are now carried into, and made a part of, the aggregate fund; and the aggregate fund is charged with the payment of the whole annuity to the crown of 800,000 l. *per annum*. Hereby the revenues themfelves, being put under the fame care and management as the other branches of the public patrimony, will produce more, and be better collected than heretofore; and the public is a gainer of upward of 100,000 l. *per annum*, by this difinterefted bounty of his majefty. The civil lift, thus liquidated, together with the four millions and three quarters, intereft of the national debt, and the two millions and a quarter produced from the finking fund, make up the feven millions and three quarters *per annum*, neat money, which were before ftated to be the annual produce of our perpetual taxes : befide the immenfe, though uncertain fums, arifing from the annual taxes on land and malt, but which, at an average, may be calculated at more than two millions and a quarter; and which, added to the preceding fum, make the clear produce of the taxes, exclufive of the charge of collecting, which are raifed yearly on the people of this country, amount to upward of ten millions fterling.

The expences defrayed by the civil lift are thofe that in any fhape relate to civil government; as the expences of the houfhold, all falaries to officers of ftate, to the judges, and every of the king's fervants; the appointments to foreign ambaffadors, the maintenance of the queen and royal family, the king's private expences, or privy purfe, and other very numerous

rous outgoings; as secret service-money, pensions, and other bounties. These sometimes have so far exceeded the revenues appointed for that purpose, that application has been made to parliament, to discharge the debts contracted on the civil list; as particularly in 1724, when one million was granted for that purpose by the statute 11 Geo. I. c. 17.

The civil list is indeed properly the whole of the king's revenue in his own distinct capacity; the rest being rather the revenue of the public, or its creditors, though collected, and distributed again, in the name, and by the officers of the crown; it now standing in the same place, as the hereditary income did formerly; and, as that has gradually diminished, the parliamentary appointments have encreased.

Of the Military and Marine strength of Great Britain.

The military state includes the whole of the soldiery; or, such persons as are peculiarly appointed among the rest of the people, for the safeguard and defence of the realm.

In a land of liberty it is extreamly dangerous to make a distinct order of the profession of arms. In such, no man should take up arms, but with a view to defend his country and its laws: he puts not off the citizen when he enters the camp; but it is because he is a citizen, and would wish to continue so, that he makes himself for a while a soldier. The laws therefore, and constitution of these kingdoms know no such state as that of a perpetual standing soldier, bred up to no other profession than that of war: and it was not till the reign of Henry VII. that the kings of England had so much as a guard about their persons.

It seems universally agreed by all historians, that king Alfred first settled a national militia in this kingdom, and by his prudent discipline, made all the subjects of his dominions soldiers.

In

In the mean time we are not to imagine that the kingdom was left wholly without defence, in cafe of domeftic infurrections, or the profpect of foreign invafions. Befide thofe, who by their military tenures, were bound to perform forty days fervice in the field, the ftatute of Winchefter obliged every man, according to his eftate and degree, to provide a determinate quantity of fuch arms as were then in ufe, in order to keep the peace: and conftables were appointed in all hundreds, to fee that fuch arms were provided. Thefe weapons were changed by the ftatute 4 and 5 Ph. and M. c. 2. into others of more modern fervice; but both this and the former provifion were repealed in the reign of James I. While thefe continued in force, it was ufual from time to time, for our princes to iffue commiffions of array, and fend into every county officers in whom they could confide, to mufter and array (or fet in military order) the inhabitants of every diftrict: and the form of the commiffion of array was fettled in parliament in the 5 Hen. IV. But at the fame time it was provided, that no man fhould be compelled to go out of the kingdom at any rate, nor out of his fhire, but in cafes of urgent neceffity; nor fhould provide foldiers unlefs by confent of parliament. About the reign of king Henry VIII. and his children, lord lieutenants began to be introduced, as ftanding reprefentatives of the crown, to keep the counties in military order; for we find them mentioned as known officers in the ftatute 4 and 5 Ph. and M. c. 3. though they had not been then long in ufe; for Camden fpeaks of them in the time of queen Elizabeth, as extraordinary magiftrates, conftituted only in times of difficulty and danger.

Soon after the reftoration of king Charles II. when the military tenures were abolifhed, it was thought proper to afcertain the power of the militia, to recognize the fole right of the crown to govern and command them, and to put the whole into a more regular

of GREAT BRITAIN. 49

regular method of military fubordination: and the order in which the militia now ftands by law, is principally built upon the ftatutes which were then enacted. It is true, the two laft of them are apparently repealed; but many of their provifions are re-enacted, with the addition of fome new regulations, by the prefent militia laws; the general fcheme of which is to difcipline a certain number of the inhabitants of every county, chofen by lot for three years, and officered by the lord lieutenant, the deputy lieutenants, and other principal landholders, under a commiffion from the crown. They are not compellable to march out of their counties, unlefs in cafe of invafion or actual rebellion, nor in any cafe compellable to march out of the kingdom. They are to be exercifed at ftated times: and their difcipline in general is liberal and eafy; but, when drawn out into actual fervice, they are fubject to the rigours of martial law, as neceffary to keep them in order. This is the conftitutional fecurity which our laws have provided for the public peace, and for protecting the realm againft foreign or domeftic violence; and which the ftatutes declare, is effentially neceffary to the fafety and profperity of the kingdom.

But, as the fafhion of keeping ftanding armies has univerfally prevailed over all Europe of late years (though fome of its potentates, being unable themfelves to maintain them, are obliged to have refource to richer powers, and receive fubfidiary penfions for that purpofe) it has alfo for many years paft been annually judged neceffary by our legiflature, for the fafety of the kingdom, the defence of the poffeffions of the crown of Great Britain, and the prefervation of the balance of power in Europe, to maintain, even in time of peace, a ftanding body of troops, under the command of the crown; who are however, *ipfo facto*, difbanded at the expiration of every year, unlefs continued by parliament. The land forces of thefe kingdoms, in time of peace, amount to about 40,000

Vol. VII. E men,

men, including troops and garrisons in Ireland, Gibraltar, Minorca, and America; but in time of war, there have been in British pay, natives and foreigners, above 150,000! The registered militia in England consists of near 200,000.

The maritime state is nearly related to the former; though much more agreeable to the principles of our free constitution. The royal navy of England hath ever been its greatest defence and ornament; it is its ancient and natural strength; the floating bulwark of the island; an army, from which, however strong and powerful, no danger can ever be apprehended to liberty: and accordingly it has been assiduously cultivated, even from the earliest ages. To so much perfection was our naval reputation arrived in the twelfth century, that the code of maritime laws, which are called the laws of Oleron, and are received by all nations in Europe, as the ground and substruction of all their marine constitutions, was confessedly compiled by our king Richard I. at the isle of Oleron on the coast of France, then part of the possessions of the crown of England. And yet, so vastly inferior were our ancestors in this point, to the present age, that even in the maritime reign of queen Elizabeth, Sir Edward Coke thinks it matter of boast, that the royal navy of England then consisted of 33 ships. The present condition of our marine is in great measure owing to the salutary provisions of the statutes, called the navigation-acts; whereby the constant increase of English shipping and seamen was not only encouraged, but rendered unavoidably necessary. The most beneficial statute for the trade and commerce of these kingdoms is that navigation-act, the rudiments of which were first framed in 1650, with a narrow partial view: being intended to mortify the sugar islands, which were disaffected to the parliament, and still held out for Charles II. by stopping the gainful trade which they then carried on with the Dutch; and at the same time

time to clip the wings of those our opulent and aspiring neighbours. This prohibited all ships of foreign nations from trading with any English plantations without licence from the council of state. In 1651, the prohibition was extended also to the mother country; and no goods were suffered to be imported into England, or any of its dependencies, in any other than English bottoms; or in the ships of that European nation, of which the merchandize imported was the genuine growth or manufacture. At the restoration, the former provisions were continued, by statute 12 Car. II. c. 18. with this very material improvement, that the master and three fourths of the mariners shall also be English subjects.

The complement of seamen, in time of peace, usually amounts to twelve or fifteen thousand. In time of war, they have amounted to no less than sixty thousand men. See at the end of this volume a list of the royal navy of England, as it stood at the end of the late war.

This navy is commonly divided into three squadrons, namely, the red, white, and blue, which are so termed from the difference of their colours. Each squadron has its admiral; but the admiral of the red squadron has the principal command of the whole, and is stiled vice-admiral of Great Britain. Subject to each admiral is also a vice and a rear-admiral. But the supreme command of our naval force is, next to the king, in the lords commissioners of the admiralty. We may venture to affirm that the British navy, during the late war, was able to cope with all the other fleets in Europe. In the course of a few years it entirely vanquished the whole naval power of France, disabled Spain, and kept the Dutch in awe.

For the protection of the British empire, and the annoyance of our enemies, it was then divided into several powerful squadrons, and so judiciously stationed, that while one fleet was successfully battering walls, hitherto reckoned impregnable, others were employed in fruſtrating the deſigns of France, and eſcorting home the riches of the eaſtern and weſtern worlds.

Notwithſtanding our favourable ſituation for a maritime power, it was not until the vaſt armament ſent to ſubdue this nation by Spain, in 1588, that the nation, by a vigorous effort, became fully ſenſible of its true intereſt and natural ſtrength, which it has ſince ſo happily cultivated. This appears more fully by the ſhort view of our naval tranſactions, which cloſes this volume; and which, beginning with the reign of queen Elizabeth, is carried down to the peace of Verſailles in 1763.

An Hiſtorical Account of the Policy and Trade of Great Britain.

The preſent ſyſtem of Engliſh politics may properly be ſaid to have taken riſe in the reign of queen Elizabeth. At this time the Proteſtant religion was eſtabliſhed, which naturally allied us to the reformed ſtates, and made all the Popiſh powers our enemies.

We began in the ſame reign to extend our trade, by which it became neceſſary for us alſo to watch the commercial progreſs of our neighbours; and, if not to incommode and obſtruct their traffic, to hinder them from impairing ours.

We then likewiſe ſettled colonies in America, which was become the great ſcene of European ambition; for, ſeeing with what treaſures the Spaniards were annually enriched from Mexico and Peru, every nation imagined, that an American conqueſt or plantation would certainly fill the mother country with gold and ſilver.

The diſcoveries of new regions, which were then every day made, the profit of remote traffic, and the neceſſity of long voyages, produced, in a few years,
a great

a great multiplication of shipping. The sea was considered as the wealthy element; and, by degrees, a new kind of sovereignty arose, called naval dominion.

As the chief trade of Europe, so the chief maritime power was at first in the hands of the Portuguese and Spaniards, who, by a compact, to which the consent of other princes was not asked, had divided the newly discovered countries between them: but the crown of Portugal having fallen to the king of Spain, or being seized by him, he was master of the ships of the two nations, with which he kept all the coasts of Europe in alarm, till the Armada, he had raised at a vast expence for the conquest of England, was destroyed; which put a stop, and almost an end, to the naval power of the Spaniards.

At this time the Dutch, who were oppressed by the Spaniards, and feared yet greater evils than they felt, resolved no longer to endure the insolence of their masters; they therefore revolted; and after a struggle, in which they were assisted by the money and forces of Elizabeth, erected an independant and powerful commonwealth.

When the inhabitants of the Low Countries had formed their system of government, and some remission of the war gave them leisure to form schemes of future prosperity, they easily perceived that, as their territories were narrow, and their numbers small, they could preserve themselves only by that power which is the consequence of wealth; and that by a people whose country produced only the necessaries of life, wealth was not to be acquired, but from foreign dominions, and by the transportation of the products of one country into another.

From this necessity, thus justly estimated, arose a plan of commerce, which was for many years prosecuted with industry and success, perhaps never seen in the world before; and by which the poor tenants of mud-walled villages and impassable bogs, erected them-

themselves into high and mighty states, who set the greatest monarchs at defiance, whose alliance was courted by the proudest, and whose power was dreaded by the fiercest nations. By the establishment of this state, there arose to England a new ally, and a new rival.

At this time, which seems to be the period destined for the change of the face of Europe, France began first to rise into power, and from defending her own provinces with difficulty and fluctuating success, to threaten her neighbours with incroachments and devastations. Henry IV. having, after a long struggle, obtained the crown, found it easy to govern nobles, exhausted and wearied with a long civil war; and having composed the disputes between the Protestants and Papists, so as to obtain, at least, a truce for both parties, was at leisure to accumulate treasure, and raise forces which he proposed to have employed in a design of settling for ever the balance of Europe. Of this great scheme he lived not to see the vanity, or feel the disappointment; for he was murdered in the midst of his mighty preparations.

The French, however, were in this reign taught to know their own power; and the great designs of a king, whose wisdom they had so long experienced, even though they were not brought to actual experiment, disposed them to consider themselves as masters of the destiny of their neighbours: and from that time he that shall nicely examine their schemes and conduct, will find that they began to take an air of superiority, to which they had never pretended before; and that they have been always employed more or less openly, upon schemes of dominion, though with frequent interruptions from domestic troubles.

When Queen Elizabeth entered upon the government, the customs produced only 36,000 l. a year; at the restoration, they were lett to farm for 400,000 l. and produced considerably above double that sum

before

before the revolution. The people of London, before we had any plantations, and but very little trade, were computed at about 100,000; at the death of queen Elizabeth, they were increased to 150,000, and are now about six times that number. In those days, we had not only our naval stores, but our ships from our neighbours. Germany furnished us with all things made of metal, even to nails; wine, paper, linen, and a thousand other things came from France. Portugal furnished us with sugars; all the produce of America was poured upon us from Spain; and the Venetians and Genoese retailed to us the commodities of the East Indies at their own price. In short, the legal interest of money was 12 per cent. and the common price of our land ten or twelve years purchase. We may add, that our manufactures were few, and those but indifferent; the number of English merchants very small, and our shipping much inferior to what now belong to the northern colonies.

Such was the state of our trade when this great princess came to the throne; but as the limits of our undertaking does not permit us to give a detail of the gradual progress of commerce, we flatter ourselves that the British reader will not be displeased with the following view of our extensive trade, at present carried on through the various nations of the globe.

Great Britain is, of all other countries, the most proper for trade; as well from its situation, as an island, as from the freedom and excellency of its constitution, and from its natural products, and considerable manufactures. For exportation: our country produces many of the most substantial and necessary commodities, as butter, cheese, corn, cattle, wool, iron, lead, tin, copper, leather, copperas, pitcoal, alum, saffron, &c. Our corn sometimes preserves other countries from starving. Our horses are the most serviceable in the world, and highly valued by all nations for their hardiness, beauty, and strength.

With

With beef, mutton, pork, poultry, bifcuit, we victual not only our own fleets, but all foreigners that come and go. Our iron we export manufactured in great guns, carcafes, bombs, &c. Prodigious, and almoft incredible, is the value likewife of other goods from hence exported; viz. hops, flax, hemp, hats, fhoes, houfhold-ftuff, ale, beer, red-herrings, pilchards, falmon, oyfters, faffron, liquorice, watches, ribbands, toys, &c.

There is fcarce a manufacture in Europe, but what is brought to great perfection in England; and therefore it is perfectly unneceffary to enumerate them all. The woollen manufacture is the moft confiderable, and exceeds in goodnefs and quantity that of any other nation. Hard-ware is another capital article; locks, edge-tools, guns, fwords, and other arms, exceed any thing of the kind; houfhold utenfils of brafs, iron, and pewter, alfo are very great articles; our clocks and watches are in very great efteem. There are but few manufactures we are defective in. In thofe of lace and paper we do not feem to excel; but we import much more than we fhould, if the duty on Britifh paper was taken off. As to foreign traffic, the woollen manufacture is ftill the great foundation and fupport of it.

The commerce between Great Britain and the countries fubject to the grand fignior is carried on by the merchants incorporated into the Levant or Turkey company; but now opened in fuch a manner by a late ftatute, as to be more capable of anfwering national purpofes, without leffening the particular advantages, which Turkey merchants ought in juftice to enjoy. The commodities we export are chiefly lead, tin, and iron, watches and clocks; and of our woollen manufactures, broad cloth and long ells. It is alfo faid, that our merchants fend thither French and Lifbon fugars, as well as bullion. We take in return raw filk in great quantities, which however is only proper for the fhute of our damafk, and other coloured

coloured filks; it will alfo ferve for making ftockings, galloons, and filver and gold lace; but it is not proper for the warp of any filk, nor even for the woof of fome of the finer forts. We import alfo grogram yarn, dying ftuffs of various kinds, drugs, foap, leather, cotton, fruit, oil, &c. While the war continued, it was a great help to us in this trade, as the French are our principal competitors therein; and as they fuffered very feverely, not only by captures, but by the high infurance they paid on all the goods they exported; fo they could not but come very dear to markets, and perhaps we preferve ftill fome of the advantages then acquired.

We export to Italy, of our own commodities, tin and lead, great quantities of fifh, fuch as pilchards, herrings, falmond, cod, &c. various kinds of Eaft India goods; and of our own manufactures, broad cloths, long ells, Bays, druggets, camblets, and other ftuffs; as alfo leather and other things. We import from thence prodigious quantities of filk, raw, thrown, and wrought; wine, oil, foap, olives, dying ftuffs, &c. It is from this country, and more efpecially from the dominions of his Sardinian majefty, that we have the fine filk called organzine, which is thrown by an engine, much truer than it can be by hand, of which we have one, and but one, at Derby. That prince, however, has taken care to preferve to his fubjects this precious commodity in its full extent; for we have no Piedmont filk raw, and what we have we pay for in ready money, at a very high rate. This therefore makes the balance of power, and the change of mafters, at leaft in the maritime parts of Italy, a thing of very great confequence to Great Britain; and as fuch, it ought always to be confidered by our minifters, and if poffible, in no other light.

We export to Spain, tin, lead, corn, &c. pilchards, herrings, cod, and other kinds of fifh; of our manufactures broad cloth, druggets, bays, and ftuffs, of various kinds; as alfo a great variety of different goods,

goods, which are re-shipped by them from Cadiz to their colonies in America. On the other hand, we import from Spain, wine, oil, and fruit, wool, indigo, cochineal, and other drugs. It appears from hence, that if the Spaniards are good customers to us, we are also the best customers they have; for it is thought we take off two-thirds of their commodities: so that considering them as a nation, nothing can distress the Spaniards so much as a war with the English. It is very true, that in time of peace we draw a considerable balance from thence in specie or in bullion; but at the same time, we furnish them with the commodities that are most necessary, with the manufactures that bring them this bullion, and take also vast quantities of commodities that must otherwise lie upon their hands; whereas the French furnish them with many trifles, as well as some costly manufactures, for which they are paid wholly in silver. Hence it appears, that it is the mutual interest of Spain and Britain to deal with each other; and if this was thoroughly inculcated, it would enrich us and serve them.

We export to Portugal, tin, lead, corn, fish, and almost all of our commodities; as also broad cloths, druggets, bays, stuffs, leather, and many other manufactures; we take from them wine, oil, salt, and fruit; so that though it is generally supposed the balance of this trade is as much in our favour as any, yet the Portuguese find their account in it: for in the first place, we take almost all the commodities they export, and for which, if we did not take them, they could hardly find another market; and we furnish them with the best part of those things they export to the Brazils, and thereby draw that immense treasure yearly, which, for its bigness, renders Portugal one of the richest countries in Europe. Beside, these reciprocal advantages have made such a connection between our interests, that upon all occasions we have been ready to espouse those of Portugal, and to protect

tect her from the only power fhe has reafon to fear, by the timely interpofition of our maritime force.

We export to France, tin, lead, corn, horn plates, and great quantities of tobacco, fome flannels; but very little elfe of our manufactures. We take from thence, in time of peace, wine, brandy, linen, lace, cambrics, lawns, (unlefs our late acts can keep them out) and an infinite number of other things which are run in upon us, and whatever elfe the French are pleafed to direct: whence it appears, that of all others, the French commerce is to us the moft dangerous and deftructive.

We export to Flanders, tin, lead, and fome iron ware, as alfo fugar and tobacco; of our manufactures, ferges, fome flannels, and a few ftuffs. On the other hand, we take from them fine lace, cambrics, lawns, linen, tape, inkles, and other goods of that kind, to a very great value; fo that there feems to be no doubt that the balance of this trade is confiderably againft us, which is chiefly owing to the prohibition of our cloth: therefore if any thing be worthy our feeking on the continent, it is the port of Oftend, with a fmall diftrict about it, which at the fame time would be of fervice to our allies, and might contribute to repair the expences we have been at in our feveral land wars. This is mentioned only incidentally.

We fend to Germany, tin, lead, and many other commodities; tobacco, fugar, ginger, and all kinds of Eaft-India goods. Of our woollen manufactures, fome of almoft every kind we make. On the other hand, we take from them tin plates, linen, kid fkins, and feveral other things. The balance of this trade is looked upon to be very much in our favour, but it might be made ftill more; for in many places of late they have prohibited different kinds of our manufactures, and in fome they have prohibited all. But in our treaties of fubfidy, if we had an article to prevent or remove fuch prohibitions, it would be but reafonable: for as we pay the Germans for fighting

their

their own battles, they might methinks in return allow a free vent to our manufactures; and as they are sure of taking our money, should give us a chance at least for seeing some of theirs.

We have a great trade with Denmark and Norway, but we export very little; a small quantity of tobacco, and a few coarse woollen goods is all; but we are forced to tack to these crown-pieces and guineas, to pay for timber and iron; and the matter is not all mended, but on the contrary grows worse; if instead of exporting our wealth, we stay till the Danes come and fetch it, for then we not only pay for their goods, but the freight also; and this evil it seems is not in our power to cure at present.

We carry on the same kind of losing trade to Sweden, where it is a maxim of state to beat out as much as possible all our commodities and manufactures; and this has been so steadily pursued, that it is now pretty near done, and gold and silver are almost our only exports. Copper, iron, and naval stores, are the goods we bring from thence, to the amount of about three hundred thousand pounds a year. We were formerly under a necessity of doing this; because their goods must be had, and could be had no where else. At present it is otherwise, we might have all these at much more reasonable rates from our own plantations, which is much the same thing as having them at home.

We export to Russia, tin, lead, and other commodities, a great quantity of tobacco; and of our manufactures, coarse cloths, long ells, worsted stuffs, &c. On the other hand, we import from thence, tallow, furrs, iron, pot-ashes, hemp, flax, linen, Russia leather, &c. Our trade to this country is managed by a company, the best constituted, and the best conducted of any that we have; for any merchant may be admitted into it for a very small consideration, and the measures they pursue are such as prove highly beneficial, and never can do any harm. The trade through

this

this empire into Perfia, may become a thing of great confequence, as it will furnifh us with that fort of filk which we want moft, at an eafy price, and may be attended with other advantages that we have not room to explain.

We export to Holland almoft all the commodities and manufactures that we have, as well as moft of our plantation goods, and of thofe we bring from the Levant and the Eaft Indies. We import prodigious quantities of fine linen, threads, tapes, inkles, whale-fins, brafs battery, cinnamon, mace, cloves, drugs, and dying ftuffs, &c. yet with refpect to the fair trade we have a large balance: the only doubt is, how far this may be abated by the great induftry of fmug-lers, who gain their bread and raife fortunes by a fteady purfuit of their private interefts, at the expence of the public.

With refpect to our African trade, it is certainly of the higheft importance to the nation, for it creates a vaft exportation of our commodities and manufac-tures, and produces a large balance in bullion from the Spaniards, as well as in gold-duft, red-wood, ivory, and other valuable commodities, fome of which are re-exported; but above all it fupplies our plan-tations with negroes, which is a thing of prodigious confequence. The old African company of Eng-land, once the moft flourifhing and profitable of all our companies, and but for bad management within, and party prejudice without, might have continued fo, has been at length diffolved by parliament, and the commerce put into a new channel, which either anfwers, or will be made to anfwer national purpofes; fince no commerce can more nearly concern Great Britain and her colonies than this does, and fcarcely any is fo much the fubject of foreign envy.

The Eaft-India trade is a prodigious thing, and of great benefit to the nation, though we export chiefly bullion; and though it is carried on by a company. But the goods we bring home are bought at low prices,

prices, are sold at high rates, and what we export is believed to produce a balance equivalent at least to the bullion that is sent out to buy them. It has been of late suggested, and not without good reason, that this commerce is capable of great improvements, by extending it to the north-east; for in that case, we might hope to vend large quantities of our manufactures, which would at once remove the only reasonable exception that was ever taken to this trade, would augment our navigation, and hinder the northern nations from interfering with us, by employing the very money we pay for naval stores, in beating us out of a very considerable branch of commerce, for the carrying on of which those stores are purchased.

As for the plantation trade, we have already spoken of it elsewhere, and without doubt it is by far the most considerable of any that we have, and is notwithstanding this, far less considerable than it might be; for with a little pains and encouragement, it might be made in its savings and in its produce, twice or thrice as beneficial at it is: for it has been computed, that by encouraging hemp and flax, pot-ashes, timber, iron, other naval stores, and silk, we might either get or keep considerably above a million annually; and by making other regulations it is demonstrable, that within a few years we might gain as much more.

In short, the advantages are infinite that redound to us from our American empire, where we have at least a million of British subjects, and between fifteen hundred and two thousand sail of ships constantly employed.

The annual exports of English and foreign goods amount to between six and seven millions sterling, and our imports do not exceed five millions. As a considerable part of this is again exported, the annual issues from England for foreign merchandize, has been estimated at four millions. Yet our foreign trade does not amount to one sixth part of the inland;

land; the annual produce of the natural products and manufactures of England amounting to above forty-two millions. The gold and filver of England is received from Portugal, Spain, Jamaica, the American colonies, and Africa; but great part of this gold and filver we again export to Holland, and the Eaft Indies; and it is fuppofed that two-thirds of all the foreign traffic of England is carried on in the port of London.

We fhall conclude this account of our trade with the following comparative view of fhipping, which, till a better table can be formed, may have its ufes.

If the fhipping of Europe be divided into twenty parts, then,

Great Britain, &c. is computed to have	6
The United Provinces — —	6
The fubjects of the northern crowns —	2
The trading cities of Germany, and the Auftrian Netherlands — — —	1
France — — — —	2
Spain and Portugal — — —	2
Italy, and the reft of Europe — —	1

A fhort View of the Stocks, or public Funds in England, with an hiftorical Account of the Eaft India, the Bank, and South Sea Companies.

As there are few fubjects of converfation more general than the value of ftocks, and hardly any thing fo little underftood, nothing can be more ufeful than a fhort account of them, which we fhall here give in as clear and concife a manner as pofiible; prefenting our readers with the rationale of the ftocks, and a fhort hiftory of the feveral companies, defcribing the nature of their feparate funds, the ufes to which they are applied, and the various purpofes they anfwer, both with refpect to the government, the companies themfelves, and the community in general.

In

In order to give a clear idea of the money tranfactions of the feveral companies, it is proper we fhould fay fomething of money in general, and particularly of paper money, and the difference between that and the current fpecie. Money is the ftandard of the value of all the neceffaries and accommodations of life, and paper-money is the reprefentative of that ftandard to fuch a degree, as to fupply its place, and to anfwer all the purpofes of gold and filver coin. Nothing is neceffary to make this reprefentative of money fupply the place of fpecie, but the credit of that office or company, who delivers it; which credit confifts in its always being ready to turn it into fpecie whenever required. This is exactly the cafe of the bank of England, the notes of this company are of the fame value as the current coin, as they may be turned into it, whenever the poffeffor pleafes. From hence, as notes are a kind of money, the counterfeiting them is punifhed with death as well as coining.

The method of depofiting money in the bank, and exchanging it for notes (though they bear no intereft) is attended with many conveniencies; as they are not only fafer than money in the hands of the owner himfelf; but as the notes are more portable and capable of a much more eafy conveyance: fince a bank note for a very large fum, may be fent by the poft, and to prevent the defigns of robbers, may, without damage, be cut in two and fent at two feveral times. Or bills, called bank poft bills, may be had by application at the bank, which are particularly calculated to prevent loffes by robberies, they being made payable to the order of the perfon who takes them out at a certain number of days after fight; which gives an opportunity to ftop bills at the bank, if they fhould be loft, and prevents their being fo eafily negotiated by ftrangers as common bank notes are: and whoever confiders the hazard, the expence and trouble there would be in fending large fums of gold of the PUBLIC FUNDS.

gold and silver to and from diftant places, muft alfo confider this as a very fingular advantage. Befide which another benefit attends them; for if they are deftroyed by time, or other accidents, the bank will, on oath being made of fuch accident, and fecurity being given, pay the money to the perfon who was in poffeffion of them.

Bank notes differ from all kinds of ftock in thefe three particulars. 1. They are always of the fame value. 2. They are paid off without being transferred; and, 3. They bear no intereft; while ftocks are a fhare in a company's funds, bought without any condition of having the principal returned. India bonds indeed (by fome perfons, though erroneoufly, denominated ftock) are to be excepted, they being made payable at fix months notice, either on the fide of the company or of the poffeffor.

By the word *ftock* was originally meant, a particular fum of money contributed to the eftablifhing a fund to enable a company to carry on a certain trade, by means of which the perfon became a partner in that trade, and received a fhare of the profit made thereby in proportion to the money employed. But this term has been extended farther, though improperly, to fignify any fum of money which has been lent to the government, on condition of receiving a certain intereft till the money is repaid, and which makes a part of the national debt. As the fecurity both of the government and of the public companies is efteemed preferable to that of any private perfon, as the ftocks are negotiable and may be fold at any time, and as the intereft is always punctually paid when due, fo they are thereby enabled to borrow money on a lower intereft than what might be obtained from lending it to private perfons, where there muft be always fome danger of lofing both principal and intereft.

But as every capital ftock or fund of a company is raifed for a particular purpofe, and limited by parliament to a certain fum, it neceffarily follows, that when that fund is compleated, no stock can be bought of the company; though shares already purchased, may be transferred from one person to another. This being the case, there is frequently a great disproportion between the original value of the shares, and what is given for them when transferred; for if there are more buyers than sellers, a person who is indifferent about selling will not part with his share without a considerable profit to himself; and on the contrary, if many are disposed to sell, and few inclined to buy, the value of such shares will naturally fall, in proportion to the impatience of those who want to turn their stock into specie.

These observations may serve to give our readers some idea of the nature of that unjustifiable and dishonest practice called *stock-jobbing*, the mystery of which consists in nothing more than this: the persons concerned in that practice, who are denominated stock-jobbers, make contracts to buy or sell, at a certain distant time, a certain quantity of some particular stock, against which time they endeavour, according as their contract is, either to raise or lower such stock, by raising rumours and spreading fictitious stories in order to induce people either to sell out in a hurry, and consequently cheap, if they are to deliver stock, or to become unwilling to sell, and consequently to make it dearer, if they are to receive stock.

The persons who make these contracts are not in general possessed of any real stock, and when the time comes that they are to receive or deliver the quantity they have contracted for, they only pay such a sum of money as makes the difference between the price the stock was at when they made the contract, and the price it happens to be at when the contract is fulfilled, and it is no uncommon thing for persons not worth 100 l. to make contracts for the buying or selling 100,000 l. stock. In the language of Exchange Alley,

Alley, the buyer in this cafe is called the Bull, and the feller the Bear.

Befide thefe, there are another fet of men, who though of a higher rank, may properly enough come under the fame denomination. Thefe are your great monied men, who are dealers in ftock and contractors with the government whenever any new money is to be borrowed. Thefe indeed are not fictitious, but real buyers and fellers of ftock; but by raifing falfe hopes, or creating groundlefs fears, by pretending to buy or fell large quantities of ftock on a fudden, by ufing the fore-mentioned fet of men as their inftruments, and other like practices, are enabled to raife or fall the ftocks one or two per cent. at pleafure.

However, the real value of one ftock above another, on account of its being more profitable to the proprietors, or any thing that will really, or only in imagination, affect the credit of a company, or endanger the government, by which that credit is fecured, muft naturally have a confiderable effect on the ftocks. Thus, with refpect to the intereft of the proprietors, a fhare in the ftock of a trading company which produces 5 l. or 6 l. per cent. per ann. muft be more valuable than an annuity with government fecurity, that produces no more than 3 l. or 4 l. per cent. per annum; and confequently fuch ftock muft fell at a higher price than fuch an annuity. Though it muft be obferved, that a fhare in the ftock of a trading company producing 5 l. or 6 l. per cent. per annum, will not fetch fo much money at market as a government annuity producing the fame fum, becaufe the fecurity of the company is not reckoned equal to that of the government, and the continuance of their paying fo much per annum, is more precarious, as their dividend is, or ought to be, always in proportion to the profits of their trade.

As the ftocks of the Eaft India, the bank, and South-Sea companies, are diftinguifhed by different denominations, and are of a very different nature, we shall give a short history of each of them, together with an account of the different stocks, each is poffeffed of, beginning with the East India company, as the first established.

Of the East India Company.

There is no trading company in Europe, the Dutch East India company excepted, which can be put in competition with this. Its was first established in the latter end of the reign of queen Elizabeth; and its privileges have been enlarged, or confirmed, by almost every monarch since. Its shares, or subscriptions, were originally only 50 l. sterling; and its capital only 369,891 l. 5 s. but the directors having a considerable dividend to make in 1676, it was agreed to join the profits to the capital, by which the shares were doubled, and consequently each became of 100 l. value, and the capital 739,782 l. 10 s. to which capital, if 963,639 l. the profits of the company to the year 1685, be added, the whole stock will be found to be 1,703,402 pounds.

However, this company having sustained several losses by the Dutch, and the subjects of the great Mogul, was in a declining way at the revolution, when the war with France reduced it so low, that it appearing scarcely possible to be supported, a new one was erected. The merchants forming the new East India company, received their charter in 1698, having in consideration of the grant thereof, lent to the government two millions at 8 per cent. per annum, and pushing their trade with vigour, they soon carried on twice the business that was ever done by the old company. But after the two companies had subsisted a few years in a separate state, means were contrived to unite them, which was effected in 1702, when a new charter was granted them under the title of the United Company of Merchants trading to the East Indies.

To

To the two millions advanced by the new company, the united company in the 6th of queen Anne, lent the government 1,200,000 l. which made their whole loan amount to 3,200,000 l. a further sum was also lent by the company in 1730, on a renewal of their charter, the interest of which is reduced to 3 per cent. and called the India 3 per cent. annuities.

As to India stock, it is of a quite different nature; for as that is not money put out to interest, but the trading stock of the company, and the proprietors of the shares, instead of receiving a regular annuity, have a dividend of the profits arising from the company's trade; which, as it is more valuable, these shares generally sell at a price much above the original value.

As to the management of this united company, all persons without exception, natives and foreigners, men and women, are admitted members of it, and 500 l. in the stock of the company, gives the owner a vote in the general court, and 2000 l. qualifies him to be chosen a director. The directors are 24 in number, including the chairman, and deputy chairman, who may be re-elected for four years successively. The chairman has a salary of 200 l. a year, and each of the directors 150 l. The meetings or courts of directors, are to be held at least once a week; but are commonly oftener, being summoned as occasion requires.

Out of the body of directors are chosen several committees, who have the peculiar inspection of certain branches of the company's business; as the committee of correspondence, a committee of buying, a committee of treasury, a house-committee, a committee of warehouses, a committee of shipping, a committee of accompts, a committee of law-suits, and a committee to prevent the growth of private trade, &c. who have under them a secretary, cashier, clerks, warehouse-keepers, &c.

Other

Other officers of the company are governors and factors abroad, some of whom have guards of soldiers, and live in all the state of sovereign princes.

Of the Bank of England.

The company of the bank was incorporated by parliament, in the 5th and 6th years of king William and queen Mary, by the name of the Governor and Company of the Bank of England; in consideration of the loan of 1,200,000 l. granted to the government; for which the subscribers received almost 8 per cent. By this charter, the company are not to borrow under their common seal, unless by act of parliament; they are not to trade, or suffer any person in trust for them, to trade in any goods, or merchandize; but they may deal in bills of exchange, in buying or selling bullion, and foreign gold and silver coin, &c.

By an act of parliament passed in the 8th and 9th year of king William III. they were impowered to enlarge their capital stock to 2,201,171 l. 10 s. It was then also enacted, that bank stock should be a personal, and not a real estate; that no contract either in word or writing, for buying or selling bank stock, should be good in law, unless registered in the books of the bank within seven days; and the stock transferred in 14 days, and that it should be felony, without benefit of clergy, to counterfeit the common seal of the bank, or any sealed bank bill, or any bank note, or to alter or erase such bills or notes.

By another act passed in the 7th of queen Anne, the company were impowered to augment their capital to 4,402,343 l. and they then advanced 400,000 l. more to the government, and in 1714, they advanced another loan of 1,500,000 l.

In the third year of the reign of king George I. the interest of their capital stock was reduced to 5 per cent. when the bank agreed to deliver up as many exchequer bills as amounted to 2,000,000 l. and to

accept

accept an annuity of 100,000 l. and it was declared lawful for the bank to call from their members, in proportion to their interests in the capital stock, such sums of money as in a general court should be found necessary. If any member should neglect to pay his share of the monies so called for, at the time appointed by notice in the London Gazette, and fixed upon the Royal exchange, it should be lawful for the bank, not only to stop the dividend of such member, and to apply it toward payment of the money in question; but also to stop the transfers of the share of such defaulter, and to charge him with an interest of 5 l. per cent. per annum, for the money so omitted to be paid: and if the principal and interest should be three months unpaid, the bank should then have power to sell so much of the stock belonging to the defaulter as would satisfy the same.

After this, the bank reduced the interest of the 2,000,000 l. lent to the government, from 5 to 4 per cent. and purchased several other annuities, which were afterward redeemed by the government, and the national debt due to the bank reduced to 1,600,000 l. But in 1742, the company engaged to supply the government with 1,600,000 l. at 3 per cent. which is now called the 3 per cent. annuities, so that the government was now indebted to the company 3,200,000 l. the one half carrying 4, and the other 3 per cent.

In the year 1746, the company agreed that the sum of 986,800 l. due to them in the exchequer bills unsatisfied, on the duties for licences to sell spirituous liquors by retail, should be cancelled, and in lieu thereof to accept of an annuity of 39,442 l. the interest of that sum at 4 per cent. The company also agreed to advance the further sum of 1,000,000 l. into the exchequer, upon the credit of the duties arising by the malt and land-tax, at 4 per cent. for exchequer bills to be issued for that purpose; in confideration of which the company were enabled to

F 4 augment

augment their capital with 986,800 l. the interest of which, as well as that of the other annuities, was reduced to 3 l. 10 s. per cent. till the 25th of December 1757, and from that time to carry only 3 per cent.

And in order to enable them to circulate the said exchequer bills, they established what is now called bank circulation. The nature of which, not being well understood, we shall take the liberty to be a little more particular in its explanation than we have been with regard to the other stocks.

The company of the bank are obliged to keep cash sufficient to answer not only the common, but also any extraordinary demand that may be made upon them; and whatever money they have by them, over and above the sum supposed necessary for these purposes, they employ in what may be called the trade of the company; that is to say, in discounting bills of exchange, in buying of gold and silver, and in government securities, &c. But when the bank entered into the above-mentioned contract, as they did not keep unemployed a larger sum of money than what they deemed necessary to answer their ordinary and extraordinary demands, they could not conveniently take out of their current cash so large a sum as a million, with which they were obliged to furnish the government, without either lessening that sum they employed in discounting, buying gold and silver, &c. (which would have been very disadvantageous to them) or inventing some method that should answer all the purposes of keeping the million in cash. The method which they chose, and which fully answers their end, was as follows.

They opened a subscription, which they renew annually, for a million of money; wherein the subscribers advance 10 per cent. and enter into a contract to pay the remainder, or any part thereof, whenever the bank shall call upon them, under the penalty of forfeiting the 10 per cent. so advanced; in consideration of which, the bank pays the subscribers

4 per

4 per cent. interest for the money paid in, and ¼ per cent. for the whole sum they agree to furnish; and in case a call should be made upon them for the whole, or any part thereof, the bank farther agrees to pay them at the rate of 5 per cent. per annum for such sum till they repay it, which they are under an obligation to do at the end of the year. By this means the bank obtains all the purposes of keeping a million of money by them; and though the subscribers, if no call is made upon them (which is in general the case) receive 6¼ per cent. for the money they advance, yet the company gains the sum of 23,500 l. per annum by the contract; as will appear by the following account.

	£.
The bank receives from the government for the advance of a million —	30,000
The bank pays to the subscribers who advance 100,000 l. and engage to pay (when called for) 900,000 l. more	6,500
The clear gain to the bank therefore is	23,500

This is the state of the case, provided the company should make no call on the subscribers; which they will be very unwilling to do, because it would not only lessen their profit, but affect the public credit in general.

Bank stock may not improperly be called a trading stock, since with this they deal very largely in foreign gold and silver, in discounting bills of exchange, &c. Beside which, they are allowed by the government very confiderable sums annually for the management of the annuities paid at their office. All which advantages render a share in their stock very valuable, tho' it is not equal in value to the East India stock. The company make dividends of the profits half yearly, of which notice is publicly given; when those who have occasion for their money may readily receive it; but private persons, if they judge convenient, are
permitted

permitted to continue their funds, and to have their intereſt added to the principal.

This company is under the direction of a governor, deputy-governor, and 24 directors, who are annually elected by the general court, in the ſame manner as in the Eaſt India company. Thirteen, or more, compoſe a court of directors for managing the affairs of the company.

The officers of this company are very numerous.

Of the South Sea Company.

During the long war with France in the reign of queen Anne, the payment of the ſailors of the royal navy being neglected, and they receiving tickets inſtead of money, were frequently obliged by their neceſſities to ſell theſe tickets to avaritious men at a diſcount of 40 l. and ſometimes 50 l. per cent. By this and other means the debts of the nation unprovided for by parliament, and which amounted to 9,471,321 l. fell into the hands of theſe uſurers. On which, Mr. Harley, at that time chancellor of the exchequer, and afterward earl of Oxford, propoſed a ſcheme to allow the proprietors of theſe debts and deficiencies 6 l. per cent. per annum, and to incorporate them in order to their carrying on a trade to the South Sea; and they were accordingly incorporated under the title of the Governor and Company of Merchants of Great Britain, trading to the South Seas, and other parts of America, and for encouraging the Fiſhery, &c.

Though this company ſeem formed for the ſake of commerce, it is certain the miniſtry never thought ſeriouſly during the courſe of the war, about making any ſettlements on the coaſt of South America, which was what flattered the expectations of the people; nor was it indeed ever carried into execution, or any trade ever undertaken by this company, except the Aſſiento, in purſuance of the treaty of Utrecht, for furniſhing the Spaniards with negroes, of which this

company

company was deprived by the late convention between the courts of Great Britain and Spain, soon after the treaty of Aix la Chapelle in 1748.

After this, some other sums were lent to the government in the reign of queen Anne at 6 per cent. In the third of George I. the interest of the whole was reduced to 5 per cent. and they advanced two millions more to the government at the same interest. By the statute of the 6th of George I. it was declared, that this company might redeem all or any of the redeemable national debts, in consideration of which the company were empowered to augment their capital according to the sums they should discharge: and for enabling the company to raise such sums for purchasing annuities, exchanging for ready money new exchequer bills, carrying on their trade, &c. the company might by such means as they should think proper, raise such sums of money as in a general court of the company should be judged necessary. The company were also impowered to raise money on contracts, bills, bonds or obligations under their common seal, on the credit of their capital stock. But if the sub-governor, deputy-governor, or other members of the company should purchase lands or revenues of the crown, upon account of the corporation, or lend money by loan or anticipation, on any branch of the revenue, other than such part only on which a credit of loan was granted by parliament, such sub-governor, or other member of the company, should forfeit treble the value of the money so lent.

The fatal South Sea scheme transacted in the year 1720, was executed upon the last-mentioned statute. The company had at first set out with good success, and the value of their stock for the first five years had risen faster than that of any other company, and his majesty, after purchasing 10,000 l. stock, had condescended to be their governor. Things were in this situation, when taking advantage of the above statute, the South Sea bubble was projected. The

pretended

pretended defign of which was to raife a fund for carrying on a trade to the South Seas, and purchafing annuities, &c. paid to the other companies: and propofals were printed and diftributed fhewing the advantages of the defign, and inviting perfons into it. The fum neceffary for carrying it on, together with the profits that were to arife from it, were divided into a certain number of fhares, or fubfcriptions to be purchafed by perfons difpofed to adventure therein. And the better to carry on the deception, the directors engaged to make very large dividends, and actually declared, that every 100 l. original ftock would yield 50 l. per annum, which occafioned fo great a rife of their ftock, that a fhare of 100 l. was fold for upward of 1000 l. This was in the month of July; but before the end of September it fell to 150 l. by which multitudes were ruined, and fuch a fcene of diftrefs occafioned as is fcarcely to be conceived. But the confequences of this infamous fcheme are too well known. We fhall pafs over all the other tranfactions of this company in the reign of king George I. as not material to our prefent purpofe.

By a ftatute of the 6th of his late majefty, it was enacted, that from and after the 24th of June 1733, the capital ftock of this company, which amounted to 14,651,103 l. 8 s. 1 d. and the fhares of the refpective proprietors, fhould be divided into four equal parts, three-fourths of which fhould be converted into a joint ftock, attended with annuities, after the rate of 4 per cent. until redemption by parliament, and fhould be called, the new South Sea annuities, and the other fourth part fhould remain in the company as a trading capital ftock, attended with the refidue of the annuities or funds payable at the exchequer to the company for their whole capital, till redemption; and attended with the fame fums allowed for charges of management, and with all effects, profits of trade, debts, privileges and advantages belonging to the South Sea company. That

the

the accomptant of the company should twice every year, at Christmas and Midsummer, or within one month after, state an account of the company's affairs, which should be laid before the next general court, in order to their declaring a dividend: and all dividends should be made out of the clear profits, and should not exceed what the company might reasonably divide, without incurring any farther debt; provided that the company should not at any time divide more than 4 per cent. per annum, until their debts were discharged; and that the South Sea company, and their trading stock, should, exclusively from the new joint stock of annuities, be liable to all the debts and incumbrances of the company; and that the company should cause to be kept within the city of London, an office and books, in which all transfers of the new annuities should be entered and signed by the party making such transfer, or his attorney, and the person to whom such transfer should be made, or his attorney, should under-write his acceptance, and no other method of transferring the annuities should be good in law.

The annuities of this company, as well as the other, are now reduced to 3 l. per cent.

This company is under the direction of a governor, sub-governor, deputy-governor, and 21 directors; but no person is qualified to be governor, his majesty excepted, unless such governor has in his own name and right, 5000 l. in the trading stock; the sub-governor is to have 4000 l. the deputy 3000 l. and a director 2000 l. in the same stock. In every general court, every member having in his own name and right 500 l. in trading stock, has one vote; if 2000 l. two votes; if 3000 l. three votes, and if 5000 l. four votes.

The East India company, the bank of England, and the South Sea company, are the only incorporated bodies to which the government is indebted, except the million bank, whose capital is only one

million,

million, conftituted to purchafe the reverfion of the long exchequer orders.

The intereft of all the debts owing by the government is now reduced to 3 per cent. excepting only the annuities for the years 1756, and 1758, the life annuities, and the exchequer orders: but the South Sea company ftill continues to divide four per cent. on their prefent capital ftock, which they are enabled to do from the profits they make on the fums allowed to them for management of the annuities paid at their office, and from the intereft of annuities which are not claimed by the proprietors.

As the prices of the different ftocks are continually fluctuating above and below par; fo when a perfon who is not acquainted with tranfactions of that nature, reads in the papers the prices of ftocks, where bank ftock is marked perhaps 127 l. India ditto 134 a 134¼. South Sea ditto 97¼, &c. he is to underftand that a 100 l. of thofe refpective ftocks fell at fuch a time for thofe feveral fums.

In comparing the prices of the different ftocks one with another, it muft be remembered, that the intereft due on them from the time of the laft payment, is taken into the current price, and the feller never receives any feparate confideration for it, except in the cafe of India bonds, where the intereft due is calculated to the day of the fale, and paid by the purchafer over and above the premium agreed for. But as the intereft on the different ftocks is paid at different times, this, if not rightly underftood, would lead a perfon not well acquainted with them into confiderable miftakes in his computation of their value; fome always having a quarter's intereft due on them more than others, which makes an appearance of a confiderable difference in the price, when, in reality, there is none at all. Thus, for inftance, old South Sea annuities fell at prefent for £.85¼ or £.85 10 s. while new South Sea annuities fetch only £.84¾, or £.84 15 s. though each of them produce

the

the same annual sum of £3 per cent. but the old annuities have a quarter's interest more due on them than the new annuities, which amounts to 15s. the exact difference. There is, however, one or two causes that will always make one species of annuities sell somewhat lower than another, though of the same real value, one of which is, the annuities making but a small capital, and there not being, for that reason, so many people at all times ready to buy into it, as into others, where the quantity is larger; because it is apprehended that whenever the government pays off the national debt, they will begin with that particular species of annuity, the capital of which is the smallest.

A stock may likewise be affected by the court of Chancery; for if that court should order the money which is under their direction to be laid out in any particular stock, that stock, by having more purchasers, will be raised to a higher price than any other of the like value.

By what has been said, the reader will perceive how much the credit and interest of the nation depends on the support of the public funds.—While the annuities, and interest for money advanced is there regularly paid, and the principal insured by both prince and people (a security not to be had in other nations) foreigners will lend us their property, and all Europe be interested in our welfare; the paper of the companies will be converted into money and merchandize, and Great Britain can never want cash to carry her schemes into execution.

In other nations, credit is founded on the word of the prince, if a monarchy; or that of the people, if a republic; but here it is established on the interests of both prince and people, which is the strongest security: for however lovely and engaging honesty may be in other respects, interest in money-matters will always obtain confidence; because many people pay great regard to their interest, who have but little veneration for virtue.

A short

A short Description of London *.

London, the metropolis of Great Britain, including Westminster and Southwark, is a city of a very surprising extent, of prodigious wealth, and of the most extensive trade; it is at once the largest and richest city in Europe. This city is now what ancient Rome once was; the seat of liberty, the encourager of arts, and the admiration of the whole world. It is situated on the banks of the Thames, a river, which, though not the largest in the world, is of the greatest service to its commerce. It being continually filled with fleets, sailing to or from the most distant climates; and its banks being from Londonbridge to Blackwall, almost one continued great magazine of naval stores, containing three large wet docks, 32 dry docks, and 33 yards for the building of ships, for the use of the merchants, beside the places allotted for the building of boats and lighters; and the king's yards lower down the river for building men of war. As this city is about sixty miles distant from the sea, it enjoys, by means of this river, all the benefits of navigation, without the danger of being surprised by foreign fleets, or of being annoyed by the moist vapours of the sea. It rises regularly from the water-side, and extending itself on both sides along its banks, reaches a prodigious length from east to west; surrounded on both sides by a number of large and populous villages, adorned with handsome commodious buildings, the country-seats of gentlemen and tradesmen; whither the latter retire for the benefit of the fresh air, and to relax their minds from the hurry of business.

---

* London is situated in 51° 30' north latitude, 400 miles south of Edinburgh, and 270 south-east of Dublin; 200 north-west of Paris, 180 miles west of Amsterdam, 500 south-west of Copenhagen, 600 north-west of Vienna, 1360 north-west of Constantinople, 800 north-east of Madrid, 850 north-east of Lisbon, and 820 north-west of Rome.

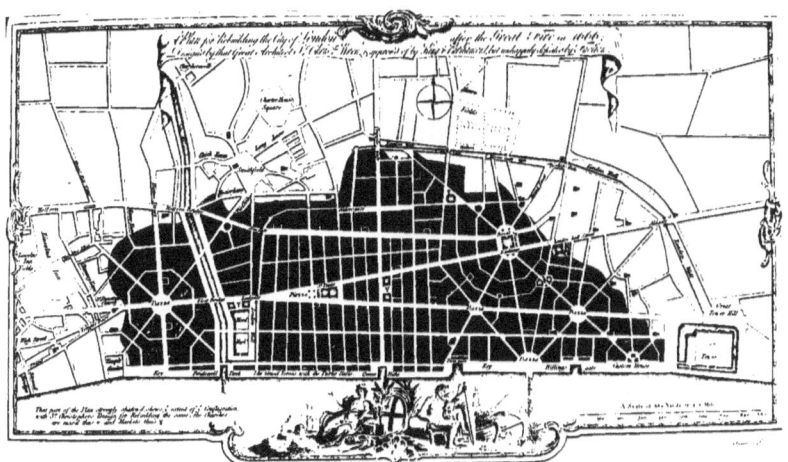

The irregular form of this city makes it difficult to ascertain its extent. However, its length from east to west, is generally allowed to be above seven miles; and its breadth, in some places, three, in other two; and in other again not much above half a mile. But it is much easier to form an idea of the large extent of a city so irregularly built, by the number of the people, who are computed to be near a million; and from the number of edifices devoted to the service of religion. Of these, beside St. Paul's cathedral, and the collegiate church at Westminster, there are 102 parish-churches, and 69 chapels of the established religion; 21 French protestant chapels; 8 chapels belonging to the Germans, Dutch, Danes, &c. 33 baptist meetings; 26 independent meetings; 28 presbyterian meetings; 14 popish chapels, and meeting-houses for the use of foreign ambassadors, and people of various sects; and 3 Jews synagogues. So that there are 318 places devoted to religious worship, in the compass of this vast pile of buildings, without reckoning the 21 out-parishes, usually included within the bills of mortality.

Of these churches the most famous is St. Paul's cathedral, which is the noblest of all the protestant churches in the world. This is an edifice equally remarkable for its beauty and magnificence, containing as few faults as the nature and extent of so large a building will admit. It is built according to the Greek and Roman orders, under the direction of that celebrated architect Sir Christopher Wren, after the model of St. Peter's at Rome. The length within is 500 feet; and its height, from the marble pavement to the cross on the top of the cupola is 340. The expence of rebuilding this cathedral after the fire of London, is computed at about 800,000 l.

Westminster-Abbey, or the collegiate church of Westminster, is a venerable pile of building, in the Gothic taste. It was first built by Edward the Confessor; king Henry III. rebuilt it from the ground, and Henry VII. added a fine chapel to the east end of it: this is the repofitory of the deceafed Britifh kings and nobility; and here are alfo monuments erected to the memory of many great and illuftrious perfonages.

Among the other churches, the moft remarkable are St. Paul's Covent-Garden, the churches of St. Mary le Bow, and St. Bride's; the two latter for having the fineft fteeples in the world. The infide of the church of St. Stephen, Walbroke, is admired all over Europe. And, in fhort, the contrivance and beauty of many other churches, confidering how they were obliged to be thruft up in corners, is furprifingly fine. It is a great misfortune, that though this city abounds with the moft elegant ftructures, and the moft magnificent public and private buildings, yet they are placed in fuch a manner as muft tempt every foreigner to believe that they were defigned to be concealed.

There are here alfo two royal palaces, St. James's and Somerfet-houfe, both of them, efpecially the firft, greatly beneath the dignity of a king of Great Britain; as to the latter, it has been generally the refidence of the queen-dowagers of England.

There are alfo in and near this city 100 almshoufes, about 20 hofpitals and infirmaries, 3 colleges, 10 public prifons, 15 flefh-markets; 1 market for live cattle, 2 other markets more particularly for herbs; and 23 other markets for corn, coals, hay, &c. 15 inns of court, 27 public fquares, befide thofe within any fingle buildings, as the Temple, &c. 49 halls for companies, 8 public fchools, called freefchools; and 131 charity-fchools; which provide education for 5034 poor children; 7000 ftreets, lanes, courts, and alleys, and 130,000 dwelling-houfes.

The bridges of London and Weftminfter are beheld with admiration by all foreigners; that of London confifts of 19 ftone arches, 20 feet between each; it is 900 feet long, 30 wide, and 60 feet high; and has a draw-bridge in the middle. The Thames in this part is 915 feet broad.

Weſtminſter-bridge is reckoned one of the moſt compleat and elegant ſtructures of the kind in the known world. It is built entirely of ſtone, and extended over the river at a place where it is 1,223 feet broad; which is above 300 feet broader than at London-bridge. On each ſide is a fine balluſtrade of ſtone, with places of ſhelter from the rain. The width of the bridge is 44 feet, having on each ſide a fine footway for paſſengers. It conſiſts of 14 piers, and 13 large, and two ſmall arches, that in the center being 76 feet wide, and the reſt decreaſing four feet each from the other; ſo that the two leaſt arches of the 13 great ones, are each 52 feet. It is computed that the value of 40,000 l. in ſtone and other materials is always under water. This magnificent ſtructure was built in 11 years and nine months, and coſt about 389,500 l.

Another elegant bridge is building at Black Friars, at the expence of the city of London; which, being ſituated near the center of this metropolis, will be of the utmoſt convenience to town and country.

Weſtminſter-hall, though on the outſide it makes a mean, and no very advantageous appearance, is a noble Gothick building, and is ſaid to be the largeſt room in the world, it being 220 feet long, and 70 broad. Its roof is the fineſt of its kind that can be ſeen. Here is held the coronation feaſts of our kings and queens; alſo the courts of chancery, king's-bench, and common-pleas, and above ſtairs, that of the exchequer.

That beautiful column, called the Monument, erected at the charge of the city, to perpetuate the memory of its being deſtroyed by fire, is juſtly worthy of notice. This column exceeds all the obeliſks and pillars of the ancients, it being 202 feet high, with a ſtair-caſe in the middle to aſcend to the balcony, which is about 30 feet ſhort of the top, from whence there are other ſteps, made for perſons to look out at the top of all, which is faſhioned like an urn, with a flame iſſuing from it. On the baſe of the

the Monument, next the street, the destruction of the city is emblematically represented in bas relief. The north and south sides of the base have each a Latin inscription, the one describing its dreadful desolation, and the other its splendid resurrection; and on the east side is an inscription, shewing when the pillar was begun and finished. The charge of erecting this monument amounted to upward of 13,000 l.

The Royal Exchange is a large noble building, and is said to have cost above 80,000 l.

We might here give a description of the Tower *, Bank of England, the New-treasury, the Admiralty-office,

---

* In examining the curiosities of the Tower of London, it will be proper to begin with those on the outside the principal gate; the first thing a stranger usually goes to visit is the wild beasts; which, from their situation, first present themselves: for having entered the outer gate, and passed what is called the spur-guard, the keeper's house presents itself before you, which is known by a painted lion on the wall, and another over the door which leads to their dens. By ringing a bell, and paying six-pence each person, you may easily gain admittance.

The next place worthy of observation is the Mint, which comprehends near one third of the Tower, and contains houses for all the officers belonging to the coinage. On passing the principal gate you see the White Tower, built by William the Conqueror. This is a large, square, irregular stone building, situated almost in the center, no one side answering to another, nor are any of its watch towers, of which there are four at the top, built alike. One of these towers is now converted into an observatory. In the first story are two noble rooms, one of which is a small armoury for the sea service, it having various sorts of arms, very curiously laid up, for above 10,000 seamen. In the other room are many closets and presses, all filled with warlike engines and instruments of death. Over this are two other floors, one principally filled with arms; the other with arms and other warlike instruments, as spades, shovels, pick-axes, and cheveaux de frize. In the upper story are kept match, sheep-skins, tanned hides, &c. and in a little room, called Julius Cæsar's chapel, are deposited some records, containing perhaps the ancient usages and customs of the place. In this building are also preserved models of the new invented engines of destruction, that have from time to time been presented to the government. Near the south-west angle of the White Tower is the Spanish armoury, in which are deposited the spoils of what was vainly called the Invincible Armada; in order to perpetuate to latest posterity,

the

office, the Banqueting-houſe at Whitehall, the Mews, where the king's horſes are kept; the Manſion-houſe

the memory of that ſignal victory, obtained by the Engliſh over the whole naval power of Spain, in the reign of Philip II.
The trophies preſerved here of this memorable victory, with ſome other curioſities, are, 1. A Spaniſh battle-ax, ſo contrived as to ſtrike four holes in a man's ſkull at once; it has beſide, a piſtol in its handle, with a match lock. 2. The Spaniſh general's halbert, covered with velvet. All the nails are double gilt, and on the top is the pope's head, curiouſly engraven. 3. The Spaniſh morning ſtar; a deſtructive engine in the form of a ſtar; of which there were many thouſands on board, and all of them with poiſoned points; deſigned to ſtrike at the Engliſh, in caſe they boarded them. 4. Thumb-ſcrews, of which there were ſeveral cheſts full on board the Spaniſh fleet. The uſe they were intended for is ſaid to have been, to extort confeſſion from the Engliſh where their money was hid, had they prevailed.——Certain it is, that, after the defeat, the whole converſation of the court and country turned upon the diſcoveries made by the Spaniſh priſoners, of the racks, the wheels, and the whips of wire, with which they were to ſcourge the Engliſh of every rank, age, and ſex. The moſt noted hereticks were to be put to death; thoſe who ſurvived were to be branded on the forehead with a hot iron; and the whole form of government, both in church and ſtate, was to be overturned. 5. A Spaniſh poll-ax, uſed in boarding of ſhips. 6. Spaniſh halberts, or ſpears, ſome of them curiouſly engraved, and inlaid with gold. 7. Spaniſh Spadas, or long ſwords, poiſoned at the points, ſo that if a man received but ever ſo ſlight a wound, it would prove certain death. 8. Spaniſh cravats, as they are called; theſe are engines of torture, made of iron, and put on board to lock the feet, arms, and heads of Engliſh hereticks together. 9. Spaniſh bilboes, alſo made of iron, to yoke the Engliſh priſoners two and two. 10. Spaniſh ſhot, which are of four ſorts; ſpike-ſhot, ſtar-ſhot, chain-ſhot, and link-ſhot; all admirably contrived, as well for the deſtruction of the maſts and rigging of ſhips, as for ſweeping the men off the decks. 11. The banner, with a crucifix upon it, which was to have been carried before the Spaniſh general. Upon it is the pope's benediction before the Spaniſh fleet ſailed; for the pope, it is ſaid, came to the water-ſide, and ſeeing the fleet, bleſſed it, and ſtiled it INVINCIBLE. 12. An uncommon piece of arms, being a piſtol in a ſhield, ſo contrived that the piſtol might be fired, and the body covered at the ſame time. It is to be fired by a match-lock, and the ſight of the enemy taken through a little grate in the ſhield, which is piſtol-proof. 13. The Spaniſh ranjeur, made

sion-house of the lord mayor, the Custom-house, India-house, and a vast number of other public buildings; beside

in different forms, and intended either to kill the men on horseback, or to pull them off their horses. At the back is a spike, which, your attendants say, was to pick the roast beef out of the Englishman's teeth. And on one of them is a piece of silver coin, which they intended to make current in England. On this coin are three heads, supposed to be the Pope's, Philip II's, and queen Mary's.——This is a curiosity which most Spaniards who arrive in London come to see, 14. The Spanish officers lances, finely engraved. These were formerly gilt, but the gilding is now almost worn off with cleaning. It is said, that when Don Pedro de Valdez, a captain of one of the Spanish ships that was taken, passed his examination before lord Burleigh, he told his lordship, that those fine polished lances were put on board to bleed the English with; to which that nobleman merrily replied, that, if he were not mistaken, the English had performed that operation better on their good friends the Spaniards, with worse instruments. 15. The common soldiers pikes, 18 feet in length, pointed with long sharp spikes, and shod with iron; designed to keep off the horse, to facilitate the landing of their foot. 16. The last thing shewn of these memorable spoils, is the Spanish general's shield, not worn by him; but carried before him as an ensign of honour. Upon it are depicted, in most curious workmanship, some of the labours of Hercules, and other allegories, which seem to throw a shade upon the boasted skill of modern artists. This was made near an hundred years before the art of printing was known in England; and upon it is the following inscription, in Roman characters, ADVLTERIO DEIANIRA CONSPURCANS OCCIDITUR CACVS AB HERCVL. OPPRIMITVR 1379. 17. The other curiosities deposited here, are Danish and Saxon clubs, weapons which each of those people are said to have used in their conquest of England. These are, perhaps, curiosities of the greatest antiquity of any in the Tower, they having lain there above 850 years. The warders call them the womens weapons, because, say they, " the British women made prize of them, when, in one night, they all conspired together, and cut the throats of 35,000 Danes; the greatest piece of secrecy the English women ever kept, for which they have ever since been honoured with the right-hand of the man, the upper end of the table, and the first cut of every dish of victuals they happen to like best." The massacre of the Danes was not, however, performed by the women alone, but by the private orders of Ethelred II. who in 1012, privately commanded his officers to extirpate those cruel and tyrannical invaders. 18.

King

beside the magnificent edifices raised by our nobility; as

King Henry VIII's walking staff, which has three match-lock pistols in it, with coverings to keep the charges dry. " With this staff, the warders tell you, the king sometimes walked round the city, to see that the constables did their duty; and one night, as he was walking near the bridge-foot, the constable stopt him, to know what he did with such an unlucky weapon, at that time of the night. Upon which the king struck him; but the constable calling the watchmen to his assistance, his majesty was apprehended, and carried to the Poultry Compter, where he lay till morning, without either fire or candle. When the keeper was informed of the rank of his prisoner, he dispatched a messenger to the constable, who came trembling with fear, expecting nothing less than to be hanged, drawn and quartered: but instead of that, the king applauded him for his resolution in doing his duty, and made him a handsome present. At the same time he settled upon St. Magnus's parish, an annual grant of 23 l. and a mark, and made a provision for furnishing 30 chaldron of coals, and a large allowance of bread annually for ever, toward the comfortable relief of his fellow-prisoners and their successors, which, the warders say, is paid them to this day." 19. A large wooden cannon, called Policy, because, as we are informed, when king Henry VIII. besieged Bouloigne, the roads being impassable for heavy cannon, he caused a number of these wooden ones to be made, and mounted on proper batteries before the town, as if real cannon; which so terrified the French commandant, that he gave up the place without firing a shot.——The truth is, the duke of Suffolk, who commanded at this siege under the king, soon made himself master of the lower town; but it was not till seven weeks afterward that the upper town capitulated, in which time the English sustained great loss in possessing themselves of the bray. The warders must therefore be greatly mistaken in their account of this piece. 20. The ax with which queen Anne Bullen, the mother of queen Elizabeth, was beheaded, on the 19th of May 1536. The earl of Essex, queen Elizabeth's favourite, was also beheaded with the same ax. 21. A small train of ten pieces of pretty little cannon, neatly mounted on proper carriages, being a present from the foundery of London to king Charles I. when a child, to assist him in learning the art of gunnery. 22. Weapons made with the blades of scythes fixed strait to the ends of poles. These were taken from the duke of Monmouth's party, at the battle of Sedgemoore, in the reign of James II. 23. The partizans that were carried at the funeral of king William III. 24. The perfect model of the admirable machine, the idea of which was brought from Italy by Sir Thomas Lombe, and first erected at Derby,

as Charlton-houfe, Marlborough-houfe, and Buckingham-

Derby, at his own expence, for making orgazine or thrown filk. This model is well worth the obfervation of the curious.
You now come to the grand ftore-houfe, a noble building, to the northward of the White Tower, that extends 245 feet in length, and 60 in breadth. It was begun by king James II. who built it to the firſt floor; but it was finifhed by king William III. who erected that magnificent room called the New, or Small Armoury, in which that prince, with queen Mary, his confort, dined in great form, having all the warrant workmen and labourers to attend them, dreffed in white gloves and aprons, the ufual badges of the order of mafonry. To this noble room you are led by a folding door, adjoining to the eaſt end of the Tower chapel, which leads to a grand ftaircafe of 50 eafy fteps. On the left-fide of the uppermoſt landing-place is the work-fhop, in which are conftantly employed about fourteen furbifhers, in cleaning, repairing, and new placing the arms. On entering the armoury, you fee what they call a wildernefs of arms, fo artfully difpofed, that at one view you behold arms for near 80,000 men, all bright, and fit for fervice: a fight which it is impoffible to behold without aftonifhment; and befide thofe expofed to view, there were, before the late war, fixteen chefts fhut up, each cheft holding about 1,200 mufkets. The arms were originally difpofed by Mr. Harris, who contrived to place them in this beautiful order, both here and in the guard-chamber of Hampton-court. He was a common gun-fmith; but after he had performed this work, which is the admiration of people of all nations, he was allowed a penfion from the crown for his ingenuity. The north and fouth walls are each adorned with eight pilafters, formed of pikes 16 feet long, with capitals of the Corinthian order, compofed of piftols. At the weft end, on the left-hand, as you enter, are two curious pyramids of piftols, ftanding upon crowns, globes, and fcepters, finely carved and placed upon pedeftals five feet high. At the eaft, or farther end, in the oppofite corner, are two fuits of armour, one made for that warlike prince Henry V. and the other for his fon Henry VI. over each of which is a femicircle of piftols; between thefe is reprefented an organ, the large pipes compofed of brafs blunderbuffes, the fmall of piftols. On one fide of the organ is the reprefentation of a fiery ferpent, the head and tail of carved work, and the body of piftols winding round, in the form of a fnake; and on the other an hydra, whofe feven heads are artfully combined by links of piftols. The inner columns that compofe the wildernefs, round which you are conducted by your guides, are, 1. Some arms taken at Bath in the year 1715, diftinguifhed
from

ham-houfe, in St. James's-park; the duke of Montague's,

from all others in the Tower, by having what is called doglocks; that is, a kind of locks with a catch, to prevent their going off at half-cock. 2. Bayonets and piftols put up in the forms of half moons and fans, with the imitation of a target in the center, made of bayonet blades. Thefe bayonets, of which feveral other fans are compofed, are of the firft invention, they having plug handles which go into the muzzle of the gun, inftead of over it, and thereby prevent the firing of the piece, without fhooting away the bayonet. Thefe were invented at Bayonne in Spain, and from that place take their name. 3. Brafs blunderbuffes for fea-fervice, with capitols of piftols over them. The waves of the fea are here reprefented in old-fafhioned bayonets. 4. Bayonets and fword-bayonets, in the form of half moons and fans, and fet in carved fcollop-fhells. The fword-bayonet is made like the old bayonet, with a plug handle, and differs from it only in being longer. 5. The rifing fun irradiated with piftols, fet in a chequered frame of marine hangers, of a peculiar make, having brafs handles, and a dog's head on their pomels. 6. Four beautiful twifted pillars, formed of piftols up to the top, which is about 22 feet high, and placed at right angles; with the reprefentation of a falling ftar on the cieling, exactly in the middle of them, being the center of this magnificent room. Into this place opens the grand ftair-cafe door, for the admiffion of the royal family, or any of the nobility, whofe curiofity leads them to view the armoury; oppofite to which opens another door into the balcony, that affords a fine profpect of the parade, the governor's houfe, the furveyor-general's, the ftore-keeper's, and other general officers in the Tower. 7. The form of a large pair of folding gates, made of ferjeant's halberts, of an antique make. 8. Horfemen's carbines, hanging very artificially in furbeloes and flounces. 9. Medufa's head, vulgarly called the Witch of Endor, within three regular ellipfes of piftols, with fnakes. The features are finely carved, and the whole figure contrived with the utmoft art. This figure terminates the north fide. 10. Facing the eaft wall, as you turn round, is a grand figure of a lofty organ, 10 ranges high, in which are contained upward of 2,000 pairs of piftols. 11. On the fouth-fide, as you return, the firft figure that attracts attention, is Jupiter riding in a fiery chariot, drawn by eagles, as if in the clouds, holding a thunder-bolt in his left-hand; and over his head is a rainbow: this figure is finely carved, and decorated with bayonets. The figures on this fide anfwer pretty nearly to thofe on the other, and therefore need no farther defcription, till you come again to the center; where, on each fide the door leading to the balcony, you fee, 12. A fine reprefentation in carved work, of the ftar and garter, thiftle, rofe and

tague's, and the duke of Richmond's, in the Privy-garden;

and crown, ornamented with piſtols, &c. and very elegantly enriched with birds, &c. 13. The arms taken from Sir William Perkins, Sir John Friend, Charnock, and others concerned in the aſſaſſination-plot in 1696; among which they ſhew the very blunderbuſs with which they intended to ſhoot king William near Turnham Green, in his way to Hampton Court: alſo the carbine with which Charnock undertook to ſhoot that monarch, as he rode a hunting. 14. Laſtly, the Highlanders arms, taken in 1715, particularly the earl of Mar's fine piece, exquiſitely wrought, and inlaid with mother of pearl: alſo a Highland broad-ſword, with which a Highlander ſtruck general Evans, and at one blow ſtruck him through the hat, wig, and iron ſkullcap; on which that general is ſaid to have ſhot him dead; others ſay, he was taken priſoner, and generouſly forgiven for his bravery. Here is alſo the ſword of juſtice, with a ſharp point, and the ſword of mercy, with a blunt point, carried before the pretender on his being proclaimed king of Scotland, in 1715. Here are likewiſe ſome of the Highlanders piſtols, the barrels and ſtocks being all iron; alſo a Highlander's Lochabor ax, with which it is ſaid that colonel Gardner was killed at the battle of Preſton Pans. A diſcerning eye will diſcover a thouſand peculiarities in the diſpoſition of ſo vaſt a variety of arms, which no deſcription can reach; and therefore it is fit that every one who has a taſte for the admirable combinations of art, ſhould gratify it with the ſight of the nobleſt curioſities of this kind in the whole world.

Upon the ground floor under the ſmall armoury, is a large room of equal dimenſions with that, ſupported by 20 pillars, all hung round with implements of war. This room, which is 24 feet high, has a paſſage in the middle 16 feet wide. At the ſight of ſuch a variety of the moſt dreadful engines of deſtruction, before whoſe thunder the moſt ſuperb edifices, the nobleſt works of art, and numbers of the human ſpecies, fall together in one common and undiſtinguiſhed ruin; one cannot help wiſhing that theſe horrible inventions had ſtill lain, like a falſe conception, in the womb of nature, never to have been ripened into birth. But when, on the other hand, we conſider, that with us they are not uſed to anſwer the purpoſes of ambition, but for ſelf defence, and in the protection of our juſt rights, our terror ſubſides, and we view theſe engines of devaſtation with a kind of ſolemn complacency, as the means Providence has put into our hands for our preſervation. 1. You are ſhewn two large pieces of cannon, employed by admiral Vernon before Carthagena; each of which has a large ſcale driven out of their muzzles by balls from the caſtle of Bocca Chica. 2. Two pieces of excellent workmanſhip, preſented by the city of London to the

garden; the earl of Chesterfield's house, near Hyde-park;

the young duke of Gloucester, son to queen Anne, to assist him in learning the art of war. 3. Four mortars in miniature, for throwing hand granadoes, invented by colonel Brown. They are fired with a lock like a common gun, but have not yet been introduced into practice. 4. Two fine brass cannon taken from the walls of Vigo in 1704, by the late lord Cobham: Their breeches represent lions couchant, with the effigy of St. Barbara, to whom they were dedicated. 5. A petard for bursting open the gates of a city or castle. 6. A large train of fine brass battering cannon, 24 pounders. 7. Some cannon of a new invention, from 6 to 24 pounders. Their superior excellence consists, first, in their lightness, the 24 pounders not weighing quite 1,700 weight, whereas formerly they weighed 5,000; the rest are in proportion; and secondly, in the contrivance for levelling them, which is by a screw, instead of beds and coins. This new method is more expeditious, and saves two men to a gun, and is said to be the contrivance of his royal highness the duke of Cumberland. 8. Brass mortars of 13 inches diameter, which throw a shell of 300 weight; with a number of smaller mortars, and shells in proportion. 9. A carcase, which they fill at sieges with pitch, tar, and other combustibles to set towns on fire. It is thrown out of an 18 inch mortar, and will burn two hours where it happens to fall. 10. A Spanish mortar of 12 inches diameter, taken on board a ship in the West Indies. 11. Six French pieces of cannon, 6 pounders, taken from the rebels at the battle of Culloden, April 16, 1745. 12. A beautiful piece of ordnance, made for king Charles I. when prince of Wales. It is finely ornamented with emblematical devices; among which is an eagle throwing a thunderbolt in the clouds. 13. A train of field-pieces, called the galloping train, carrying a ball of a pound and a half each. 14. A destroying engine, that throws 30 hand-granadoes at once, and is fired by a train. 15. A most curious brass cannon, made for prince Henry, the eldest son of king James I. the ornamenting of which is said to have cost 200 l. 16. A piece with seven bores, for throwing so many balls at once, and another with three, made as early as Henry VIII's time. 17. The drum-major's chariot of state, with kettle-drums placed. It is drawn by four white horses at the head of the train, when upon a march. 18. Two French field-pieces taken at the battle of Hochstadt in 1704. 19. An iron cannon of the first invention, being bars of iron hammered together, and hooped from top to bottom with iron hoops, to prevent its bursting. It has no carriage, but was to be moved from place to place by means of six rings, fixed to it at proper distances. 20. A very large mortar, weighing upward of 6,600 weight, and throwing a shell of 500 weight two miles. This
mortar

park; the duke of Devonshire's, and the earl of Bath's,

mortar was fired so often at the siege of Namur by king William, that the very touch-hole is melted, for want of giving it time to cool. 21. A fine twisted brass cannon, 12 feet long, made in Edward VI's time, called queen Elizabeth's pocket-pistol; which the warders, by way of joke, tell you she used to wear on her right-side when she rode a hunting. 22. Two brass cannon, three bores each, carrying six pounders, taken by the duke of Marlborough at the glorious battle of Ramelies. 23. A mortar that throws nine shells at a time; out of which the baloons were cast at the fire-works, for the last peace.

Beside those above enumerated, there were in the stove-room, before the present war, a vast number of new brass cannon; together with spunges, ladles, rammers, handspikes, wadhooks, &c. with which the walls were lined round; and under the cieling there hang on poles upward of 4,000 harness for horses, beside men's harness, drag-ropes, &c. And beside the trophies of standards, colours, &c. taken from the enemy, it is now adorned with the transparent pictures brought hither from the fire-works played off at the conclusion of the peace in 1748.

The horse-armoury is a plain brick-building, a little to the eastward of the White Tower; and is an edifice rather convenient than elegant, where the spectator is entertained with a representation of those kings and heroes of our own nation, with whose gallant actions it is to be supposed he is well acquainted; some of them equipped and sitting on horseback, in the same bright and shining armour they were used to wear when they performed those glorious actions that give them a distinguished place in the British annals. In ascending the stair-case, just as you come to the landing-place, on casting your eye into the room, you see the figure of a grenadier in his accoutrements, as if upon duty, with his piece rested upon his arm; which is so well done, that at the first glance you will be apt to mistake it for real life. When you enter the room, your conductor presents to your notice, 1. The figures of the horse and foot on your left-hand, supposed to be drawn up in military order, to attend the kings on the other side of the house. These figures are as big as the life, and have been lately new painted. 2. A large tilting lance of Charles Brandon, duke of Suffolk, king Henry VIII's general in France; a nobleman who excelled at the then fashionable diversion of tilting. 3. A compleat suit of tilting armour, such as the kings, nobility, and gentlemen at arms used to wear; with the tilting lance, the rest for the lance, and grand guard. 4. A compleat suit of armour, made for king Henry VIII. when he was but 18 years of age, rough from the hammer. It is at least six feet high, and the joints in the hands, arms and thighs, knees and feet, play like the joints of

a rattle-

Bath's, in Piccadilly; Northumberland-house, in the

a rattle-snake, and are moved with all the facility imaginable. The method of learning the exercise of tilting, was upon wooden horses set upon castors, which by the sway of the body could be moved every way; so that by frequent practice, the rider could shift, parry, strike, unhorse, and recover with surprising dexterity. Some of the horses in this armoury have been used for this purpose; and it is but lately that the castors have been taken from their feet. 5. A little suit of armour made for king Charles II. when prince of Wales, and about seven or eight years of age; with a piece of armour for his horse's head; the whole most curiously wrought and inlaid with silver. 6. Lord Courcy's armour. This nobleman, as the warders tell you, was champion of Ireland, and as a proof, shew you the very sword he took from the French champion; for which valiant action, he and all his successors have the honour to wear their hats in the king's presence; which privilege is still enjoyed by the lord Kinsale, as head of that ancient and noble family. 7. Real coats of mail, called brigantine jackets. They consist of small bits of steel, so artfully quilted one over another, as to resist the point of a sword, and perhaps a musket-ball, and yet are so flexible, that the wearer might bend his body as well as in his ordinary cloaths. 8. An Indian suit of armour, sent by the great mogul as a present to king Charles II. This is very great curiosity; it is made of iron quills about two inches long, finely japanned and ranged in rows, one row slipping easily over another: these are bound very strong together with silk twist, and are used in that country as a defence against darts and arrows. 9. A neat little suit of armour, worn by a carved figure, representing Richard duke of York, the youngest son of king Edward IV. who, with his brother Edward V. were smothered in the Tower, by order of their uncle and guardian, Richard III. 10. The armour of John of Gaunt duke of Lancaster, who was the son of a king, the father of a king, and the uncle of a king, but was never king himself: and Dugdale observes, that more kings and sovereign princes sprang from his loins, than from any king of Christendom. The armour here shewn is seven feet high, and the sword and lance of an enormous size. 11. The droll figure of Will Somers, who, as the warders tell you, was king Henry VIII's jester. They add, " he was an honest man of a woman's making —— he had a handsome woman to his wife, who made him a cuckold; and he wears his horns on his head, because they should not wear holes in his pockets.—— He would neither believe king, queen, nor any about the court, that he was a cuckold, till he put on his spectacles to see, being a little dim-sighted, as all cuckolds should be:" in which antic manner he is here represented. 12. What your conductors call a collar of torments, which, say they, " used formerly to be put

about

the Strand; the houſes of the duke's of New-caſtle

about the womens necks that cuckolded their huſbands, or ſcolded at them when they came home late; but that cuſtom is left off now-a-days, to prevent quarrelling for collars, there not being ſmiths enough to make them, as moſt married men are ſure to want at one time or other."

You now come to the line of kings, which your conductor begins by reverſing the order of chronology; ſo that in following them we muſt place the laſt firſt. 1. His late majeſty king George I. in a compleat ſuit of armour, ſitting with a truncheon in his hand, on a white horſe richly capariſoned, having a fine Turky bridle gilt, with a globe, creſcent and ſtar; velvet furniture laced with gold, and gold trappings. 2. King William III. dreſſed in the ſuit of armour worn by Edward the Black Prince, ſon to Edward III. at the glorious battle of Creſſey. He is mounted on a ſorrel horſe, whoſe furniture is green velvet embroidered with ſilver, and holds in his right-hand a flaming ſword. 3. King Charles II. dreſſed in the armour worn by the champion of England, at the coronation of his preſent majeſty. He ſits with a truncheon in his hand, on a fine horſe richly capariſoned, with crimſon velvet laced with gold. 4. King Charles I. in a rich ſuit of his own armour gilt, and curiouſly wrought, preſented to him by the city of London when he was prince of Wales, and is the ſame that was laid on the coffin at the funeral proceſſion of the late great duke of Marlborough, on which occaſion a collar of SS was added to it, and is now round it. 5. James I. who ſits on horſeback, in a compleat ſuit of figured armour, with a truncheon in his right-hand. 6. King Edward VI. dreſſed in a curious ſuit of ſteel armour, whereon are depicted, in different compartments, a great variety of ſcripture hiſtories. He ſits like the reſt on horſeback, with a truncheon in his hand. 7. King Henry VIII. in his own armour, which is of poliſhed ſteel, with the foliages gilt or inlaid with gold. He holds a ſword in his right-hand. 8. King Henry VII. who alſo holds a ſword. He ſits on horſeback in a compleat ſuit of armour, finely wrought, and waſhed with ſilver. 9. King Edward V. who with his brother Richard was ſmothered in the Tower, and having been proclaimed king, but never crowned, a crown is hung over his head. He holds a lance in his right-hand, and is dreſſed in a rich ſuit of armour. 10. King Edward IV. father to the two unhappy princes above-mentioned, is diſtinguiſhed by a ſuit of bright armour ſtudded. He holds a drawn ſword in his hand. 11. King Henry VI. who, though crowned king of France at Paris, loſt that kingdom, and was at laſt murdered in the Tower by the duke of Glouceſter, afterward Richard III. 12. The victorious Henry V. who by his conqueſts in France cauſed himſelf to be acknowledged regent,

and

and presumptive heir to that kingdom. 13. Henry IV. the son of John of Gaunt. 14. King Edward III. John of Gaunt's father, and father to Edward the Black Prince, is represented here with a venerable beard, and in a suit of plain bright armour, with two crowns on his sword, alluding to his being crowned king both of England and France. 15. King Edward I. dressed in a very curious suit of gilt armour, and in shoes of mail. He has a battle-axe in his hand. 16. William the Conqueror, the first in the line, though last shewn, sits in a suit of plain armour. 17. Over the door where you go out of the armoury is a target, on which are engraved, by a masterly hand, the figures, as it should seem, of Justice, Fortune, and Fortitude; and round the room, the walls are every where lined with various uncommon pieces of old armour, for horses heads and breasts, targets, and many pieces that now want a name.

In a dark, strong, stone room, about 20 yards to the eastward of the grand store-house or new armoury, the crown jewels are deposited. I. The imperial crown, with which it is pretended that all the Kings of England have been crowned since Edward the Confessor, in 1042. It is of gold, enriched with diamonds, rubies, emeralds, saphires and pearls: the cap within is of purple velvet, lined with white taffety, turned up with three rows of ermine. They are however mistaken in shewing this as the ancient imperial diadem of St. Edward; for that, with the other most ancient regalia of this kingdom, was kept in the arched room in the cloisters in Westminster Abbey till the grand rebellion; when in 1642, Harry Martin, by order of the parliament, broke open the iron chest in which it was secured, took it thence, and sold it, together with the robes, sword, and scepter of St. Edward. However, after the restoration, king Charles II. had one made in imitation of it, which is that now shewn. II. The golden orb or globe, put into the king's right-hand before he is crowned; and borne in his left with the scepter in his right, upon his return into Westminster Hall, after he is crowned. It is about six inches in diameter, edged with pearl, and enriched with precious stones. On the top is an amethyst, of a violet colour, near an inch and a half in height, set with a rich cross of gold, adorned with diamonds, pearls, and precious stones. The whole height of the ball and cup is 11 inches. III. The golden scepter, with its cross set upon a large amethyst of great value, garnished round with table diamonds. The handle of the scepter is plain; but the pummel is set round with rubies, emeralds, and small diamonds. The top rises into a *fleur de lis* of six leaves, all enriched with precious stones, from whence issues a mound or ball, made of the amethyst already mentioned. The cross is quite covered with precious stones. IV. The scep-

Wade, in Saville-row; the earl of Granville's, Mr. Pelham's,

ter with the dove, the emblem of peace, perched on the top of a small Jerusalem crofs, finely ornamented with table diamonds and jewels of great value. This emblem was first used by Edward the Confeffor, as appears by his feal; but the ancient fcepter and dove was fold with the reft of the regalia, and this now in the Tower was made after the reftoration. V. St. Edward's ftaff, four feet seven inches and a half in length, and three inches three quarters in circumference, all of beaten gold, which is carried before the king at his coronation. VI. The rich crown of ftate, worn by his majefty in parliament; in which is a large emerald seven inches round; a pearl efteemed the fineft in the world, and a ruby of ineftimable value. VII. The crown belonging to his royal highnefs the prince of Wales. The king wears his crown on his head while he fits upon the throne; but that of the prince of Wales is placed before him, to fhew that he is not yet come to it. VIII. The late queen Mary's crown, globe and fcepter, with the diadem fhe wore at her coronation with her confort king William III. IX. An ivory fcepter, with a dove on the top, made for king James II's queen, whofe garniture is gold, and the dove on the top gold, enamelled with white. X. The *curtano*, or fword of mercy, which has a blade 32 inches long, and near two broad, is without a point, and is borne naked before the king at his coronation, between the two fwords of juftice, fpiritual and temporal. XI. The golden fpurs, and the armillas, which are bracelets for the wrifts. Thefe, though very antique, are worn at the coronation. XII. The *ampullo*, or eagle of gold, finely engraved, which holds the holy oil the kings and queens of England are anointed with; and the golden fpoon that the bifhop pours the oil into. Thefe are two pieces of great antiquity. The golden eagle, including the pedeftal, is about nine inches high, and the wings expand about feven inches. The whole weighs about 10 ounces. The head of the eagle fcrews off about the middle of the neck, which is made hollow, for holding the holy oil; and when the king is anointed by the bifhop, the oil is poured into the fpoon out of the bird's bill. XIII. A rich falt-feller of ftate, in form like the fquare White Tower, and fo exquifitely wrought, that the workmanfhip of modern times is in no degree equal to it. It is of gold, and ufed only on the king's table at the coronation. XIV. A noble filver font, double gilt, and elegantly wrought, in which the royal family are chriftened. XV. A large filver fountain, prefented to king Charles II. by the town of Plymouth, very curioufly wrought; but much inferior in beauty to the above. Befide thefe, which are commonly fhewn, there are in the jewel office, all the crown jewels worn by the prince and princeffes at coronations, and a great variety of curious old plate.

The

ham's, the duke of Bedford's, and Montague-houſe [*], in Bloomſbury; with a great number of others of the

The Record Office conſiſts of three rooms, one above another, and a large round room, where the rolls are kept. Theſe are all handſomely wainſcoted, the wainſcot being framed into preſſes round each room, within which are ſhelves, and repoſitories for the records; and for the eaſier finding of them, the year of each reign is inſcribed on the inſide of theſe preſſes, and the records placed accordingly. Within theſe preſſes, which amount to 56 in number, are depoſited all the rolls, from the firſt year of the reign of king John, to the beginning of the reign of Richard III. but thoſe after this laſt period are kept in the rolls chapel. The records in the Tower, among other things, contain, the foundation of abbies, and other religious houſes; the ancient tenures of all the lands in England, with a ſurvey of the manors; the original of laws and ſtatutes; proceedings of the courts of common law and equity; the rights of England to the dominion of the Britiſh ſeas; leagues and treaties with foreign princes; the atchievements of England in foreign wars; the ſettlement of Ireland, as to law and dominion; the forms of ſubmiſſion of ſome Scottiſh kings; ancient grants of our kings to their ſubjects; privileges and immunities granted to cities and corporations during the period above-mentioned; enrollments of charters and deeds made before the conqueſt; the bounds of all the foreſts in England, with the ſeveral reſpective rights of the inhabitants to common of paſture, and many other important records, all regularly diſpoſed, and referred to in near a thouſand folio indexes. This office is kept open, and attendance conſtantly given, from ſeven o'clock till one, except in the months of December, January and February, when it is open only from eight to one, Sundays and holidays excepted. A ſearch here is half a guinea, for which you may peruſe any one ſubject a year.

[*] The Britiſh Muſeum is depoſited in Montague-houſe. Sir Hans Sloane, bart. (who died in 1753) may not improperly be accounted the founder of the Britiſh Muſeum: for its being eſtabliſhed by parliament, was only in conſequence of his leaving by will his noble collection of natural hiſtory, his large library, and his numerous curioſities, which coſt him 50,000 l. to the uſe of the public on condition that the parliament would pay 20,000 l. to his executors. To this collection were added the Cottonian library, the Harleian manuſcripts, and a collection of books given by the late major Edwards. His late majeſty, in conſideration of its great uſefulneſs, was gracious ly pleaſed to add thereto, the royal libraries of books and manuſcripts collected by the ſeveral kings of England.

The Sloanian collection conſiſts of an amazing number of curioſities; among which are, the library, including books of drawings,

the nobility and gentry; but thefe would be fufficient to fill a large volume.

London is the center of trade, it has an intimate connection with all the countries in the kingdom; it is the grand mart of the nation, to which every part fend their commodities, from whence they again are fent back into every town in the nation, and to every part in the world. From hence innumerable carriages, by land and water, are conftantly employed, and from hence arifes that circulation in the national body, which renders every part healthful, vigorous, and in a profperous condition; a circulation that is equally beneficial to the head, and the moft diftant members. Merchants are here as rich as noblemen; and there is no place in the world in which the fhops of tradefmen make fuch a noble and elegant appearance.

No expence has been fpared to give this city all the effential advantages that could be procured by art and induftry. And in particular, no place in the world is better fupplied with water from the Thames and the New River; which is not only of inconceivable fervice to every family, but, by means of fire-plugs every where difperfed, the keys of which are

drawings, manufcripts and prints, amounting to about 50,000 volumes. Medals and coins, ancient and modern, 23,000. Cameos and intaglios, about 700. Seals, 268. Veffels, &c. of agate, jafper, &c. 542. Antiquities, 1,125. Precious ftones, agates, jafpers, &c. 2,256. Metals, minerals, ores, &c. 2,725. Cryftals, fpars, &c. 1,864. Foffils, flints, ftones, 1,275. Earths, fands, falts, 1,035. Bitumens, fulphurs, ambers, &c. 399. Talcs, micæ, &c. 388. Corals, fpunges, &c. 1,421. Teftacea, or fhells, &c. 5,843. Echini, echinitæ, &c. 659. Afteriæ, trochi, entrochi, &c. 241. Cruftaceæ, crabs, lobfters, &c. 363. Stellæ marinæ, ftar-fifhes, &c. 173. Fifh and their parts, &c. 1,555. Birds and their parts, eggs and nefts, of different fpecies, 1,172. Quadrupeds, &c. 1,886. Vipers, ferpents, &c. 521. Infects, &c. 5,439. Vegetables, 12,506. Hortus ficcus, or volumes of dried plants, 334. Humana, as calculi, anatomical preparations, 756. Mifcellaneous things, natural, 2,098. Mathematical inftruments, 55. A catalogue of all the above is written in 38 volumes in folio, and 8 in quarto.

depofited

depofited with the parifhes officers, the city is, in a great meafure, fecured from the fpreading of fire; for thefe plugs are no fooner opened than there is vaft quantities of water to fupply the engines.

This plenty of water has been attended with another advantage, it has given rife to feveral companies, who infure houfes and goods, from fire; an advantage, that is not to be met with in any other nation on earth: the premium is fmall, and the recovery, in cafe of lofs, is eafy and certain. Every one of thefe offices, keep a fet of men in pay, who are ready at all hours to give their affiftance in cafe of fire; and who are on all occafions extreamly bold, dexterous, and diligent; but though all their labours fhould prove unfuccefsful, the perfon who fuffers by this devouring element, has the comfort that muft arife from a certainty of being paid the value of what he has infured.

OF NORTH BRITAIN, OR SCOTLAND, WITH ITS ISLANDS.

THE kingdom of Scotland, or North Britain, comprehends all the northern part of this ifland beyond the counties of Cumberland and Northumberland, together with a multitude of iflands, which amount to about 300; fome of them are very inconfiderable. This country is bounded on all fides by the ocean, except on the fouth, where it is feparated from England, beginning at the eaft, by the river Tweed, Cheviot-

Cheviot-hills, the river Erſk, and Solway Frith. Near Carliſle it is generally reckoned to extend 300 miles in length, from Aldermouth head, near the iſle of Mull, to Buchaneſs, and 150 in breadth, where broadeſt. The coaſt is much indented, and the land in ſeveral places nearly cut through by bays, gulphs, and rivers, the firſt of which form excellent harbours, and the latter abound with freſh water fiſh.

North Britain, excluſive of its iſlands, lies between the fifty-fourth degree forty minutes, and the fifty-eight degree thirty minutes north latitude, and between the firſt degree thirty minutes, and the ſixth degree weſt longitude. The longeſt day is upwards of eighteen hours, and the ſhorteſt five hours forty-five minutes: but the brightneſs of the northern lights in a great meaſure remedy the inconvenience of the ſhort days of winter.

The air is very temperate, and not half ſo cold as might be imagined from its being ſeated ſo far to the north. This, as in England, is owing to the warm vapours and moderate breezes that continually come from the ſea; which alſo ſerve to purify the air, and put it in ſuch a conſtant agitation, as preſerves the inhabitants from any remarkable epidemic diſeaſes.

Great part of the country, particularly toward the north and weſt, is mountainous, and covered with heath; this is called the Highlands, but theſe in ſeveral places yield good paſture: between the higher grounds are many rich valleys, which produce corn and cattle. The ſouth parts of Scotland are far preferable to the north parts of England, and there are every where all things neceſſary for human life; and not only ſufficient for the inhabitants, but alſo to export. They do not want wheat, but the grain moſtly cultivated is oats, as it will grow in the mountainous parts. The productions in Scotland are in general much the ſame as in England. In the Lowlands there is little timber, but in the more northern parts there are foreſts of fir-trees, that might afford

maſts

mafts for the largeft men of war; but it is difficult to bring them to the fea-fide. There are alfo many large woods of oaks, afh, and elms, fit for building, and abundance of fruit-trees in their gardens and orchards. The foil likewife in many places produces great plenty of hemp and flax.

Befide the frefh-water fifh found in the lakes and rivers, feveral of the iflands are frequented by whales; and cod, ling, haddock, fturgeon, turbot, mackrel, fcate, fea-urchins, cat-fifh, &c. are caught in great plenty on all their coafts. Lobfters, crabs, and oyfters, are found in vaft quantities on the Weftern Iflands; and cockles, muffels, limpets, wilks, fcallops, and fpouts, are caft by the tide in fuch numbers on the ifles, that the people cannot confume them.

In this country fprings of clear and wholefome water are every where in plenty, not only on the fides, but on the tops of many of the mountains. Thefe in their defcent fwell into pleafant rills, and augmenting their ftreams become rivers. Many of thefe meeting with hollow places in their paffage, expand themfelves into lakes, till finding a proper channel they refume their form of rivers, and, as the nature of the foil directs, fometimes expand themfelves again and again, or continue their progrefs in the fame form to the fea.

The moft remarkable lochs or lakes in Scotland are Lochtay, Lochnefs, and Lochlevin, which fend forth rivers of the fame name with themfelves; Lochlomond, which fends forth the river Lomond; and Lochiern, from which flows the river Iern. There is a lake in Straitherrach, which never freezes, however fevere the froft, till February, and then in one night it freezes all over, and if it continues two nights, the ice grows very thick. Another lake at a place called Glencanich, is feated on a high ground between the tops of two mountains, and it is remarkable that the middle of this lake is always frozen

H 3 through-

throughout the summer, notwithstanding the strong reflection of the sun-beams from the mountains, which melts the ice at the sides of the lake. Round the lake the ground has a constant verdure, as if it enjoyed a perpetual spring; and by feeding on that grass, cattle grow sooner fat than any where else.

In Linlithgowshire is a lake called Lochoat, from whence a stream runs under a neighbouring mountain, and after it has pursued its course about two hundred paces, issues with great force from a spring about three feet broad, when it forms a stream that turns a mill.

The capital rivers, particularly the Forth, Clyde, Tay, and Nefs, &c. divide the country into peninsulas; these running so far within land as to be intercepted only by a small isthmus, or neck of land.

The kingdom of Scotland, notwithstanding the union of the crowns on the accession of their king James VI. to that of England, continued an entirely separate and distinct kingdom for above a century, though an union had been long projected: this was judged to be the more easy to be done, as both kingdoms were antiently under the same government, and still retained a very great resemblance, though far from an identity, in their laws. By an act of parliament 1 Jac. I. c. 1. it is declared, that these two, mighty, famous, and antient kingdoms were formerly one. And Sir Edward Coke observes, how marvellous a conformity there was, not only in the religion and language of the two nations, but also in their antient laws. the descent of the crown, their parliaments, their titles of nobility, their officers of state and of justice, their writs, their customs, and even the language of their laws. Upon which account he supposes the common law of each to have been originally the same, especially as their most antient and authentic book, called *Regiam Majestatem*, and containing the rules of their antient common law, is extreamly similar to that of Glanvil, which contains

the

the principles of ours, as it stood in the reign of Henry II. The many diverfities, fubfifting between the two laws at prefent, may be well enough accounted for, from a diverfity of practice in two large and uncommunicating jurifdictions, and from the acts of two diftinct and independent parliaments, which have in many points altered and abrogated the old common law of both kingdoms.

However, Sir Edward Coke, and the politicians of that time, conceived great difficulties in carrying on the projected union: but thefe were at length overcome, and the great work was happily effected in 1707, in the fifth of queen Anne; when twenty-five articles of union were agreed to by the parliaments of both nations: the purport of the moft confiderable being as follows:

1. That on the firft of May 1707, and for ever after, the kingdoms of England and Scotland fhall be united into one kingdom, by the name of Great Britain.

2. The fucceffion to the monarchy of Great Britain fhall be the fame as was before fettled with regard to that of England.

3. The united kingdom fhall be reprefented by one parliament.

4. There fhall be a communication of all rights and privileges between the fubjects of both kingdoms, except where it is otherwife agreed.

9. When England raifes 2,000,000 l. by a land tax, Scotland fhall raife 48,000 l.

16, 17. The ftandards of the coin, of weights, and of meafures, fhall be reduced to thofe of England, throughout the united kingdoms.

18. The laws relating to trade, cuftoms, and the excife, fhall be the fame in Scotland as in England. But all the other laws of Scotland fhall remain in force; but alterable by the parliament of Great Britain. Yet with this caution: that laws relating to public policy are alterable at the difcretion of the
parlia-

parliament; laws relating to private right are not to be altered but for the evident utility of the people of Scotland.

22. Sixteen peers are to be chosen to represent the peerage of Scotland in parliament, and forty-five members to sit in the house of commons.

23. The sixteen peers of Scotland shall have all privileges of parliament: and all peers of Scotland shall be peers of Great Britain, and rank next after those of the same degree at the time of the union, and shall have all privileges of peers, except sitting in the house of lords and voting on the trial of a peer.

These are the principal of the twenty-five articles, of union, which are ratified and confirmed by statute 5 Ann. c. 8. in which statute there are also two acts of parliament recited; the one of Scotland, whereby the church of Scotland, and also the four universities of that kingdom, are established for ever, and all succeeding sovereigns are to take an oath inviolably to maintain the same; the other of England, 5 Ann. c. 6. whereby the acts of uniformity of 13 Eliz. and 13 Car. II. (except as the same had been altered by parliament at that time) and all other acts then in force for the preservation of the church of England, are declared perpetual; and it is stipulated, that every subsequent king and queen shall take an oath inviolably to maintain the same within England, Ireland, Wales, and the town of Berwick upon Tweed. And it is enacted, that these two acts " shall for ever be " observed as fundamental and essential conditions of " the union."

Upon these articles, and act of union, it is to be observed, 1. That the two kingdoms are now so inseparably united, that nothing can ever disunite them again; unless perhaps an infringement of those points which, when they were separate and independent nations, it was mutually stipulated should be " funda-
" mental and essential conditions of the union."
2. That whatever else may be deemed " fundamental
" and

" and essential conditions," the preservation of the two churches, of England and Scotland, in the same state that they were in at the time of the union, and the maintenance of the acts of uniformity which establish our common prayer, are expressly declared so to be. 3. That therefore any alteration in the constitutions of either of those churches, or in the liturgy of the church of England, would be an infringement of these " fundamental and essential conditions," and greatly endanger the union. 4. That the municipal laws of Scotland are ordained to be still observed in that part of the island, unless altered by parliament; and, as the parliament has not yet thought proper, except in a few instances, to alter them, they still (with regard to the particulars unaltered) continue in full force. Wherefore the municipal or common laws of England are, generally speaking, of no force or validity in Scotland.

The courts of civil judicature in Scotland are,

The college of justice, commonly called the session, which consists of a president, and fourteen fixed senators or judges, called ordinary lords of session, with two extraordinary lords. Under these are seven clerks of session, and six inferior officers. Before this court are tried at stated times, all civil causes, which they determine by acts of parliament, and the custom of the nation; and where these are defective, they decide according to the civil law, and the rules of equity. There lies no appeal from this court but to the parliament; and the presence of nine judges is required to make their decrees valid.

The justiciary, usually called the justice or criminal court, consists of five lords of the session, the justice-general, and justice-clerk. These are joined by a pannel of fifteen out of forty-five, cited like juries in England, by whom all causes of a criminal nature are tried. They hold assizes all over the kingdom twice every year, and from thence are called lords of the circuit.

The

The court of exchequer, which is like that of England, and confifts of a chief and four other barons, &c.

The court of chancery. The officers of ftate are, the keeper of the feal, and lord privy-feal, the lord clerk-regifter, and the lord advocate.

Befide the above national judges, every county or fhire has a chief magiftrate or his deputy, who is ordinary judge in all civil and criminal caufes; but, in moft cafes, an appeal lies from this magiftrate to the feffion and court of jufticiary. The fheriff is in effect the fupream juftice of peace, to whom the law principally intrufts the fecuring the quiet and tranquillity of that part of the kingdom of which he is fheriff. Bailiffs, ftewards, and conftables, in their refpective diftricts, have the fame liberty as fheriffs in their fhires.

The court of admiralty is a fupream court, in which all maritime caufes, crimes, trefpaffes, quarrels, &c. may be tried before the lord high admiral's judge, for he himfelf never judges; he forms his decifions on the civil law, and the cuftoms of Scotland.

There are alfo in Scotland what are called commiffary courts, which are a kind of ecclefiaftical courts, in which caufes are tried by commiffaries. The principal of thefe is at Edinburgh. The four commiffaries of that metropolis particularly try caufes of matrimony and adultery, in order to a plenary divorce, fo that the innocent perfon may marry, as if the offending party were naturally dead.

The Scots nation in general is of the reformed religion, except a fmall part ftill adhering to the church of Rome. The government of their church is denominated prefbyterian, becaufe they allow of no higher office than a preaching prefbyter, who with the elders of the people perform the whole government. The Scots writers declare this to be their primitive form, when the nation firft turned chriftian in the fecond century, and was never altered by the

popifh

of SCOTLAND.   107

popish prelates till the fourteenth century: and that the church of Scotland was reformed from popery by presbyters, without settling any prelacy instead thereof, is evident from the acts of parliament and general assemblies. The ecclesiastical courts are the four following.

1. The general assembly, which meets at Edinburg annually in May, and consists of ministers and elders deputed from every presbytery in the nation. These determine all appeals from inferior church judicatures, and make laws and regulations for the government of the kirk. A lord commissioner, who is always a nobleman of the first quality, presides here as a representative of the king's person. The power of this court is very great, and from it there is no appeal.

2. The provincial synod, which is composed of the members of several adjacent presbyteries, meeting twice a year, at a principal place within the bounds, and like the general assembly is opened by a sermon. Their business is to receive correspondents from the neighbouring synods, who are a check upon one another; to determine appeals from the presbyteries within their district; and to enquire into and censure the behaviour of the presbyteries themselves. They have likewise power to remove a minister from one place to another: but appeals lie from the synod to the general assembly.

3. The presbytery, which consists of a minister and one elder from five to ten or more neighbouring parishes, who, being assembled, chuse one of the ministers to be præses, or moderator. Here are tried appeals from the kirk-session; and here they inspect into the behaviour of the ministers and elders within their respective bounds. They supply vacant parishes, ordain pastors, examine and licenfe school-masters and young students for probationary preachers.

4. The kirk session consists of the minister and elders in each parish, who consider the affairs of the parish

as

as a religious fociety. They judge in all leffer matters efteemed fcandalous, can fufpend from the communion, and regulate every thing relating to public worfhip and the poor.

The number of kirks or churches in Scotland amounts to about nine hundred and fifty, befide a few chapels, which make up fixty-eight prefbyteries, included in thirteen provincial fynods.

There are here however feveral fects of diffenters from the eftablifhed worfhip, the principal of which are the epifcopalians, who ufe the form of prayer of the church of England: but the nonjurers among thefe are not permitted to have public meeting-houfes, but are only fuffered to preach and read the divine fervice to very fmall congregations; while thofe who take the oaths, and pray for his majefty in exprefs terms, have meeting-houfes. There are alfo the Erfkinites and Gibbonites, fo called from the minifters of thofe names, who have broke off from the church of Scotland, and upon that account they are alfo called feceders. There are likewife mountaineers, thus named from their preaching in the open fields, and on the mountains; thefe are alfo called covenanters.

The law of Scotland has provided againft pluralities, and throughout the whole country there are no benefices worth lefs than fifty pounds fterling per annum; which in that county is a good maintenance; nor any that exceed a hundred and fifty pounds a year.

The members of this ecclefiaftical republic (who are all upon an equality in point of dignity and power) are efteemed to be very fincere in their principles, indefatigable in their minifterial labours, and are greatly refpected by their parifhioners. Befide difcharging their fpiritual duties, thefe gentlemen frequently act in the capacity of arbitrators in matters of difpute between man and man; their healing advice is generally attended with fuccefs, and both

parties

parties return to their families fully reconciled to each other. Where such pastors preside there are few instances of irregularity among the lower classes of the people: adultery, swearing, and fighting, are so very uncommon, that the persons guilty of such practices are considered as the most incorrigible miscreants, despised and shunned by the whole neighbourhood.

The union with England was strongly opposed by the people of Scotland in general, and occasioned such tumults, that the nation was threatned with a civil war. One of the nobles declared in parliament, that his degenerate countrymen were about to give up in half an hour what their warlike predecessors had so bravely defended, and so hardly earned during a contest of many centuries. But the chief grounds of opposition proceeded from a consideration of the heavy taxes that must be levied upon them to pay the interest of debts they never had contracted. Before this time, taxes were almost unknown in that kingdom, provisions were cheap, and by means of their fisheries, mines, and manufactures, they carried on a beneficial trade with Holland and France: but in consequence of the union they were to renounce this trade, and drink port at 2 s. per bottle, in preference to claret at 10 d. because the English carried on a lucrative trade with Portugal. By this treaty the parliament of Scotland, which was annually held at Edinburgh, was to be dissolved, and a limited number of their nobility, together with 45 commoners, were to represent Scotland in the British parliament. It was easy to foresee that so many of their nobility and gentry residing at London would spend one third of the rents of the kingdom in that metropolis.

Such were the objections made by the people of Scotland against this famous treaty, but upon the other hand, the advantages resulting therefrom, though at first they seemed remote and precarious, are many and substantial. An increase of trade has, in the course of 60 years, given a new face to the whole

whole kingdom, but more particularly in the weſtern parts, where the inhabitants ſoon availed themſelves of a free commerce with America. Inſtead of dark Gothick caſtles inhabited by a nobility more diſtinguiſhed for their valour than by wealth, and under whoſe protection exiſted a poor, oppreſſed commonalty, we now behold an incredible number of villas, ſurrounded with incloſures, and laid out in a manner that does honour to the taſte of a trading people. Inſtead of a few inconſiderable boroughs, remarkable only for the antiquity of their charters, or ſome ruinous abbey, we meet large and populous towns, well known in the mercantile world for the variety and beauty of their manufactures.

Scotland produces moſt of the neceſſaries of life, and ſupplies other nations with black cattle, ſheep, pork, ſalmon, herrings, and other kinds of fiſh, corn, barley, ſalt, tallow, hides, butter, eggs, lead, coals, and freeſtone; it likewiſe exports linen cloth, hollands, cambrics, gauzes, ſilk and worſted ſtockings, printed cloths, carpets, books, hats, plaid, and coarſe woollen cloth, &c. Theſe and many other commodities are chiefly manufactured at Glaſgow, a large and beautiful city, ſituated upon the river Clyde; in point of commerce the firſt in Scotland. This city likewiſe carries on a very extenſive foreign trade, particularly to America, by means of which, and her own natural productions, Scotland is enabled to remit incredible ſums to England, where the fruits of her induſtry chiefly centers; ſo that in reality the people of South Britain owe a conſiderable part of their riches to the very people whoſe poverty they are ſo apt to deſpiſe. The difficulty of procuring bills upon London, and the high premiums they bear, are convincing proofs that the balance of trade is greatly in favour of England. It may not be improper in this place to obſerve alſo, how groſsly this country has been miſrepreſented by late writers, ſome wilfully, and others through ignorance,

rance, by literally copying from Camden and other old authors, without making proper allowances for the changes and improvements which have taken place, from a gradual increase of trade, and an uncommon attention to agriculture during a period of near two centuries. These compilers of geographical systems would do well to convince us of their extensive knowlege of foreign countries, by giving a more just account of our own. The best modern description of this island seems to be that written by Mr. S. Richardson, intitled, *A Tour through Great Britain*.

The Scots are in general well shaped, strongly made, hardy and robust. They live well, though not grosly, and are wholly unacquainted with some diseases, as well as some vices too common in many other countries. They are, for the most part, an active, industrious, and religious people; and having a great share of natural good sense and sagacity, they generally succeed in their undertakings. The women of inferior rank, and some in higher life, are so remarkable for their industry, that their whole families are generally clothed with their own manufacture. The fidelity of this people is such, that the kings of France, for near 300 years, committed the immediate care of their royal persons to a regiment of Scottish guards. And in 1746, the young pretender wandered several months from place to place, during which time there was not one attempt made toward a discovery, though he was known to many persons, and a reward of 30000l. offered for his head. The Scotch, however, are not without their faults, and the inferior gentlemen among them have often a greater share of pride than the first English peers; this, however, wears off soon after they have crossed the Tweed, or have visited other countries. Many of them likewise too much affect to imitate their more wealthy neighbours in luxury, and in the other prevailing vices of the times.

Scotland has produced many persons eminent for genius and learning, but no period was ever so distinguished

tinguished as the present, which, if we may use the expression, may be considered as the golden age of literature in that kingdom.

The Scots music is universally admired; love is generally the subject, and many of the airs have been brought upon the English stage, under new names, but with this disadvantage, that they are mostly altered for the worse; being strip'd of that original simplicity which is their essential characteristic, which is so agreeable to the ear, and has such powers over the human breast.

With regard to the original inhabitants of Scotland, we have no certain accounts; it is probable that they came in colonies from the neighbouring continent. The Picts seem to be no other than such of the bravest Britons as would not submit to the Roman yoke, and were driven northward by these invaders. The history of Scotland, says Dr. Robertson, may be properly divided into four periods. The first reaches from the origin of that monarchy to the reign of Kenneth II. who subdued the Picts in the year 838, and united under one monarchy all that country now called Scotland. The second, from Kenneth's conquest of the Picts to the death of Alexander III. when the competitors for the crown put themselves under the arbitration of Edward I. of England. The third extends to the death of James V. The last, from thence to the accession of James VI. to the crown of England. It has been much regretted, that this celebrated writer confined his history to this last period, containing only two reigns. It is observable, that Innes, and other Scottish writers since his time, have affected to doubt the very existence of no less than forty of their first kings. But it is not very probable that 30000 Caledonians, who opposed Agricola, could be brought together in these barbarous ages without a leader invested with sovereign authority; and that these people should, during several centuries, sustain the hostile attacks of united armies, and at last oblige the Romans to bound their

empire

of SCOTLAND.

empire northward by a wall, which neither their legions, nor the trembling Britons could guard.

This might lead us to a review of the Scots in their military capacity, in which light they are truly great. Their brave defence when attacked by superior arms; their noble ſtruggles in ſupport of the independency and liberties of their country, when reduced to the moſt diſtreſsful circumſtances, have gained them a reputation in the annals of Europe, that reflects honour upon their country and their name.

Such were the people whom the wiſeſt of the Engliſh monarchs, from various motives of policy, laboured to unite with their own ſubjects. The Scots, as early as the reign of Charlemagne, had engaged in a league with France, and their inflexible adherence to that nation proved the ſource of their greateſt miſery; agriculture, manufactures, and commerce, were ſacrificed to their darling profeſſion of arms. Nor did England eſcape the unhappy conſequences of this foreign alliance. At length the wiſdom of Henry VII. effected by a marriage, what his predeceſſors had in vain endeavoured to accompliſh by force of arms; and the memorable 1707 united more firmly both nations in one great kingdom. The happy effects of this great event were more eaſily perceived from a conſideration that both nations inhabited the ſame iſland, profeſſed the reformed religion, ſpoke one language, were equally diſtinguiſhed for bravery, love of liberty, and a ſimilitude in capacity and manners. Since this period, the inhabitants of both nations have mutually exerted themſelves in ſupport of the liberties of Europe and of Britain.

AN ACCOUNT
OF
IRELAND.

IRELAND is bounded by the Deucaledonian Sea, on the north; and on the weft and fouth by the great Atlantic Ocean, which feparates it from America; and on the eaft, by St. George's Channel, which divides it from Britain; and is diftant from Scotland not full 30 miles, and from Wales, about 60 miles. The whole area, or fuperficial content of this ifland, is computed to take up about 11,067,712 Irifh acres, plantation meafure; the difference between Englifh and Irifh acres, being as 16 and an half is to 21; and it is held to bear proportion to England and Wales, as 18 is to 30.

The air is much the fame with thofe parts of England that lie under the fame parallel; only in fome parts it is more grofs and unhealthy, efpecially to ftrangers, on account of its many lakes, bogs, and marfhes. It is remarkable, that no venomous creatures can live in this country, as appears from repeated experiments.

There are fome bogs in this country fo deep, as entirely to fwallow up a man and horfe, who fink an unknown depth, though they are covered with turf, which feems to promife folid ground; however, roads have been made for horfes and carriages over thefe dreadful bogs, by ranging rows of faggots faftened together, and covered with earth, which forms a kind of bridge that fhakes under the feet of the paffenger. There are other bogs that have too ftrong a cruft of turf to be eafily broken, and are conftantly paffed in fafety, though they fhake and quiver at every ftep of the foot.

Ireland is in general a fine level country, abounding in navigable rivers, numerous bays and harbours.

The inhabitants, aided by parliament, have of late years applied in good earnest to sundry improvements, as draining of bogs, making canals, building market-towns, inclosing the country, and enriching the soil; so that this kingdom bids fair to rival England in point of beauty and fertility. Its pastures feed prodigious numbers of cattle, whence Ireland is enabled to supply the ships of all European nations with beef and butter: but however advantageous this trade may be in one respect, it is carried on to an excess that is very prejudicial to that kingdom in general, as it causes agriculture to be neglected, which would employ many more hands, and prevent the necessity of importing corn from England, from whence Ireland is likewise supplied with potatoes, in considerable quantities.

The roads in this country are excellent; but there are few or no good inns in the kingdom.

Dublin, whether we consider it in point of extent, beauty, or the wealth of its inhabitants, claims a place among the first cities in Europe. The Liffey, which divides it, is generally covered with the ships of various nations, and the streets that run along both sides of this river, afford a very agreeable prospect.

The Irish were first converted to Christianity in the fifth century, by a zealous and devout person from * North Britain, whom his new disciples distinguished by the name of St. Patrick. The established religion is the same as in England; but the inhabitants of the northern counties still adhere to the church of Scotland. However, the most numerous body are the Papists, who will not submit to the king's supremacy even in temporals, but place the same in a foreign jurisdiction. They have their bishops and other dignitaries, like the established church: but neither they, nor the inferior clergy of that communion, have any other revenues than the voluntary contributions of their poor disciples. It is supposed, that throughout Ire-

* According to his own account, he was born at Kilpatric, a small village on the river Clyde, near Dumbarton.

land, there are eight Papists to one Protestant. From such a disproportion, the latter, ever since the memorable 1641, have placed their security in the military and a Protestant militia.

The present inhabitants of Ireland may be divided into three different classes; First, The original natives, who, from a similitude of language and customs, are supposed to be descended from the Britains and Caledonians; particularly the latter, who antiently inhabited the most barren parts of Scotland, and being in all ages desirous of possessing better countries than their own, it is natural to suppose that many of them might quit the bleak mountains of Argyleshire, for the more fertile plains of Ulster, being within the view of these parts. This opinion, of being anciently the same people, still prevails among the Highlanders and the Irish; and it is said, that, during the massacre of English Protestants in 1641, some proposals were made to except the Scots from this dreadful butchery. The old Irish are generally represented as an ignorant, uncivilized people. We may, at least, with equal justice represent them as the most oppressed subjects under the British government, and the only people who do not enjoy the benefits of our excellent constitution. This, however, partly proceeds from their adherence to Popery, but more especially from the inhumanity and tyranny of their more immediate landlords or leaseholders.

Human invention could not contrive a more effectual method for the instruction of these people in the real principles of Christianity, and for the inuring them to industry, labour and obedience to their sovereign, than the institution of English Protestant working-schools over the whole kingdom.

The next class of people are the descendants of the English, who, since the conquest, gradually extended themselves over the country, and to whose arts and industry Ireland is infinitely indebted; of these are most of the nobility, gentry, and merchants.

The third class are descended from a colony of Scots, who were sent thither by king James I. and inhabit Belfast, Londonderry, and a great part of the province of Ulster. These people first introduced the linen manufactory into Ireland, which has been so very beneficial to that kingdom. They are the people who so bravely defended Londonderry and Inniskillen against the Popish army under James II.

Notwithstanding these supplies from Great Britain, Ireland is in general but thinly inhabited, and according to the latest computations, does not contain above one million of people.

The inhabitants of Ireland are by no means deficient in genius and bravery. To the Irish brigades the French were indebted for their boasted victory at Fontenoy; and it cannot be yet forgot that generals of this nation led on the Austrian troops and boldly faced the greatest warrior of modern times.

Ireland is still a distinct, though a dependent, subordinate kingdom. It was only entitled the dominion or lordship of Ireland, and the king's stile was no other than *dominus Hiberniæ*, lord of Ireland, till the 33d year of king Henry VIII. when he assumed the title of King, which is recognized by act of parliament, 35 Hen. VIII. But, as Scotland and England are now one and the same kingdom, and yet differ in their municipal laws; so England and Ireland are, on the other hand, distinct kingdoms, and yet in general agree in their laws. After the conquest of Ireland by king Henry II. the laws of England were received and sworn to by the Irish nation, assembled at the council of Lismore. And as Ireland, thus conquered, planted, and governed, still continues in a state of dependence, it must necessarily conform to, and be obliged by, such laws as the superior state thinks proper to prescribe.

But this state of dependence being almost forgotten, and ready to be disputed by the Irish nation, it

became

became neceffary, fome years ago, to declare how that matter really ftood: and therefore by ftatute 6 Geo. I. it is declared, that the kingdom of Ireland ought to be fubordinate to, and dependent upon, the imperial crown of Great Britain, as being infeparably united thereto; and that the king's majefty, with the confent of the lords and commons of Great Britain in parliament, hath power to make laws to bind the people of Ireland.

The conftitution of the Irifh government is nearly the fame with that of England. The power of the lord-lieutenant, who reprefents the king, is in fome meafure reftrained, and in others enlarged, according to the king's pleafure, or the exigencies of the times. On his entering upon this honourable office, his letters patent are publicly read in the council chamber, and having taken the ufual oath before the lord chancellor, the fword, which is to be carried before him, is delivered into his hands, and he is feated in the chair of ftate, attended by the lord chancellor, the members of the privy council, the peers and nobles, the king at arms, a ferjeant at mace, and other officers of ftate; and he never appears publicly without being attended by a body of horfe-guards. Hence, with refpect to his authority, his train and fplendor, there is no viceroy in Chriftendom that comes nearer the grandeur and majefty of a king. He has a council compofed of the great officers of the crown; namely the chancellor, treafurer, and fuch of the archbifhops, earls, bifhops, barons, judges, and gentlemen, as his majefty is pleafed to appoint.

The parliament here as well as in England, is the fupream court, which is convened by the king's writ; but the reprefentatives of the people enjoy their feat in the houfe during life, or till the death of the king. The laws are made in Ireland by the houfe of lords and commons, after which they are fent to England for the royal approbation; when, if approved by his

majefty

majesty and council, they pass the great seal of England, and are returned. Thus the two houses of parliament make laws which bind the kingdom, raise taxes for the support of government, and for the maintenance of an army of 16,000 men, who are placed in barracks in several parts of the kingdom.

For the regular distribution of justice, there are also in Ireland, as well as in England, four terms held annually for the decision of causes; and four courts of justice, the chancery, king's-bench, common-pleas, and exchequer.

With respect to the trade of Ireland, the discouragements laid upon it by the act of navigation, and other laws made in England, are so numerous, that it cannot be expected it should flourish to such a degree as its natural situation, extended coasts, commodious harbours, bays and rivers seem to promise. The chief exports of Ireland consist of linen cloth and yarn, lawns and cambricks, which are manufactured to great perfection, and exported to considerable advantage; the English laws giving great encouragements to this branch of trade, which, with a few exceptions, may be said to be the source of all the wealth in Ireland. To these may be added, wool and woollen yarn exported to England only; beef, pork, green hides, some tanned leather, calf-skins dried, great quantities of butter, tallow, candles, ox and cow horns, ox hair, a small quantity of lead, copper-ore, herrings, dried fish, rabbit-skins, and fur; otter-skins, goat-skins, salmon, and a few other particulars. Wool and yarn are allowed to be exported only to England; but from the thirst of gain, many ship-loads are sent by stealth to France, to the great detriment of the woollen trade; and perhaps the best method of preventing it for the future, would be to restore the woollen manufacture to Ireland, at least in the coarse branches of it, and to make it the interest of the Irish to employ their wool at home.

The

The Irish, however, enjoy many advantages unknown to Britons. If they are denied some privileges in trade, they are not saddled with our taxes and heavy duties. The productions of their country are cheap; in the metropolis of the kingdom beef sells at two-pence per pound, turkies at one shilling and six-pence, and a variety of fish, at a trifling rate. French claret is landed at little more than one shilling per bottle, and all other foreign commodities (that have not been blessed with a British excise) may be had in the same proportion.

With regard to the other adjacent islands which are subject to the crown of Great Britain, some of them (as the isle of Wight, of Portland, of Thanet, &c.) are comprized within some neighbouring county, and are therefore to be looked upon as annexed to the mother island, and part of the kingdom of England. Likewise the Orkneys, and many more that belong to Scotland. But there are others which require a more particular consideration.

And, first, the Isle of Man is a distinct territory from England, and is not governed by our laws; neither doth any act of parliament extend to it, unless it be particularly named therein; and then an act of parliament is binding there. It was formerly a subordinate feudatory kingdom, subject to the kings of Norway; then to king John and Henry III. of England; afterward to the kings of Scotland; and after various grants, it fell at last into the hands of the duke of Athol. But the distinct jurisdiction of this little subordinate royalty being found inconvenient for the purposes of public justice, and for the revenue (it affording a commodious asylum for debtors, outlaws, and smugglers) authority was given to the treasury by statute 12 Geo. I. c. 28. to purchase the interest of the then proprietors for the use of the crown: which purchase was at length compleated in the year 1765, and confirmed by statute 5 Geo. III. c. 26 and 39. whereby the whole island and all its dependencies, so granted as aforesaid

said (except the landed property of the Athol family, their manerial rights and emoluments, and the patronage of the bishopric, and other ecclesiastical benefices) are unalienably vested in the crown, and subjected to the regulations of the British excise and customs.

The islands of Jersey, Guernsey, Sark, Alderney, and their appendages, were parcel of the dutchy of Normandy, and were united to the crown of England by the first princes of the Norman line. They are governed by their own laws, which are, for the most part, the ducal customs of Normandy, being collected in an ancient book of very great authority, intitled, *le Grand Couſtumier*. The king's writ, or process from the courts of Westminster, is there of no force; but his commission is. They are not bound by common acts of our parliaments, unless particularly named. All causes are originally determined by their own officers, the bailiffs and jurats of the islands; but an appeal lies from them to the king in council, in the last resort.

Beside these adjacent islands, our more distant plantations in America and elsewhere, are also in some respects subject to the English laws. Plantations, or colonies in distant countries, are either such where the lands are claimed by right of occupancy only, by finding them desart and uncultivated, and peopling them from the mother country; or where, when already cultivated, they have been either gained by conquest, or ceded to us by treaties. And both these rights are founded upon the law of nature, or at least upon that of nations. But there is a difference between these two species of colonies, with respect to the laws by which they are bound. For it hath been held, that if an uninhabited country be discovered and planted by English subjects, all the English laws then in being, which are the birthright of every subject, are immediately there in force. But this must be understood with many and very great restrictions. Such colonists carry with them only so much

much of the English law, as is applicable to their own situation, and the condition of an infant colony; such, for instance, as the general rules of inheritance, and of protection from personal injuries. The artificial refinements and distinctions incident to the property of a great and commercial people, the laws of police and revenue (such especially as are inforced by penalties) the mode of maintenance for the established clergy, the jurisdiction of spiritual courts, and a multitude of other provisions, are neither necessary nor convenient for them, and therefore are not in force. What shall be admitted and what rejected, at what times, and under what restrictions, must, in case of dispute, be decided in the first instance, by their own provincial judicature, subject to the revision and control of the king in council; the whole of their constitution being also liable to be new-modelled and reformed, by the general superintending power of the legislature in the mother country. But in conquered or ceded countries, that have already laws of their own, the king may indeed alter and change those laws; but, till he does actually change them, the ancient laws of the country remain, unless such as are against the law of God, as in the case of an infidel country. Our American plantations are principally of this latter sort, being obtained in the last century, either by right of conquest, and driving out the natives (with what natural justice shall not at present be decided) or by treaties. And therefore the common law of England, as such, has no allowance or authority there; they being no part of the mother country, but distinct (though dependent) dominions. They are subject, however, to the control of the parliament; though (like Ireland, Man, and the rest) not bound by any acts of parliament, unless particularly named.

With respect to their interior polity, our colonies are properly of three sorts. 1. Provincial establishments, the constitutions of which depend on the respective commissions issued by the crown to the governors,

vernors, and the inftructions which ufually accompany thofe commiffions; under the authority of which, provincial affemblies are conftituted, with the power of making local ordinances, not repugnant to the laws of England. 2. Proprietary governments, granted out by the crown to individuals, in the nature of feudatory principalities, with all the inferior regalities, and fubordinate powers of legiflation, which formerly belonged to the owners of counties palatine: yet ftill with thefe exprefs conditions, that the ends for which the grant was made, be fubftantially purfued, and that nothing be attempted, which may derogate from the fovereignty of the mother country. 3. Charter governments, in the nature of civil corporations, with the power of making byelaws for their own interior regulation, not contrary to the laws of England; and with fuch rights and authorities as are fpecially given them in their feveral charters of incorporation. The form of government in moft of them is borrowed from that of England. They have a governor named by the king (or in fome proprietary colonies by the proprietor) who is his reprefentative or deputy. They have courts of juftice of their own, from whofe decifions an appeal lies to the king in council here in England. Their general affemblies, which are their houfes of commons, together with their councils of ftate, being their upper houfes, with the concurrence of the king or his reprefentative the governor, make laws fuited to their own emergencies. But it is particularly declared by ftatute 7 and 8 W. III. c. 22. that all laws, bye-laws, ufages, and cuftoms, which fhall be in practice in any of the plantations, repugnant to any law, made or to be made in this kingdom relative to the faid plantations, fhall be utterly void and of none effect. And, becaufe feveral of the colonies had claimed the fole and exclufive right of impofing taxes upon themfelves, the ftatute 6 Geo. III. c. 12. exprefsly declares, that all his majefty's colonies and plantations

tations in America have been, are, and of right ought to be, subordinate to and dependent upon the imperial crown and parliament of Great Britain; who have full power and authority to make laws and statutes of sufficient validity to bind the colonies and people of America, subjects of the crown of Great Britain, in all cases whatsoever.

These are the several parts of the dominions of the crown of Great Britain, in which the municipal laws of England are not of force or authority, merely as the municipal laws of England. Most of them have probably copied the spirit of their own law from this original; but then it receives its obligation, and authoritative force, from being the law of the country.

As to any foreign dominions which may belong to the person of the king by hereditary descent, by purchase, or other acquisition, as the territory of Hanover, and his majesty's other property in Germany; as these do not in any wise appertain to the crown of these kingdoms, they are entirely unconnected with the laws of England, and do not communicate with this nation in any respect whatsoever. The English legislature had wisely remarked the inconveniencies that had formerly resulted from dominions on the continent of Europe; from the Norman territory which William the Conqueror brought with him, and held in conjunction with the English throne; and from Anjou, and its appendages, which fell to Henry II. by hereditary descent. They had seen the nation engaged for near four hundred years together in ruinous wars for defence of these foreign dominions; till, happily for this country, they were lost under the reign of Henry VI. They observed, that, from that time, the maritime interests of England were better understood, and more closely pursued: that, in consequence of this attention, the nation, as soon as she had rested from her civil wars, began at this

period

period to flourish all at once; and became much more considerable in Europe, than when her princes were possessed of a larger territory, and her councils distracted by foreign interests. This experience, and these considerations, gave birth to a conditional clause in the act of settlement, which vested the crown in his present majesty's illustrious house, " That in case the crown and imperial dignity of " this realm shall hereafter come to any person " not being a native of this kingdom of England, " this nation shall not be obliged to engage in any " war for the defence of any dominions or terri- " tories which do not belong to the crown of Eng- " land, without consent of parliament."

[AFTER this review of the British empire, we have, though not introduced by any historical narrative, given a view of the English dress at two remarkable periods, which when compared with that of our own times, may amuse some of our readers.]

A SHORT

of a Wealthy Merchant of London in 1588.

Habit of a Nobleman of England, in 1640

Habit of the Lady Mayoress of London in 1640.

'bit of an Oliverian an English Partisan in 1650.

A

SHORT VIEW

OF THE

NAVAL TRANSACTIONS

OF

BRITAIN:

Beginning with the Reign of Queen ELIZABETH, and ending with the PEACE of VERSAILLES in 1762.

THE extensive commerce of Great Britain having increased her riches and power, and thence enabled her to acquire a very respectable influence among the European states; some of them much her superiors in extent of territory and numbers of people: it is a very natural subject of inquiry to ask what peculiar circumstances operated so happily in her favour? In this investigation, it will not be long before it is discovered, that whatever causes beside might co-operate; the prosperity of Britain is primarily owing to its insular situation; and to its being an island of such a size, as to possess sufficient internal strength to make proper improvement of its exterior advantages.

These advantages were indeed enjoyed but in part, before the two kingdoms understood their mutual interest so well as to unite together in one empire. England, it is true, was always formidable before; but it is since that happy period that Great Britain has shone with superior lustre; and shewn, what a brave

brave and a free people, fo fortunately fituated, can perform, under prudent conduct, for their common intereft.

After a general collection of voyages and travels, in which we have ranged the globe at large, and informed ourfelves concerning diftant nations; as we find our own ifland fo peculiarly calculated for a maritime power, and fo eminently diftinguifhed as one; it will certainly be a very interefting amufement to a Britifh reader, to trace, in a hiftorical view, thofe fignal naval tranfactions, from which our mariners have derived fo much glory, and our country fuch capital emoluments, and fuch afcendancy on the ocean.

England from the earlieft ages was diftinguifhed as a maritime nation, compared with her cotemporaries at the feveral periods. But it was not until the time of Queen Elizabeth, that the conftitution began to fettle; and a commercial intereft to take place of the old feudal fyftem. This infpired the government with a vigour heretofore little known; the effects of which were fhewn to great advantage under the refolute princefs with whom we fhall commence a review of the Britifh marine.

Perhaps there never was a kingdom in a more diftreffed condition than England, at the acceffion of Queen Elizabeth. It was engaged in a war abroad for the intereft of a foreign prince; at home the people were divided and diftracted about their religious and civil concerns. Thofe of the reformed religion had been lately expofed to the flames, and thofe of the Roman community found themfelves now in a declining ftate. On the continent we had no allies; in this very ifland the Scots were enemies, and their queen claimed the Englifh crown. The exchequer was exhaufted; moft of the forts and caftles throughout the kingdom mouldering into ruins; at fea we had loft much of our ancient reputation; and a too
fharp

sharp sense of their misfortunes, had dejected the whole nation to the last degree.

Elizabeth was about twenty-five years of age, had quick parts, an excellent education, much prudence, and withal, what she inherited from her father, a high and haughty spirit, qualified by a warm and tender affection for her people, and an absolute contempt of those pleasures, by the indulging which, princes are too commonly misled. She received the compliments on her accession, with majesty; and she supported her dignity even in her dying moments.

The first act of the queen's government was asserting her independency. She made an order in council, in the preamble of which it was recited, that the distresses of the kingdom were chiefly owing to the influence of foreign counsels in the late reign; and therefore the queen thought fit to declare, that she was a free princess, and meant so to act, without any farther applications to Spain, than the concerns of her people absolutely required. On the twenty-first of November, when she had worn the crown but three days, she sent orders to vice-admiral Malyn, to draw together as many ships as he could for the defence of the narrow seas, and for preventing likewise all persons from entering into, or passing out of the kingdom without licence; which he performed so strictly, that in a short time the council were forced to relax their orders, and to signify to the warden of the Cinque-ports, that the queen meant not to imprison her subjects, but that persons might pass and repass about their lawful concerns.

With like diligence, provision was made for the security of Dover, Portsmouth, and the Isle of Wight, so that by the end of the year, the kingdom was out of all danger from any sudden insult, and the queen at leisure to consider how she might farther strengthen it, so as to render all the projects of her enemies abortive. Her entrance on government had the same appearance of wisdom as if she had been years upon the throne,

throne, and the hopes raifed by her firft actions were fupported and even exceeded by the fteadinefs of her conduct; fo that by a firm and uniform behaviour fhe fecured the reverence and affection of her fubjects at home, and eftablifhed a character abroad that prevented any immediate enterprizes upon her dominions in that feeble and fluctuating condition in which fhe found them.

In the month of April 1559, peace was concluded with France; and therein, amongft other things, it was provided, that, after the term of eight years, the French fhould render to the queen the town of Calais, or pay her fifty thoufand crowns by way of penalty. In this treaty, the Dauphin and the queen of Scots were alfo included: but this was very indifferently performed; for the French immediately began to fend over great forces into Scotland, where they intended, firft to root out the proteftant religion, and then to have made themfelves entirely mafters of the kingdom. This proceeding fo alarmed the nobility of Scotland, that they applied for protection to Queen Elizabeth; who forefeeing the confequence of fuffering the French to eftablifh an intereft in Scotland, determined to fend thither affiftance both by land and fea.

In the mean time a ftrict but legal inquiry was made into the lofs of Calais in the late reign. The Lord Wentworth, on whom many afperfions had fallen, was very fairly tried and honourably acquitted by his peers; but the captains Chamberlain and Harlefton, were condemned, though the queen thought fit to pardon them. As for Lord Grey, his gallant defence of the fortrefs, wherein he was governor, exempted him from any profecution; inftead of which, he was appointed commander in chief of the forces that were to march into Scotland. The fleet was commanded by Admiral Winter, which failed up the Frith of Forth, blocked up Leith by fea, while the army of the Scots lords, and the Englifh auxiliaries under
Lord

Lord Grey, befieged it by land, and in a very fhort fpace forced the French garrifon to capitulate. Thus all the defigns of France on that fide, were entirely broken, and the queen left to look to her own concerns, which fhe did with fuch diligence, that in two years fpace, religion was reftored, the principal grievances felt under the former government redrefied; bafe money taken away, the forts throughout the kingdom repaired, and trade brought into a flourifhing condition.

But above all, the navy was the queen's peculiar care; fhe directed a moft exact furvey of it to be made, a very ftrict enquiry into the caufes of its decay, and the fureft means by which it might be recovered. She iffued orders for preferving timber fit for building, directed many pieces of brafs cannon to be caft, and encouraged the making gunpowder here at home, which had been hitherto brought from abroad at a vaft expence. For the fecurity of her fleet, which generally lay in the river Medway, fhe built a ftrong fortrefs, called Upnore-Caftle. The wages of the feamen fhe raifed, enlarged the number, and augmented the falaries of her naval officers; drew over foreigners fkilled in the arts relating to navigation, to inftruct her people, and by the pains fhe took in thefe affairs, excited a fpirit of emulation among her fubjects, who began every where to exert themfelves in like manner, by repairing of ports, and building veffels of all fizes, efpecially large and ftout fhips, fit for war, as well as commerce. From all which, as Mr. Camden tells us, the queen juftly acquired the glorious title of the RESTORER of NAVAL POWER, and SOVEREIGN of the NORTHERN SEAS; infomuch, that foreign nations were ftruck with awe at the queen's proceedings, and were now willing refpectfully to court a power, which had been fo lately the object of their contempt.

The civil diffentions in the kingdom of France, which gave the court a pretence for oppreffing thofe of the reformed religion, whom they called Huguenots, produced in the year 1562, very deftructive confequences to their neighbours. The French proteftants had long fued to Elizabeth for protection, and offered to put the port of Havre de Grace, then called Newhaven, into her hands; which fhe at length accepted, and fent over Ambrofe Dudley, earl of Warwick, in the month of September 1562, with a confiderable fleet, and a good body of troops on board, who entered into the town, and kept poffeffion of it till the twenty-ninth of July following.

The taking into our hands this place, proved of infinite detriment to the French; for the court having declared all Englifh fhips good prize, fo long as the queen held that port, fhe found herfelf obliged to iffue a like proclamation; whereupon, fuch numbers of privateers were fitted out from Englifh ports, and from Newhaven, that the fpoil they made is almoft incredible. A maritime power injured, inftead of expoftulating, immediately makes reprifals, and thereby extorts apologies from the aggreffors made fenfible of their paft miftake. But by degrees this fpirit of privateering grew to fuch a height, that the queen for her own fafety, and the honour of the nation, was obliged to reftrain it.

Philip II. of Spain, from the time of Queen Elizabeth's acceffion to the throne, had dealt with her very deceitfully, fometimes pretending to be her firm friend, at others, feeking every occafion to injure and moleft her fubjects, which he had more frequent opportunities of doing, from the great commerce they carried on in Flanders. Yet, while thefe things difturbed the nation's tranquillity in a certain degree, France and the Low Countries, were much more grievoufly torn through religious difputes, which by degrees kindled a civil war. The proteftants being the weakeft, and withal the moft injured party, the queen was inclined to favour them, and to afford them fome affiftance, though fhe was not willing abfolutely

to

to break either with the moſt Chriſtian, or with the Catholic king.

In the midſt of theſe difficulties, the queen took every opportunity to encourage her people, in proſecuting new ſchemes of trade abroad, or purſuing what might be an improvement of their lands at home. With this view ſhe ſometimes contributed ſhips, ſometimes gave money, at others, entered into partnerſhip: in ſhort, ſhe neglected nothing which might ſhew her maternal tenderneſs for all her ſubjects.

The provinces of Zealand and Holland had now delivered themſelves from the Spaniſh bondage, and were growing conſiderable in the world by their maritime power. This however, had a bad effect on the diſpoſition of the common people, who became inſufferably inſolent to all their neighbours, and particularly to us who had been their principal benefactors. Their pretence for this was, our correſponding with the inhabitants of Dunkirk, who were their enemies. At firſt, therefore, they took only ſuch ſhips as were bound to that port; but by degrees they went farther, and committed ſuch notorious piracies, that the queen was again forced to ſend the comptroller of the navy, Mr. Holſtock, with a ſmall ſquadron to ſea, who quickly drove the Dutch frigates into their harbours, and ſent two hundred of their ſeamen to priſon. The queen, not ſatisfied with this puniſhment, ſent Sir William Winter, and Robert Beale, Eſq; to demand reſtitution of the goods taken from her ſubjects; which, however, they did not obtain; and on this account the Dutch factors here ſuffered ſeverely.

But as for ſuch refugees of all nations, as fled hither for the ſake of religion, ſhe not only received them kindly, but granted them various privileges, in order to induce them to ſtay, and fix here the manufactures in which they had laboured in their own countries. This policy ſucceeded ſo well, that Colcheſter, Norwich,

wich, Yarmouth, Canterbury, and many other places were filled with those induftrious foreigners, who taught us to weave variety of filk and worfted ftuffs; while many alfo from Germany were fent into the North, where they employed themfelves in mining, making falt-petre, forging all forts of tools made of iron, which were arts abfolutely unknown to us before their arrival.

The growth of this kingdom's power and commerce, being fo confpicuous, left King Philip of Spain, the moft penetrating prince of his time, no room to doubt, that his projects for affuming the fupream dominion of Europe, or at leaft the abfolute direction of it, would be rendered entirely abortive, unlefs fome method could be contrived for ruining England at once. The catholic king had three points in view, not for diftreffing only, but for deftroying Queen Elizabeth, and utterly fubverting the Englifh ftate. The firft of thefe was, uniting againft her, under colour of religion, moft of the princes and ftates abroad; which, by the affiftance of the pope, joined to his own extenfive influence, he, in a good meafure, effected. His fecond point was, perplexing the queen at home, by countenancing the popifh faction, and by maintaining, at a vaft expence, fuch fugitives as fled from hence, in which he was likewife for fome time fuccefsful. The laft thing King Philip had at heart was the providing, as fecretly as might be, fuch a force as, with the affiftance of his other fchemes, might enable him to make himfelf entirely mafter of England at once: to which end he with great diligence fought to increafe his maritime power, and upon the pretence of his wars in the Netherlands, to keep under the command of the prince of Parma, one of the ableft generals that, or perhaps any age ever produced, fuch an army in conftant readinefs there, as might be fufficient to atchieve this conqueft, when he fhould have a fleet ftrong enough to protect them in their paffage. In the profecution

fecution of thefe deep laid projects, Philip met with many favourable circumftances, which might, and very probably did, ftrongly flatter his hopes: particularly, the death of the queen of Scots, which ftained the character of Elizabeth in foreign courts; and his own acquifition of the kingdom of Portugal, by which he gained a vaft acceffion of naval ftrength.

Queen Elizabeth and her minifters, were too penetrating, and had too quick, as well as certain intelligence, to be at all in the dark, as to the purpofe of the king of Spain; and their prudence was fuch, that by every method poffible, they prepared to difappoint him, without difclofing their apprehenfions to the world. With this intent they laboured to convince foreign ftates, that King Philip was a common enemy, and that he aimed alike at fubduing all his neighbours; which being alfo ftrictly true, had, undoubtedly, a proper weight. In the next place, pains were taken to cultivate a clofer correfpondence with his difcontented fubjects in the Netherlands, and to furnifh them with money, and fecretly with other aids, whereby they were enabled to give fome check to his power, both by fea and land. Our own privateers were allowed to pafs into the Weft Indies, where they carried on an illicit trade, not more to their own profit than the public benefit: for, by this means, they gained a perfect acquaintance with the ports, rivers, and fortreffes in the Weft Indies, with the nature of the commerce tranfacted there, the method of fharing it by fair means, or of deftroying it by force. Thus, notwithftanding their immenfe wealth, and extenfive dominions, the Englifh were in fome meafure a match for the Spaniards, in all places and at all points.

But ftill, the great fecret by which the queen defeated all King Philip's political inventions, feems to have been fcarcely known, to moft of the writers, who have undertaken to acquaint us with the tranfactions of her reign. It was in reality this; fhe difcovered

the

the principal inftruments he intended to make ufe of for her deftruction; but inftead of expofing or deftroying them, fhe contrived fo to manage them by her creatures, as to make them actually fulfill her purpofes, though they remained all the time tools and penfioners to Spain.

The queen's apprehenfions of the Spaniard's defigns, were certainly conceived much earlier than moft of our hiftorians imagine, as appears from the state-papers in her reign; among which, from the year 1574, we meet with nothing more frequent, than inftructions for viewing fortifications, examining the condition of our forts, enquiring into the ftrength, and pofture of our militia, taking frequent mufters; and, in fine, forming from all thefe enquiries, a brief ftate of the military and naval power of her dominions: whereby it appears, that the able men throughout England, were computed to be one hundred, eighty-two thoufand, nine hundred, twenty-nine, by which were intended ferviceable men; and of fuch as were armed, and in a continual capacity of acting, there were fixty-two thoufand, four hundred, and fixty-two; and of light-horfe two thoufand five hundred fixty-fix. In an account of the royal navy in 1578, it alfo appears, that it confifted of no more than twenty-four fhips of all fizes. The largeft was called the Triumph, of the burthen of a thoufand tons; the fmalleft was the George, which was under fixty tons. At the fame time, all the fhips throughout England, of an hundred tons and upward, were but one hundred thirty-five; and all under an hundred, and upward of forty tons, were fix hundred and fixty-fix.

It muft give every candid and attentive reader a very high idea of the wifdom and fortitude of Queen Elizabeth, and her minifters, when he is told, that during the whole time Spain was providing fo formidable an invafion, they were affiduoufly employed in cherifhing the commerce and naval power of England;

land; without suffering themselves to be at all intimidated, either by the enemy's boasts, or by the intelligence they had of their great strength and vast preparations. To distress King Philip in bringing home his treasures from the West Indies, many adventurers were licensed to cruise in those seas, and the queen herself lent some ships for this purpose. To delay the invasion as much as possible, or if it had been practicable, to defeat it, the queen sent a stout fleet under Sir Francis Drake, in 1587, to Cadiz; where that admiral performed rather more than could be expected: for he forced six gallies which were designed to have guarded the port, to shelter themselves under the cannon of their castles, and then burnt a hundred ships and upward in the bay, all of which were laden with ammunition and provisions. From thence he sailed to Cape St. Vincent, where he surprized some forts, and entirely destroyed the fishing craft in the neighbourhood.

Arriving at the mouth of the Tayo, and understanding that the Marquis de Santa Cruz lay hard by, with a squadron of good ships, he challenged him to come out and fight; but the marquis, who was one of the best seamen in Spain, adhering closely to his master's orders, chose rather to let Drake burn and destroy every thing on the coast than hazard an engagement. Sir Francis, having done this, steered for the Azores, where he took a large ship homeward bound from the East Indies, which added as much to his profit, as his former glorious exploits had done to his reputation; and so returned home in triumph. This expedition delayed the Spaniards for some months; but in the spring of the next year, his enormous fleet being almost ready, King Philip gave orders that it should rendezvous at Lisbon, in order to pass from thence to England.

His catholic majesty presumed so much on the force of this extraordinary fleet, superior certainly to any thing that had been fitted out for ages before, that
instead

instead of concealing its strength, he caused a very accurate account of it to be published in Latin, and most of the languages spoken in Europe, except English. This piece was dated May 20th, 1588; and according to it, the most happy Armada, as it was therein stiled, (afterward christened by the pope the Invincible Armada) consisted of 130 ships, in all 57,868 tons; on board which were 8450 mariners, 19,295 soldiers, 2088 slaves, and 2630 pieces of cannon. Beside, there was a large fleet of tenders, with a prodigious quantity of arms on board, intended for such as should join them. There were also on board this fleet 124 volunteers of quality, and about 180 monks of several orders.

The command of the whole was originally designed to have been vested in the abovementioned marquis de Santa Cruz, a nobleman of known valour, and great experience, of which he had given high proofs in the famous battle of Lepanto: but he dying, the duke of Medina Sidonia, Don Alphonso de Gusman, was appointed in his stead, rather on account of his superior quality than his distinguished merit. Under him served Don Martinez de Ricalde, an old experienced Biscaneer, who had the direction of all things, and by whose advice the general was entirely led.

In the first place, the queen took care to give proper information to all foreign states, of the nature and intent of this project of the king of Spain's, pointing out to them, not her own, but their danger, in case that monarch should prevail; which method being as prudently carried into practice, as it was wisely contrived, the king of Denmark, at the request of her ambassador, laid an embargo on a very strong squadron of ships hired for the use of King Philip in his dominions. The Hanse-Towns, determined enemies at that time to England, retarded, however, the ships they were to have sent to Spain, which, though a very seasonable act of prudence then, proved fatal to them afterward. King James VI. of Scotland
buried

buried all his refentments for his mother's death, and fteadily adhered to his own, by following the queen's interefts. The French were too wife to afford the Spaniards any help; and the Dutch fitted out a confiderable navy, for the fervice of the queen, under the command of Count Juftin of Naffau.

A Lift of the Englifh Fleet, under the Command of Charles Lord Howard of Effingham, Lord High Admiral.

Men of war belonging to her majefty,	17
Other fhips hired by her majefty for this fervice,	12
Tenders and ftore-fhips,	6
Furnifhed by the city of London, being double the number the queen demanded, all well-manned, and throughly provided with ammunition and provifion,	16
Tenders and ftore-fhips,	4
Furnifhed by the city of Briftol, large and ftrong fhips, and which did excellent fervice,	3
A tender,	1
From Barnftaple, merchant-fhips converted into frigates,	3
From Exeter,	2
A ftout pinnace,	1
From Plymouth, ftout fhips, every way equal to the queen's men of war,	7
A fly-boat,	1
Under the command of Lord Henry Seymour, in the narrow feas, of the queen's fhips and veffels in her fervice,	16
Ships fitted out at the expence of the nobility, gentry, and commons of England,	43
By the merchant-adventurers, prime fhips, and excellently well furnifhed,	10
Sir William Winter's pinnace,	1
In all	143

The lift at large given by Mr. Entick, makes them amount to 197 ships. The quantity of guns carried by the English fleet is not to be found; but though we outnumbered the Spaniards in veffels, the English fleet was greatly inferior both in tonnage, and in the number of men.

The English fleet was commanded by Charles Lord Howard of Effingham, then high-admiral, who had under him for his vice-admiral, Sir Francis Drake; for his rear-admiral, Sir John Hawkins, and abundance of experienced officers, who had fignalized their courage and conduct: their orders were to lie on the weftern coaft, that they might be ready to receive the enemy. Lord Henry Seymour, in conjunction with Count Naffau, cruized on the coaft of Flanders, the better to prevent the prince of Parma from making any defcent, as it was expected he would attempt to do with the army under his command.

In regard to a land-force, the queen had three armies; the firft confifted of 20,000 men, cantoned along the fouthern coaft; another of 22,000 foot and 1000 horfe, which was encamped near Tilbury, under the command of the earl of Leicefter; the third, which was made up of 34,000 foot, and 2000 horfe, all chofen men, was for the guard of the queen's perfon, their commander being the Lord Hunfdon, a brave, active, and refolute nobleman, the queen's near relation.

The Spanifh fleet failed from the river of Lifbon, on the firft of June, N. S. with as great pómp, and as fanguine hopes, as any fleet ever did. The king's inftructions to the duke of Medina Sidonia, were to repair to the road of Calais, in order to be joined there by the prince of Parma, and then to purfue fuch further orders as he fhould find in a fealed letter delivered to the general with his inftructions. It was further recommended to him, to keep as clofe as poffible to the French fhore, in order to prevent the English from having any intelligence of his approach;

I and

and in cafe he met our fleet, he was to avoid fighting to the utmoft of his power, and to endeavour only to defend himfelf. But in doubling the North-cape, the fleet was feparated by foul weather, which obliged the general to fail to the Groyne, where he re-affembled his fhips, and had intelligence, that the Englifh fleet, believing their expedition laid afide, was put into Plymouth.

Upon this he held a council of war, to confider whether they fhould adhere ftrictly to the king's order, or embrace this favourable opportunity of burning the Englifh fleet in their harbour; an attempt certainly not impracticable. After a long debate, wherein many were of a contrary opinion, it was refolved to attempt the Englifh fleet; and this chiefly at the inftigation of Don Diego Flores de Valdes, admiral of the Andalufian fquadron. The pretence, indeed, was very plaufible; and, but for an unforefeen accident, they had certainly carried their point. The firft land they fell in with was the Lizard, which they miftook for the Ram's-head near Plymouth; and being toward night, ftood off to fea, till the next morning. In this fpace of time they were defcried by a Scots pirate, one Captain Fleming, who bore away immediately for Plymouth, and gave the lord admiral notice; which proved the utter ruin of their defign, as well as the fole caufe of the prefervation of the Englifh fleet.

The feafon was fo far advanced, and the Englifh had fo little intelligence of the Spaniard's departure, that their fleet was not only returned into port, but feveral of their fhips alfo were already laid up, and their feamen difcharged. The admiral, however, failed on the firft notice, and though the wind blew hard into Plymouth Sound, got out to fea, with great difficulty. The next day, being the 20th of July, they faw the Spanifh navy drawn up in a half-moon, failing flowly through the channel, its wings being near feven miles afunder. The admiral fuffered them

to

to pafs by quietly, that, having the advantage of the wind, he might the better attack them in the rear; which he performed with equal courage and fuccefs: and though Don Martinez de Ricalde, did all that it was poffible for a brave officer to do, yet they were put into the utmoft diforder, and many of them received confiderable damage. More had been done, but that a great part of the Englifh fleet lay at too great a diftance, fo that the admiral was forced to wait for them.

The night following, a Dutch gunner, who had been ill treated by fome Spanifh officers, fet fire to the fhip on board which was their treafure; nor was it without great difficulty, that the flames were extinguifhed. The greateft part of the money was put on board a galleon commanded by Don Pedro de Valdez, which foon after fprung her foremaft; and being thus difabled, and the night very dark, fell into the hands of Sir Francis Drake. He fent her captain to Dartmouth, and left the money on board to be plundered by his men. The next day was fpent by the Spanifh general in difpofing his fleet, iffuing orders to his officers, and difpatching an advice-boat to haften the duke of Parma; by giving him an account of the great lofs he had already fuffered, and the extream danger he was in. On the twenty-third they fought again, with variety of fuccefs, which however demonftrated to the Spaniards, that the mighty bulk of their fhips was a difadvantage to them, their fhot flying over the heads of the Englifh, while every bullet of theirs took place.

On the twenty-fourth, the Englifh were able to do little for want of ammunition; but a fupply arriving in the evening, the admiral made all neceffary difpofitions for attacking the Spaniards in the midft of the night; dividing his fleet into four fquadrons, the firft commanded by himfelf, the fecond by Sir Francis Drake, the third by Admiral Hawkins, and the fourth by Captain Martin Frobifher; but a dead calm prevented

vented the execution of his defign. On the twenty-fifth, one of the Spanifh fhips was taken; and on the twenty-fixth, the admiral refolved to make no further attempts upon them, till they fhould enter the ftreights of Dover, where he knew Lord Henry Seymour, and Sir William Winter, waited for them with a frefh fquadron. He alfo took this opportunity of knighting Lord Thomas Howard, Lord Sheffield, Roger Townfend, Admiral Hawkins, and Captain Frobifher, for their gallant behaviour throughout the engagement.

The wind favouring the Spanifh fleet, they continued their courfe up the channel, with the Englifh fhips clofe in their rear. The ftrength of the Spaniards had not only alarmed, but excited the courage of the whole nation; infomuch, that every man of quality and fortune was ambitious of diftinguifhing himfelf, by appearing upon this occafion, againft the common enemy. With this public fpirited view, the earls of Oxford, Northumberland, and Cumberland, Sir Thomas Cecil, Sir Robert Cecil, Sir Walter Raleigh, Sir Thomas Vavafor, and many others, fitted out fhips at their own expence, and went, moft of them in perfon, to attend the admiral. Men of lower rank fhewed their zeal and loyalty by fending ammunition and provifions; and fo unanimous were all men againft thefe foreigners, that even the papifts, whom the Spaniards expected to have found in arms, were glad to wipe away the afperfions which had been thrown upon them, by ferving as common foldiers.

When, therefore, the Spanifh fleet anchored on the twenty-feventh of July before Calais, the Englifh admiral had with him near a hundred and forty fhips, which enabled him to gall the enemy extreamly. But, perceiving on the twenty-eighth, that the Spaniards had fo difpofed their larger fhips, that it would be a very difficult matter to put them again into diforder, he refolved to practife an expedient long before in contemplation in cafe the enemy fhould have come up the river Thames; which was converting some of their worst vessels into fire-ships. This method he accordingly pursued, filling eight large barks with all sorts of combustible matter, and sending them under the command of the Captains Young and Prowse, about midnight, into the thickest part of the Spanish fleet, where they speedily began to blaze; and, as the admiral had foreseen, obliged the navy to separate, and each ship, by steering a different course, to seek its own safety. This is the first account we meet with of fire-ships being used in sea-engagements.

The next day a large galeass ran ashore on the sands of Calais, where she was plundered by the English. Desirous, however, of attempting somewhat, the Spaniards again rendezvoused near Graveling; where they waited some time, in hopes the prince of Parma would have come out: but in this they were disappointed, whether through the want of power, or of will, in that great general, is uncertain. At last, finding themselves hard pressed by the English fleet, which continued to make a terrible fire upon them, they made a bold attempt, to have retreated through the streights of Dover: but the wind, coming about with hard gales at north-west, drove them on the coast of Zealand; but soon after steering to the south-west, they tacked and got out of danger. The duke de Medina Sidonia took this opportunity of calling a council of war; wherein, after mature deliberation, it was resolved, that there were now no hopes left of succeeding, and therefore, the most prudent thing they could do, was to drop their design and to save as many ships as possible.

This resolution being once fixed, was immediately carried into execution, and the whole Spanish navy made all the sail they could for their own coast, going north about, which exposed them to variety of unforeseen dangers. The English admiral very prudently sent Lord Henry Seymour with a strong squa-

dron

dron to cruize on the coaſt of Zealand, to prevent any danger from their joining with the prince of Parma, and afterward left them to purſue their courſe. When the Spaniſh fleet arrived on the Scots coaſt, and found that care was every where taken they ſhould meet with no ſupply, they threw their horſes and mules overboard; and ſuch of them as had a proper ſtore of water, bore away directly for the bay of Biſcay, with the duke of Medina Sidonia, making in all about twenty-five ſhips. The reſt, about forty ſail, under the command of the vice-admiral, ſtood over for the coaſt of Ireland, intending to have watered at Cape Clare. On the ſecond of September, however, a tempeſt aroſe, and drove moſt of them aſhore, ſo that upward of thirty ſhips, and many thouſand men, periſhed on the Iriſh coaſt.

Some likewiſe were forced a ſecond time into the Engliſh channel, where they were taken, ſome by the Engliſh, and ſome by the Rochellers. Several very large veſſels were loſt among the weſtern iſles, and upon the coaſt of Argyleſhire. Out of theſe, about five hundred perſons were ſaved; who came into Edinburgh, in a manner naked; and, out of mere charity, were cloathed by the inhabitants of that city; who alſo attempted to ſend them home to Spain. But, as if misfortunes were always to attend them, they were forced in their paſſage upon the coaſt of Norfolk, and obliged to put into Yarmouth; where they ſtayed, till advice was given to the queen and council: who conſidering the miſeries they had already felt, and not willing to appear leſs compaſſionate than the Scots, ſuffered them to continue their voyage.

Thus, in the ſhort ſpace of a month, this mighty fleet, which had been no leſs than three years preparing, was deſtroyed and brought to nothing. Of one hundred and thirty ſhips, there returned but fifty-three or four; and of the people embarked there periſhed twenty thouſand men at leaſt. We may beſt form an idea of their lofs, from the precaution taken by King Philip to hide it, which was publifhing a proclamation to prohibit mourning. As to the courage and conftancy he expreffed upon this occafion, it is certain, that the lord treafurer Burleigh received intelligence " That the king fhould fay, after mafs, " that he would fpend the wealth of Spain, to one of " thofe candlefticks upon the altar, rather than not " revenge himfelf upon the Englifh." His future conduct agreed fo exactly with this threatning, that we may well conclude, if he did not fay, he thought fo, and was therefore far from being fo unmoved at this difafter as is commonly reported. What might in fome meafure juftify his refentment, was, the falling out of this mifchief, through the breach of his orders, which is well remarked by a writer of our own: for, if the king's inftructions had been purfued, it is more than probable, that Queen Elizabeth's government had run the utmoft hazard of being overturned.

The duke of Medina Sidonia efcaped punifhment, through the intereft of his wife; but as for Don Diego Flores de Valdez, whofe perfuafions induced the general to take that rafh ftep, he was arrefted as foon as he fet foot on fhore, and conducted to the caftle of St. Andero; after which, he was never heard of more. The fame writer, from whom we have this particular, remarks alfo an error in the conduct of the Englifh; viz. that they did not attack the Spanifh fleet after it arrived before Graveling; which, however, he affures us, was not through any fault in the admiral, but was occafioned through the negligence of fome under-officers, who had the direction of the military ftores, and had been too fparing of powder and ammunition. Otherwife, he tells us, it was thought, the duke de Medina Sidonia, at the perfuafion of his confeffor, would have yielded both himfelf and his fhips, which, it feems, were, in that particular, not at all better provided. This would have

have been a conquest indeed, a conquest equally glorious and important, the loss of which, ought to teach posterity, not to be too hasty in censuring great officers, or too remiss in punishing little ones.

The queen having intelligence that the Spaniards meditated a second attempt upon her dominions, resolved, like a wise princess, to find them work at home; in order to which, in the spring of the year 1589, she expressed her royal intention of assisting Don Antonio to recover his kingdom of Portugal. The expedition was undertaken partly at the queen's charge, and partly at the expence of private persons. Sir Francis Drake, and Sir John Norris, were joint commanders; and the whole navy consisted of 146 sail. To which also the Dutch, as much interested as we, joined a small squadron.

This armament landed near Corunna, commonly called the Groyne, which place they attacked, burnt the adjacent country, together with many magazines of naval stores: they then reimbarked their forces, and sailed, as they had at first designed, for the river of Lisbon. On their arrival before Peniche, the troops were landed; the place quickly surrendered to Don Antonio; and from thence the whole army marched by land toward Lisbon; where they expected to have met the fleet under the command of Sir Francis Drake: but he finding it impossible to proceed up the river with safety to her majesty's ships, staid at the castle of Cascais, which place he took, and also seized sixty sail of ships belonging to the Hanse-Towns, laden with corn and ammunition; which, with about 150 pieces of cannon, were the principal fruits of this voyage. It was indeed, intended, to have gone to the Canaries; but by this time the soldiers and sailors were so weakened with sickness, that it was thought more expedient to return. In their passage home they landed at Vigo, took and plundered it; and having made some addition to their booty, reached England; after having been about ten weeks abroad.

This expedition was inexpreffibly deftructive to the Spaniards, difappointed all their defigns, weakened their naval force, and fpread a mighty terror of the Englifh arms through their whole dominions. But as to any advantages which the proprietors reaped, they were but very inconfiderable; and the generals met with a cold reception in England. The chief grounds of their mifcarriage were in thofe days, when men could beft judge, held to be thefe. Firft, They were but indifferently manned and victualled. Secondly, Their landing at the Groyne was contrary to their inftructions; gave the men an opportunity of drinking new wines, and expofed them to a great and unneceffary lofs. Thirdly, The difagreement of the generals before Lifbon, defeated the remaining part of their defign; whereas, if in purfuance of their inftructions, they had failed directly to the coafts of Portugal, and landed their forces there, it is more than probable, they had effectually placed Don Antonio upon the throne of Portugal, which would have given a deadly ftroke to the power of Spain.

The difappointments which happened in this voyage, did not difcourage either the queen or her fubjects from purfuing the war by fea. In order to this, her majefty fettled a part of her revenue for the ordinary fupply of the navy, amounting to about nine thoufand pounds a year: and by expreffing a very high efteem for fuch young lords, and other perfons of diftinction, as had fhewn an inclination to the fea-fervice, fhe encouraged others to undertake yet greater things. Amongft thefe, the earl of Cumberland particularly diftinguifhed himfelf by fitting out a ftout fquadron, in the fummer of the year 1589, with which he failed to the Tercera iflands, where he did the Spaniards incredible mifchief, and obtained confiderable advantages for himfelf, and for his friends.

In 1590, Sir John Hawkins and Sir Martin Frobifher were at fea with two fquadrons; and by impeding the return of the Spanifh plate-fleets from America,

America, and other services, kept King Philip entirely employed at home, though his thoughts were still busy in contriving another expedition against England. The succeeding year, Lord Thomas Howard, second son to the duke of Norfolk, sailed with a squadron to the islands, in hopes of intercepting the Spanish fleet from the West Indies, which now was forced to return home. In this he had probably succeeded, if his force had been greater; but having no more than seven of the queen's ships, and about as many fitted out by private adventurers, he very narrowly escaped being totally destroyed by the Spaniards.

In 1591, the earl of Cumberland made another expedition: and in 1592, Sir Martin Frobisher, and Sir John Boroughs, infested the Spanish coast, and did much mischief. In 1594, the queen sent a small squadron to sea, under the command of Sir Martin Frobisher, to reduce the port of Brest in Bretagne, which the king of Spain had taken, by the assistance of the Leaguers in France, from King Henry IV. A place that if it had been long kept, must have been very troublesome to that monarch, and would have given the Spaniards great advantages against us. It was strong, as well by situation, as by the art and expence employed in fortifying it; and had, beside, a numerous garrison of Spanish troops. Sir John Norris, with a small English army, formed the siege by land; Sir Martin Frobisher, with only four men of war, forced an entrance into the harbour; and having thus blocked up the place by sea, landed his sailors, and in conjunction with Sir John Norris, stormed the fort; which, though gallantly defended, was taken; with the loss of abundance of brave men; and amongst them, may be reckoned Sir Martin himself, who died in the wounds he received in that service. The same year Sir Francis Drake, and Sir John Hawkins sailed on their last expedition into the West Indies.

The Spaniards, who seldom abandon any design they once undertake, were all this time employed in assembling and equipping another fleet for England; and as an earnest of their intentions, in the year 1595, Don Diego Brochero, with four gallies, arrived in Mount's-Bay, in Cornwall, and landing with all his men, burnt three little places; but without killing or taking so much as a single man. This, however, alarmed the nation, and engaged the queen to undertake an invasion of the Spanish dominions, to prevent any such future visits to her own; in order to which, a stout fleet and a numerous army were provided, under the most experienced officers of those times.

The true design of this expedition, was, to destroy the Spanish fleet in the port of Cadiz, and to make themselves masters of that rich city. The force employed was very great, not less in all than 150 sail; of which, 126 were men of war; but of these, only seventeen were the queen's ships, the rest were hired from traders and fitted for this voyage. On board this mighty fleet, were embarked upward of 7000 men. The joint commanders of the expedition were, the earl of Essex, and the lord high-admiral (Howard) assisted by a council of war. There was beside, a Dutch squadron, under the command of Admiral Van Duvenvoord, consisting of twenty-four ships, well manned and victualled. This navy lay for some time at Plymouth, till all things could be got ready; and then, on the first of June 1596, sailed for the coast of Spain with a fair wind, and the good wishes of all their countrymen.

They were so happy as to arrive in sight of Cadiz on the twentieth of the same month, before they were either looked for, or so much as apprehended. They found the town indifferently well fortified, and defended by a strong castle. In the port were fifty-nine Spanish ships; amongst them, many laden with treasure, and nineteen or twenty gallies. Some time was lost before their coming to a resolution how to act,

owing

owing to the joint command : for the earl of Effex, who was young and warm, affected to dictate; while the admiral, who had as much courage, and more experience, could not brook being controuled. At laft, it was determined to attack the fhips in the haven, before any attempt was made upon the town; whereupon a new difficulty arofe, which was, who fhould command this attack. In the execution, fome errors were committed, through the too great heat and emulation of the commanders; but others much more grofs and fatal by the Spaniards; who, when they found themfelves compelled to fly, did it without any of thofe precautions whereby they might have provided for their fafety : for inftead of running their fhips afhore under the town, where they would have been covered by their own artillery, and where at leaft their men might have gone afhore in fafety, they ran them up the bay, as far from the enemy as poffible; by which means, part fell into the hands of the Englifh, and the reft were burnt.

In the mean time, the earl of Effex landed his men quietly, the enemy deferting a ftrong fort, from which they might have done him much mifchief: three regiments alfo were fent to make themfelves mafters of the caufeway which unites the ifland to the main. This they performed with very fmall lofs; but afterward quitted it again, which gave the gallies an opportunity of efcaping; another overfight, for which no account can be given. The lord admiral, hearing the earl was landed, landed alfo with the remainder of the forces, doubting much whether his lordfhip could have kept the place : and while the two generals were employed in reducing the city, Sir Walter Raleigh was fent to feize the fhips in the harbour of Port-Real; to prevent which, the duke of Medina Sidonia caufed them to be fet on fire, and burnt, whereby twenty millions were buried in the fea. The city and its forts they poffeffed for a fortnight; and the earl of Effex was very defirous of being

ing left there with a garrifon, however fmall; which was, notwithftanding, over-ruled by the council of war. It was then agreed to fail to Faro, in the kingdom of Algarve, where they found the place deferted by its inhabitants, and void of any thing that could be made plunder. To repair this difappointment, the earl of Effex was for failing to the Azores, there to wait for the Eaft India fhips; but in this too he was over-ruled, becaufe there was a great complaint of the want of provifion and ammunition on board the fleet. In their return, they looked into the ports of Groyne, St. Andero, and St. Sebaftian, where they expected to find fhips, but met with none; and after this, nothing remarkable happened till their arrival in England, which was on the eighth of Auguft the fame year. They brought with them two galleons, one hundred brafs guns, and an immenfe booty; the defire of keeping which, is conceived to have hindered them from performing more.

In the fpring of the year 1597, the king of Spain fitted out a frefh armada from Lifbon, compofed not only of his own fhips and gallies, but alfo of all that he could take up, and hire in Italy, or elfewhere. On board of thefe, he embarked a great body of troops, efpecially of the Irifh, intending to have invaded both England and Ireland; but the winds difappointed him, fcattered his fleet, and thirty-fix fail were caft away. In the mean time the queen fitted out another fleet of 40 men of war under the command of the earl of Effex, with an intent to intercept the plate-fleet near the Azores, after burning fuch veffels as were in the harbours of the Groyne and Ferrol. They failed from Plymouth the 9th of July; but a ftorm arifing, they were forced back thither again, and did not fail the fecond time till the 7th of Auguft. They ufed their beft endeavours to perform the firft part of their inftructions, but finding it impracticable, they thought it expedient to fteer for the iflands. In this voyage Sir Walter Raleigh's
fhip

ship sprung her mast, which, however, did not hinder him, when he had repaired his loss, from proceeding to the place of rendezvous. He had scarce begun to wood and water there, before the earl of Essex sent him orders to follow him to Fayal, which island the general himself intended to attempt. Raleigh obeyed him; but not finding Essex on his arrival, and perceiving that the people were securing their goods, throwing up retrenchments, and making every other preparation necessary for their defence, he with the advice of his officers resolved, in case Essex did not arrive in four days, to attempt the reduction of the island, which accordingly he performed: but though he got reputation by this exploit, yet he lost the general's friendship, so that a coldness thenceforth prevailed, which afterward encreased to open opposition and the most rancorous hatred.

After Essex's arrival they sailed together to Graciosa, which immediately submitted. Here the general intended to have staid; and if he had done so, undoubtedly it had answered his purpose, and he had taken the whole Spanish fleet: but being too easily brought to alter his purposes, he took another method, which gave the Spaniards, who arrived the next day, an opportunity of proceeding for Tercera, with the loss of no more than three ships, which were taken by Sir William Monson. The rest of the fleet, consisting of about thirty-seven sail, arrived safely in the port of Angra, which was well defended by several forts; so that on mature deliberation, it was judged impracticable to attempt any thing there with reasonable hopes of success.

The earl of Essex, vexed at this disappointment, resolved to do somewhat of consequence before he returned; and therefore landing, surprised the town of Villa Franca and plundered it: after which he reimbarked his forces, and prepared for his return home. In his passage he had the good luck to take a very rich Spanish ship, which fell into his fleet,
mistaking

mistaking it for their own. In the mean time, the Spaniards were meditating great designs. The absence of the English fleet gave them an opportunity of sending out their squadrons from the Groyne and Ferrol. With these they intended to have made a descent in Cornwall, and to have possessed themselves of the port of Falmouth. The Spanish admiral proceeded to the islands of Scilly, almost within sight of our shore: but it so happened, that a very high storm arose, which entirely separated their fleet. In this storm eighteen capital ships were lost, several forced into English ports were taken, and the Spanish admiral's schemes thereby entirely disconcerted. Nor did our fleet escape the fury of this tempest; but with much difficulty reached the western coast in the latter end of the month of October.

In 1598, the earl of Cumberland fitted out a squadron of eleven sail at his own expence; with which he first attempted to intercept the Lisbon fleet in its passage to the East Indies. Being disappointed in that, he sailed to the Canaries, where he made a descent on the island of Lancerota, plundered it, and then proceeded to America, where he promised himself great things. The place he fixed upon was the island of Puerto Rico, where he landed, and took the capital with small loss. This city he determined to keep, with an intent to have cruised from thence upon the Spanish coasts; but he was quickly convinced that the design was impracticable, diseases spreading amongst his soldiers and seamen to such a degree, that he was obliged to abandon his conquest.

In 1599, there was a great fleet fitted out by the queen's command: but it seems rather with an intent to watch the Spaniards, than to undertake any other enterprize of importance; since after remaining about three weeks in the Downs, it was again laid up. Yet the equipping this fleet had a great effect upon Spain, and all the powers of Europe; for it was drawn together in twelve days time, well victualled, and

throughly

throughly manned, which shewed the strength of our maritime power, and how much it was improved since 1588. The next year, being 1600, Sir Richard Levison was sent to intercept the plate-fleet; which design, though it was well contrived and wisely executed, yet failed. In 1601, the same admiral was employed in Ireland, where he did good service, in obliging the Spaniards, who had landed a considerable body of forces, to relinquish their design, and withdraw out of that island.

In 1602, the same admiral, in conjunction with Sir William Monson, was employed in an expedition for intercepting the galleons, which had infallibly taken effect, if the Dutch had sent their squadron, agreeable to their engagements with the queen. Notwithstanding this disappointment, they continued on the coast of Portugal, and at length resolved to attack a galleon which lay with eleven gallies in the road of Cerimbra; which was one of the most gallant exploits performed in the whole war. The town of Cerimbra was large and well built with free-stone, defended by a good citadel well furnished with artillery. Above the town, on the top of a mountain, stood the abbey, so fortified as to command the place, the citadel, and the road. The galleon was moored close to the shore, so as to defend by its fire, part of the citadel and part of the town : the gallies had so flanked and fortified themselves, that they were able to make a great fire upon the English fleet, without receiving any damage themselves, till such time as our ships were just before the town. Yet, in spite of these and many other disadvantages, the English admirals resolved to attack them; which they did on the 3d of June. A gale of wind blowing fresh about two in the morning, the admiral weighed, and made the signal for an attack. The vice-admiral did the like, and soon after they fell upon the enemy with great fury; and though the Spaniards defended themselves with much resolution, yet in the end several

of

of the gallies were burnt, the garrison driven from the castle, and the rich galleon, for which all this struggle was made, taken, with about a million of pieces of eight on board. Frederic Spinola, in the St. Lewis, sailed from Cerimbra, with the rest of the gallies that had escaped, viz. The St. John Baptist, the Lucera, the Padilla, the Philip, and the St. John, for the coast of Flanders; and on the 23d of September entered the British channel. Here they fell in with some English and Dutch ships; by whom three of them were sunk: the rest with great difficulty reached Dunkirk in safety.

This was the last great exploit performed by sea in this reign; for the queen, now far in years, and worn out with the cares and fatigues of government, died on the 24th of March following, in the forty-fifth year of her reign, and in the seventieth of her life: when she had settled the protestant religion throughout her kingdom, had restored the crown to its ancient reputation, supported her allies with the greatest firmness, and humbled her enemies, so as to compel them to think of soliciting for peace.

Her attention to trade appears in many instances, of some of which it may not be amiss to treat more particularly. The merchants of the Hanse-towns complained loudly in the beginning of her reign, of the ill-treatment they had received in the days of Edward and queen Mary; to which she very prudently answered, " That as she would not innovate any " thing, so she would protect them still in the im- " munities and condition she found them:" which not contenting them, their commerce was soon after suspended for a time, to the great advantage of the English merchants. At last the Hanse-towns prevailed so far in virtue of their German connections as to gain an imperial edict, whereby the English merchants were prohibited all commerce in the empire; this was answered by a proclamation, in consequence of which, sixty sail of their ships were taken in the river of Lisbon, laden with contraband goods for the

use

use of the Spaniards. These ships the queen intended to have restored, as sincerely desiring to have compromised all differences with those trading cities: but when she was informed that a general assembly was held at the city of Lubeck, in order to concert measures for distressing the English trade, she caused the ships and their cargoes to be confiscated; only two of them were released to carry home this news, and that the queen had the greatest contempt imaginable for all their proceedings.

After this, Sigismond king of Poland interposed in their behalf, sending hither an ambassador, who talking in a very high stile; the queen, in her answers told him plainly, that the king his master made no right estimate of his own power, and that himself was very little fit for the employment in which she found him. Thus were we ridded for ever of these incorporated foreign factors, and our own merchants established in the right of managing our commerce. In the latter end of her reign, some disputes happening with the king of Denmark, and he most unadvisedly seizing the English ships that were in his ports, the queen sent one Dr. Parkins to demand immediate and adequate satisfaction: which he did in so peremptory a stile, that the Dane was glad to compound the matter for forty thousand dollars, which he paid her majesty, and which she caused to be proportionably divided among the merchants who were injured.

These are instances of her noble spirit in obtaining redress of grievances in foreign countries, even in the most perillous times, and when her affairs were in the utmost embarrassment. As to her care of trade and navigation within her own dominions we have already mentioned many particulars; however, it may not be amiss to observe, that in 1563, an act was made for the better regulation, maintenance, and increase of the navy; and in 1566, there was a law to enable the master, wardens, and the assistants of the Trinity-house, to set up beacons and sea-marks. The same year there passed an act for incorporating, and

more

more effectually establishing the company of merchant adventurers. In 1581, there likewise passed an act for the increase of mariners, and for the maintenance of navigation, and more especially for recovering the trade to Iceland, which began then to decay, and in which there had been employed annually upward of two hundred sail of stout ships. In 1585, the queen erected by her letters patent, a new company for the management of the trade to Barbary; and in the year 1600, she incorporated a society of merchants trading to the East Indies, whence the present East India company is derived *.

Beside these numerous marks of her royal favour, and the strict attention to the commerce of her subjects, the queen afforded others continually, by sending envoys and agents to the Czar, to the Shah of Persia, to several great princes in the East Indies: and in short, wherever her interposition could be of any use to open, to promote, or to recover any branch of traffic; as appears by all the histories that are extant of her reign. It may be said, and which is more, may be said with truth and justice, that in the midst of these great things done for industry and trade, the prerogative was carried very high: many monopolies erected, and several exclusive privileges granted, which have been found injurious to trade. But the discussing these points belong to general history.

This disposition of the queen, excited a like spirit throughout the whole nation. Not only persons bred to trade, and some of the middle gentry of the kingdom, launched out into expeditions for discoveries, and planting new-found countries; but even persons of the first distinction, became encouragers and adventurers in those designs: such as the lord-treasurer Burleigh, the earl of Warwick, the earl of Leicester, &c. and some of them actually engaged in the exe-

* See the first voyage on account of the English East India company, under Sir James Lancaster; in the second volume of this Collection.

cution

cution of such projects, amongst whom were the earls of Cumberland, Essex, and Southampton, Sir Walter Raleigh, Sir Richard Grenville, Sir Humphry Gilbert, Sir Robert Dudley, &c. And therefore we need not wonder at the surprising increase of our maritime power, or the number of remarkable undertakings of this sort, within so short a period of time. Let us mention only a few. In 1575, Sir Humphry Gilbert attempted the discovery of a north-west passage; in 1577, Sir Martin Frobisher sought one the same way; Pet and Jackman sailed on a like design in 1580, by the direction of the governor and company of merchant-adventurers: an expedition was undertaken at a great expence by Sir Humphry Gilbert, in order to settle Florida; nor did it miscarry through any error of the undertaker. The great Sir Walter Raleigh would have settled Virginia in 1584, if prudence, industry, and public spirit could have effected it; but though he failed in the extent, yet he was not totally defeated in his hopes, since he laid the foundation of that settlement, which hath since so happily succeeded.

It may in this place contribute not a little to our satisfaction, if we enquire what quantity of coin, both gold and silver, there might be in the nation, toward the close of her reign; that is, at the beginning of the last century, because it is of very great consequence to have a just notion of what was the nation's stock in ready money at that period, when our great foreign commerce began. We have indeed an authentic account of her entire coinage in silver, amounting to above four millions and a half; but then if we consider that she recoined almost all the silver specie of the kingdom, and that there was a small alteration in the standard in the latter end of her reign, which raised silver from five shillings, to five and two-pence an ounce, which occasioned a new fabrication; so that much of the former coin came into the mint again as bullion: we may, with the judicious Dr. Davenant, estimate the filver coin at that time in this kingdom, at two millions and a half; to which, if we add the gold of her own and her predeceffors coin, and eftimate this at a million and a half, we may be pretty fure that we are not much wide of the truth; and that one hundred and fifty years ago, the current coin of England amounted in the whole, to four millions or thereabout.

King James, at his acceffion to the Englifh throne, was about thirty-fix years of age; and, if he had been a private perfon, would not have rendered himfelf very remarkable either by his virtues or his vices. The greateft of his failings were timidity, diffimulation, and a high opinion of his own wifdom: thefe, however, were more excufable than modern writers are willing to allow, if we confider the accident that happened to his mother before his birth, the ftrange treatment he met with in Scotland, from the feveral factions prevailing in that kingdom during his junior years, and the exceffive flatteries that were heaped on him after he came hither, by all ranks of people. It was impoffible for him to have made himfelf much acquainted with maritime affairs while he continued in Scotland, yet it does not at all appear, that he was negligent of naval concerns, after he was feated on the Englifh throne; unlefs his hafty conclufion of a peace with Spain fhould be thought liable to the like cenfure.

The acceffion of king James gave a fair opportunity to the houfe of Auftria, to make an end of the long quarrel which had fubfifted with England; becaufe, during all that time, they had been in peace and amity with king James as king of Scots. Immediately on his arrival at London, the arch-duke fent over a minifter to the Englifh court, and in confequence of his negotiations, a peace was foon after concluded with Spain. Some of the writers of thofe times tell us, that it was chiefly brought about by the large bribes given to all the king's minifters and favourites,

vourites. It seems, however, more reasonable to conclude, that this peace was in reality the effect of the king's inclination, supported by the advice of his most eminent statesmen; some of whom were known to have been for this measure in the queen's time. There were two treaties, one of peace and alliance, the other of commerce, both signed at London, the 18th of August, 1604; the constable of Castile, the greatest subject in Spain, being sent for that purpose. All the trading part of the nation were very well pleased with this proceeding, and would have been much more so, if the king had not taken a very strange step upon its conclusion. He erected a company of merchants, who were to carry on the Spanish commerce exclusively, which gave both an universal and very just offence; for as the whole nation had borne the expence of the war, and trade in general had suffered thereby, it was but reasonable, that the benefits of peace should be as diffusive. This evil, however, was of no long continuance. But if this treaty gave some dissatisfaction at home, it raised no less discontent abroad. The Hollanders, who were left to shift for themselves, and who had reaped so great advantages from the favour of queen Elizabeth, were exceedingly exasperated at a step so much to their immediate disadvantage. But as they found themselves still strong enough, not only to cope with the Spaniards, but also to make a greater figure than most other nations at sea; they lost that respect which was due to the English flag, and began to assume to themselves a kind of equality even in the narrow seas. This was quickly represented to the king as an indignity not to be borne; and thereupon he directed a fleet to be fitted out, the command of which was given to Sir William Monson, with instructions to maintain the honour of the English flag, and that superiority which was derived to him from his ancestors in the British seas. This fleet put to sea in the spring of 1604, and was continued annually under the same admiral,

admiral, who appears to have been a man of great spirit and much experience; for, as he tells us in his own memoirs, he served in the first ship of war fitted out in the reign of queen Elizabeth, and was an admiral in the last fleet she ever sent to sea. Yet he found it a very difficult matter to execute his commission; the Dutch, whenever he conferred with any of their chief officers, gave him fine language, and fair promises: but they minded them very little, taking our ships on very frivolous pretences, and treating those they found on board them with great severity, till such time as it appeared the admiral would not bear such usage, and began to make reprisals, threatening to hang, as pirates, people who shewed themselves very little better in their actions. There were also high contests about the flag, which began through some accidental civilities shewn to the Hollanders, in the late reign, when they sailed under the command of English admirals, upon joint expeditions, and were on that account treated as if they had been her majesty's own subjects; which favours they now pretended to claim as prerogatives due to them in quality of an independent state.

These disputes continued for many years; and though, through the vigilance of admiral Monson, the Dutch were defeated in all their pretensions, and the prerogatives of the British sovereignty at sea were thoroughly maintained; yet the republic of Holland still kept up a spirit of resentment, which broke out in such acts of violence, as would not have been past by in the days of queen Elizabeth. Nevertheless our admiral does not seem to charge the king, or his ministry in general, with want of inclination to do themselves justice; but lays it expresly at the door of secretary Cecil, afterward earl of Salisbury; who thought it, says he, good policy, to pass by such kind of offences: but he does not report any reasons upon which that kind of policy was grounded. However it did not absolutely or constantly prevail, even in the councils

cils of king James; for upon some surmises that foreigners took unreasonable liberties in fishing in our seas, a proclamation was published in the year 1608, asserting the king's sovereignty in that point, and prohibiting all foreign nations to fish on the British coast. This, though general in appearance, had yet a more particular relation to the Dutch, who found themselves greatly affected thereby, especially when the king appointed commissioners at London, for granting licences to such foreigners as would fish on the English coast; and at Edinburgh, for granting licences of the like nature to such as would fish in the northern sea. To these regulations, though with great reluctance, they submitted for the present; the reason of which seems to be, their having affairs of great moment to manage with the court of Great Britain. In these important concerns, notwithstanding all that had passed, they succeeded; and two treaties were concluded on the 26th of June, 1608, between the crown of Great Britain and the States-General: the one of peace and alliance, the other for stating and settling the debt due to king James. One would have imagined, that the advantages obtained by these treaties, should have brought the republic to a better temper, in respect to other matters; but they did not: for within a short time after, they disputed paying the assize-herring in Scotland, and the licence-money in England; and to protect their subjects from the penalties which might attend such a refusal, they sent ships of force to escort their herring-busses. These facts, as they are incontestable, are related, though without the least prejudice against the Dutch; who are a people certainly to be commended for all instances of public spirit, when they are not inconsistent with the rights of their neighbours, and the law of nations.

But at this time of day, ministers were too much afraid of parliaments to run the hazard of losing any of the nation's rights, for want of insisting upon them;

them; and therefore they prevailed upon the king to republish his proclamation, that a parliament, whenever they met, might see they had done their duty, and advise the king thereupon, as they should think fit.

There were also some struggles in this reign with the French, about the same rights of fishery, and the sovereignty of the sea; in which, through the vigorous measures taken by Sir William Monson, the nation prevailed, and the French were obliged to desist from their practices of disturbing our fishermen, and otherwise injuring our navigation. In 1614, the same admiral was sent to scour the Scotch and Irish seas, which were much infested with pirates. The noise, however, of their depredations far exceeded the damage; for when, on the first of June, Sir William Monson made the coast of Cathness, the most northern part of Scotland, he found that, instead of twenty pirates, of whom he expected to have intelligence in those parts, there were in fact but two; one of whom immediately surrendered, and the other was afterward taken by the admiral on the coast of Ireland: where, by a proper mixture of clemency and severity, he extirpated these rovers, and reclaimed the inhabitants of the sea-coast from affording shelter and protection to pirates, furnishing them with provisions, and taking their plunder in exchange.

In 1617, Sir Walter Raleigh was released from his imprisonment in the Tower, and had a commission from the king, to discover and take possession of any countries in the south of America, which were inhabited by heathen nations, for the enlargement of commerce, and the propagation of religion; in the undertaking which expedition, his expences were borne by himself, his friends, and such merchants as entertained a good opinion of the voyage. His design has been variously represented; but it is sufficiently evident, that the complaints of the Spanish minister, don Diego Sarmiento d'Acuna, so well known afterward

ward by the title of Count Gondemar, were not so much grounded on any notions of the injustice of this design, as on a piece of Spanish policy, by raising a clamour on false pretences, to discover the true scope and intent of Sir Walter's voyage. In this he was but too successful; for upon his representations, that excellent person was obliged to give a distinct account, as well of his preparations for executing, as of the design he was to execute: and this (by what means is not clear) was communicated to the Spaniards, who thereby gained an opportunity, first of disappointing him in America, and then of taking off his head upon his return, to the lasting dishonour of this reign, as well as the great detriment of the nation: for, without all doubt, this project of Sir Walter Raleigh's, for settling in Guiana, was not only well contrived, but well founded; and, if it had been followed, might have been as beneficial to Britain, as Brazil is to Portugal.

The disputes with the states of Holland, in reference to the right of fishing, broke out again, in the year 1618, from the old causes; which were plainly a very high presumption of their own maritime force, and an opinion they had entertained, of the king's being much addicted to peace. Mr. Camden, in his annals of the reign of this prince, says, that the deputies of the states, at their audience of the king, on the 31st of December, 1618, intreated that nothing might be done in respect to the herring-fishing; as it was the great support of their commonwealth, and the only succour and relief of the common people, in regard to the troubles then amongst them.

King James however asserted his rights through the course of this negotiation, and brought the states themselves to acknowledge, that these rights had a just foundation. If it should be enquired how it came to pass, that after carrying things so far, and to such a seeming height, they should fall again into silence and oblivion; the best answer that can be given to this queftion is, that in the midft of this difpute, the prince of Orange afked Sir Dudley Carleton a very fhrewd queftion, viz. Whether this claim about the fifhery might not be quieted for a fum of money? That gentleman, who was afterward created Vifcount Dorchefter, was certainly a man of honour; but whether fome men in power might not find a method by agents of their own, to convey an anfwer to fo plain a demand, is more than at this diftance of time can be determined. Sir William Monfon tells us, that in reference to the difputes about the flag, the Dutch found a kind of protector in the great earl of Salifbury; nor is it at all impoffible, that they might alfo find an advocate in this important bufinefs of the fifhery: but if they did, this muft have been a minifterial and not a national bargain, fince we fhall find, that in the next reign, this claim was infifted upon as warmly, and with fomewhat better effect.

We come now to the only naval expedition of confequence, undertaken during the time this king fat upon the throne, which was the attempt upon Algiers. What the real grounds were of this romantic undertaking, feem not eafy to be difcovered. The common ftory is, that count Gondemar, having gained an afcendancy over his majefty's underftanding, perfuaded him, contrary to his natural inclination, which feldom permitted him to act vigoroufly againft his own enemies, to fit out a formidable fleet, in order to humble the foes of the king of Spain. But we have it from other hands, that this was a project of much older ftanding: that the earl of Nottingham had follicited the king to fuch an expedition, before he laid down his charge of lord high admiral; and that Sir Robert Manfel infufed it into the head of his fucceffor Buckingham, that it would give a great reputation to his management of naval affairs, if fuch a thing was entered upon in the dawn of his adminiftration. As Buckingham eafily brought the king to confent to whatever himfelf approved, there is the

utmoft

utmoft probability, that it was by his influence this defign was carried into execution.

In the month of October, 1620, this fleet failed from Plymouth. It confifted of fix men of war, and twelve ftout fhips hired from the merchants. Of thefe Sir Robert Manfel, then vice-admiral of England, had the command in chief: Sir Richard Hawkins was vice, and Sir Thomas Button, rear-admiral. On the 27th of November, they came to an anchor in Algier-road, and faluted the town; but without receiving a fingle gun in anfwer. On the 28th, the admiral fent a gentleman with a white flag to let the Turkifh viceroy know the caufe of his coming; who returned him an anfwer by four commiffioners, that he had orders from the Grand Seignior to ufe the Englifh with the utmoft refpect, to fuffer their men to come on fhore, and to furnifh them with what provifions they wanted. Upon this, a negotiation enfued; in which it is hard to fay, whether the Turks or the admiral acted with greater chicanery. The former refufed to difmifs the gentleman firft fent, unlefs an Englifh conful was left at Algiers; and the latter, to rid himfelf of this difficulty, prevailed upon a feaman to put on a fuit of good cloaths, and to pafs for a conful: this cheat not being difcovered by the Turks, they fent forty Englifh flaves on board the admiral, and promifed to give him fatisfaction as to his other demands; upon which, he failed again for the Spanifh coaft, attended by fix French men of war, the admiral of which fquadron had ftruck to the Englifh fleet on his firft joining it, which feems to have been the greateft honour, and perhaps the greateft advantage too that attended this whole expedition.

It had been well if this enterprize had ended thus; but after receiving a fupply of provifions from England, it was refolved to make another attempt upon Algiers in the fpring, and, if poffible, to burn the fhips in the mole. Accordingly in the month of May the fleet left the coaft of Majorca, and upon the 21ft

of

of the fame month, anchored before Algiers, and began to prepare for the execution of this defign. Two ships taken from the Turks, one of an hundred, the other of fixty tons, were fitted up for this purpofe. Seven armed boats followed to fuftain thofe of the fire-fhips, in cafe they were purfued at their coming off. Thefe were likewife furnifhed with fireworks to deftroy the fhips without the mole.

The wind not being favourable, the attempt was put off till the 24th, and blowing then at S. S. W. the fhips advanced with a brifk gale toward the mole; but when they were within lefs than a mufket-fhot of the mole's head, the wind died away, and it grew fo calm they could not enter. However, the boats and brigantines finding they were difcovered, by the brightnefs of the moon, which was then at full, and being informed by a chriftian flave, who fwam from the town, that the Turks had left their fhips unguarded, with only a man or two in each of them, they refolved to proceed; which they did, but performed little or nothing, and then retired with the lofs of fix men. After a day or two's flay they put to fea, and in the month of June returned to England. This ill-concerted enterprize had no other effect, than that of expofing our own commerce to the infults of the Algerines, who did us a great deal of mifchief, while we did them little or none. Two other fleets were afterward fent againft them, one under the command of the lord Willoughby, and the other under that of the earl of Denbigh; but both did fo fmall fervice, that very few of our hiftories take any notice of them. Sir William Monfon has made fome fevere, but juft obfervations, upon thefe undertakings; and particularly remarks, that notwithftanding the whole nation was grievoufly offended, as they will always be at fuch mifcarriages, yet they never had any fatisfaction given them; which irritated them exceedingly, and contributed not a little to raife that fpirit, which vented itfelf afterward in a civil war.

In

In 1623, happened the bloody affair of Amboyna; of which we have given a detail in vol. 2. p. 421.

It is indeed ſtrange, that, conſidering the ſtrength of the nation at ſea at the time we received this inſult, and the quick ſenſe the Engliſh always have of any national affront; no proper ſatisfaction was obtained, nor any vigorous meaſures entered into, in order to exact it. But the wonder will in a great meaſure ceaſe, when we conſider the ſtate of the crown, and of the people at that period. Therefore, though it made a great noiſe, and occaſioned much expoſtulation with that republic, yet the attention of the crown to the propoſed war with Spain, and its concern for the recovery of the Palatinate, joined to the neceſſity there was of managing the Dutch at ſo critical a juncture, hindered our proceeding any farther than remonſtrances, while our competitors kept excluſively ſo very conſiderable a branch of trade.

Nothing of importance relating to naval affairs in this reign remains unmentioned, except the ſending a fleet to bring home prince Charles from Spain, may be reckoned in that number. It conſiſted, however, of a few ſhips only, but in good order, and well manned; ſo that the Spaniards are ſaid to have expreſſed great ſatisfaction at the ſight of it: which, however, true or falſe, is a matter of no great conſequence. This voyage, though a ſhort one, gave prince Charles ſome idea of maritime affairs; which proved afterward of benefit to the nation. The breaking the Spaniſh match made way for a war with that kingdom, much to the ſatisfaction of the Engliſh; but in the midſt of the preparations that were making for it, the king ended his days at Theobald's, on the 27th of March, 1625, in the 59th year of his age, and in the 23d of his reign. His pacific temper occaſioned our having but little to ſay at this period; but it will be proper to give the reader a conciſe view of the improvement of trade and navigation,

gation, as well as a brief account of the colonies settled, while this prince sat upon the throne.

It has been already shewn, that under the public-spirited administration of queen Elizabeth, this nation first came to have any thing like a competent notion of the benefits of an extensive commerce; and began to think of managing their own trade themselves, which down to that period had been almost entirely in the hands of foreigners. So long as the war continued with Spain, our merchants went on in a right way; they prosecuted their private advantage in such a manner, as that it proved likewise of public utility, by increasing the number of seamen, and of stout ships belonging to this kingdom: but after king James's accession, and the taking place of that peace which they had so long and so earnestly expected, things took a strange turn. Our traders saw the manifest advantage of using large and stout ships; but instead of building them, were contented to freight those of their neighbours, because a little money was to be saved by this method. In consequence of this notion, our shipping decayed in proportion as our trade encreased; till in the year 1615, things were come to so strange a pass, that there were not ten ships of 200 tons belonging to the port of London. Upon this, the Trinity-house petitioned the king, setting forth the matter of fact, and the dreadful consequences it would have, with respect to our naval power, through the decay of seamen; and praying, that the king would put in execution some good old laws, which were calculated for the redress of this evil: suggesting also the example of the state of Venice, which, on a like occasion, had prohibited their subjects to transport any goods in foreign bottoms. The merchants unanimously opposed the mariners in this dispute, and, having at this juncture better interest at court, prevailed. Yet, in a year's time, the tables were turned, and the merchants convinced

vinced of their own miftake, joined with the mariners in a like application. An extraordinary accident produced this happy effect. Two fhips, each of the burden of three hundred tons, came into the river Thames, laden with currants and cotton, the property of fome Dutch merchants refiding here. This immediately opened the eyes of all our traders: they faw now, that, through their own error, they were come back to the very point from which they fet out; and if fome bold and effectual remedy was not immediately applied, our commerce would be gradually driven again by foreigners on foreign bottoms. They inftantly drew up a reprefentation of this, and laid it before the king and his council; upon which a proclamation was iffued, forbidding any Englifh fubject to export or import goods in any but Englifh bottoms.

When a people have once entered into a courfe of induftry, the benefits accruing from it, will generally keep them in that road; and even the difficulties they meet with, turn to their advantage. Thus, after the Englifh merchants had built a few large fhips in their own ports, and furnifhed them with artillery and other neceffaries, they found themfelves in a condition to launch into many trades, that were unthought of before. For fome time, indeed, they fuffered not a little by the pirates of Barbary; yet, in the end, it put them upon building ftill larger fhips, as well as taking more care in providing and manning fmall ones. This had fuch an effect in the fpace of feven years, that whereas fhips of a hundred tons had been before efteemed very large veffels, and were generally built and brought from beyond the feas; there were now many merchantmen of three, four, and five hundred tons belonging to feveral ports. So that before the death of king James, our trade was fo far increafed, that, in the opinion of Sir William Monfon, we were little, if at all inferior in maritime force to the Dutch.

In

In refpect to the encouragements given by the crown, for promoting commerce and plantations in the Eaft Indies, and America, they were as great under this reign, as under any fucceeding one. Several voyages were made on account of the Eaft India company, and the king did not fpare fending an ambaffador into thofe parts for their fervice *. Virginia and New England were in a great meafure planted; Barbadoes poffeffed and fettled, and Bermudas difcovered in his time. Even the attempts made for fixing colonies in Newfoundland, and Acadia, or New Scotland, though ineffectual, occafioned building a great many good fhips, increafed the Newfoundland fifhery, added to the number of our failors, and kept alive that fpirit of difcovering, which is effential to a beneficial commerce. Befide, they engaged abundance of knowing and experienced perfons to write upon all branches of traffic; and their books, which yet remain, fufficiently prove, that there were numbers in thofe days, who thoroughly underftood all the arts neceffary to promote manufactures, navigation and ufeful commerce.

As to the navy, which was more particularly the care of the crown, we find it frequently engaged the attention of the king himfelf, as well as of his minifters. In moft of our naval hiftories, we have a lift of nine fhips added to the royal navy of England by this prince. But of the greateft fhip built in this king's reign, we have fo exact, and at the fame time fo authentic an account, in Stow's Annals, that it may not be amifs to tranfcribe it.

" This year, 1610, the king built a moft goo'ly fhip for war; the keel whereof was one hundred and fourteen feet long, and the crofs-beam was forty-four feet in length : fhe will carry fixty-four pieces of great ordinance, and is of the burthen of fourteen hundred tons. This royal fhip is double built, and is moft fumptuoufly adorned, within and without, with all
man-

* See Sir Thomas Roe's embaffy, in vol. 6.

manner of curious carving, painting, and rich gilding, being in all refpects the greateft and goodlieft fhip that ever was built in England; and this glorious fhip the king gave unto his fon Henry prince of Wales. The 24th of September, the king, the queen, the prince of Wales, the duke of York, and the lady Elizabeth, with many other lords, went unto Woolwich, to fee it launched; but becaufe of the narrownefs of the dock, it could not then be launched: whereupon the prince came the next morning by three o'clock, and then, at the launching thereof, the prince named it after his own dignity, and called it The Prince. The great workmafter in building this fhip, was mafter Phineas Pet, gentleman, fometime mafter of arts of Emanuel College in Cambridge."

In the fame author, we have an account of the king's going on board the great Eaft India fhip of twelve hundred tons, which was built here, and feems to have been the firft of that fize launched in this kingdom. The king called it, The Trade's Increafe; and a pinnace of two hundred and fifty tons, which was built at the fame time, he called, The Pepper-Corn. This fhews that he was a favourer of navigation. The king alfo granted a commiffion of enquiry, for reforming the abufes in the navy; the proceedings upon which are ftill preferved in the Cottonlibrary. He was liberal alfo to feamen, and naturally inclined to do them honour; but as in other things, fo in this, he was too much governed by his favourites.

Upon the demife of king James, his only fon Charles prince of Wales fucceeded him; not only quietly; and without difturbance, but with the general approbation of his fubjects. He was then in the flower of his age, had fhewn himfelf poffeffed of great abilities; and after the breaking off the Spanifh match, he rendered himfelf for a time very popular by his conduct. His father left him in a fituation much incumbered

cumbered at the time of his deceafe ; for the government was deeply in debt, a war with Spain was juft begun, and his prime minifter, the duke of Buckingham, who had been likewife his father's, was generally hated. In this fad ftate of public affairs, every thing was fubject to wrong conftructions. Eight thoufand men, raifed for the fervice of the Palatinate, were ordered to rendezvous at Plymouth; and in their paffage thither, coat and conduct-money were demanded of the country, to be repaid out of the Exchequer. The behaviour of thefe troops was very licentious; and the long continuance of peace, made it appear ftill a greater grievance. The clamour thereupon grew high; and the king, to remedy this evil, granted a commiffion for executing martial-law; which, inftead of being confidered as a remedy, was taken for a new grievance, more heavy than any of the reft.

During the time that Buckingham remained in the king's council, all things were attributed to him; and the nation was fo prejudiced againft him, that whatever was reputed to be done by him, was thought a grievance: and though no man faw this more clearly than the king, yet by an infatuation, not eafily to be accounted for, he trufted him as much, and loved him much more than his father had ever done.

The marriage of Charles with the princefs Henrietta-Maria, daughter to Henry IV. of France, had been concluded in the life-time of king James; and after his deceafe, the king was married to her by proxy. In the month of June, 1625, Buckingham went to attend her with the royal navy, and brought her to Dover; from thence fhe came to Canterbury, where the marriage was confummated: and on the 16th of the fame month, their majefties entered London privately, the plague daily increafing in the fuburbs. It was not long before an unfortunate tranfaction rendered this marriage difagreeable to the people, and as this related to the navy, it falls particularly under our cognizance; which we shall therefore handle more at large, becaufe in moſt of our general hiſtories it is treated very confuſedly.

The marquis d'Effiat, ambaſſador from France to king James, had repreſented to his majeſty, that the power of the catholic king in Italy was dangerous to all Europe; that his maſter was equally inclined with his Britannic majeſty to curtail it: but wanting a ſufficient maritime force, was deſirous of borrowing from his majeſty a few ſhips, to enable him to execute the deſign he had formed againſt Genoa. To this the king condeſcended; and it was agreed, that the Great Neptune, a man of war, commanded by Sir Ferdinando Gorges, and ſix merchant ſhips, each of between three and four hundred tons burden, ſhould be lent to the French: but ſoon after this agreement, the Rochellers made an application here, ſignifying, that they had juſt grounds to apprehend, that this Engliſh ſquadron would be employed for deſtroying the proteſtant intereſt in France, inſtead of diminiſhing the king of Spain's power in Italy.

The duke of Buckingham, knowing that this would be little reliſhed by captain Pennington, who was to go admiral of the fleet, and the owners of the ſhips; he gave them private inſtructions, contrary to the public contract with France, whereby they were directed not to ſerve againſt Rochelle: but upon their coming into a French port, in the month of May, they were told by the duke of Montmorency, that they were intended to ſerve, and ſhould ſerve againſt Rochelle; upon which, the ſailors on board the fleet ſigned, what is called by them, a round Robin, that is, a paper containing their reſolution not to engage in that ſervice, with their names ſubſcribed in a circle, that it might not be diſcerned who ſigned firſt.

Upon this, Pennington fairly failed away with the whole ſquadron, and returned into the Downs in the

VOL. VII.   R   be-

beginning of July; from whence he sent a letter to the duke of Buckingham, defiring to be excufed from that fervice. The duke, without acquainting the king, or confulting the council, directed lord Conway, then fecretary of ftate, to write a letter to captain Pennington, commanding him to put all the ships into the hands of the French. This, however, not taking effect, the duke fuperftitioufly, and without the king's knowing any thing of the defign upon Rochelle, procured his letter to captain Pennington, to the fame effect. Upon this, in the month of Auguft, he failed a fecond time to Dieppe, where, according to his inftructions, the merchant fhips were delivered to the French; but Sir Ferdinando Gorges, who commanded the king's fhip, weighed anchor and put to fea: and fo honeft were all the feamen on board thefe fhips, that, except one gunner, they all quitted them, and returned to England: but as for the fhips, they remained with the French, and were actually employed againft Rochelle, contrary to the king's intention, and to the very high difhonour of the nation. This affair made a great noife, and came at laft to form an article in an impeachment againft the duke of Buckingham.

In the mean time the defign ftill went on of attacking and invading Spain, and a ftout fleet was provided for that purpofe; but as Buckingham, in quality of lord high-admiral, had the fupream direction of that affair, the nation looked upon it with an evil eye, and were not fo much difpleafed at its mifcarriage, as glad of an opportunity of railing at the duke, and thofe who, by his influence, were entrufted with the command of the fleet, and forces on board it. The whole of this tranfaction has been very differently related, according to the humours of thofe who penned the accounts; however, there are very authentic memoirs remaining, which inform us that this war with Spain was chiefly of the duke of
Buck-

Buckingham's procuring, and seems to have proceeded more from his perfonal diftafte to count Olivarez, than any folid or honourable motive.

While the clamour fubfifted on the want of fuccefs attending this fleet abroad, the duke of Buckingham fell into another error, in the execution of his office as lord high-admiral at home. He was vexed at the noife that had been made about the merchant fhips put into the hands of the French, and employed againft Rochelle; and therefore took occafion in the latter end of the year 1626, to caufe a French fhip, called the St. Peter, of Havre de Grace, to be arrefted. The pretence was, that it was laden with Spanifh effects; which, however, the French denied, and afferted, that all the goods in the fhip belonged to French merchants, or to Englifh and Dutch. Upon this a commiffion was granted to hear evidence as to that point; and it appearing plainly, there was no juft ground of feizure, the fhip was ordered to be releafed, but not before the French king made fome reprifals: which fo irritated the nation, that this alfo was made an article in the duke's impeachment. The matter, however, was compromifed between the two kings, and the good correfpondence between their fubjects for a time reftored; but at the bottom, there was no cordial reconciliation: and fo this quarrel, like a wound ill cured, broke quickly out again with worfe fymptoms than before.

The war in which the king was engaged, in order to have procured the reftitution of the Palatinate to his brother-in-law, had drawn him into a league with Denmark, which obliged him to fend a fquadron of fhips to that king's affiftance; and this being attended with fmall fuccefs, he was called upon for farther fupplies. His parliaments all this time were little inclined to affift him, becaufe he would not part with Buckingham; and this obliged him to have recourfe to fuch methods for fupply, as his lawyers affured him were juftifiable. Amongft the reft, he obliged all the sea-ports to furnish him with ships: of the city of London he demanded twenty, and of other places in proportion.

The inhabitants thought this so hard, that many, who had no immediate dependence on trade, were for quitting their residence in maritime places, and retiring up into the country. This conduct of theirs made the burden still more intolerable upon those who staid behind; and the consequence of their remonstrances was a proclamation, requiring such as had quitted the sea-coast, to return immediately to their former dwellings: and this it was gave rise to the first disturbances in this unfortunate reign. They were quickly increased by the rash management of Buckingham; who, though he saw his master so deeply embarrassed with the wars in which he was already engaged, yet plunged him into another with France, very precipitately, and against all the rules of true policy.

The queen's foreign servants, who were all bigotted papists, had not only acted indiscreetly in matters relating to their religion, but had likewise drawn the queen to take some very wrong, to say the truth, some ridiculous and extravagant steps; upon which Buckingham engaged his majesty to dismiss her French servants, which he did the first of July, 1626, and then sent the lord Carleton to represent his reasons, for taking so quick a measure, to the French king. That monarch refused him audience, and to shew his sense of the action, immediately seized one hundred and twenty of our ships which were in his ports, and undertook the siege of Rochelle; though our king had acted but a little before, as a mediator between him and his protestant subjects. Upon this, the latter applied themselves to king Charles, who ordered a fleet of thirty sail to be equipped for their relief, and sent it under the command of the earl of Denbigh: but this being so late in the year as the month of October, his lordship found it impracticable

cable to execute his commiffion; and fo, after continuing fome time at fea in hard weather, returned into port; which not only difappointed the king's intention, but alfo blemifhed his reputation, as the Rochellers began to fufpect the fincerity of this defign.

The duke of Buckingham, to put the thing out of difpute, caufed a great fleet to be drawn together the next year, and an army of feven thoufand men to be put on board it; refolving to go himfelf as admiral and commander in chief. He failed from Portfmouth the 27th of June, and landed on the ifland of Rhe; though at firft he intended to have made a defcent on Oleron, and actually promifed fo much to the duke of Soubife, whom he fent to Rochelle, to acquaint the inhabitants of his coming to their relief. They received this meffage coldly; for the French king having corrupted fome by his gold, and terrifying many more by his power, the Rochellers were now afraid to receive the very fuccours they had demanded.

The town of St. Martin's however was fpeedily taken by the Englifh, and his grace then invefted the citadel; but gave evident proofs of his want of military fkill in managing the fiege. By this time the Rochellers had declared for the Englifh; and this declaration of theirs, and the expectation he had of fuccours from England, engaged Buckingham to remain fo long in his camp, that his troops were much diminifhed. At length, on the 6th of November, he made a general affault; when it appeared, that the place was impregnable to forces under fuch circumftances as his were. Two days after, he refolved upon a retreat; which was as ill conducted as the reft of the expedition. With equal fhame and lofs therefore, the duke concluded this unlucky expedition, embarking all his forces on the 9th of the fame month, and fending the Rochellers a folemn promife, that he would come back again to their relief; which, however, he did not live to perform. To compleat his misfortune, as he entered Plymouth, he met the

earl

earl of Holland with the promised succours failing out, who now returned with him.

To remedy those evils, a parliament was called in the beginning of 1628, wherein there passed nothing but disputes between the king and the commons; so that at last it was prorogued without granting supplies. The king, however, exerted himself to the utmost, in preparing a naval force to make good what the duke of Buckingham had promised to the inhabitants of Rochelle. With this view a fleet of fifty sail was assembled at Plymouth in the spring, and a large body of marines embarked; the command of it was given to the earl of Denbigh, who was brother-in-law to Buckingham, and who sailed from that port on the 17th of April, coming to anchor in the road of Rochelle on the 1st of May. On his arrival, he found twenty sail of the French king's ships riding before the harbour; and being much superior in number and strength, he sent advice into the town, that he would sink the French ships as soon as the wind came west, and made a higher flood. About the 8th of May, the wind and tide served accordingly, and the Rochellers expected and sollicited that deliverance: but the earl, without remembering his promise, or embracing the opportunity, weighed anchor and sailed away, suffering four of the French ships to pursue, as it were, the English fleet, which arrived at Plymouth on the 26th of May.

This second inglorious expedition was still a greater discouragement to the poor Rochellers; and increased the fears and jealousies of a popish interest at home. One Le Brun, a Frenchman, but captain in the English fleet, gave in depositions before the mayor of Plymouth, on the 6th of May, which argued treachery, or apparent cowardice, in the management of this late expedition. This account was certified by the mayor of Plymouth, and the two burgesses of that town in parliament, by whom it was communicated to the council-table; from whence a letter was

directed

directed to the duke of Buckingham, as lord high-admiral, dated the 30th of May, 1628, to fignify his majefty's pleafure, that the earl of Denbigh fhould return back to relieve the town of Rochelle, with the fleet under his charge, and with other fhips prepared at Portfmouth and Plymouth. But, notwithftanding this order of council, no fuch return was made; nor any enquiry into the difobedience of the king's order for it.

Notwithftanding thefe repeated defeats, the cries of the Rochellers, and the clamours of the people were fo loud, that a third fleet was prepared for the relief of that city, now, by a clofe fiege, reduced to the laft extremity. The duke of Buckingham chofe to command in perfon, and to that end came to Portfmouth; where, on the 23d of Auguft, he was affaffinated by one Felton, an enthufiaftic officer of the army.

This accident did not prevent the king's profecuting his defign; the very next day his majefty made the earl of Lindfey admiral, Monfon and Mountjoy, vice and rear admirals: and, as an illuftrious foreign writer affures us, his care and prefence had fuch an effect in the preparing for this voyage, that more was difpatched now, in ten or twelve days, than in many weeks before. This expedition, however, was not more fortunate than the former. The fleet failed the 8th of September, 1628, and arriving before Rochelle, found the boom raifed to block up the entrance of the port, fo ftrong, that though many attempts were made to break through it, yet they proved vain; fo that the Rochellers were glad to accept of terms from their own prince, and actually furrendered the place on the 18th of October, the Englifh fleet looking on, without being able to help them. With this expedition ended the operations of the war with France.

From this time, the French began to be ambitious of raifing a maritime power, and to be extreamly uneafy at the growth of the Englifh fhipping. This

R 4 was

was the effect of Richlieu's politics, who best understood the different interests of the several European powers, of any minister that nation ever had, or, it is to be hoped, for the peace of Christendom, will ever have. He revived the dispute between the Dutch and us, respecting the fishery; and the famous Hugo Grotius was induced to write a treatise, under the title of *Mare Liberum*, wherein, with great eloquence, he endeavoured to shew the weakness of our title to dominion over the sea: which, according to his notion, was a gift from God, common to all nations. This was answered by Selden, in his famous treatise, entitled, *Mare Clausum*; wherein he has effectually demonstrated, from the principles of the law of nature and nations, and from history, that a dominion over the sea may be, and has been, acquired. This book of Mr. Selden's was published in 1634, and by the countenance then, and afterward, shewn by king Charles toward this extraordinary performance, we may fairly conclude, that he had very just and generous notions of his own, and his people's rights in this respect, though he was very unfortunate in taking such methods as he did to support them.

The French minister persisted steadily in his Machiavellian scheme, of using the power and industry of the Dutch, to interrupt the trade, and lessen the maritime force of Britain. With this view also, a negotiation was begun between that crown and the states of Holland, for dividing the Spanish Netherlands between them; and under colour of thus assisting them, in support of their pretensions to an equal right over the sea, and in promoting their trade, to the prejudice of ours, Richlieu carried on secretly and securely his darling object of raising a naval force in France: to promote which, he spared not either for pains or expence, procuring from all parts the ablest persons in all arts and sciences, any way relating to navigation, and fixing them in the French service, by giving them great encouragement.

The

The apprehenfions which the king had entertained of this new league between the French and Dutch, were fo heightened in the year 1635, by the junction of the fleets of thofe two powers, and the intelligence he had, that France was fhortly to declare war againft Spain, and from thence to derive that occafion they had been fo long feeking to divide the Netherlands between themfelves and their new allies; all whofe pretenfions, in refpect to the right of fifhing in, and ufing an unreftrained navigation in the feas, they had undertaken to fupport, that he refolved to be no longer paffive. In order to defeat this defign, and maintain the fovereignty annexed to the Englifh crown, as well as the nation's credit, as a maritime power; the king faw, that it was neceffary to equip and put to fea a fuperior naval force.

This it feemed exceeding hard to do, without the affiftance of a parliament; and yet the delays in granting aids had been fo great in former parliaments, that his majefty was very doubtful of fucceeding, if for this he trufted to a parliamentary fupply. His lawyers, knowing both the nature of the cafe, and his deep diftrefs, fuggefted to him, that upon this occafion, he might have recourfe to his prerogative; which opinion having been approved by the judges, he thereupon directed writs to be iffued, for the levying of fhip-money. Thefe writs were, for the prefent, directed only to fea-ports, and fuch places as were near the coaft; requiring them to furnifh a certain number of fhips, or to grant the king an equivalent thereto. The city of London was directed to provide feven fhips for twenty-fix days, and other places in proportion. To make the nation more eafy under this tax, the king directed, that the money raifed thereby, fhould be kept apart in the exchequer; and that a diftinct account fhould be given of the fervices to which it was applied. Yet, in fpite of thefe precautions, the people murmured grievoufly;
which,

which, however, did not hinder this project from being carried into execution.

With the help of this money, the king, in the month of May, 1635, fitted out a fleet of forty sail, under the command of Robert earl of Lindsey, who was admiral; Sir William Monson, vice-admiral, Sir John Pennington, rear-admiral: as also another of twenty sail, under the earl of Essex. The first of these fleets sailed from Tilbury-Hope on the 26th of May. Their instructions were, to give no occasion of hostility and to suffer nothing that might prejudice the rights of the king and kingdom. The French and Dutch fleets joined off Portland, the last of this month; and made no scruple of giving out, that they intended to assert their own independency, and to question that prerogative which the English claimed in the narrow seas; but as soon as they were informed that the English fleet was at sea, and in search of them, they quitted our coast, and repaired to their own.

Our admiral sent a bark upon the coast of Britany, to take a view of them; and from the time of the return of this bark, to the 1st of October, this fleet protected our own seas and shores, gave laws to the neighbouring nations, and effectually asserted that sovereignty which the monarchs of this kingdom have ever claimed. The good effect of this armament, and the reputation we gained thereby abroad, in some measure quieted the minds of the people; as it convinced them, that this was not an invention to bring money into the exchequer, without respect had to the end for which it was raised.

The king, perfectly satisfied with what had been done this year, and yet well knowing that it would signify little if another, and that at least as good a fleet, was not set out the next; to raise the money necessary for equipping such a force, had recourse again to his writs for levying of ship-money: but now the aid was made more extensive. The burden, indeed,

in

in itself, was far from being pressing: at the utmost it did not amount to above 236,000 l. per annum, which was not quite 20,000 l. a month throughout the whole kingdom; yet the making it an universal aid, and the assessing and collecting it in the parliamentary methods, without parliamentary authority, gave it an air of oppression, and made it extreamly odious.

In order to prevent all doubts from his own subjects, and also to prevent any false surmises gaining ground in foreign nations, as to the design of this potent armament; the king thought fit to express his royal intentions to the world, in the most public, and in the most authentic manner: that, at one and the same time, it might appear what himself demanded, and what had been paid in acknowledgment of the right of his ancestors in regard to those things, as to which these demands were made.

In 1636, the king sent a fleet of sixty sail to sea, under the command of the earl of Northumberland, admiral; Sir John Pennington, vice-admiral, and Sir Henry Marom, rear-admiral. They sailed first to the Downs, and from hence to the north, where the Dutch busses were fishing upon our coast. The admiral required them to forbear; which they not seeming disposed to do, he fired upon them: this put them into great confusion, and obliged them to have recourse to other methods. The Dutch, therefore, applied themselves to the earl of Northumberland; desired him to mediate with the king, that they might have leave to go on with their fishing this year, for which they were content to pay 30,000 l. and expressed also a willingness to obtain a grant from the king, for his permission for their vessels to fish there for the time to come, paying an annual tribute.

Such is the best account that can be collected of the causes and consequences of this expedition, from our best historians. But the earl of Northumberland delivered a journal of his whole proceedings, signed

with

with his own hand; which is, or at least was preserved in the paper-office. In that journal, there are several memorable particulars. The Dutch fishing-busses, upon the appearance of his lordship's fleet, did take licences, to the number of two hundred, though he arrived amongst them pretty late in the year. He exacted from them twelve pence per ton, as an acknowledgment; and affirms that they went away well satisfied. It was pretended by the Dutch in king Charles the second's time, that this was an act of violence; and that nothing could be concluded as to the right of this crown, from that transaction: since the Dutch did not pay, because they thought what was insisted upon to be due, but, because they were defenceless. His lordship's journal sets this pretence entirely aside; since it appeared from thence, that they had a squadron of ten men of war for their protection; as also, that August the 20th, 1636, the Dutch vice-admiral Dorp, came with a fleet of twenty men of war: but instead of interrupting the earl in his proceedings, he saluted him by lowering his topsails, striking his flag and firing his guns; after which he came on board, and was well entertained by the earl of Northumberland. It is farther mentioned in that journal, that upon his lordship's return from the north, and anchoring in the Downs, he had notice of a Spanish fleet of twenty-six sail, bound for Dunkirk; to reconnoitre which he sent one of the ships of his squadron, called the Happy Entrance; to which single ship, that fleet paid the marks of respect, which were due to the English flag whenever it appeared.

The king meant to have continued both this method of raising money, and of fitting out fleets annually; and by giving several young noblemen commands at sea, to have rendered them the more capable of serving their country in times of greater danger: but he quickly found this impracticable. The nation grew so exceedingly dissatisfied with this

method

method of raising money, and the great case of Mr. Hampden made it so clear, that a constant and regular levying of this tax was dangerous to the constitution, and to the freedom of the subject; that the king was obliged to lay aside this scheme, and to content himself with using all the methods that could be thought of, to awaken the people's attention in regard to the sovereignty of the sea. With this view, his majesty made an order in council, that a copy of Mr. Selden's book upon that subject, should be kept in the council-chest, that another copy should be kept in the court of exchequer, and a third in the court of admiralty; there to remain as perpetual evidence of our just claim to the dominion of the seas.

Nothing of consequence occurs in regard to naval affairs till the year 1639, when the Spaniards fitted out a powerful fleet, consisting of sixty-seven sail of large ships, manned with 25,000 seamen, and having on board 12,000 land forces, designed for the relief of Flanders. The Dutch had two or three squadrons at sea; the Spanish fleet coming up the channel, was met in the streights by one of them, consisting of seventeen sail, under the command of Martin, the son of Herbert Van Tromp, who, notwithstanding the enemy's great superiority, attacked them: but finding himself too weak, was obliged to sheer off towards Dunkirk; where, being joined by the other squadrons, he so roughly handled the Spanish fleet, under the command of Don Antonio de Oquendo, that at last he forced them on the English coast near Dover.

Admiral Van Tromp finding himself in want of powder and ball, stood away for Calais; where he was liberally supplied by the governor, and then returned to attack the enemy. Upon his approach, the Spaniards got within the South-Foreland, and put themselves under the protection of our castles. Things being in this situation, the Spanish resident importuned king Charles, that he would oblige the

Dutch

Dutch to forbear hoftilities for two tides, that the Spaniards might have an opportunity of bearing away for their own coaft; but the king being in amity with both powers, was refolved to ftand neuter: and whereas the Spaniards had hired fome Englifh fhips to tranfport their foldiers to Dunkirk, upon complaint made thereof by the Dutch ambaffadors, ftrict orders were given, that no fhips or veffels belonging to his majefty's fubjects, fhould take any Spaniard on board, or pafs below Gravefend without licence.

However, after much plotting and counterplotting on both fides, the Spaniard at length outwitted his enemy; and found means, by a ftratagem in the night, to convey away through the Downs, round by the North-Sand-Head, and the back of the Godwin, twelve large fhips to Dunkirk, and in them four thoufand men. In excufe of this grofs neglect of the Dutch admirals, in leaving that avenue from the Downs unguarded; they affirmed they were affured by the Englifh, that no fhips of any confiderable burden could venture by night to fail that way. The two fleets had now continued in their ftations near three weeks, when king Charles fent the earl of Arundel to the admiral of Spain, to defire him to retreat upon the firft fair wind: but by this time the Dutch fleet was, by continual reinforcements from Zealand and Holland, increafed to an hundred fail; and feeming difpofed to attack their enemies, Sir John Pennington, admiral of his majefty's fleet, who lay in the Downs with thirty-four men of war, acquainted the Dutch admiral, that he had received orders to act in defence of either of the two parties, which fhould be firft attacked.

The Spaniards, however, growing too prefumptuous on the protection they enjoyed, a day or two after, fired fome fhot at Van Tromp's barge, when himfelf was in her; and killed a man with a cannon-ball on board of a Dutch fhip, whofe dead body was prefently fent on board Sir John Pennington, as a proof that the Spaniards were the firſt aggreſſors, and had violated the neutrality of the king of England's harbour. Soon after this the Dutch admiral, on receiving freſh orders from the ſtates, came to a reſolution of attacking the Spaniards; but before he put it in execution, he thought fit to write to admiral Pennington, telling him, that the Spaniards having infringed the liberties of the king of England's harbours, and being clearly become the aggreſſors, he found himſelf obliged to repel force by force, and attack them; in which, purſuant to the declaration he had made to him, he not only hoped for, but depended on his aſſiſtance: which, however, if he ſhould not pleaſe to grant, he requeſted the favour, that he would at leaſt give him leave to engage the enemy; otherwiſe he ſhould have juſt cauſe of complaint to all the world, of ſo manifeſt an injury.

This letter being delivered to the Engliſh admiral, Van Tromp immediately weighed and ſtood to the Spaniards in ſix diviſions, cannonading them furiouſly, and vigorouſly preſſing them at the ſame time with his fire-ſhips; ſo that he quickly forced them all to cut their cables, and of fifty-three, which the Spaniards were in number, twenty-three ran aſhore and ſtranded in the Downs: of theſe, three were burnt, two ſunk, and two periſhed on the ſhore. The remainder of the twenty-three, which were ſtranded and deſerted by the Spaniards, were manned by the Engliſh, to ſave them from falling into the hands of the Dutch. The other Spaniſh ſhips, with Don Antonio de Oquendo, the commander in chief, and Lopez, admiral of Portugal, got out to ſea, and kept in good order, till a thick fog ariſing, the Dutch took advantage thereof, interpoſed between the admirals and their fleet, and fought them valiantly till the fog cleared up, when only ten eſcaped. The firſt hoſtility having been indiſputably committed by the Spaniards, was a plea of which the Dutch made uſe in

their

their juftification to us; and at the fame time became a fufficient argument to defend the conduct of the Englifh government, in fuffering one friend to deftroy another within its harbours.

It may not be amifs to obferve, that in reality the people of England were not forry for this misfortune that befel the Spaniards, though the court took all the care imaginable to prevent it: and the reafon of this was, that fome furmifed this to be a new Spanifh Armada, fitted out nominally againft the Dutch; but in truth, intended to act againft heretics in general.

The expedition of the marquis of Hamilton againft the Scots, was undertaken this year; in which there is very little worth mentioning. He arrived in the Frith of Forth the firft of May: there he continued for fome time, treating with the Scots to little or no purpofe, till the feafon being loft, he returned without effecting any thing.

The fleet was from this time forward fo entirely out of the king's power, that the naval hiftory of this reign ends properly here: and therefore having already related, the feveral expeditions undertaken by his authority, we come now to mention the progrefs of trade, the increafe of fhipping, and the encouragement of our plantations, during the fame fpace.

This prince, before the rebellion broke out, among others, added one fhip to the royal navy of England; which on account of its fize, and other remarkable particulars, deferves to be mentioned in this place, more efpecially as it has efcaped the notice of all our naval writers. This famous veffel was built at Woolwich in 1637. She was in length by the keel 128 feet; in breadth 48 feet; in length, from the fore-end of the beak-head, to the after-end of the ftern, 232 feet: and in height, from the bottom of the keel to the top of her lanthorn, 76 feet. Bore five lanthorns, the biggeft of which would hold ten perfons upright: had three flufh-decks, a forecaftle, half-deck, quarter-deck and round-houfe. Her lower tier had thirty

ports,

ports, middle tier thirty ports, third tier twenty-fix ports, forecaftle twelve ports, half-deck fourteen ports; thirteen or fourteen ports more within board, befide ten pieces of chace-ordnance forward, and ten right aft, with many loop-holes in the cabins for mufket-fhot. She had eleven anchors, one of four thoufand four hundred pounds weight. She was of the burthen of one thoufand fix hundred and thirty-feven tons; and was built by Peter Pett, Efq; under the infpection of Captain Phineas Pett, one of the principal officers of the navy.

It appears from Sir William Monfon, and indeed from all the unprejudiced writers of thofe times, who were competent judges of thefe matters, that the commerce of this ifland increafed exceedingly during the firft fifteen years of this king's reign; infomuch that the port of London only could have fupplied a hundred fail, capable of being eafily converted into men of war, and well furnifhed with ordnance. The trade to the Eaft Indies, which was but beginning in his father's time, became now very lucrative; and our fhips gave law in thofe parts to almoft all foreign nations. The trade to Guinea grew likewife to be of confiderable benefit to the Englifh fubjects; and our intercourfe with Spain, after the ending of the war, proved of infinite advantage likewife. It is true, there happened fome confiderable difputes between the government and the merchants, about cuftoms, which fome of the minifters of the crown thought depended immediately thereupon, and might be taken by virtue of the prerogative only; whereas others conceived, as moft of the merchants themfelves did, that nothing of this kind could be levied but by the confent of parliament: But thefe very difputes fhew that trade was in a flourifhing condition; for if the cuftoms had not rifen to a confiderable height, beyond what they did in former times, no miniftry would have run the hazard of fuch a conteft.

But the principal fource of our naval ftrength then, (as it has been ever fince) was our plantations, to the encouragement and augmentation of which, even thofe accidents highly contributed, which might have been otherwife fatal to fociety; fuch as our civil and ecclefiaftical divifions, which inclined numbers of fober, induftrious, and thinking people, to prefer liberty, and whatever they could raife in diftant and hitherto uncultivated lands, to the uneafy fituation in which they found themfelves at home.

The colony of Virginia had ftruggled under great difficulties, from the time it fell under the direction of a company, till the king was pleafed to take it into his own hands; which he did very foon after his coming to the crown, and then directed the conftitution of that colony to be a governor, council, and affembly, conformable to that of this kingdom, and under which the colony quickly began to flourifh. That of New England had its name beftowed by his majefty when prince, and was better fettled in King James's time, than any other of our colonies; and throughout the whole reign of King Charles I. was conftantly fupplied with large draughts of people; fo that by degrees it was divided into four governments.

The papifts in England, finding themfelves liable to many feverities, were defirous of having an afylum in the new world, as well as other nonconformifts; and this gave rife to the planting of Maryland, a country which had been hitherto accounted part of Virginia, between 37° and 40° of N. L. It was granted by King Charles, the 20th of June, 1632, to the anceftor of the prefent Lord Baltimore, and derived its name of Maryland, from his queen Henrietta-Maria.

The Summer Iflands which were planted in the laft reign, and fettled under a regular government in the year 1619, flourifhed exceedingly, the country being extreamly pleafant and fruitful, and the air

much

much more wholesome than in any other part of America. As for the island of Barbadoes, which had been regularly planted about the beginning of the king's reign, it was granted to the earl of Carlisle, who gave such encouragement to all who were inclined to go thither, and most of those who went became so speedily rich, that it was quickly well peopled, and even within this period, was esteemed the most populous of all our plantations. The island of St. Christopher and Nevis were also settled about this time.

Upon the commencement of violence between Charles and his parliament; it was natural for each party to be solicitous about the fleet, for many reasons; and for this particularly, that whoever was master of that, would be considered as the supream power by foreign princes. The earl of Northumberland was at this time lord high-admiral: the king had given him that commission, to satisfy the house of commons, who had a confidence in him; and granted it during pleasure only, because his intention was to confer that office on his son the duke of York, as soon as he became of age. Sir Robert Mansel was vice-admiral of England; a gentleman very loyal, but withal very infirm and far in years. Sir John Pennington was vice-admiral of the fleet, then in the Downs, and Sir John Mennes was rear admiral; both well affected to his majesty.

The parliament having formed a project of dispossessing the king of his fleet, executed it successfully; notwithstanding these circumstances so favourable for his majesty, and though he had the affections of the seamen, whose wages he had raised, and for whom he had always shewn a very particular regard. In the spring of the year, 1641, the parliament desired, that is, in effect directed, the earl of Northumberland to provide a strong fleet for the nation's security by sea, and appropriated a proper fund for this service. They next desired, that he would appoint the earl of

Warwick admiral of that fleet, on account of his own indifpofition, which rendered it impoffible for him to command in perfon. The king took this ill, and infifted on Sir John Pennington's keeping his command; but the earl had fo much refpect to the parliament's recommendation, that he ordered the fleet to be delivered up to the earl of Warwick, and granted him a commiffion to command it, as by his own he had power to do. This was one great point gained. The parliament then would have made Captain Cartwright comptroller of the navy, vice-admiral in the room of Sir John Pennington; but he refufing to undertake this fervice without the king's permiffion, his majefty was pleafed to fignify his pleafure, that he fhould decline it; which he did, and the parliament thereupon appointed one Batten, vice-admiral, who was remarkably difaffected toward the king: and their orders being complied with, the fleet in the fpring 1642, fell into their hands; though the king was perfuaded in his own mind that he could at any time recover it, which was the true reafon of his not removing at that time, as he afterward did, the earl of Northumberland from his high office. It was not long before he had good reafon to change his opinion; for the queen, fending his majefty a fmall fupply from Holland, in the Providence, the only fhip the king had left, the fhips from the Downs chafed the veffel into the Humber, and there forced the captain to run her afhore. Upon this the king refolved to attempt feizing the fleet; and the defign, had it been executed as well as it was laid, might very probably have taken effect; but through the mifmanagement of Sir John Pennington it mifcarried, and ferved only to defeat the king's hopes for the future, by affording the earl of Warwick an opportunity of removing all the king's friends, which he had long wanted.

The parliament, as they had difcovered great care and induftry in fecuring, fo they fhewed no lefs wifdom

dom in the conduct of the fleet, which they always kept in good order and well paid. In 1643, vice-admiral Batten having intelligence, that the queen intended to go by sea from Holland into the north of England, he did his utmost to intercept her, though on board a Dutch man of war. This proving ineffectual, he chased the ship into Burlington-Bay; and when the queen was landed, having intelligence that she lodged in a house upon the key, he fired upon it, so that many of the shot went through her chamber; and she was obliged, though very much indisposed, to retire for safety into the open fields. This service, which was performed in the month of February, was very grateful to the parliament, because it shewed how much the officers of the fleet were in their interest.

While the presbyterian party remained uppermost, all affairs relating to the navy went on smoothly. The earl of Warwick was entirely devoted to them, and so were all the officers by him appointed. Every summer a stout squadron was fitted out to serve as occasion required, and by this means the trade of the nation was tolerably protected. But in the year 1648, when the independents came by their intrigues to prevail, things took a new turn, and it was resolved to remove the earl of Warwick from his command, notwithstanding the services he had performed, and to make Colonel Rainsborough admiral. This gentleman had been bred a seaman, and was the son of a commander of distinction; but had for some time served as an officer in the parliament-army, and was then a colonel of foot. When this news came to the fleet in the Downs, it put the seamen into great confusion; and their officers, the earl of Warwick, and vice-admiral Batten, were so little pleased with the usage they had met with, that instead of softening, they augmented their discontents: insomuch, that they seized upon Rainsborough, and such officers as adhered to him, set them on shore, and resolved to
sail

fail over to Holland, in order to take on board the duke of York, whom they called their admiral; becaufe the king's intention of making him fo, was a thing generally known.

Though the king was then a prifoner, and his affairs reduced to a very low ebb, yet, if this revolt of the fleet had been properly managed, it might have had very happy effects: but as it was conducted, it is fcarcely poffible to conceive how little advantage was drawn from an incident which promifed fo much. The great misfortune was, that this ftrange turn was entirely concerted by the feamen; fo that when they declared for the king, they had very few officers among them; and as they were little inclined to ufe the advice of any who were not of their own profeffion, there was a good deal of time loft before they pofitively refolved what to do. This gave the parliament an opportunity of recovering themfelves from the confternation into which this unexpected event had thrown them; and the firft refolution they took was a very wife one, viz. the reftoring the earl of Warwick to his title and command, fending him orders to draw together a fleet as foon as poffible.

It was about this time that the parliament, if the affembly which then met as one, could be confidered as the national body, brought the king to a public trial; in confequence of which he was executed at Whitehall, January 30th 1649: a tranfaction fo fingular in its nature, and fo much being to be faid on both fides; that it is not eafy to decide on; nor can we pretend to enter on the merits of it in our brief narrative. Thus much however may be obferved; that Charles did not fuffer fo extraordinary a fate, fo much for violating the old conftitution, as to make way for the introduction of a new one: one, which after the commotions fo naturally to be expected, in fuch an undertaking, has happily fettled in that moderate frame of government, under which we now live. But to proceed in our detail.

The

The parliament recovered their sovereignty at sea; where they kept such strong squadrons continually cruising, that it was not thought adviseable for King Charles II. to venture his person on that element, in order to go to Ireland, where his presence was necessary. Yet the earl of Warwick, who had served them so faithfully, and with such success, was removed from the command of the fleet, which was put into the hands of land-officers, such as Blake, Deane, and Popham; who, notwithstanding, behaved well, quickly gained the love of the sailors, and grew in a short time very knowing seamen themselves.

Blake was a man of heroic courage and a generous disposition, the same person who had defended Lyme and Taunton with such unshaken obstinacy against the king; and though he had hitherto been accustomed only to land service, into which too he had not entered till past fifty years of age, he soon raised the naval glory of the nation to a higher pitch than it had ever attained in any former period. A fleet was committed to him; and he received orders to pursue Prince Rupert, to whom the king had given the command of that squadron, which had deserted to him. Rupert took shelter in Kinsale; and escaping thence, fled toward the coast of Portugal. Blake pursued, and chased him into the Tagus; where he intended to attack that prince: but the king of Portugal, moved by the favour, which, throughout all Europe, attended the royal cause, refused Blake admittance, and aided Prince Rupert in making his escape. To be revenged of this partiality, the English admiral made prize of twenty Portuguese ships richly laden, and threatened still farther vengeance. The king of Portugal, dreading so dangerous a foe to his new acquired dominion, and sensible of the unequal contest, in which he was engaged, made all possible submissions to the haughty republic, and was at last admitted to negotiate the renewal of his alliance with England. Prince Rupert, having lost a great part of his squadron on the coaft of Spain, made fail toward the Weft Indies. His brother, Prince Maurice, was there fhip-wrecked in a hurricane. Every where, this fquadron fubfifted by privateering, fometimes on Englifh, fometimes on Spanifh veffels. And Rupert at laft returned to France; where he difpofed of the remnants of his fleet, together with all his prizes.

All the fettlements in America, except New England, which had been planted entirely by the puritans, adhered to the royal party, even after the fettlement of the republic; and Sir George Ayfcue was fent with a fquadron to reduce them to obedience Bermudas, Antigua, Virginia, were foon fubdued. Barbadoes, commanded by Lord Willoughby of Parham, made fome refiftance; but was at laft obliged to fubmit.

With equal eafe were Jerfey, Guernfey, Scilly, and the ifle of Man, brought under fubjection to the republic; and the fea, which had been much infefted by privateers from thefe iflands, was rendered entirely fafe to the Englifh commerce. The countefs of Derby defended the ifle of Man; and with great reluctance yielded to the neceffity of furrendring to the enemy. This lady, a daughter of the illuftrious houfe of Trimoüille in France, had, during the civil wars, difplayed a manly courage by her obftinate defence of Latham Houfe againft the parliamentary forces; and fhe retained the glory of being the laft perfon in the three kingdoms, and in all their dependant dominions, who fubmitted to the victorious commonwealth.

The movements of great ftates are often directed by as flender fprings as thofe of individuals. Though war with fo confiderable a naval power as the Dutch, who were in peace with all their other neighbours, might feem dangerous to the yet unfettled commonwealth, there were feveral motives, which at this time induced the Englifh parliament to embrace hoftile meafures.

The

The causes of this war are differently related, according to the humours and opinions of different writers: the truth, however, seems to be, that the old commonwealth grew quickly jealous of the new one, and began to apprehend, that, whatever the rest of the world might be, Holland was like to be no gainer by this change of government in England. The parliament, on the other side, was no less jealous of its new acquired sovereignty, and expected, therefore, extraordinary marks of regard from all the powers with which it corresponded. To divert the attention of the public from domestic quarrels toward foreign transactions, seemed also in the present disposition of mens minds to be good policy. The superior power of the English commonwealth, together with the advantages of situation, promised it success; and the parliamentary leaders hoped to gain many rich prizes from the Dutch, to distress and sink their flourishing commerce, and by victories to throw a lustre on their establishment, which was so new and unpopular.

To cover these hostile intentions, the parliament, under pretence of providing for the interests of commerce, embraced such measures as they knew would give disgust to the States. They framed the famous act of navigation; which prohibited all nations to import into England in their bottoms any commodity, which was not the growth and manufacture of their own country. By this law, though the terms, in which it was conceived, were general, the Dutch were principally hurt; because their country produces few commodities, and they subsist chiefly by being the general carriers and factors of the world. Letters of reprizal were granted to several merchants, who complained of injuries, which, as they pretended, they had received from the States; and above eighty Dutch ships fell into their hands, and were made prize of. The cruelties practised on the English at Amboyna, which were certainly enormous, but which

seemed

seemed to be buried in oblivion by a thirty years silence, were again, with some other matters, made the grounds of complaint. The minds of men, in both states, were every day more and more irritated against each other; and it was not long before these malignant humours broke forth into action.

Tromp, an admiral of great renown, received from the States the command of a fleet of forty-two sail, in order to protect the Dutch navigation against the privateers of the English. He was forced by stress of weather, as he alleged, to take shelter in the road of Dover; where he met with Blake, who commanded an English fleet much inferior in number. Who was the aggressor in the action, which ensued between these two admirals, both of them men of such prompt and fiery dispositions, it is not easy to determine; since each of them sent to his own state a relation totally opposite in all its circumstances to that of the other, and yet supported by the testimony of every captain in his fleet. Blake pretended, that, having given a signal to the Dutch admiral to strike, Tromp, instead of complying, fired a broad-side at him. Tromp asserted, that he was preparing to strike; and that the English admiral, nevertheless, began hostilities. It is certain, that the admiralty of Holland, who are distinct from the council of state, had given Tromp no orders to strike, but had left him to his own discretion with regard to that vain, but much contested ceremonial. They seemed willing to introduce the claim of an equality with the new commonwealth, and to interpret the former respect, which they had ever payed the English flag, as a deference due only to the monarchy. This circumstance forms a strong presumption against the narrative of the Dutch admiral. The whole Orange party, it must be remarked, to which Tromp was suspected to adhere, were desirous of a war with England.

Blake, though his squadron consisted only of fifteen vessels, re-inforced, after the battle began, by eight
under

under Captain Bourne, maintained the fight with great bravery for five hours, and funk one ship of the enemy, and took another. Night parted the combatants, and the Dutch fleet retired toward the coast of Holland. The populace of London were enraged, and would have insulted the Dutch ambassadors, who lived at Chelsea, had not the council of state sent guards to protect them.

When the States heard of this action, of which the fatal consequences were easily foreseen, they were in the utmost consternation. They immediately dispatched Paw, pensionary of Holland, as their ambassador extraordinary to London; and ordered him to lay before the parliament the narrative which Tromp had sent of the late rencounter. They entreated them, by all the bands of their common religion, and common liberties, not to precipitate themselves into hostile measures, but to appoint commissioners, who should examine every circumstance of the action, and clear up the truth, which lay in obscurity. And they pretended, that they had given no orders to their admiral to offer any violence to the English, but would severely punish him, if they found upon enquiry, that he had been guilty of an action, which they so much disapproved. The parliament would hearken to none of these reasons or remonstrances. Elated with the numerous successes, which they had obtained over their domestic enemies, they thought, that every thing must yield to their fortunate arms; and they gladly seized the opportunity, which they sought, of making war upon the States. They demanded, that, without any farther delay or enquiry, reparation should be made for all the damages which the English had sustained. And when this demand was not complied with, they dispatched orders for commencing war against the United Provinces.

Blake sailed northward with a numerous fleet, and fell upon the herring busses, which were escorted by twelve men of war. All these he either took or dispersed.

perfed. Tromp followed him with a fleet of above a hundred fail. When thefe two admirals were within fight of each other, and preparing for battle, a furious ftorm attacked them. Blake took fhelter in the Englifh harbours. The Dutch fleet was difperfed and received great damage.

Sir George Ayfcue, though he commanded only forty fhips according to the Englifh accounts, engaged near Plymouth the famous de Ruyter, who had under him fifty fhips of war, with thirty merchant-men. The Dutch fhips were indeed of inferior force to the Englifh. De Ruyter, the only admiral in Europe, who has attained a renown equal to that of the greateft general, defended himfelf fo well, that Ayfcue gained no advantage over him. Night parted them in the greateft heat of the action. De Ruyter next day failed off with his convoy. The Englifh had been fo fhattered in the fight, that they were not able to purfue.

Near the coaft of Kent, Blake, feconded by Bourne and Pen, met the Dutch fleet, nearly equal in number, commanded by de Witte and de Ruyter. A battle was fought much to the difadvantage of the Dutch. Their rear-admiral was boarded and taken. Two other veffels were funk, and one blown up. The Dutch fleet next day made fail toward Holland.

The Englifh were not fo fuccefsful in the Mediterranean. Van Galen with much fuperior force attacked Captain Badily, and defeated him. He bought, however, his victory with the lofs of his life.

Sea-fights are feldom fo decifive as to difable the vanquifhed from making head in a little time againft the victors. Tromp, feconded by de Ruyter, met near the Goodwins, with Blake, whofe fleet was inferior to the Dutch; but who was refolved not to decline the combat. A furious battle commenced, where the admirals on both fides, as well as the inferior officers and feamen, exerted extraordinary bravery. In this action, the Dutch had the advantage. Blake

himfelf

himself was wounded. The Garland and Bonaventure were taken. Two ships were burned, and one sunk; and night came very opportunely to save the English fleet. After this victory, Tromp, in a bravado, fixed a broom to his main-mast; as if he were resolved to sweep the sea entirely of all English vessels.

Great preparations were made in England, in order to wipe off this disgrace. A gallant fleet of eighty sail was fitted out. Blake commanded, and Dean under him, together with Monk, who had been sent for from Scotland. When the English lay off Portland, they descried near break of day the Dutch fleet of seventy-six vessels, sailing up the channel, along with a convoy of 300 merchant-men, who had received orders to wait at the isle of Rhé, till the fleet should arrive to escort them. Tromp and de Ruyter commanded the Dutch. This battle was the most furious which had yet been fought, between these warlike and rival nations. Three days was the battle continued with the utmost rage and obstinacy: and Blake, who was victor, gained not more honour than Tromp, who was vanquished. The Dutch admiral made a skilful retreat, and saved all the merchant ships, except thirty. He lost however eleven ships of war, had 2000 men slain, and 1500 taken prisoners. The English, though many of their ships were extreamly shattered, had but one sunk. Their slain were not much inferior in number to those of the enemy.

All these successes of the English were chiefly owing to the superior size of their vessels; an advantage which all the skill and bravery of the Dutch admirals could not compensate. By means of ship-money, an imposition, which had been so much complained of, and in some respects with reason, the late king had put the navy into a situation, which it had never attained in any former reign: and he ventured to build ships of a size which was then unusual. But the misfortunes which the Dutch met with in battle, were

small

small in comparison of those which their trade sustained from the English. Their whole commerce by the Channel was cut off. Even that to the Baltic was much infested by the English privateers. Their fisheries were totally suspended. A great number of their ships, above 1600, had fallen into the enemy's hands. And all this distress they suffered, not for any national interest or necessity; but from vain points of honour and personal resentments, of which it was difficult to give a satisfactory account to the public. They resolved therefore to gratify the pride of the parliament, and to make some advances toward a peace. Their reception, however, was not favourable; and it was not without pleasure, that they learned the dissolution of that haughty assembly by the violence of Cromwel; an event from which they expected a more prosperous turn to their affairs.

The Dutch, however, did not instantly receive any great benefit from this sudden revolution; but then it must be considered, that the chief officers of the fleet concurred in this measure. The government of the parliament, was a government of order and laws, (however they came by their authority) the government of the general, afterward protector, was entirely military: no wonder, therefore, that both the navy and the army were pleased with him. Some advantage, however, the enemy certainly reaped from this change in English affairs; for Van Tromp conveyed a great fleet of merchant-men to the north, (for they were now forced to try that rout rather than the channel) and though our navy followed him to the height of Aberdeen, yet it was to no purpose: he escaped them both going and coming back, which gave him an opportunity of coming into the Downs, making some prizes, and battering Dover castle. This scene of triumph lasted but a bare week; for Tromp came thither on the 26th of May, and on the last of that month he had intelligence, that Monk and Deane, who commanded the English fleet, were approaching, and

and that their whole fleet confifted of ninety-five fail of men of war, and five fire-fhips. The Dutch had ninety-eight men of war, and fix fire-fhips; and both fleets were commanded by men the moft remarkable for courage and conduct in either nation.

On the 2d of June in the morning, the Englifh fleet difcovered the enemy, whom they immediately attacked with great vigour. The action began about 11 o'clock; and the firft broadfide from the enemy, carried off the brave admiral Deane, whofe body was almoft cut in two by a chain-fhot. Monk, with much prefence of mind, covered his body with his cloak: and here appeared the wifdom of having both admirals on board the fame fhip; for as no flag was taken in, the fleet had no notice of this accident, but the fight continued with the fame warmth as if it had not happened. The fight continued very hot till three o'clock, when the Dutch fell into great confufion, and Tromp faw himfelf obliged to make a kind of running fight till nine in the evening, when a ftout fhip, commanded by Cornelius van Velfen, blew up. This increafed the confternation in which they were before; and though Tromp ufed every method in his power to oblige the officers to do their duty, and even fired upon fuch fhips as drew out of the line; yet it was to no purpofe, but rather ferved to increafe their misfortune. In the night, Blake arrived in the Englifh fleet, with a fquadron of eighteen fhips, and fo had his fhare in the fecond day's engagement.

Admiral Tromp did all that was confiftent with his honour, to avoid fighting the next day; but the Englifh fleet came up with him again by eight in the morning, and engaged with the utmoft fury for about four hours; and vice-admiral Penn boarded Tromp twice, and had taken him, if he had not been feafonably relieved by de Witte and de Ruyter. At laft the Dutch fell again into confufion, which was fo great, that a plain flight quickly followed; and they efcaped to Zealand. Our writers agree, that the Dutch had

fix

six of their best ships sunk, two blown up, and eleven taken; six of their principal captains were made prisoners, and upward of fifteen hundred men. Among the ships before mentioned, one was a vice, and two were rear-admirals. We need not wonder then, that the Dutch, whilst in such circumstances, sent ambassadors into England, to negotiate a peace almost on any terms. These Cromwell received with haughtiness enough, talked high, and assumed to himself the credit of former victories, in which he could have little share, but of which he very ably availed himself now. The States, however, were far from trusting entirely to negotiations; but at the time they treated, laboured with the utmost diligence to repair their past losses, and to fit out a new fleet. This was a very difficult task; and in order to effect it, they were forced to raise the seamens wages, though their trade was at a full stop: they came down in person to their ports, and saw their men embarked, and advanced them wages beforehand; and promised them, if they would fight once again, they would never ask them to fight more. The scheme laid down by the States was this, that to force the English fleet to leave their ports, this navy of theirs should come and block up ours. But first it was resolved, Van Tromp should sail to the mouth of the Texel, where de Ruyter, with twenty-five sail of stout ships, was kept in by the English fleet, in order to try if they might not be provoked to leave their station, and give the Dutch squadron thereby an opportunity of coming out.

On the 29th of July 1653, the Dutch fleet appeared in sight of the English, upon which the latter did their utmost to engage them: but Van Tromp, having in view the release of de Witte, rather than fighting, kept off; so that it was seven at night before General Monk in the Resolution, with about thirty ships, great and small, came up with them, and charged through their fleet. It growing dark soon after, there passed nothing more that night, Monk

failing

failing to the south, and Van Tromp to the northward; and this not being suspected by the English, he both joined de Witte's squadron, and gained the weather-gage. The next day proving very foul and windy, the sea ran so high, that it was impossible for the fleets to engage, the English particularly, finding it hard enough to avoid running upon the enemy's coasts.

On Sunday July 31, the weather being become favourable, both fleets engaged with terrible fury. The battle lasted at least eight hours, and was the most hard-fought of any that had happened throughout the war. The Dutch fire-ships were managed with great dexterity; many of the large vessels in the English fleet were in the utmost danger of perishing by them; and the Triumph was so effectually fired, that most of her crew threw themselves into the sea, and yet those few who staid behind, were so lucky as to put it out. Lawson engaged de Ruyter briskly, killed and wounded above half his men, and so disabled his ship, that it was towed out of the fleet: yet the admiral did not leave the battle so, but returned in a galliot, and went on board another ship. About noon, Van Tromp was shot through the body with a musket-ball, as he was giving orders. This miserably discouraged his countrymen; so that by two, they began to fly in great confusion, having but one flag standing amongst them. The lightest frigates in the English fleet pursued them closely, till the Dutch admiral, perceiving they were but small, and of no great strength, turned his helm, and resolved to engage them; but some bigger ships coming into their assistance, the Dutchman was taken. It was night by that time their scattered fleet recovered the Texel.

This was a terrible blow to the Dutch, of whom, according to Monk's letter, no less than thirty ships were lost; but, from better intelligence, it appeared, that four of these had escaped, two into a port of Zeland, and two into Hamburgh. Their loss, however, was very great: between four and five thousand men killed, twenty-six ships of war either burnt or sunk. On the side of the English, there were two ships only, viz. the Oak and the Hunter frigate burnt, and upward of five hundred seamen.

Some very singular circumstances attended this extraordinary victory, and deserve therefore to be mentioned. There were several merchant-men in the fleet, and Monk, finding occasion to employ them, thought proper to send their captains to each other's ships, in order to take off their concern for their owners vessels and cargoes; a scheme which answered his purpose perfectly well, no ships in the fleet behaving better. He had likewise issued his orders in the beginning of the fight, that they should not either give or take quarter; which, however, were not so strictly observed, but that twelve hundred Dutchmen were taken out of the sea, while their ships were sinking.

The parliament then sitting, who were of Cromwell's appointment, upon the eighth of August 1653, ordered gold chains to be sent to the generals Blake and Monk, and likewise to vice-admiral Penn, and rear-admiral Lawson; they sent also chains to the rest of the flag-officers, and medals to the captains. The 25th of August was appointed for a day of solemn thanksgiving, and Monk being then in town, Cromwell, at a great feast in the city, put the gold chain about his neck, and obliged him to wear it all dinner-time. As for the States, they supported their loss with inexpressible courage and constancy: they buried Tromp very magnificently at the public expence.

From the rigorous terms prescribed by the parliament, the negotiation carried on by the Dutch ministers at London, met at first with many difficulties: but an accident (if indeed the effect of Cromwell's intrigues ought to be called so) delivered them out of their distress. The parliament, on the 12th of December 1653, took a sudden resolution of delivering up their power to him from whom it came, viz. the

lord

lord general Cromwell; who foon after took upon him the fupreme magiftracy, under the title of protector. He quickly admitted the Dutch to a treaty upon fofter conditions, though he affected to make ufe of high terms; and this treaty ended in a peace, which was made the fourth of April 1654. In this negotiation it was in the firft place ftipulated, that fuch as could be found of the perfons concerned in the maffacre at Amboyna, fhould be delivered up to juftice. This was very fpecious, and calculated to give the people a high idea of the protector's patriotifm, who thus compelled the Dutch to make fatisfaction for an offence, which the two former kings could never bring them to acknowlege. But as this article was never executed, fo we may reafonably conclude, that the Dutch knew the protector's mind before they made him this boafted conceffion. They acknowleged the dominion of the Englifh at fea, by confenting to ftrike the flag, fubmitted to the act of navigation, undertook to give the Eaft India company fatisfaction for the loffes they had fuftained; and by a private article bound themfelves, never to elect any of the houfe of Orange to the dignity of Stadtholder.

The war between England and Holland had not continued quite two years; and yet, in that time, the Englifh took no lefs than one thoufand feven hundred prizes, valued by the Dutch themfelves at fixty-two millions of guilders, or near fix millions fterling. On the contrary, thofe taken by the Dutch could not amount to the fourth part, either in number or value. Within that fpace the Englifh were victorious in no lefs than five general battles, whereas the Hollanders cannot juftly boaft of having gained one. For the action between de Ruyter and Ayfcue, in which they pretended fome advantage, was no general fight; and the advantage gained by Tromp in the Downs, is owned to have been gained over a part only of the Englifh fleet. As fhort as this quarrel was, it brought

T 2   the

the Dutch to greater extremities, than their fourscore years war with Spain.

Hostilities between France and England still continued; our ships of war taking, sinking, or burning theirs wherever they met them; and the French privateers disturbing our commerce as much as they were able. An attempt was made by the French ministry, to have got France, as well as Denmark, included in the peace made with the states: but Cromwell would not hear of this, because he knew how to make his advantage of the difficulties the French then laboured under another way; in which he succeeded perfectly well, obliging them in 1655, to submit to his own terms, and to give up the interests of the royal family, notwithstanding their near relation to the house of Bourbon. He likewise obtained a very advantageous treaty of commerce; and without question his conduct with regard to France would have deserved commendation, if, for the sake of securing his own government, he had not entered too readily into the views of cardinal Mazarine, and thereby contributed to the aggrandizing of a power which has been troublesome to Europe ever since. It is generally supposed, that the primary as well as principal instigation to the Spanish war came from him; who gave the protector to understand, that the English maritime force could not be better employed, than in conquering part of the Spanish West Indies, while France attacked the same crown in Europe; and to purchase his assistance, would readily relinquish the royal family, and so rid him from all fears of an invasion.

No sooner was the Dutch war ended, than the protector ordered his navy to be repaired, augmented, and put into good condition; whence it was evident enough, that he intended not to be idle, though nobody knew against whom this new force was to be exerted. In the summer of the year 1654, he ordered two great fleets to be provided: and while he

was

was making these preparations, all the neighbouring nations, ignorant of his intentions, remained in suspence, and looked with anxious expectation on what side the storm would discharge itself. One of the squadrons, consisting of thirty capital ships, was sent into the Mediterranean under Blake; whose fame was now spread over all Europe. No English fleet, except during the Croisades, had ever before sailed those seas; and from one extremity to the other, there was no naval force, Christian or Mahometan, able to resist them. The Roman pontiff, whose weakness and whose pride, equally provoke attacks, dreaded invasion from a power, which professed the most inveterate enmity against him; and which so little regulated its movements by the common motives of interest and prudence. Blake, casting anchor before Leghorn, demanded and obtained of the duke of Tuscany satisfaction for some losses, which the English commerce had formerly sustained from him. He next sailed to Algiers, and compelled the Dey to make peace; and to restrain his pyratical subjects from all farther violences on the English. He presented himself before Tunis, and having made the same demands, the Dey of that republic bade him look to the castles of Porto-Farino and Goletta, and do his utmost. Blake needed not to be rouzed by such a bravado: he drew his ships close up to the castles, and tore them in pieces with his artillery. He sent a numerous detachment of seamen in their long-boats into the harbour, and burned every ship which lay there. This bold action, which its very temerity, perhaps, rendered safe, was executed with very little loss; and filled that part of the world with the renown of English valour.

The other squadron was not equally successful. It was commanded by Pen; and carried on board 4000 men, under the command of Venables. About 5000 more joined them from Barbadoes and St. Christophers. Both these officers were inclined to the king's service;

service; and it is pretended, that Cromwel was obliged to hurry the soldiers on board, in order to prevent the execution of a conspiracy, which had been formed among them, in favour of the exiled family. The ill success of this enterprize, may justly be ascribed, as much to the injudicious contrivance of the protector, who planned it, as to the bad execution of the officers, by whom it was conducted.

It was agreed by the admiral and general to attempt St. Domingo, the only place of strength in the island of Hispaniola. On the approach of the English, the Spaniards in a fright deserted their houses, and fled into the woods. Contrary to the opinion of Venables, the soldiers were disembarked without guides ten leagues distant from the town. They wandered four days through the woods without provisions; and what was still more intolerable in that sultry climate, without water. The Spaniards gathered courage, and attacked them. The English, discouraged with the bad conduct of their officers, and scarce alive from hunger, thirst, and fatigue, had no spirit to resist. A very inconsiderable number of the enemy put the whole army to rout; killed 600 of them, and chaced the rest on board their vessels.

The English commanders, in order to atone, if possible, for this unprosperous attempt, bent their course to Jamaica, which was surrendered to them without a blow. Pen and Venables returned to England, and were both of them sent to the Tower by the protector, who, though commonly master of his fiery temper, was thrown into a violent passion at this disappointment. He had made a conquest of much greater importance, than he was himself at that time aware of; yet was it much inferior to the vast projects, which he had formed. He gave orders, however, to support it by men and money; and that island has ever since remained in the hands of the English: the chief acquisition which they owe to the enterprising spirit of Cromwel.

As

As soon as the news of this enterprize, which was a moſt unwarrantable violation of treaty, arrived in Europe, the Spaniards declared war againſt England; and ſeized all the ſhips and goods of Engliſh merchants, of which they could make themſelves maſters. The Spaniſh commerce, ſo profitable to the nation, was cut off; and near 1500 veſſels, it is computed, fell in a few years into the hands of the enemy. Blake, to whom Montague was now joined in command, after receiving new orders, prepared himſelf for hoſtilities againſt the Spaniards.

Blake lay ſome time off Cadiz, in expectation of intercepting the plate-fleet; but was obliged, for want of water, to make ſail toward Portugal. Captain Steyner, whom he had left on the coaſt with a ſquadron of ſeven veſſels, came in ſight of the galleons, and immediately ſet ſail to purſue them. The Spaniſh admiral ran his ſhip aſhore; two others followed his example: the Engliſh took two ſhips, valued at near two millions of pieces of eight: two galleons were ſet on fire; and the marquis of Bajadox, viceroy of Peru, with his wife and his daughter, betrothed to the young duke of Medina Celi, were deſtroyed in them. The marquis himſelf might have eſcaped; but ſeeing theſe unfortunate women, aſtoniſhed with the danger, fall in a ſwoon, and periſh in the flames, he choſe rather to die with them, than drag out a life, embittered with the remembrance of theſe diſmal ſcenes. When the treaſures, gained by this enterprize, arrived at Portſmouth, the protector, from a ſpirit of oſtentation, ordered them to be tranſported by land to London.

The next action againſt the Spaniards was more glorious, though leſs profitable to the nation. Blake, having heard that a Spaniſh fleet of ſixteen ſhips, much richer than the former, had taken ſhelter in the Canaries, immediately made ſail toward them. He found them in the bay of Santa Cruz, diſpoſed in a moſt formidable poſture. The bay was ſecured with

with a strong castle, well fortified with cannon; beside seven forts in several parts of it, all united by a line of communication, manned with musqueteers. Don Diego Diagues, the Spanish admiral, ordered all his smaller vessels to moor close to the shore; and posted the larger galleons farther off, at anchor, with their broadsides to the sea.

Blake was rather animated, than daunted with this appearance. The wind seconded his courage; and blowing full into the bay, in a moment brought him among the thickest of his enemies. After a resistance of four hours, the Spaniards yielded to the English valour; and abandoned their ships, which were set on fire, and consumed with all their treasures. The greatest danger still remained to the English. They lay under the fire of the castles and all the forts, which must, in a little time, have torn them in pieces. But the wind suddenly shifting, carried them out of the bay; where they left the Spaniards in astonishment at the happy temerity of their audacious victors.

This was the last and greatest action of the gallant Blake. He was consumed with a dropsy and scurvy, and hastened home, that he might yield up his last breath in his native country; which he so passionately loved, and which he had so much adorned by his valour. As he came within sight of land, he expired. Never man, so zealous for a faction, was so much respected and esteemed even by the opposite factions. He was by principle an inflexible republican; and the late usurpations, amidst all the trust and caresses which he received from the ruling powers, were thought to be very little grateful to him. " It is still our duty (he said to the seamen) to fight for our country, into whatever hands the government may fall." Disinterested, generous, liberal; ambitious only of true glory; dreadful only to his avowed enemies: he forms one of the most perfect characters of that age, and the least stained with those errors and violences, which were then so predominant. The
pro-

protector ordered him a pompous funeral at the public charge: but the tears of his countrymen were the moſt honourable panegyric on his memory.

When the confuſions of a diſtracted ſtate, rendered the reſtoration of the king, the moſt eligible alternative; the ſeamen ſhewed greater readineſs than any other ſort of men to execute this ſalutary deſign: and without waiting for any farther orders, than thoſe which came from their own officers, chearfully carried the fleet over to the Dutch coaſt; where, after giving new names to the ſhips, they received his majeſty, the duke of York, and other perſons of principal quality, who had attended him, on board, the 23d of May, 1660, and ſafely landed them in Kent. For this ſervice, Mr. Montague, who commanded that fleet, was created earl of Sandwich; had a garter, and was appointed vice-admiral of England, under his royal highneſs the duke of York. Sir John Lawſon, Sir Richard Stayner, and other officers, received the honour of knighthood; and the king was pleaſed to promiſe the ſeamen in general, a particular ſhare in his favour. In September, 1660, the earl of Sandwich went, with a ſquadron of nine men of war, to Helvoetſluys, to bring over the king's ſiſter, the princeſs of Orange; who not long after died.

A treaty of marriage having been concluded between his majeſty and the infanta of Portugal, with whom he was to receive a portion of three hundred thouſand pounds, the iſland of Bombay in the Eaſt Indies, and the city of Tangier in Africa; it became neceſſary to ſend a fleet to bring over the queen, and to ſecure the laſt mentioned city againſt any attempt from the Moors. For this purpoſe, the earl of Sandwich was again ſent with a numerous fleet, which ſailed on the 19th of June, 1661, from the Downs. His lordſhip ſailed firſt to Liſbon, and from thence to Tangier; which place was put into the hands of the Engliſh on the 30th of January, 1662, when the earl of Peterborough marched into it with an Engliſh

garriſon,

garrifon, and had the keys delivered to him by the Portuguefe governor. The admiral then returned to Lifbon, where he received the queen's portion; confifting in money, jewels, fugars, and other commodities, in bills of exchange, and then failed with her majefty for England, and arrived at Spithead the 14th of May, 1662.

It is apparent that there was no occafion for fo large a fleet, merely to bring over the queen; but as it afforded a fair pretence for fending fuch a force into the Mediterranean, this opportunity was feized to execute things of greater moment. The Algerines, and other pyratical ftates of Barbary, taking advantage of our inteftine confufions, had broke the peace they made with admiral Blake. To put an end to their depredations, the earl of Sandwich, with his fleet, came before Algiers the 29th of July, 1661, and fent captain Spragge with the king's letter to the principal perfon in the government, and a letter of his own, with orders alfo to bring off Mr. Brown, the conful; which was accordingly done. Anfwer was returned, that the government of Algiers would confent to no peace, whereby they were deprived of the right of fearching our fhips. This infolence of thefe fea-robbers fprung out of the jealoufy of the chriftian powers, who would never unite to crufh this neft of pirates, and give the beautiful and rich country they inhabit to fome prince of their own faith; which would be a common benefit to all commercial nations.

In the mean time, to fhew they were in earneft, they wrought very hard at a boom, which, with much ado, they brought over from the mole-head, to the oppofite corner of the port; that, by the help of this, and many other new works which they had raifed, they might be able to defend themfelves from any attempts that could be made by fea. The earl of Sandwich, however, refolved to make a bold trial to burn the fhips in the harbour; but the wind prevented him:

him: so that after a good deal of firing on both sides, wherein more hurt was done to the city than the ships, the admiral thought fit to sail for Lisbon on the first of August, leaving Sir John Lawson, with a strong squadron to protect the English trade, and harrass the enemy. This he performed with such success, that, after taking many of their ships, he, by degrees, forced all these pyratical states to conclude a peace with Great Britain, without any reservation as to their favourite article of searching our ships.

On his first return to the throne of his ancestors, king Charles and his ministers had certainly shewn a great concern for the true interest of the nation; as will appear to any attentive reader of our history, who observes the advantages we gained by the treaties of commerce which he concluded with Spain and Holland. He also restored to the nation the advantages they drew from the Spanish trade: and the affection of this people to the English, preferable to any other nation, appeared in this, that they immediately fell out with the Dutch, and even forbade their ships of war to enter their ports, as the Dutch writers themselves tell us. The treaty with Holland not only secured the respect due to the English flag, but likewise procured some other concessions very honourable for the nation, and the island of Poleron, more correctly Pulo-Ron, i. e. the isle of Ron, for the East India company. His majesty had also an intention to have secured absolutely and for ever the fishery on the British coast to his own subjects: but, before that could be effectually done, the war broke out; for the true grounds of which, it is not easy to account.

The Dutch quickly began to conceive jealous prejudices against the king's government; and in reality to apprehend our becoming their superiors in commerce, in which we were every day visibly increasing. These sentiments engaged them, and especially their East and West India companies, to take various steps in those parts of the world to the prejudice of the

English,

English. The East India company particularly delayed the liquidation of the damages the English were to receive; peremptorily refused to deliver up the island before mentioned: and pretended to prescribe the places where, and the terms on which the English should trade in the rest of the ports of India. The other company trod exactly in their steps; and proceeded so far as to get Cape Corse-castle into their hands, which belonged to the English African company.

Charles confined not himself to memorials and remonstrances. Sir Robert Holmes was secretly dispatched with a squadron of twenty-two ships to the coast of Africa. He not only expelled the Dutch from Cape Corse, but he likewise seized the Dutch settlements of Cape Verde and the isle of Goree, together with several ships trading on that coast. And having sailed to America, he possessed himself of Nova Belgia, since called New York; a territory which James the first had given by patent to the earl of Sterling, but which had never been planted but by the Hollanders. When the states complained of these hostile measures, the king pretended to be totally ignorant of Holmes's enterprize. He likewise confined Holmes to the Tower; but some time after restored him to his liberty.

The Dutch, finding that their applications for redress were likely to be eluded, and that a ground of quarrel was industriously sought for by the English, began to arm with diligence. They even exerted, with some precipitation, an act of vigour, which hastened on the rupture. Sir John Lawson and de Ruyter had been sent with combined squadrons into the Mediterranean, in order to chastise the pyratical states on the coast of Barbary; and the time of their separation and return was now approaching. The states secretly dispatched orders to de Ruyter, that he should take in provisions at Cadiz; and sailing toward the coast of Guinea, should retaliate on the English,

lish, and put the Dutch in poffeffion of thofe fettlements whence Holmes had expelled them. De Ruyter, having a confiderable force on board, met with no oppofition in Guinea. All the new acquifitions of the Englifh, except Cape Corfe, were recovered from them: they were even difpoffeffed of fome old fettlements. Such of their fhips as fell into his hands, were feized by de Ruyter. That admiral failed next to America: he attacked Barbadoes, but was repulfed: he afterward committed hoftilities on Long Ifland.

Meanwhile, the Englifh preparations for war were advancing with vigour and induftry. The king had received no fupplies from parliament; but by his own funds and credit, he was enabled to equip a fleet: the city of London lent him 100,000 pounds: the fpirit of the nation feconded his armaments: he himfelf went from port to port, infpecting with great diligence, and encouraging the work: and in a little time the Englifh navy was put in a very formidable condition. Eight hundred thoufand pounds are faid to have been expended on this armament. When Lawfon arrived, and communicated his fufpicion of de Ruyter's enterprife, orders were iffued for feizing all Dutch fhips; and 135 fell into the hands of the Englifh. Thefe were not confifcated, nor declared prizes, till afterward, when war was proclaimed.

The Dutch faw, with the utmoft regret, a war approaching, whence they might dread the moft fatal confequences, but which afforded no profpect of advantage. They tried every art of negotiation, before they would come to extremity. Their meafures were at that time directed by John de Wit; a minifter equally eminent for greatnefs of mind, for capacity, and for integrity. By his management, a fpirit of union was preferved in all the provinces; great fums were levied; and a navy was equipped, compofed of larger fhips than the Dutch had ever built before, and able to cope with the fleet of England.

When certain intelligence arrived of de Ruyter's enterprizes, Charles declared war againſt the ſtates, 22d Feb. 1665. His fleet, confiſting of 114 fail, befide fire-ſhips and ketches, was commanded by the duke of York, and under him prince Rupert and the earl of Sandwich. It had about 22,000 men on board. Opdam, who was admiral of the Dutch navy, of nearly equal force, declined not the combat. In the heat of action, when engaged in cloſe fight with the duke of York, Opdam's ſhip blew up. This accident much difcouraged the Dutch, who fled toward their own coaſt. Tromp alone, ſon of the famous admiral, killed during the protectorſhip, bravely fuſtained with his ſquadron the efforts of the Engliſh, and protected the rear of his countrymen. The vanquiſhed had nineteen ſhips funk and taken: the victors loſt only one. Sir John Lawfon died ſoon after of his wounds.

It is affirmed, and with great appearance of reaſon, that this victory might have been rendered much more compleat; had not orders been iſſued to ſlacken ſail by Brounker, one of the duke's bedchamber, who pretended authority from his maſter. The duke difclaimed the orders; but Brounker never was ſufficiently puniſhed for his temerity. It is allowed, however, that the duke behaved with great bravery during the action: he was long in the thickeſt of the fire. The earl of Falmouth, lord Muſkerry, and Mr. Boyle, were killed by one ſhot at his ſide, and covered him all over with their brains and gore. And it is not likely, that in a purſuit, where even perſons of inferior ſtation, and of the moſt cowardly difpoſition acquire courage; a commander ſhould feel his ſpirits to flag, and ſhould turn from the back of an enemy, whoſe face he had not been afraid to encounter.

This difaſter threw the Dutch into conſternation, and determined dé Wit, who was the foul of all their councils, to exert his military capacity, in order to

ſupport

support the declining courage of his countrymen. He went on board the fleet, which he took under his command; and he soon remedied all those disorders which had been occasioned by the late misfortune. The genius of this man was of the most extensive nature. He quickly became as much master of naval affairs, as if he had from his infancy been educated in them; and he even improved some parts of pilotage and sailing, beyond what men expert in those arts had ever been able to attain.

The misfortunes of the Dutch determined their allies to act for their assistance and support. The king of France was engaged in a defensive alliance with the States; but as his naval force was yet in its infancy, he was extremely averse, at that time, from entering into a war with so formidable a power as England. He tried long to mediate a peace between the two parties; and for that purpose sent an embassy to London, which returned without effecting any thing.

The king of France, though he was resolved to support the Hollanders in that unequal contest, in which they were engaged; yet protracted his declaration, and employed the time in naval preparations, both in the ocean and in the Mediterranean. The king of Denmark mean while was resolved not to remain an idle spectator of the contest between the maritime powers. The part which he acted was extraordinary: he made a secret agreement with Charles to seize all the Dutch ships in his harbours, and to share the spoils with the English; provided they would assist him in executing this measure. In order to increase his prey, he perfidiously invited the Dutch ships to take shelter in his ports; and accordingly the East India fleet, very richly laden, had put into Bergen. Sandwich, who now commanded the English navy (the duke having gone ashore) dispatched Sir Thomas Tiddiman with a squadron to attack them; but whether from the king of Denmark's delay in sending orders to the governor, or

what

what is more probable, from his avidity in endeavouring to engrofs the whole booty, the Englifh admiral, though he behaved with great bravery, failed of his purpofe. The Danifh governor fired upon him; and the Dutch, having had leifure to fortify themfelves, made a very gallant refiftance.

The king of Denmark, feemingly afhamed of his conduct, concluded with Sir Gilbert Talbot, the Englifh envoy, an offenfive alliance againft the States; and at the very fame time, his refident at the Hague, by his orders, concluded an offenfive alliance againft England. To this laft alliance he adhered, probably from jealoufy of the increafing naval power of England; and he feized and confifcated all the Englifh fhips in his harbours. This was a very fenfible check to the advantages which Charles had obtained over the Dutch; a great blow was given to the Englifh commerce: the king of Denmark's naval force was alfo confiderable, and threatened every moment a conjunction with the Hollanders. That prince ftipulated to affift his allies with a fleet of thirty fail; and he received in return a yearly fubfidy of 1,500,000 crowns, of which 300,000 were paid by France.

The king endeavoured to counterbalance thefe confederacies, by acquiring new friends and allies. He had difpatched Sir Richard Fanfhaw into Spain, who met with a very cold reception. That monarchy was funk into a great degree of weaknefs, and was menaced with an invafion from France; yet could not any motive prevail with Philip to enter into a cordial friendfhip with England. Charles's alliance with Portugal, the detention of Jamaica and Tangiers, the fale of Dunkirk to the French; all thefe offences funk fo deep into the mind of the Spanifh monarch, that no motive of intereft was fufficient to outweigh them. The bifhop of Munfter was the only ally that Charles could acquire.

The Dutch, encouraged by all thefe favourable circumftances, continued refolute to exert themfelves

to

to the utmost in their own defence. De Ruyter, their great admiral, was arrived from his expedition to Guinea; their India fleet was come home in safety; their harbours were crowded with merchant ships; faction at home was appeased; the young prince of Orange had put himself under the tuition of the states of Holland, and of de Wit, their penfionary, who executed his trust with great honour and fidelity: and the animosity which the Hollanders entertained against the attack of the English so unprovoked, as they thought it, made them thirst for revenge, and hope for better success in their next enterprize. Such vigour was exerted in the common cause, that, in order the better to man the fleet, all merchant ships were prohibited to sail, and even the fisheries were totally suspended.

The English likewise continued in the same disposition, though another more grievous calamity had joined itself to that of war. The plague had broke out in London; and that with such violence as to cut off, in less than a year, near 100,000 inhabitants. The king was obliged to summon the parliament at Oxford.

After France had declared war, England was evidently over-matched in force. Yet she possessed this advantage by her situation, that she lay between the fleets of her enemies; and might be able, by speedy and well-concerted operations, to prevent their junction. But such was the unhappy conduct of her commanders, or such the want of intelligence in her ministers, that this circumstance turned rather to her prejudice. Lewis had given orders to the duke of Beaufort, his admiral, to sail from Toulon; and the French squadron, under his command, consisting of above forty sail, was now commonly supposed to be entering the channel. The Dutch fleet, to the number of seventy-six sail, was at sea, under the command of de Ruyter and Tromp, in order to join him. The Duke of Albemarle and prince Rupert commanded the Englifh fleet, which exceeded not feventy-four fail. Albemarle, who, from his fucceffes under the protectorfhip, had too much learned to defpife the enemy, propofed to detach prince Rupert with twenty fhips, in order to oppofe the duke of Beaufort. Sir George Ayfcue, well acquainted with the bravery and conduct of de Ruyter, protefted againft the temerity of this refolution: but Albemarle's authority prevailed. The remainder of the Englifh fet fail to give battle to the Dutch; who, feeing the enemy advance quickly upon them, cut their cables, and prepared for the combat. The battle, which enfued, is one of the moft memorable which we read of in hiftory; whether we confider its duration, or the defperate courage with which it was fought. Albemarle made here fome atonement by his valour for the rafhnefs of the attempt. No youth, animated by glory and ambitious hopes, could exert himfelf more than did this man; who was now in the decline of life, and who had reached the fummit of honours. We cannot enter minutely into particulars. It will be fufficient to mention the chief events of each day's engagement.

In the firft day, Sir William Berkeley, vice-admiral, leading the van, fell into the thickeft of the enemy, was over-powered, and his fhip taken. He himfelf was found dead in his cabin, all covered with blood. The Englifh had the weather-gage of the enemy; but as the wind blew fo high, that they could not ufe their lower tire, they received fmall advantage from this circumftance. The Dutch fhot, however, fell chiefly on their fails and rigging; and few fhips were funk or much damaged. Chain-fhot was at that time a new invention; which is commonly attributed to de Wit. Sir John Harman exerted himfelf extreamly this day. The Dutch admiral, Evertz, was killed in engaging him. Darknefs parted the combatants.

The second day, the wind was somewhat fallen, and the combat became more steady and more terrible. The English now found, that the most heroic valour cannot compensate the superiority of numbers, against an enemy who is well conducted, and who is not defective in courage. De Ruyter and Van Tromp, rivals in glory, and enemies from faction, exerted themselves in emulation of each other; and de Ruyter had the advantage of disengaging and saving his antagonist, who had been surrounded by the English, and was in the most imminent danger. Sixteen fresh ships joined the Dutch fleet during the action: and the English were so shattered, that their fighting ships were reduced to twenty-eight, and they found themselves obliged to retreat toward their own coast. The Dutch followed them, and were just on the point of renewing the combat; when a calm, which came a little before night, prevented the engagement.

Next morning, the English were necessitated to continue their retreat; and a proper disposition was made for that purpose. The shattered ships were ordered to stretch a-head; and sixteen of the most entire followed them in good order, and kept the enemy in awe. Albemarle himself closed the rear, and presented an undaunted countenance to his victorious foes. The earl of Ossory, son to Ormond, a gallant youth, who sought honour and danger in every action throughout Europe, was then on board the admiral. Albemarle confessed to him his intention rather to blow up his ship and perish gloriously, than yield to the enemy. Ossory applauded this desperate resolution.

About two o'clock, the Dutch had come up with their enemy, and were ready to renew the fight; when a new fleet was descried from the south, crowding all their sails to reach the scene of action. The Dutch flattered themselves that Beaufort was arrived, to cut off the retreat of the vanquished: the English hoped, that prince Rupert had come to turn the scale of action. Albemarle, who had received intelligence of the prince's approach, bent his courſe toward him. Unhappily, Sir George Ayſcue, in a ſhip of a hundred guns, the largeſt in the fleet, ſtruck on the Galloper ſands, and could receive no aſſiſtance from his friends, who were haſtening to join the reinforcement. He could not even reap the conſolation of periſhing glorioully, and revenging his death on his enemies. They were preparing fireſhips to attack him, and he was obliged to ſtrike. The Engliſh ſailors, ſeeing the neceſſity, with the utmoſt indignation ſurrendered themſelves priſoners.

Albemarle and prince Rupert were now determined to face the enemy; and next morning, the battle began afreſh, with more equal force, and with equal valour. After long cannonading, the fleets came to a more cloſe combat; which was continued with great violence, till parted by a miſt. The Engliſh retired firſt into their harbours.

Though the Engliſh, by their obſtinate courage, reaped the chief honour in this engagement, it is ſomewhat uncertain, who obtained the victory. The Hollanders took a few ſhips; and having ſome appearances of advantage, expreſſed their ſatisfaction by all the ſigns of triumph and rejoicing. But as the Engliſh fleet was repaired in a little time, and put to ſea more formidable than ever, together with many of thoſe ſhips which the Dutch had boaſted to have burned or deſtroyed; all Europe ſaw, that thoſe two brave nations were engaged in a conteſt, which was not likely to prove deciſive.

It was the conjunction of the French alone, which could give the ſuperiority to the Dutch. In order to facilitate this junction, de Ruyter, having repaired the fleet, poſted himſelf at the mouth of the Thames. The Engliſh, under prince Rupert and Albemarle, were not long in coming to the attack. The numbers of each fleet amounted to about eighty ſail; and the valour and experience of the commanders, as

well

well as of the seamen, rendered the engagement fierce and obstinate. Sir Thomas Allen, who commanded the white squadron of the English, attacked the Dutch van, whom he entirely routed; and he killed the three admirals who commanded it. Van Tromp engaged Sir Jeremy Smith; and during the heat of action, he was separated from de Ruyter and the main body, whether by accident or design was never certainly known. De Ruyter, with great conduct and valour, maintained the combat against the main body of the English; and though over-powered by numbers, kept his station, till night ended the engagement. Next day, finding the Dutch fleet scattered and discouraged, his high spirit was obliged to submit to a retreat; which yet he conducted with such skill, as to render it equally honourable to himself as the greatest victory. Full of indignation however for yielding the superiority to the enemy, he frequently exclaimed, " My God! what a wretch am I? among " so many thousand bullets, there is not one to put " an end to my miserable life!" One de Witte, his son-in-law, who stood near, exhorted him, since he sought death, to turn upon the English, and render his life a dear purchase to the victors. But de Ruyter esteemed it more worthy a brave man to persevere to the uttermost, and, as long as possible, to render service to his country. All that night and next day, the English pressed upon the rear of the Dutch; and it was chiefly by the redoubled efforts of de Ruyter, that the latter saved themselves in their harbours.

The loss of the Hollanders in this action was not very considerable; but as violent animosities had broke out between the two admirals, who engaged all the officers on one side or other, the consternation which took place, was very great among the provinces. Tromp's commission was at last taken from him; but though several captains had misbehaved, they were so well protected by their friends in the magistracy of the towns, that moſt of them eſcaped puniſhment: many were ſtill continued in their commands.

The Engliſh now rode inconteſtible maſters of the ſea, and inſulted the Dutch in their harbours. A detachment under Holmes was ſent into the road of Vlie, and burned a hundred and forty merchantmen, two men of war, together with Bandaris, a large and rich village on the coaſt. The merchants, who loſt by this enterprize, uniting themſelves to the Orange faction, exclaimed againſt an adminiſtration, which, they pretended, had brought ſuch diſgrace and ruin on their country. None, but the firm and intrepid mind of de Wit, cou'd have ſupported itſelf under ſuch a complication of calamities.

The deſtroying the Dutch ſhips, and the burning the town of Bandaris, though done by Engliſhmen, was no Engliſh project. One captain Heemſkerk, a Dutchman, who fled hither, for fear of his being called to an account for miſbehaviour under Opdam, was the author of that diſmal ſcene. After the return of the fleet, he was one day at court, and boaſting, in the hearing of king Charles the ſecond, of the bloody revenge he had taken upon his country: that monarch, with a ſtern countenance, bid him withdraw, and never preſume to appear again in his preſence. He ſent him, however, a very conſiderable ſum of money for the ſervice; with which he retired to Venice. This inſtance of magnanimity, in that generous prince, has been long and highly applauded by the Dutch.

As ſoon as the fleet was ready, the command was beſtowed on Michael de Ruyter; Tromp having at that time, in conſequence of his diſpute with de Ruyter, laid down his commiſſion. This navy conſiſted of ſeventy-nine men of war and frigates, and twenty-ſeven fire-ſhips. The firſt deſign they had, was to join the French ſquadron, which Louis XIV. had promiſed to fit out for their aſſiſtance; in this they were moſt egregiouſly diſappointed, and after a dan-

gerous

gerous navigation, in which they were more than once chafed by a fuperior Englifh fleet, they were glad to return, though fired with indignation at fuch ufage: which, it is faid, wrought fo powerfully on the mind of the gallant de Ruyter, as to throw him into a fit of ficknefs.

When the French thought the coaft was become pretty clear, they ventured out with their fleet; but Sir Thomas Allen attacking them with his fquadron, boarded the Ruby, a fine fhip of a thoufand tons, and fifty-four guns, and carrying her in a fhort time, it fo difcouraged the French miniftry, that they fcarcely trufted their navy afterward out of fight of their own fhores.

Charles began to be fenfible, that all the ends for which the war had been undertaken, were likely to prove entirely ineffectual. The Dutch, even when alone, had defended themfelves with great vigour, and were every day improving their military fkill and preparations. Though their trade had fuffered extreamly, their extenfive credit enabled them to levy prodigious fums; and while the feamen of England loudly complained for want of pay, the Dutch navy was regularly fupplied with every thing requifite for its fubfiftence. As two powerful kings now fupported them, every place, from the extremity of Norway to the coafts of Bayonne, was become hoftile to the Englifh. And Charles, neither fond of action, nor ftimulated by any violent ambition, gladly fought for means of reftoring tranquillity to his people; heartily difgufted with a war, which, being joined with the plague and fire of London, had proved fo fruitlefs and deftructive.

The firft advances toward an accommodation were made by England. When the king fent for the body of Sir William Berkeley, he infinuated to the ftates his defire of peace on reafonable terms; and their anfwer correfponded in the fame amicable intentions. Charles, however, to maintain the appearance of fuperiority, ftill still insisted, that the states should treat at London; and they agreed to make him this compliment so far as concerned themselves: but being engaged in an alliance with two crowned heads, they could not, they said, prevail with these to depart in that respect from their dignity. It was in the end agreed to treat at some other place; and Charles made choice of Breda.

Whatever projects might have been formed by Charles for secreting the money granted him by parliament, he had hitherto failed in his intention. The expences of such vast armaments had exhausted all the supplies; and even a great debt was contracted to the seamen. The king therefore was resolved to save, as far as possible, the last supply of 1,800,000 pounds; and to employ it for payment of his debts, as well those occasioned by the war, as those which either necessity, pleasure, or generosity, had formerly engaged him to contract. In this situation, Charles rashly remitted his preparations, and exposed England to one of the greatest affronts, which it has ever received. Two small squadrons alone were equipped; and during a war with such potent and martial enemies, every thing was left almost in the same situation as in times of the most profound tranquillity.

De Wit protracted the negotiations at Breda, and hastened the naval preparations. The Dutch fleet appeared in the Thames under the command of de Ruyter, and threw the English into the utmost consternation. A chain had been drawn cross the river Medway; some fortifications had been added to Sheerness and Upnore castle: but all these preparations were unequal to the present necessity. Sheerness was soon taken; nor could it be saved by the valour of Sir Edward Spragge, who defended it. Having the advantage of a spring-tide, and an easterly wind, the Dutch pressed on, and broke the chain, though fortified by some ships, which had been there sunk by order of the duke of Albemarle. They burned the three ships, which lay to guard the chain, the Matthias, the Unity, and the Charles the Fifth. After damaging several veffels, and poffeffing themfelves of the hull of the Royal Charles, which the Englifh had burned, they advanced with fix men of war and five fire-fhips, as far as Upnore-caftle, where they burned the Royal Oak, the Loyal London, and the Great James. Captain Douglas, who commanded on board the Royal Oak, perifhed in the flames, though he had an eafy opportunity of efcaping. " Never was it known," he faid, " that a Douglas " had left his poft without orders." The Hollanders fell down the Medway without receiving any confiderable damage; and it was apprehended, that they might next tide fail up the Thames, and extend their hoftilities even to the bridge of London. Nine fhips were funk at Woolwich, four at Blackwall: platforms were raifed in many places, furnifhed with artillery; the train-bands were called out; and every place was in the utmoft diforder. The Dutch failed next to Portfmouth, where they made a fruitlefs attempt: they met with no better fuccefs at Plymouth: they infulted Harwich: they failed again up the Thames as far as Tilbury, where they were repulfed by Sir Edward Spragge, who had with him five frigates, and feventeen fire-fhips. This proved a very fharp action, at leaft between the fire-fhips; of which the Dutch writers themfelves confefs, they fpent eleven to our eight.

The next day the Englifh attacked the Dutch in their turn; and, notwithftanding their fuperiority, forced them to retire, and to burn the only fire-fhip they had left, to prevent her being taken. On the twenty-fifth they bore out of the river, with all the fail they could make, followed at a diftance by Sir Edward Spragge, and his remaining fire-fhips. On the twenty-fixth, in the mouth of the river, they were met by another Englifh fquadron from Harwich, confifting of five men of war, and fourteen fire-fhips.
They

They boldly attacked the Dutch, and grappled the vice-admiral of Zealand, and another large ship; but were not able to fire them, though they frightened a hundred of their men into the sea. The rear-admiral of Zealand was forced on shore, and so much damaged thereby, as to be obliged to return home.

The Dutch fleets, notwithstanding these disappointments, and though it was now very evident that no impression could be made, as had been expected, on the English coasts, continued still hovering about, even after they were informed that the peace was actually signed, and ratifications exchanged at Breda. Our writers are pretty much at a loss to account for this conduct; but a Dutch historian has told us very plainly, that Cornelius de Wit ordered all our ports, on that side, to be sounded, and took incredible pains to be informed of the strength of our maritime forts, and the provision made for protecting the mouths of our rivers: This shewed plainly, that though this was the first visit, it was not intended to be the last. The whole coast was in alarm; and had the French thought proper at this time to join the Dutch fleet, and to invade England, consequences the most fatal might justly have been apprehended. But Lewis had no intention to push the victory to such extremities. His interest required, that a ballance should be kept between the two maritime powers; not that an uncontrouled superiority should be given to either.

Great indignation prevailed amongst the English, to see an enemy, whom they regarded as inferior, whom they had expected totally to subdue, and over whom they had gained many honourable advantages; now of a sudden ride undisputed masters of the ocean, burn their ships in their very harbours, fill every place with confusion, and strike a terror into the capital itself. But tho' the cause of all these disasters could be ascribed neither to bad fortune, to the misconduct of admirals, nor the misbehaviour of seamen, but solely to the avarice, at least to the improvidence

of

of the government; no dangerous symptoms of discontent appeared, and no attempt for an insurrection was made by any of those numerous sectaries, who had been so openly branded for their rebellious principles, and who upon that suppofition had been treated with such severity.

But the figning the treaty at Breda, extricated the king from his prefent difficulties. The English ambaffadors received orders to recede from thofe demands, which, however frivolous in themfelves, could not now be relinquifhed, without acknowledging a fuperiority in the enemy. Polerone remained with the Dutch; fatisfaction for the fhips, Bonaventure and Good Hope, the pretended grounds of the quarrel, was no longer infifted on: Acadie was yielded to the French. The acquifition of New York, a fettlement fo important by its fituation, was the chief advantage which the Englifh reaped from a war, in which the national character of bravery fhone out with great luftre; but where the mifconduct of the government, efpecially in the conclufion, had been no lefs apparent.

The Dutch war being over, his majefty fent Sir Thomas Allen with a ftout fquadron into the Mediterranean, to reprefs the infults of the Algerines, who taking advantage of our differences, had difturbed both the Englifh commerce and the Dutch. The latter fent admiral Van Ghendt with a fquadron to fecure their trade. Thefe fquadrons having engaged fix corfairs, forced them to fly to their own coafts, where they were attacked by the Englifh and the Dutch in their boats; and being abandoned by their refpective crews, were all taken, and a great number of chriftian flaves of different nations releafed. The fame year fome of our frigates attacked feven of the enemies beft fhips near cape Gaeta. The admiral and vice-admiral of the Algerines carried fifty-fix guns each; their rear-admiral, the biggeft fhip in the fquadron, carried fixty, and the leaft forty. Yet, after

after a sharp engagement, the vice-admiral was sunk, and the rest forced to retire, most of them miserably disabled.

At last, Sir Edward Spragge was sent, in 1670, with a strong squadron of men of war and frigates, to put an end to the war. He cruised for some days before their capital, without receiving any satisfactory answer to his demands. Upon this, he sailed from thence, with six frigates and three fire-ships, to make an attempt upon a considerable number of those corsairs, which lay in the haven of Bugia. By the way, he lost the company of two of his fire-ships; yet not discouraged by this accident, he persisted in his resolution. Being come before the place, he broke the boom at the entrance of the haven, forced the Algerines a-ground, and (notwithstanding the fire of the castle) burnt seven of their ships, which mounted from twenty-four to thirty-four guns, together with three prizes: after which he destroyed another of their ships of war near Teddeller. These and other misfortunes caused such a tumult among the Algerines, that they murdered their dey, and chose another, by whom the peace was concluded to the satisfaction of the English, on the ninth of December in the same year: and as they were now sufficiently humbled, and saw plainly enough that the continuance of a war with England must end in their destruction, they kept this peace better than any they had made in former times.

We are now come to the third Dutch war (more frequently called the second, because it was so in respect to this reign) and to account for the beginning of it, will be no easy matter. The last treaty of peace was made by king Charles against his will, and on terms, to which force only made him content. We need not wonder, therefore, that he still retained a dislike to the Dutch. Beside, there had been many other things done, sufficient to give distaste to any crowned head. For instance, their factory at Gambron

bron in Perfia, after the peace, burnt the king in effigy; having firſt dreſſed up the image in an old ſecond-hand ſuit, to expreſs the diſtreſs in which they knew him in his exile: for this, as the king thought it beneath him to demand, ſo the ſtates-general looked upon themſelves as above giving him, any ſatisfaction.

They likewiſe ſuffered ſome medals to be ſtruck, in which their vanity was very apparent. Amongſt others, becauſe the triple alliance had given a check to the power of France, and their mediation had been accepted in the treaty of Aix-la-Chapelle, they were pleaſed to arrogate to themſelves the ſole honour of giving peace to Europe, and of being arbiters among contending princes. Here, however, it muſt be owned that, in making war upon them, at this juncture, king Charles acted too much under the direction of French counſels. He had about him the worſt ſet of miniſters that ever curſed this, or perhaps any other nation. Men of different faiths, (if bad ſtateſmen have any) and who agreed only in promoting thoſe arbitrary acts, which, while they ſeemed to make their maſter great, in reality ruined his, and, if they could have been ſupported, would have exalted their power.

This infamous crew (for however decked with titles by their maſter, no Engliſhman will tranſmit their names to poſterity with honour) were then called, the CABAL; and theſe engaged the king to liſten to the propoſitions of his moſt chriſtian majeſty, who, as he had before deceived him to ſerve the Dutch, ſo he now offered to deceive the Dutch, to gratify our king. That Charles might not heſitate at this ſtep, Louis le Grand betrayed his creature de Wit, and diſcovered a project he had ſent him for entering into an offenſive alliance againſt England; which, with other articles for his private advantage, moſt unhappily determined our monarch to take a ſtep prejudicial to the proteſtant intereſt, repugnant to that of

the

the nation, and dangerous to the balance of power in Europe.

By virtue of secret engagements with France, this war was to end in the total deftruction of the republic of Holland. Part of her dominions was to be added to thofe of France, and the reft to fall to the fhare of England. In order to have a pretence for breaking with them, the captain of the Merlin-yatcht, with Sir William Temple's lady on board, had directions to pafs through the Dutch fleet in the channel; and, on their not ftriking to his flag, was commanded to fire; which he did: yet this not being thought enough, he was blamed inftead of being rewarded for it; and for not fufficiently afferting the king's right, he was, on his arrival in England, committed to the Tower. The pretence, however, thus fecured, the French next undertook to lull the Dutch afleep, as they had done us, when our fhips were burnt at Chatham; and this too they performed, by offering their mediation to accommodate that difference which they had procured, and upon which the execution of all their fchemes depended. Yet de Wit trufted to this; till, as the dupe of France, and the fcourge of his own nation, he fell a facrifice to the fury of an enraged people. The war once refolved on, Sir Robert Holmes, who began the former by his reprifals in Guinea, had orders to open this too, though as he did that, without any previous declaration, by attacking the Smyrna fleet.

That fleet confifted of feventy fail, valued at a million and a half; and the hopes of feizing fo rich a prey had been a great motive for engaging Charles in the prefent war, and he had confidered that capture as a principal refource for fupporting his military enterprizes. Holmes, with nine frigates and three yatchts, had orders to go in fearch of this fleet; and he paffed Spragge in the channel, who was returning home with a fquadron from a cruize in the Mediterranean. Spragge informed him of the near approach

of

of the Hollanders; and had not Holmes, from a defire of engroffing all the honour and profit of the enterprize, kept the fecret of his orders, the conjunction of thefe fquadrons had rendered the fuccefs infallible. When Holmes approached the Dutch, he put on an amicable appearance, and invited the admiral, Van Nefs, who commanded the convoy, on board of him : one of his captains gave a like infidious invitation to the rear-admiral. But thefe officers were on their guard. They had received an intimation of the hoftile intentions of the Englifh, and had already put all the fhips of war and merchantmen in an excellent pofture of defence. Three times were they valiantly affailed by the Englifh ; and as often did they as valiantly defend themfelves. In the third attack one of the Dutch fhips of war was taken ; and three or four of their moft inconfiderable merchantmen fell into the enemies hands. The reft, fighting with great fkill and courage, continued their courfe ; and, favoured by a mift, got fafe into their own harbours. This attempt is denominated perfidious and piratical by the Dutch writers, and even by many of the Englifh. It merits at leaft the appellation of irregular; and as it had been attended with bad fuccefs, it brought double fhame upon the contrivers. The Englifh miniftry endeavoured to cover the action, by pretending that it was a cafual rencounter, arifing from the obftinacy of the Dutch, who refufed the honours of the flag : but the contrary was fo well known, that even Holmes himfelf had not the affurance to perfift in this affeveration.

War againft the Dutch was declared on the 28th of March, 1672, in the cities of London and Weftminfter ; and great pains were taken to impofe upon the world a grofs and groundlefs notion, that it was undertaken at the inftance, or, at leaft, with the concurrence, of the people in general : whereas they knew their intereft too well, not to difcern how little this meafure agreed with it. And therefore, though the

the king had then a parliament much to his mind, yet he found it extreamly difficult to obtain supplies; while the Dutch, in the midst of all their miseries, went on receiving sixty millions of their money (which is between five and six millions of ours) annually from their subjects. So great difference there is between taxes levied by authority, and money chearfully paid to preserve the common-wealth. The French king's declaration of war contained more dignity, if undisguised violence and injustice could merit that appellation. He pretended only, that the behaviour of the Hollanders had been such, that it did not consist with his glory any longer to bear it.

In the mean time de Ruyter put to sea with a formidable fleet, consisting of ninety-one ships of war and forty-four fire-ships. Cornelius de Wit was on board, as deputy from the states. They sailed in quest of the English, consisting of sixty-five ships, who were under the command of the duke of York, and who had already joined the French squadron of thirty-six sail, under mareschal d'Etrées. The combined fleets lay at Solebay in a very negligent posture; and Sandwich, being an experienced officer, had given the duke warning of the danger; but received, it is said, such an answer as intimated, that there was more of caution than of courage in his apprehensions. Upon the appearance of the enemy, every one ran to his post with precipitation; and many ships were obliged to cut their cables, in order to be in readiness. Sandwich commanded the van; and though determined to conquer or perish, he so tempered his courage with prudence, that the whole fleet was visibly indebted to him for its safety. He hastened out of the bay, where it had been easy for de Ruyter with his fire-ships to have destroyed the combined fleets, which were crowded together; and by this wise measure he gave time to the duke of York, who commanded the main body, and to mareschal d'Etrées, admiral of the rear, to disengage themselves

selves. He himself meanwhile was engaged in close fight with the Hollanders; and by presenting himself to every danger, had drawn upon him all the bravest of the enemy. He killed Van Ghendt, the Dutch admiral, and beat off his ship: he sunk another ship, which ventured to lay him aboard: he sunk three fire-ships, which endeavoured to grapple with him: and though his vessel was torne in pieces with shot, and of a thousand men she contained, near six hundred lay dead upon the deck; he continued still to thunder with all his artillery in the midst of the enemy. But another fire-ship, more fortunate than the preceding, having laid hold of his vessel, her destruction was now inevitable: Warned by Sir Edward Haddock, his captain, he refused to make his escape; and bravely embraced death as a shelter from that ignominy, which a rash expression of the duke, he thought, had thrown upon him.

During this fierce engagement with Sandwich, de Ruyter remained not inactive. He attacked the duke of York, and fought him with such fury for above two hours, that of two and thirty actions, in which he had been engaged, he declared this combat to be the most obstinately disputed. The duke's ship was so shattered, that he was obliged to leave her, and remove his flag to another. His squadron was overpowered with numbers, till Sir Joseph Jordan, who had succeeded to Sandwich's command, came to his assistance; and the fight, being more equally balanced, was continued till night; when the Dutch retired, and were not followed by the English. The loss sustained by the fleets of the two maritime powers was nearly equal, if it did not rather fall more heavy on the English. The French suffered very little, because they had scarce been engaged in the action; and as this backwardness is not their national character, it was concluded, that they had received orders to spare their ships, while the Dutch and English should weaken themselves by their mutual animosity.

Almost all the other actions during the present war tended to confirm this suspicion.

It brought great honour to the Dutch to have fought with some advantage the combined fleets of two such powerful nations; but nothing less than a compleat victory could serve the purpose of de Wit, or save his country from those calamities, which from every quarter threatened to overwhelm her. Lewis invaded the Dutch territories by land, and took their towns as fast as he appeared before them. A general astonishment seized the Hollanders, from the combination of such powerful princes against the republic; and no where was resistance made, suitable to the antient glory or present greatness of the state. Governors without experience commanded troops without discipline; and despair had universally extinguished that sense of honour, by which alone, men in such dangerous extremities can be animated to a valorous defence. Every hour brought to the states news of the rapid progress of the French, and of the cowardly defence of their own garrisons.

The Prince of Orange, with his small and discouraged army, retired into the province of Holland; where he expected, from the natural strength of the country, since all human art and courage failed, to be able to make some resistance. Three provinces were already in the hands of the French; Guelderland, Overyssel, and Utrecht; Groninghen was threatened; Friezland lay exposed: The only difficulty lay in Holland and Zealand; and the monarch deliberated concerning the proper measures for reducing them.

The town of Amsterdam alone seemed to retain some courage; and by forming a regular plan of defence, endeavoured to infuse spirit into the other cities: and the sluices being opened, the neighbouring country, without regard to the great damage sustained, was laid under water. All the province followed this example; and scrupled not, in this
extre-

extremity, to reftore to the fea thofe fertile fields, which with infinite art and expence had been won from it.

The ftates of Holland met to confider, whether any means were left to fave the remains of their lately flourifhing, and now diftreffed commonwealth. The nobles gave their vote, that, provided their religion, liberty, and fovereignty could be faved, every thing elfe fhould without fcruple be facrificed to the conqueror: eleven towns concurred in the fame fentiments. Amfterdam fingly declared againft all treaty with infolent and triumphant enemies: but notwithftanding that oppofition, they refolved once more to try the force of intreaties; with which view they fent four deputies to England, and as many to the French king. The bufinefs of the former, was to fhew the danger of the proteftant religion, the apparent and near approaching ruin of the balance of Europe, and the difmal confequences which muft follow, even to England, from the further profecution of the war. As to the latter, they were charged to offer any fatisfaction to his moft chriftian majefty, that he fhould require.

The terms infifted on by Lewis were fuch as totally deftroyed, not only the exiftence, but the very appearance, of independence in the ftates: and the ambaffadors, who came 'to London, met with ftill worfe reception. No minifter was allowed to treat with them; and they were retained in a kind of confinement. But notwithftanding this rigorous conduct of the court, the prefence of the Dutch deputies excited the fentiments of tender compaffion, and even indignation among the people in general, but efpecially among thofe who could forefee the aim and refult of thofe dangerous councils. The two moft powerful monarchs, they faid, in Europe, the one by land, the other by fea, have, contrary to the faith of folemn treaties, combined to exterminate an illuftrious republic: what a dismal prospect does their success afford to the neighbours of the one, and to the subjects of the other? Charles had formed the triple league, in order to restrain the exorbitant power of France: a sure proof, that he does not now err from ignorance.

But though the fear of giving offence to his confederate had engaged Charles to treat the Dutch ambassadors with such rigour, he was not altogether without uneasiness, on account of the rapid and unexpected progress of the French arms. Were Holland entirely conquered, its whole commerce and naval force, he saw, must become an accession to France; the Spanish Low Countries must soon follow; and Lewis, now independent of his ally, would no longer think it his interest to support him against his discontented subjects. Charles, though he never stretched his attention to very distant consequences, could not but foresee these obvious events; and though incapable of envy or jealousy, he was touched with anxiety, when he found every thing yield to the French arms, while such vigorous resistance was made to his own. He soon dismissed the Dutch ambassadors, lest they should cabal among his subjects, who bore them great favour: but he sent over Buckingham and Arlington, and soon after lord Halifax, to negotiate anew with the French king, in the present prosperous situation of that monarch's affairs.

These ministers passed through Holland; and as they were supposed to bring peace to the distrest republic, they were received every where with the loudest acclamations. " God bless the king of England! God bless the prince of Orange! Confusion to the States!" This was every where the cry of the populace. The ambassadors had several conferences with the States and the prince of Orange; but made no reasonable advances toward an accommodation. They went to Utrecht, where they renewed the

league

league with Lewis; and agreed, that neither of the kings should ever make peace with Holland, but by common consent.

The terms proposed by Lewis bereaved the republic of all security against any land invasion from France: those demanded by Charles exposed them equally to an invasion by sea from England: and when both were joined, they appeared absolutely intolerable; and reduced the Hollanders, who saw no means of defence, to the utmost despair. What extreamly augmented their distress, were the violent factions with which they continued to be every where agitated. Their rage at last broke all bounds, and bore every thing before it. They rose in an insurrection at Dort; and this proved a signal of general revolt throughout all the provinces. The two brothers of de Wit were assassinated, and the prince of Orange invested with the stadtholdership.

In the mean time the French and English fleets sailed again for the Dutch coasts, with a design to make a descent on Zealand, the only province into which the French had not carried their arms by land. Here they found the Dutch fleet; but not thinking proper to attack them among the sands, they deferred the execution of their design, and blocked up the Maese and Texel; which de Ruyter (having strict orders from the States not to hazard a battle) saw with concern, yet wanted power to prevent. The duke of York was resolved to debark on the isle of Texel, the body of troops on board his fleet. The occasion was favourable in all respects; the French and the bishop of Munster were in the heart of the Dutch territories, so that no great force could be drawn together to resist them on shore.

It was upon the 3d of July this resolution was taken; and it was intended, that their forces should have landed the next flood. But providence interposed in favour of a free people, and saved them from a yoke, which seemed already to press upon their

their necks. The ebb, inſtead of ſix, continued twelve hours, which defeated the intended deſcent for that time; and the ſtorm, that roſe the night following, forced the fleet out to ſea, where they ſtruggled for ſome time with very foul weather, and, the opportunity being quite loſt, returned, without performing any thing of conſequence, to the Engliſh ſhore. The Dutch clergy magnified this accident into a miracle; and, though ſome of our writers have thereupon arraigned them of ſuperſtition, yet their exceſs of piety was, in this reſpect, very pardonable; eſpecially, if we conſider, there could not be a higher ſtroke of policy, at that time, than to perſuade a nation, ſtruggling againſt ſuperior enemies, that they were particularly favoured by heaven.

After this diſappointment, there was no other action thought of at ſea for this year, except the ſending Sir Edward Spragge, with a ſquadron, to diſturb the Dutch herring-fiſhery; which he performed with a degree of moderation that became ſo great a man: contenting himſelf with taking one of their veſſels, when he ſaw that was ſufficient to diſperſe the reſt. But while the war ſeemed to ſlumber in Europe, it raged ſufficiently in the Weſt and Eaſt Indies. All this time commerce in general ſuffered exceedingly on both ſides: noble plantations were ruined; and the French, who, before this war, had very little ſkill in navigation, and ſcarcely at all underſtood the art of fighting at ſea, as their own writers confeſs, improved wonderfully in both, at the joint expence of Britain and Holland. Thus their ſelf-intereſted political end was plainly anſwered, while the maritime powers were fighting with, and weakening each other; and this too as much againſt their inclinations, as their intereſts.

The money, granted by parliament, ſufficed to equip a fleet, 1673, of which prince Rupert was declared admiral: for the duke was ſet aſide by the teſt. Sir Edward Spragge and the earl of Oſſory
com-

commanded under the prince. A French squadron joined them, commanded by d'Etrées. The combined fleets set sail toward the coast of Holland, and found the enemy, lying at anchor, within the sands of Schonvelt. There is a natural confusion attending sea-fights, even beyond other military transactions; derived from the precarious operations of winds and tides, as well as from the smoke and darkness, in which every thing is there involved. No wonder, therefore, that relations of these battles are apt to contain uncertainties and contradictions; especially when composed by writers of the hostile nations, who take pleasure in exalting their own advantages, and suppressing those of the enemy. All we can say with certainty of this battle, is, that both sides boasted of the victory; and we may thence infer, that the action was not decisive. The Dutch, being near home, retired into their own harbours. In a week, they were refitted, and presented themselves again to the combined fleets. A new action ensued, not more decisive than the foregoing. It was not fought with great obstinacy on either side; but whether the Dutch or the allies first retired, seems to be a matter of uncertainty. The loss in the former of these actions fell chiefly on the French, whom the English, diffident of their intentions, took care to place under their own squadrons; and they thereby exposed them to all the fire of the enemy. There seems not to have been a ship lost on either side in the second engagement.

It was sufficient glory to de Ruyter, that with a fleet much inferior to the combined squadrons of France and England, he could fight without any notable disadvantage; and it was sufficient victory, that he could defeat the project of another descent in Zealand; which, had it taken place, had endangered, in the present circumstances, the total overthrow of the Dutch commonwealth. Prince Rupert also was suspected not to favour the king's project of subduing Holland, or enlarging his authority at home; and from these motives, he was thought not to have pressed so hard on the enemy, as his well-known valour gave reason to expect. It is indeed remarkable, that, during this war, though the English with their allies much over-matched the Hollanders, they were not able to gain any advantage over them; while in the former war, though often over-borne by numbers, they still exerted themselves with the most heroic courage, and always acquired great renown, sometimes even signal victories. But they were disgusted with the present measures, which they esteemed pernicious to their country; they were not satisfied in the justice of the quarrel; and they entertained a perpetual jealousy of their confederates, whom, had they been permitted, they would with much more pleasure have destroyed than even the enemies themselves.

If prince Rupert was not favourable to the designs of the court, he enjoyed as little favour from the court, at least from the duke, who, though he could no longer command the fleet, still possessed the chief authority in the admiralty. The prince complained of a total want of every thing, powder, shot, provisions, beer, and even water; and he went into harbour, that he might refit the fleet, and supply its numerous necessities. After some weeks he was refitted; and he again put to sea. The hostile fleets met at the mouth of the Texel, and fought the last battle, which, during a course of so many years, these neighbouring maritime powers have disputed with each other. De Ruyter, and under him Tromp, commanded the Dutch in this action, as in the two former: for the prince of Orange had reconciled these two gallant rivals; and they retained nothing of their former animosity, except that emulation, which made them exert themselves with more distinguishing bravery against the enemies of their country. Brankert was opposed to d'Etrées, de Ruyter to prince Rupert,

Rupert, Tromp to Spragge. It is remarkable, that in all actions these brave admirals last mentioned had still selected each other, as the only antagonists worthy each others valour; and no decisive advantage had as yet been gained by either of them. They fought in this battle, as if there were no mean between death and victory.

D'Etrées and all the French squadron, except rear-admiral Martel, kept at a distance; and Brankert, instead of pressing on them, bore down to the assistance of de Ruyter, who was engaged in furious combat with prince Rupert. On no occasion did the prince acquire more deserved honour: his conduct, as well as valour, shone out with signal lustre. Having disengaged his squadron from the numerous enemies, with which he was every where surrounded, and having joined Sir John Chichely, his rear-admiral, who had been separated from him, he made haste to the relief of Spragge, who was very hard pressed by Tromp's squadron. The Royal Prince, in which Spragge first engaged, was so disabled, that he was obliged to hoist his flag on board the St. George; while Tromp was, for a like reason, obliged to quit his ship, the Golden Lion, and to go on board the Comet. The fight was renewed with the utmost fury by these valorous rivals, and by the rear-admirals, their seconds. Ossory, rear-admiral to Spragge, was preparing to board Tromp, when he saw the St. George terribly torn, and in a manner disabled. Spragge was leaving her, in order to hoist his flag on board a third ship, and return to the charge; when a shot, which had passed through the St. George, took his boat, and sunk her. The admiral was drowned, to the great regret of Tromp himself, who bestowed on his valour the deserved praises.

Prince Rupert found affairs in this dangerous situation, and saw most of the ships in Spragge's squadron disabled from fight. The engagement was renewed,

newed, and became very close and bloody. The prince threw the enemy into great disorder: to increase it, he sent among them two fire-ships; and at the same time made a signal to the French to bear down, which if they had done, a total victory must have ensued. But the prince, when he saw that they neglected his signal, and observed that most of his ships were in no condition to keep the sea long, wisely provided for their safety, by making easy sail toward the English coast. The victory in this battle was as doubtful, as in all the actions fought during the present war.

The turn, which the affairs of the Hollanders took by land, was more favourable. The prince of Orange, by his conduct and success, obliged Lewis to recal his forces, and to abandon all his conquests, with greater rapidity than he had at first made them.

The king plainly saw, that he could expect no supply from the commons for carrying on a war, which was so odious to them. He resolved therefore to make a separate peace with the Dutch, on the terms which they had proposed through the canal of the Spanish ambassador. With a cordiality, which, in the present disposition on both sides, was probably but affected, but which was obliging, he asked advice of parliament. The parliament unanimously concurred, both in thanks for this gracious condescension, and in their advice for peace. Peace was accordingly concluded at London, February 9th, 1674. The honour of the flag was yielded by the Dutch in the most extensive terms: a regulation of trade was agreed to: all possessions were restored to the same condition as before the war: the English planters in Surinam were allowed to remove at pleasure: and the States agreed to pay to the king the sum of eight hundred thousand patacoons, near three hundred thousand pounds. Thus ended the last of our Dutch wars, which, though made against the interest and will of the people, terminated highly to

their

their advantage; whereas the former war, though it was begun at the inſtance of the nation, ended but indifferently: ſo little correſpondence there is between the grounds and iſſues of things.

The corſairs of Tripoli having for ſome time committed great outrages on the Engliſh trade, Sir John Narborough was ſent, in the latter end of the year 1675, to reduce them to reaſon. The 14th of January following, Sir John came before the place, and having blocked up the port in the night, ſo that no ſhip could go in, or come out, he manned all his boats, and ſent them under the command of lieutenant Shovel (afterward Sir Cloudeſly, the famous admiral) into the harbour; where he ſeized the guard-ſhip, and afterward burnt the veſſels, which lay at that time in the harbour: after which, he ſafely returned to the fleet without the loſs of a ſingle man. This extraordinary action ſtruck the Tripolines with amazement, and made them inſtantly ſue for peace; which, however, did not immediately take place, becauſe they abſolutely refuſed to make good the loſſes ſuſtained by the Engliſh. Sir John, thereupon, cannonaded the town; and, finding that ineffectual, landed a body of men about twenty leagues from thence, and burnt a vaſt magazine of timber, which was to have ſerved for the building of ſhips. When all this failed of reducing theſe people, Sir John ſailed to Malta; and, after remaining there for ſome time, returned ſuddenly upon the enemy, and diſtreſſed them ſo much, that they were glad to ſubmit to a peace, on the terms preſcribed.

However, ſoon after the concluſion of this treaty, ſome of their corſairs, returning into port, not only expreſſed a great diſlike thereto, but actually depoſed the dey for making it; and, without any regard to it, began to take all Engliſh ſhips, as before. Sir John remaining ſtill in the Mediterranean, and having immediate notice of what paſſed, ſuddenly appeared with eight frigates before Tripoli, and began

with

with such violence to batter the place, that the inhabitants were glad once more to renew the peace, and deliver up the authors of the late disturbance to condign punishment.

In 1679, we had some differences with the Algerines; upon which Sir John Narborough was sent with a squadron to demand satisfaction: this he procured, as it must always be procured, by dint of force. This peace, however, did not last long; but commodore Herbert, afterward so well known to the world by the title of earl of Torrington, went thither with a few ships, and compelled them to make satisfaction for the breach of it, and to give the strongest assurances of their future conduct. That expedition, which was performed in 1682, proved the last in this reign.

There is yet one transaction more which calls for our notice, and that is, the demolition of the strong and expensive fortress of Tangier. In the space of twenty years it cost the nation an immense sum of money; and yet many doubted, all things considered, whether, after all, it was of any real use to us, or not. When we first had it, the harbour was very dangerous; to remedy which, there was a fine mole run out at a vast charge. Several societies, or copartnerships, which undertook to perfect this work, raised great sums for that purpose; and, after wasting them, miscarried. At last, however, all difficulties were, in a manner, overcome; and this work finished in such a manner, that it might be said to vie with those of the Romans. But the house of commons, in 1680, having expressed a dislike to the management of the garrison kept there, which they suspected to be no better than a nursery for a popish army; and discovering, withal, no thoughts of providing for it any longer; the king began, likewise, to entertain thoughts of quitting, destroying, and bringing home his forces from thence. In 1683, the lord Dartmouth was constituted captain-general of his

his majesty's forces in Africa, and governor of Tangier, and sent, as admiral of an English fleet, to demolish the works, blow up the mole, and bring home the garrison from thence; all which he very effectually performed: so that the harbour is, at this time, entirely spoiled; and, though now in the hands of the Moors, is a very inconsiderable place. One circumstance, attending its demolition, deserves to be remarked, because it shews the temper and spirit of the king. He directed a considerable number of new-coined crown-pieces to be buried in the ruins, that if (through the vicissitudes of fortune, to which all sublunary things are liable) this city should ever be restored, there might remain some memorial of its having had once the honour of depending on the crown of Britain. Thus, through disputes between the king and parliament, whatever party-suspicions might suggest, the British nation lost a place and port of great importance.

It is on all hands confessed, that never any English, perhaps it might, without distinction of countries, be said, any prince, understood maritime concerns so well as Charles the second. He piqued himself very much on making, as occasion offered, minute enquiries into whatever regarded naval affairs: he understood ship-building perfectly, and made draughts of vessels with his own hands: he was no stranger to the conveniencies and inconveniencies of every port in his dominions. But he was so expensive in his pleasures, the jealousies raised against him were so strong, he was so much in the hands of favourites and mistresses, he was so frequently and so egregiously betrayed by both, and his finances, through his whole reign, were so cramped, and in such disorder; that he was not able to accomplish any great designs.

How intent he was, for the first ten years of his reign, in promoting whatever had a tendency to increase the naval power of his kingdom, appears, from all the candid histories of those times; and from the

collections

collections of orders, and other public papers relating to the direction of the navy, while the duke of York was admiral, published of late years, and in every body's hands. The lord keeper Bridgman affirmed, that, from 1660 to 1670, the charge of the navy had never amounted to less than half a million a year. But after the second Dutch war, the king grew more saving in this article; and yet, in 1678, when the nation in general expected a war with France, his navy was in excellent order. The judicious Mr. Pepys, secretary to the admiralty, has left us a particular account of its state in the month of August that year; which as it is very short, it may not be amiss to insert.

ABSTRACT of the FLEET.

	Rates.	Number.	Men.
	1	5	3135
	2	4	1555
	3	16	5010
	4	33	6460
	5	12	1400
	6	7	423
Fire-ships		6	340
	Total	83	18323

Of these, seventy-six were in sea-pay, the storehouses and magazines in compleat order; and, which is still more to the purpose, thirty capital ships were then actually on the stocks.

The East India company were exceedingly favoured and protected, especially in the beginning of this reign: the African company was in the zenith of its glory, and brought in vast profits to the proprietors, and the nation. Many of our plantations were settled by his majesty's favour; such as Pensilvania, Carolina,

lina, &c. Others were reftored to this nation by his arms; fuch as New York and the Jerfeys: and all had fuch encouragement, that they made quite another figure than in former times, as we may guefs from what a modern writer (no way partial to this prince) fays of Barbadoes; that, during his reign, it maintained four hundred fail of fhips, produced two hundred thoufand pounds a year clear profit to this nation, and maintained one hundred thoufand people there and here.

Thefe are high calculations: Sir William Petty calculated our exports at ten millions per annum. This agrees very well with the ftate of our cuftoms, which fell then little fhort of a million; though in 1660, they were farmed out for four hundred thoufand pounds, as they were once let by queen Elizabeth at thirty-fix thoufand. Dr. Davenant, an excellent judge in thefe matters, having duly weighed thefe calculations, and compared them with all the lights he had received from long experience; pronounces the balance of trade to have been in our favour, in this reign, two millions a year. The bounds prefcribed to this work, will not allow more to be faid on this fubject.

Few princes have ftruggled with greater difficulties, before they afcended their thrones, than king James II. and few ever fuftained a greater load of trouble afterward. He fucceeded his brother the 6th of February, 1685, with the general acclamations of his fubjects, who expected great things from a king who came to the throne with fuch advantages. He was then turned of fifty-one, had good natural parts, improved and ftrengthened both by education and experience; inclined to, and very diligent in bufinefs; an able œconomift: in fine, a prince, who, if he had conducted public affairs with the fame eafe and dexterity which he fhewed in the management of his private concerns, his reign might have been as

happy

happy and glorious, as it proved troublesome and unfortunate.

It was his great foible, that he was constantly influenced by foreign councils, which is what the English nation cannot endure; and, indeed, it is impossible they should: for, as our constitution differs from the constitution of all the states upon the continent, it is simply impracticable to govern us well, by any other system of politics than our own. King James knew this well enough; and yet his fondness for the popish religion, threw him into the arms of France, and engaged him, while a subject, to act as a tool; when a king, to rule as a viceroy to Lewis XIV. and this at a juncture, when, if he had been of the religion of his fathers, and had complied with the desires of his people, he might have given law to that haughty monarch, and been esteemed the deliverer of Europe.

Nevertheless, wrong as his conduct was, in almost every other particular, the care he took of naval affairs deserves to be mentioned. He had long exercised the office of lord high-admiral, in the reign of his brother, and understood it thoroughly: he knew, too, the disorders which had crept into the whole œconomy of the fleet, in the six years immediately preceding his accession; and was well acquainted, beside, with the difficulties the late king had found, in applying remedies to these mischiefs.

As soon, therefore, as he was seated on the throne, he began to consider how a total reformation might be wrought, and the affairs of the navy be not only set right for the present, but also be put into such a settled course, as that they might not suddenly go wrong again. With this view, he consulted Mr. Pepys, and some other persons, on whose abilities and integrity he could depend; and having learned from them what was necessary to be done to bring about the ends at which he aimed, he first assigned a

stated

stated fund of four hundred thousand pounds a year, payable quarterly out of the treasury, for the service of the navy; and then issued a special commission for settling all things relating to it, and for putting the management thereof into such a method, as might need few or no alterations in succeeding times.

This was the wisest act of his whole reign, and answered very effectually all that could be expected from it; and was grounded, as to form, on a commission which had issued, for the same purpose, in the reign of his grandfather. This commission was dated the 17th of April, 1686, and by it the commissioners were directed to enquire into, and remedy all the disorders that were then in the navy, to restore it, in every respect, to good order, and from time to time to report the proceedings to his majesty and the privy council.

The commissioners vested with these powers lost no time, but fell immediately on a diligent inspection into the state of the navy, enquired strictly into the causes of past miscarriages, with respect rather to things than men; and taking such measures for the immediate remedy of the mischiefs they discovered, that the old ships were perfectly repaired; the new ones altered and mended; the yards properly supplied with the ablest workmen; all the storehouses filled with whatever was requisite, bought at the best hand, and, in all respects, the best in their kind: the estimates brought into proper order, and the whole œconomy of the navy reduced into so clear a method, that it was impossible any officer could mistake in his duty, the public service suffer in any of its various branches, or the king run any hazard of being cheated.

While this commission subsisted, the king issued new instructions to the officers commanding his ships of war; these are dated the 15th of July, 1686, and are extreamly well calculated for promoting the public service, securing discipline, and preserving proper memorials of every man's particular merit, by obliging all captains, and superior officers, to deposit a perfect copy of their journals with the secretary of the admiralty. As many things, in these regulations, might seem to bear hard upon commanders, and to deprive them of those emoluments which their predecessors had long enjoyed; his majesty was pleased to grant them very considerable favours: such as a settled allowance for their tables, several advantages in respect to prizes, &c. and, in the close, promised to reward every instance of courage, care, or diligence, in any of his officers, upon proper attestations deposited with the secretary of the admiralty.

We need not wonder, that, in consequence of so unwearied an attention, the British fleet was in very good order when king James had the first notice of the prince of Orange's intended invasion; but we may be justly surprised at the strange management of maritime affairs from that time. A squadron of ships was, indeed, immediately ordered to sea, under the command of Sir Roger Strickland, then rear-admiral of England; who was, perhaps, the most improper man in the world to command them, on account of his being obnoxious to the seamen, by the readiness he had shewn in bringing priests on board the fleet. His squadron was ordered to the Downs very indifferently manned; and when he complained of it, and desired to have soldiers at least sent on board, even this was very slowly complied with.

When the danger appeared more clearly, this fleet was directed to retire to the Buoy in the Nore; and lord Dartmouth was ordered to sea, with such a reinforcement as made the whole fleet, under his command, consist of forty men of war: of which, thirty-eight were of the line of battle, and eighteen fire-ships. A council of war was called, wherein Sir William Jenings, who commanded a third rate, proposed to put to sea, and stand over to the Dutch coasts, as the shortest and surest way to prevent an

inva-

invasion. This proposition, however, was rejected, by a great majority; and so it was resolved to continue there. The true ground of this, as Mr. secretary Burchet fairly tells us, was, the secret resolution of the greatest part of the captains to hinder the admiral, in case he had come up with the Dutch fleet, from doing them much damage: and thus it appears, how ineffectual fleets and armies are, when princes have lost the confidence of their subjects.

In the mean time, the prince of Orange had about his person abundance of English noblemen and gentlemen. The fleet that was to carry these, consisted of about fifty sail, most of them third or fourth rates, and the transports were about five hundred. These, with twenty-five fire-ships, made up the whole navy: the land forces embarked, were four thousand horse and dragoons, and ten thousand foot. It was very remarkable, that though all the captains of these vessels were Dutch, yet the chief command was given to admiral Herbert; who very lately commanded the English fleet; and this with a view, either to engage ships to come over, or, at least, to encourage the seamen to desert.

In order to do this more effectually, Herbert first addressed a letter to his countrymen in the sea-service, and then stood with the Dutch fleet over to the Downs, in order to look at the English squadron, and try what effects his exhortation had produced. At that time his success did not promise much; and, after a fortnight's cruizing, he returned to the Dutch coasts, with a better opinion of the king's fleet, and a worse of his own, than when he sailed. But, for all this, his epistle did almost as much service as the force he commanded: for though the desertion was inconsiderable; yet, by degrees, the sailors lost their spirits, and their officers began to cabal.

On the first of November the fleet sailed. The prince intended to have gone northward, and to have landed his forces in the mouth of the Humber; but a strong east wind rendered this impracticable, and seemed to direct them to a better course. His highness then sailed westward, the same wind which brought him to the English coast keeping in the king's ships. They passed the English navy, during a fog, undiscerned, except a few transports which sailed in sight, while the English fleet rode with their yards and top-masts down, and could not, by reason of the extraordinary violence of the wind, purchase their anchors. The prince and his army landed safely in Torbay, on the fifth of November, the anniversary of the gun-powder plot.

The conduct of the king, after the arrival of the Dutch fleet, was unaccountable: since, if we except the care he took in sending away his family, it does not appear that he issued any orders relating to the fleet, which will seem still the more extraordinary, if we consider, that his admiral was not only a man of quality, and one on whose fidelity he could absolutely depend; but also an experienced officer, and a man extreamly beloved by the sailors. In all probability, he was deterred from taking any measures, of this sort, by what happened at the docks, where the workmen employed in the service of the royal navy, rose on a sudden, and, without any other arms than the tools belonging to their trades, drove out the regiment of regular troops quartered at Rochester, and Chatham, and declared for the protestant religion, and the prince of Orange. To say the truth, the sea-faring people declared unanimously against his measures, and did all in their power to prevent the most obnoxious of his ministers, such as chancellor Jefferies, and father Petre, from making their escape: which can be attributed to nothing but the just sense they had of the iniquitous measures these people had pursued: for, as to themselves, they had no particular grievances.

The mistakes committed on this side, were heightened, in their appearance, by the great caution and wise-wife management on the other, as well as by the foreseen and unforeseen consequences of the whole transaction. The embarkation was made with ease; the passage better regulated by the winds, than it could have been by their prudence; the descent in the fittest place in England for landing of horse; so that it was performed without difficulty, as well as without danger.

In Holland, they triumphed on the exact execution of the plan laid down by the states; and the most eminent news-writer they then had, made this observation on the success of the prince's enterprize, in his reflections on the history of Europe, for November, 1688. " The expence bestowed on the fleet
" and army set out from Holland, is a sign they are
" morally assured of the success of the expedition,
" which, I am apt to think, has been a long time
" in agitation, though it was carried with that pru-
" dence and secrecy, as not to be discovered, till it
" could be no longer concealed." When skill, industry, and zeal, were visibly on the part of the prince; and weakness, irresolution, and diffidence apparent in all the king's measures; it was impossible things should continue long in dispute, or that his highness, who knew so well how to use all the advantages that were in his hands, should not prevail.

When lord Dartmouth saw the disposition of his officers, and how little it was in his power to serve his master; he wisely yielded to necessity: and, failing once again into the Downs, held a council of war, in which it was resolved, first, to dismiss from their commands, all such officers as were known to be papists, or suspected so to be; and then to send up an address to his highness, setting forth their steady affection to the protestant religion, and their sincere concern for the safety, freedom, and honour of their country. Not long after this, the ships were dispersed, some to the dock-yards, to be dismantled and laid up, others to be cleaned and repaired; and such as were in the beft condition for the fea, were appointed for neceffary fetvices.

Thefe were all the exploits performed by the Englifh navy, during the reign of a prince, who, while a fubject, had ferved and acquired a reputation at fea; who underftood maritime affairs perfectly well, and who attended to them with extraordinary diligence. But it ought to be remembered, that though this fleet was ufelefs to him, yet it was of the higheft advantage to the nation. If he had been lefs careful in this refpect; if he had left the navy in a low condition; nay, if he had left it as he found it at his brother's deceafe, it would have been impoffible for us to have withftood the naval power of France, which had been for feveral years growing: and about the time of the revolution, or a little before, it had attained to its greateft height.

An abftract of the lift of the royal navy of England, upon the 18th of December, 1688, with the force of the whole.

Ships and veffels. Rates.	Number.	Force. Men.	Guns.
1	9	6705	878
2	11	7010	974
3	39	16545	2640
4	41	9480	1908
5	2	260	60
6	6	420	90
Bombers,	3	120	34
Fire-fhips,	26	905	218
Hoys,	6	22	00
Hulks,	8	50	00
Ketches,	3	115	24
Smacks,	5	18	00
Yatchts,	14	353	104
Total.	173	42003	6930

No sooner was the crown placed on the head of the prince of Orange, than he began to feel the weight of it, and found himself obliged to embark in a war, as soon as he was seated on the throne. A war in which all Europe was engaged; for the ambitious designs of Lewis XIV. were now so evident, that even the powers, least inclined to action, saw themselves obliged to provide for their own safety, by entering into a confederacy for effectually opposing the encroachments of that aspiring prince.

The French king, on the other hand, instead of discovering any dread of this formidable alliance, began first by falling upon the empire, and declaring war against Spain, at the same time that he provided for his ally, king James, whom he sent over into Ireland, with a considerable force, escorted by a fleet of thirty sail of men of war, and seven frigates. On the 12th of March, 1688-9, that monarch landed at Kingsale, from whence he went to Cork.

Admiral Herbert, who commanded the English fleet, in the beginning of the month of April, 1689, sailed for Cork, with a squadron which consisted of no more than twelve ships of war, one fire-ship, two yatchts, and two smacks. Here he received information, that king James had landed at Kingsale, about two months before. He then thought it proper to attempt the cutting off the convoy that had attended him from France: with this view he sailed for Brest, and cruised off that port for some time; but hearing nothing of the French men of war from the advice-boats he daily received, and having increased his force to nineteen sail, he again steered for the Irish coast, and toward the latter end of April, appeared off Kingsale.

On the 29th of that month, he discovered a fleet of forty-four sail, which he judged were going into Kingsale, and therefore did his utmost to prevent it. The French shipped the stores and money they had brought for James's army, on board six fire-ships, and some merchantmen they had with them, to land at a place in the bay, seven leagues distant, while they engaged the English squadron, that at all events they might be safe.

Authors vary not a little as to the strength of both fleets; but bishop Kennet reckons the English ships twenty-two, wherein he agrees with the French relations. The enemy's fleet consisted, according to our accounts, of twenty-eight; according to their own, of no more than twenty-four sail. The English had certainly the wind, and might therefore have avoided fighting, if they had so pleased; but this was by no means agreeable to admiral Herbert's temper: he therefore endeavoured all he could to get into the bay, that he might come to a close engagement; but the French saved him the labour, by bearing down upon him in three divisions, about ten in the morning on the first of May. The fight was pretty warm for about two hours; but then slackened, because a great part of the English fleet could not come up; but they continued firing on both sides till about five in the afternoon, when the French fleet stood into the bay, which put an end to the fight. The English writers ascribe this either to want of courage, or to the admiral's being restrained by his orders; but the French inform us, that he retired in order to take care of the ships under his convoy; and that after they had entirely debarked the supply they had brought, he disposed every thing in order to put to sea the next morning, which he did. This is the battle in Bantry Bay, which though inconsiderable enough in itself, (since the English, who had certainly the worst of it, lost only one captain, one lieutenant, and ninety-four men) is yet magnified by some writers into a mighty action.

After the action, admiral Herbert bore away for the Scilly islands, and having cruised there for some time, returned to Spithead; upon which occasion, king William went down in person to Portsmouth, where,

where, to shew he would distinguish and reward merit, though not pointed out to him by success, he declared admiral Herbert earl of Torrington, and knighted captain John Ashby of the Defiance, and captain Cloudesly Shovel of the Edgar; giving, at the same time, a bounty of ten shillings to each seaman, and making a provision for Mrs. Ailmer, relict of captain Ailmer, and for the rest of the widows of such as had been killed in the action. This was perfectly well judged by that prince, and was indeed an act of his own, flowing from the thorough knowlege he had of mankind, and the necessity there is of keeping up the spirits of the seamen, if we expect they should perform great things.

When king James landed in Ireland, his affairs had certainly a very promising aspect on that side. He brought with him a very considerable supply, and he found there an army of 40,000 men compleat. There were but two places in the north that held out against him, viz. London-Derry and Inniskilling. Of these he determined to make himself master; and might have easily done it, if he had been well advised: but, as bishop Burnet justly observes, there was a kind of fatality that hung on his councils.

Commodore Rooke, who had been sent with a squadron in the month of May to the coast of Ireland, performed all that could be expected from him there, by keeping king James and his army from having any intercourse with the Scots; and on the eighth of June, he failed in with the Bonaventure, Swallow, Dartmouth, and a fleet of transport-ships, under the command of major-general Kirke, who was come with his force to relieve London-Derry. When they came to examine the method taken by the enemy to prevent their relieving the place, they found they had laid a boom cross the river, composed of chains and cables, and floated with timber, there being strong redoubts at each end, well provided with cannon. Major-general Kirke having properly disposed

the

the men of war, on the 30th of July, sent the Mountjoy of Derry, captain Browning, and the Phœnix of Colrain, captain Douglas, both deeply laden with provisions, under the convoy of the Dartmouth frigate, to attempt breaking the boom. The Irish army made a prodigious fire upon these ships as they passed, which was very briskly returned, 'till the Mountjoy struck against the boom, and broke it, and was by the rebound run ashore; upon this, the Irish gave a loud huzza, made a terrible fire upon her, and with their boats attempted to board her: but the sailors firing a broadside, the shock loosened her so, that they floated again, and passed the boom, as did the Phœnix also, under cover of the Dartmouth's fire. This seasonable supply saved the remains of that brave garrison, which, after a hundred and five days close siege, and being reduced from seven thousand five hundred, to four thousand three hundred, had subsistence for only two days left, the enemy raising the siege on the last of July.

The naval transactions of 1690, will commence properly with an account of admiral Ruffel's sailing into the Mediterranean, though this is, generally speaking, accounted a transaction of the former year; but the reason for placing it here, is the fleet's not putting to sea 'till the spring, though orders were given for it in the preceding winter. His catholic majesty, Charles II. having espoused a princess of the house of Neubourg, sister to the reigning empress, and to the queen of Portugal, demanded an English fleet to conduct her safely to his dominions, which was readily granted; and indeed such a compliment never had been refused even to the states in war with us, because it was always taken as a tacit confession of our dominion at sea. On the 24th of November, admiral Ruffel sailed with seven large men of war, and two yatchts, to Flushing, in order to receive her catholic majesty, and her attendants; and had orders, as soon as the queen came on board, to hoist the

union

union flag at the main-top-maft head, and to wear it there as long as her majefty was on board. The admiral had orders to put to fea with the firft fair wind, and was inftructed to block up the harbour of Toulon, in order to prevent the French fquadron there from coming out. He failed, after fome delays for want of a fair wind, on the 7th of February, with a ftout fquadron of thirty men of war, under his command, and a fleet of four hundred merchantmen, bound for the Streights; and after a very tempeftuous paffage, landed her catholic majefty, on the 16th, at the Groyne. From thence he failed to execute his other commiffion; which having effected, and having left vice-admiral Killegrew, with the Mediterranean fquadron, behind him; bore away with the firft fair wind for England.

Vice-admiral Killegrew arrived at Cadiz on the 8th of April, where having, according to his inftructions, taken all poffible care of the trade, and having been joined by two Dutch men of war, the Guelderland and Zurickzee, he was next to proceed from thence in order to attend the motions of the Toulon fquadron. In this, however, he met with no fmall difficulty, by reafon of the ftormy weather, which injured feveral fhips of his fquadron extreamly; and the two Dutch fhips, one of 72, and the other of 62 guns, after lofing all their mafts, except a mizen, foundered. In repairing thefe unlucky accidents, a great deal of time was wafted; and, when he afterward got fight of the French fhips, they ftretched away, and being cleaner fhips, would not let our fquadron come up with them: on which our admiral gave over the chace.

The French had been very induftrious this year, in fending a large fleet to fea, early in the feafon; for on the 1ft or 2d of March, they embarked a great fupply for Ireland, under the convoy of a fquadron of 36 men of war, attended by four fire-fhips, and five flutes, which were afterward joined by another fquadron from Provence, with feveral tranfports; fo that

that in all, they convoyed over 6000 men, befide ammunition and money. On the 8th of April, they left the coafts of that ifland, in order to return into the road of Breft; which they did fafely on the 23d, and then prepared to join their grand fleet, which had orders to affemble under the command of the count de Tourville.

While the French were thus employed, our councils were chiefly bent in fending over a royal army, to be commanded by king William in perfon, to Ireland. This great defign was brought to bear about the beginning of the month of June; when his majefty left London, and embarked his forces on board 288 tranfports on the 11th, efcorted by a fquadron of fix men of war, under Sir Cloudefly Shovel: he failed for Carrickfergus, where he fafely arrived on the 14th of the fame month, and foon after difmiffed rear-admiral Shovel, with the Plymouth fquadron, with orders to join the grand fleet; which he could not do, till it was too late.

There was nothing better underftood in England, than the abfolute neceffity of affembling early in the year, a ftrong fleet in the channel. The nation's fafety depended on this meafure, fince the king, and the greateft part of his forces were abroad. Yet, for all this, our maritime proceedings were very flow, for which, various, and fome fcarcely credible caufes are affigned. On the other hand, it was late before the Dutch fent their fleet to fea; and the Englifh, knowing that nothing of confequence could be done, till after their junction, were the lefs folicitous about putting themfelves in order, till they heard of their being at fea.

The conduct of the French, in the mean time, was of quite another kind; for while the fquadron before mentioned was gone to Ireland, orders were given for equipping a fleet of fixty fail at Breft, which was to put to fea by the end of May: and though they were forced by contrary winds, to put back again, yet on the

the 12th of June, they put to sea in three squadrons, each squadron being divided into three divisions: in all there were 78 men of war, 22 fire-ships, and the whole fleet carried upward of 4700 pieces of cannon, under admiral Tourville. On the 13th of June, they steered for the English coast, and the 20th found themselves off the Lizard. The next day the admiral took some English fishing-boats, and after having paid the people who were on board for their fish, he set them at liberty again; and these were the men, such was our supineness! that first brought advice of the arrival of the French fleet on our coast.

The earl of Torrington was at St. Helen's, when he received this news, which must have surprized him very much, since he was so far from expecting any advice of this kind, that he had no scouts to the westward. He put to sea, however, with such ships as he had, and stood to the south-east, on Midsummer-day, leaving his orders, that all the English and Dutch ships which could have notice, should follow him. His whole strength, when collected, consisted of about 34 men of war of several sizes; and the three Dutch admirals had under their command 22 large ships. We need not wonder, therefore, that seeing himself out-numbered by above twenty sail, he was not willing to risk his own honour, and the nation's safety, upon such unequal terms. But the queen, who was then regent, having been informed, that her father's adherents intended a general insurrection; and that if the French fleet continued longer on the coast, this would certainly take effect; by advice of the privy-council, sent him orders to fight at all events, in order to force the French fleet to withdraw. In obedience to this order, as soon as it was light, on the 30th of June, the admiral threw out the signal for drawing into a line, and bore down upon the enemy, while they were under sail.

The signal for a battle was made about eight, when the French braced their head sails to their masts, in order

order to lie by. The action began about nine, when the Dutch squadron, which made the van of the united fleets, fell in with the van of the French, and put them into some disorder. About half an hour after, our Blue squadron engaged their rear very warmly; but the Red, commanded by the earl of Torrington in person, which made the center of our fleet, could not come up till about ten: so that the Dutch were almost surrounded by the enemy. The admiral seeing their distress, drove between them and the enemy; and in that situation, anchored about five in the afternoon, when it grew calm: but discerning how much the Dutch had suffered, and how little probability there was of regaining any thing by renewing the fight, he weighed about nine at night, and retired eastward with the tide of flood.

The next day it was resolved in a council of war, held in the afternoon, to preserve the fleet, by retreating; and rather to destroy the disabled ships, if they should be pressed by the enemy, than to hazard another engagement, by endeavouring to protect them. This resolution was executed with as much success as could be expected; which, however, was chiefly owing to want of experience in the French admirals: for by not anchoring when the English did, they were driven to a great distance, and by continuing to chace in a line of battle, instead of leaving every ship at liberty to do her utmost, they could never recover what they lost by their first mistake.

As soon as the earl of Torrington came to town, he was examined before the council; where he justified himself with great presence of mind. The council, however, thought proper to commit his lordship to the Tower; and that they might lessen the clamours of the crowd, and give some satisfaction to the Dutch, they directed a committee to repair to Sheerness, where they were to make a thorough enquiry into the real causes of this disaster.

After

After raising the siege of Limerick, king William returned into England; where, in a council held on the affairs of Ireland, which were still in a very precarious condition, many of the great cities, and most of the convenient ports being still held for king James, the earl of Marlborough proposed a plan for the immediate reduction of that island. He observed first, that our fleet was now at sea, and that of the French returned to Brest; in which situation, therefore, there was nothing to be feared in relation to descents. He farther remarked, that there were at least 5000 land forces lying idle in England, which might be embarked on board the fleet, even in this late season of the year, and land time enough to perform considerable service. The king readily accepted this offer, gave the command of the troops to the earl of Marlborough, and sent orders to the admirals to send the great ships about to Chatham, and to take on board the remainder of the fleet, the forces ordered for this service.

The admirals hoisted their flag on board the Kent, a third rate; and having embarked the troops with all imaginable expedition, arrived with them before the harbour of Cork, on the 21st of September, in the afternoon. On the 23d, the forces were landed, and joined a body of between 3 and 4000 men, under the command of the duke of Wirtemberg; who, by an ill-timed dispute about the command, had like to have ruined the whole expedition. The city of Cork was very well fortified, and had in it a body of 4000 men: but the earl of Marlborough having observed that the place was commanded by an adjacent hill, he ordered a battery to be erected there on the 24th; and after playing on the town for a few hours, made so considerable a breach, that on the 25th the generals resolved to attack it. The besieged were so terrified at this, that the Irish instantly capitulated. The reduction of Kingsale followed soon after.

The

The fleet arrived in the Downs on the 8th of October, bringing over with them, by the earl of Marlborough's defire, the governor of Cork, and feveral perfons of quality, who were made prifoners when that city was taken. There the admirals received orders to divide their fleet into fmall fquadrons for feveral fervices, and leave only a ftrong fquadron in the Downs, under the command of Sir Cloudefly Shovel, who cruifed the remaining part of the year in the Soundings, without any fuccefs remarkable enough to deferve notice.

The care of the adminiftration to repair all paft errors in naval affairs, and to retrieve the honour of the maritime powers, appeared vifibly in the meafures taken for fending a great fleet early to fea, in the fpring of the year 1691. In order to this, after the earl of Torrington was difmiffed from his command, Edward Ruffel, Efq; was appointed admiral and commander in chief, and immediately received inftructions to ufe the utmoft expedition in drawing together the fhips of which his fleet was to be compofed; and a lift of them, to the number of 91, of which 57 were of the line of battle, was annexed to his inftructions. He executed thefe directions with the utmoft fkill and diligence, and by the 7th of May was ready to put to fea. His orders were to proceed in the Soundings, as foon as he fhould be joined by the Dutch; and he was likewife directed to take care to block up the port of Dunkirk, in order to prevent the French privateers from difturbing our trade. Thefe directions, however, were but indifferently executed; which our writers attribute to the flownefs of the Dutch in fending their fhips to join the confederate fleet, which they had ftipulated to do by the beginning of May. It is certain, that notwithftanding all his fkill and care, admiral Ruffel found his fleet but indifferently manned, and fcantily victualled; at the fame time that he was fo perplexed by his orders,

orders, and with the difficulties ſtarted upon every occaſion by the Dutch admiral, who very probably was as much cramped by his; that a great part of the months of May and June were ſpent to very little purpoſe: and though the French fleet was not in ſuch forwardneſs this year as it had been the laſt, yet it was at ſea ſome time before ours had any intelligence of it.

Lewis XIV. ſeemed at this time to ſhew a ſingular vanity in maintaining a prodigious naval force, to make all Europe ſee how ſoon, and how effectually, his councils had been able to create a maritime power. He had at this time to deal with the Engliſh, Spaniards, and Dutch; and as he was now in the zenith of his glory, he exhauſted his treaſures, in order, had it been poſſible, to render himſelf maſter at ſea. He appointed the count d'Eſtrees, vice-admiral of France, to command in the Mediterranean a fleet conſiſting of four large men of war, 5 frigates, 26 gallies, and three bomb-veſſels: and, on the other hand, count Tourville was directed to aſſemble the grand fleet intended for the ocean. This fleet, though very conſiderable, and excellently provided with every thing neceſſary, yet was inferior in force to that of the confederates; and therefore count Tourville was inſtructed to avoid an engagement as much as poſſible, and to amuſe the enemy, by keeping as long as might be in the channel. It muſt be obſerved alſo, that a ſquadron had been ſent, under the command of the marquis de Neſmonde, to carry ſupplies of all ſorts for the relief of king James's army in Ireland.

The Smyrna fleet was expected home this ſpring; and as the Engliſh and Dutch had a joint concern therein; to the amount of upward of four millions ſterling, both nations were extreamly apprehenſive of its being attacked by the French. Preciſe orders were therefore ſent to admiral Ruſſel, to uſe his utmoſt care for its preſervation: this he performed with equal induſtry and ſucceſs; and then ſteered his courſe for the coaſt of France.

Arriving in this station, Sir Cloudesley Shovel was sent to look into Brest, where he saw about forty sail coming out of that port; which proved to be a fleet of merchant-ships from Bretagne, escorted by three men of war. Sir Cloudesley, to decoy these ships into his hands, made use of an excellent stratagem: he knew the French had intelligence that a small squadron of their fleet had made prizes of several English merchantmen; laying hold, therefore, of this piece of false news, he ordered part of his squadron to put out French colours, and the rest to take in theirs. By this method he thought to deceive the French, who might naturally suppose it that squadron with their prizes. This succeeded in part; but the enemy discovered the cheat before he was near enough to do much mischief.

About the latter end of July, admiral Russel fell in with a convoy going to the French fleet with fresh provisions; some of these were taken, and from them he learnt that count Tourville had orders to avoid fighting, which he very punctually obeyed, keeping scouts at a considerable distance on all points of the compass by which he could be approached, and these being chased by ours, they immediately ran, making signals to others, that lay within them; so that it was impossible to come up with the body of their fleet.

Being sensible of the dangers that might attend this situation, the admiral wrote home for fresh orders, which he received; but found them so perplexed, that having intelligence of the French fleet's being gone into Brest, he, in the beginning of August, pursuant to the resolution of a council of war, returned to Torbay, from whence he wrote up to court to have his last orders explained. In return he was directed to put to sea again, which he did; and notwithstanding his frequent representations of the inconvenience of having such large ships exposed to the rough weather, which usually happens about the equinox; he was obliged to continue in the Soundings to the 2d of Sep-

September, when he met with such a violent storm, that after doing all that could be done for the preservation of the fleet, it sustained considerable damage, the Coronation, a second rate, and the Harwich, a third rate, being lost.

The whole nation were now convinced, that with respect to our honour and interest in this war, the management of affairs at sea was chiefly to be regarded; and yet, by an unaccountable series of wrong councils, the management of these affairs was worse conducted than any other. The absolute reduction of Ireland, and the war in Flanders, seemed to occupy the king's thoughts entirely; and the care of the navy was left wholly to the board of admiralty, who, to speak in the softest terms, did not manage it much to the satisfaction of the nation. There were, beside, some other things which contributed to hurt our maritime proceedings. A faction was grown up in the fleet against the admiral, and at the same time the government entertained a great jealousy of many of the officers; though to this hour it remains a secret, whether it was, or was not, well founded. The truth appears to be, that king James was better known to the officers of the fleet, than to any other set of men in England; most of them had served under him when lord high-admiral, and many had been preferred by him; which rendered it highly probable, they might have an esteem for his person: but that any of these officers intended to act in his favour, in conjunction with a French force, against their country, is very unlikely: especially if we consider the unanimity with which they went into the revolution, which had been openly acknowleged, and they solemnly thanked for it by the convention. However it was, this is certain, that in parliament, at court, and in the navy, nothing was heard of but jealousies, ill conduct, and want of sufficient supplies for the service; a kind of discourse that lasted all the winter, and which answered very bad purposes.

In the spring of the year 1692, a little before the king went to Holland, he began to communicate his intentions, as to the employment of the fleet, to admiral Ruffel, who, however, was very far from standing in high favour: but his character, as an officer, and his known steadiness in revolution-principles, supported him; and the king resolved to confide the fleet to his care.

When Lewis XIV. perceived, that it was impossible to support the war in Ireland any longer to advantage, he came to a resolution of employing the forces that were still left king James, to serve his purpose another way. With this view he concerted with the malecontents in England, an invasion on the coast of Suffex; and though for this design it was necessary to draw together a great number of transports, as well as a very considerable body of forces, yet he had both in readiness, before it was so much as suspected here. In short, nothing was wanting to the execution of this design in the beginning of April, but the arrival of count d'Estrees's squadron of 12 men of war, which was to escort the embarkation; while the count de Tourville cruized in the channel with the grand fleet, which was also ready to put to sea, but was detained by contrary winds. Things being in this situation, king James sent over some agents to give his friends intelligence of his motions; and some of these people, in hopes of reward, gave the first clear account of the whole design to the government at home: upon which, order after order was sent to admiral Ruffel to hasten out to sea, in whatever condition the fleet might be at this time.

King William, as soon as he arrived in Holland, took care to hasten the naval preparations with unusual diligence; so that the fleet was ready to put to sea much sooner than had been expected. As for our admiral, he went on board in the beginning of May; and observing how great advantage the French might reap by the division of our fleet, his first care was to

write

write to court to defire, that a certain place might be fixed for their conjunction. In return to this, he had orders fent him to cruize between Cape la Hogue and the Ifle of Wight, till the fquadrons fhould join with him, though he had propofed the junction fhould be made off Beachy-head. However, he obeyed his orders as foon as he received them, and plyed it down through the fands, with a very fcanty wind, contrary to the opinion of many of his officers, and all the pilots, who were againft hazarding fo great a fleet in fo dangerous an attempt; and yet to this bold ftroke of the admiral's, was owing all his following fuccefs.

On the 11th day of May, Ruffel failed from Rye to St. Helen's, where he was joined by the Englifh fquadrons under Delaval and Carter; and by the Dutch fquadrons, commanded by Allemonde, Callembergh, and Vandergoes. He fet fail for the coaft of France on the 18th day of May, with a fleet of 99 fhips of the line, befide frigates and fire-fhips.

Next day, about three o'clock in the morning, he difcovered the enemy, under the count de Tourville, and threw out the fignal for the line of battle, which by eight o'clock was formed in good order, the Dutch in the van, the blue divifion in the rear, and the red in the center. The French fleet did not exceed 63 fhips of the line, and as they were to windward, Tourville might have avoided an engagement; but, he had received a pofitive order to fight, on the fuppofition that the Dutch and Englifh fquadrons had not joined. Tourville, therefore, bore down along-fide of Ruffel's own fhip, which he engaged at a very fmall diftance. He fought him with great fury till one o'clock, when his rigging and fails being confiderably damaged, his fhip, the Rifing Sun, that carried 104 cannon, was towed out of the line in great diforder. Neverthelefs, the engagement continued till three, when the fleets were parted by a thick fog. When this abated, the enemy were defcried flying to the northward; and Ruffel made the fignal for chafing. Part of the blue fquadron came up with the enemy about eight in the evening, and engaged them half an hour, during which admiral Carter was mortally wounded. At length, the French bore away for Conquet-Road, having loft four fhips in this day's action. Next day, about eight in the morning, they were difcovered crowding away to the weftward, and the combined fleets chafed with all the fail they could carry, until Ruffel's foretop-maft came by the board. Though he was retarded by this accident, they ftill continued the purfuit, and he anchored near Cape la Hogue. On the 22d of the month, about feven in the morning, part of the French fleet was perceived near the Race of Alderney, fome at anchor, and fome driving to the eaftward with the tide of flood. He, and the fhips neareft him, immediately flipt their cables and chafed. The Rifing-Sun, having loft her mafts, ran afhore near Cherbourg, where fhe was burned by Sir Ralph Delaval, together with the Admirable, another firft rate, and the Conquerant of eighty guns. Eighteen other fhips of their fleet ran into La Hogue, where they were attacked by Sir George Rooke, who deftroyed them, and a great number of tranfports loaded with ammunition, in the midft of a terrible fire from the enemy, and in fight of the Irifh camp. Sir John Afhby, with his own fquadron and fome Dutch fhips, purfued the reft of the French fleet, which efcaped through the Race of Alderney, by fuch a dangerous paffage as the Englifh could not attempt, without expofing their fhips to the moft imminent hazard.

This was a very mortifying defeat to the French king, who had been fo long flattered with an uninterrupted feries of victories: and reduced James to the loweft ebb of defpondence, as it fruftrated the whole fcheme of his embarkation, and overwhelmed his friends in England with grief and defpair. Some hiftorians allege, that Ruffel did not improve his
.victory

victory with all advantages that might have been obtained before the enemy recovered of their confternation. But this is a malicious imputation; and a very ungrateful return for his manifold services to the nation. He acted in this whole expedition with the genuine spirit of a British admiral: and, in a word, obtained such a decisive victory, that during the remaining part of the war, the French would not hazard another battle by sea with the English.

Ruffel having ordered Sir John Ashby, and the Dutch admiral Callembergh, to steer toward Havre de Grace, and endeavour to destroy the remainder of the French fleet, failed back to St. Helen's, that the damaged ships might be refitted, and the fleet furnished with fresh supplies of provision and ammunition: but, his principal motive was to take on board a number of troops provided for a descent upon France, which had been projected by England and Holland, with a view to alarm and distract the enemy in their own dominions. In the latter end of July, 7000 men, commanded by the duke of Leinster, embarked on board of transports, to be landed at St. Maloe's, Brest, or Rochfort; and the nation conceived the most sanguine hopes of this expedition. A council of war, consisting of land and sea-officers, being held on board the Breda, to deliberate upon the scheme of the ministry, the members unanimously agreed, that the season was too far advanced to put it in execution.

Nothing could be more inglorious for the English than their operations by sea in the course of the summer 1693. The king had ordered the admirals to use all possible dispatch in equipping the fleets, that they might block up the enemy in their own ports, and protect the commerce, which had suffered severely from the French privateers. They were, however, so dilatory in their proceedings, that the squadrons of the enemy failed from their harbours before the English fleet could put to sea. About the

the middle of May it was affembled at St. Helen's, and took on board five regiments, intended for a defcent on Breft; but this enterprize was never attempted. When the Englifh and Dutch fquadrons joined, fo as to form a very numerous fleet, the public expected they would undertake fome expedition of importance; but the admirals were divided in their opinion, nor did their orders warrant their executing any fcheme of confequence. Killigrew and Delaval did not efcape the fufpicion of being difaffected to the fervice; and France was faid to have maintained a fecret correfpondence with the malecontents in England. Lewis had made furprifing efforts to repair the damage which his navy had fuftained. He had purchafed feveral large veffels, and converted them into fhips of war; he had laid an embargo on all the fhipping of his kingdom, until his fquadrons were manned: he had made a grand naval promotion, to encourage the officers and feamen; and this expedient produced a wonderful fpirit of activity and emulation. In the month of May his fleet failed to the Mediterranean, in three fquadrons, confifting of 71 capital fhips, befide bomb-ketches, fire-fhips, and tenders.

In the beginning of June, the Englifh and Dutch fleets failed down the channel. On the 6th, Sir George Rooke was detached to the Streights, with a fquadron of 23 fhips, as convoy to the Mediterranean trade. The great fleet returned to Torbay, while he purfued his voyage, having under his protection about 400 merchant fhips belonging to England, Holland, Denmark, Sweden, Hamburgh, and Flanders. On the 16th, his fcouts difcovered part of the French fleet under Cape St. Vincent: next day their whole navy appeared, to the amount of 80 fail. Rooke avoided engaging them, which he thought could only tend to their ruin; he directed the veffels neareft land to put into the firft Spanifh ports, while he ftood off with the remainder; however a great number fell into the enemy's hands. The value of the lofs fuftained on this occasion amounted to one million sterling. Mean while Rooke stood off with a fresh gale, and on the 19th sent home the Lark ship of war, with the news of his misfortune; then he bore away for the Madeiras, where having taken in wood and water, he set sail for Ireland; and in pursuance of orders, he joined the great fleet then cruising in the chops of the channel. On the 25th day of August, they returned to St. Helen's, and the four regiments were landed.

The French admirals, instead of pursuing Rooke to Madeira, made an unsuccessful attempt upon Cadiz, and bombarded Gibraltar, where the merchants sunk their ships, that they might not fall into the hands of the enemy. Then they sailed along the coast of Spain, destroyed some English and Dutch vessels at Malaga, Alicant, and other places; and returned in triumph to Toulon. About this period, Sir Francis Wheeler returned to England with his squadron, from an unfortunate expedition in the West Indies. In conjunction with colonel Codrington, governor of the Leeward islands, he made unsuccessful attempts upon the islands of Martinique and Dominique. Then he sailed to Boston in New England, with a view to concert an expedition against Quebec, which was judged impracticable. He afterward steered for Placentia in Newfoundland, which he would have attacked without hesitation; but the design was rejected by a majority of voices in the council of war. Thus disappointed, he set sail for England; and arrived at Portsmouth in a very shattered condition.

In November another effort was made to annoy the enemy. Commodore Benbow sailed with a squadron of 12 capital ships, four bomb-ketches, and ten brigantines, to the coast of St. Malo; and anchoring within half a mile of the town, cannonaded and bombarded it for three days successively. Then they landed on an island, where they burnt a convent. On the 19th, they took the advantage of a dark night,

night, a fresh gale, and a strong tide, to send in a fire-ship, of a particular contrivance, stiled the Infernal, in order to burn the town; but, she struck upon a rock before she arrived at the place, and the engineer was obliged to set her on fire, and retreat. She continued burning for some time, and at last blew up, with such an explosion as shook the whole town like an earthquake, unroofed 300 houses, and broke all the glass and earthen ware for three leagues round. A capstan, that weighed 200 pounds, was transported into the place, and falling upon a house, levelled it to the ground; the greatest part of the wall toward the sea tumbled down; and the inhabitants were overwhelmed with consternation: so that a small number of troops might have taken possession without resistance; but there was not a soldier on board. Nevertheless, the sailors did considerable damage to the town of St. Malo, which had been a nest of privateers that infested the English commerce. Though this attempt was executed with great spirit, and some success, the clamours of the people became louder and louder. But if the English were discontented, the French were miserable, in spite of all their victories. That kingdom laboured under a dreadful famine, occasioned partly from unfavourable seasons, and partly from the war, which had not left hands sufficient to cultivate the ground. Notwithstanding all the diligence and providence of their ministry, in bringing supplies of corn from Sweden and Denmark, their care in regulating the price, and furnishing the markets, their liberal contributions for the relief of the indigent; multitudes perished of want, and the whole kingdom was reduced to poverty and distress. Lewis pined in the midst of his success. He saw his subjects exhausted by a ruinous war, in which they had been involved by his ambition. He tampered with the allies apart, in hope of dividing and detaching them from the grand confederacy: he solicited the northern crowns to engage as mediators

OF KING WILLIAM III.   347

for a general peace. A memorial was actually prefented by the Danifh minifter to king William, by which it appears, that the French king would have been contented to purchafe a peace with fome confiderable conceffions. But the terms were rejected by the king of England, whofe ambition and revenge were not yet gratified; and whofe fubjects, though heavy laden, could ftill bear additional burdens.

King William having received intelligence of the defign of the French upon Barcelona, endeavoured to prevent the junction of the Breft and Toulon fquadrons, by fending Ruffel to fea as early as the fleet could be in a condition to fail : but before he arrived at Portfmouth, the Breft fquadron had quitted that harbour. And a body of land-forces, intended for a defcent upon the coaft of France, under the command of general Tollemache, failed on the 29th of May, 1694, but effected nothing, and loft their general.

After this unfortunate attempt, lord Berkeley, with the advice of a council of war, failed back for England; and at St. Helen's received orders from the queen to call a council, and deliberate in what manner the fhips and forces might be beft employed. They agreed to make fome attempt upon the coaft of Normandy. With this view they fet fail on the 5th day of July. They bombarded Dieppe, and Havre de Grace; and haraffed the French troops, who marched after them along-fhore. They alarmed the whole coaft, and filled every town with fuch confternation, that they would have been abandoned by the inhabitants, had not they been detained by military force.

During thefe tranfactions, admiral Ruffel with the grand fleet failed for the Mediterranean; and being joined by rear-admiral Neville from Cadiz, together with Callembergh and Evertzen, he fteered toward Barcelona, which was befieged by the French fleet and army. At his approach, Tourville retired with precipitation into the harbour of Toulon; and Noailles

aban-

abandoned his enterprize. The Spanish affairs were in such a deplorable condition, that without this timely assistance, the kingdom must have been undone. While he continued in the Mediterranean, the French admiral durst not venture to appear at sea; and all his projects were disconcerted. After having asserted the honour of the British flag in those seas during the whole summer, he sailed in the beginning of November to Cadiz, where, by an express order of the king, he passed the winter; during which he took such precautions for preventing Tourville from passing the Streights, that he did not think proper to risque the passage.

While admiral Russel asserted the British dominion in the Mediterranean-sea, the French coasts were again insulted in the channel by a separate fleet, under the command of lord Berkeley, of Straton, assisted by the Dutch admiral Allemonde. On the fourth day of July, 1695, they anchored before St. Malos, which they bombarded from nine ketches covered by some frigates, which sustained more damage than was done to the enemy. On the 6th, Granville underwent the same fate; and then the fleet returned to Portsmouth. The bomb-vessels being refitted, the fleet sailed round to the Downs, where 400 soldiers were embarked for an attempt upon Dunkirk, under the direction of Meesters, the famous Dutch engineer: but to no effect, owing to the ill understanding between the Dutch engineer and the English officers.

A squadron had been sent to the West Indies, under the joint command of captain Robert Wilmot and colonel Lilingston, with 1200 land-forces. They had instructions to co-operate with the Spaniards in Hispaniola, against the French settlements on that island, and to destroy their fisheries on the banks of Newfoundland, in their return. They were accordingly joined by 1700 Spaniards, raised by the president of St. Domingo; but, instead of proceeding against

against Petit-Guavas, according to the directions they had received, Wilmot took poſſeſſion of Fort-Francois, and plundered the country for his own private advantage, notwithſtanding the remonſtrances of Lilingſton.

Notwithſtanding the great efforts the nation had made to maintain ſuch a number of different ſquadrons for the protection of commerce, as well as to annoy the enemy, the trade ſuffered ſeverely from the French privateers, which ſwarmed in both channels, and made prize of many rich veſſels. The marquis of Carmarthen being ſtationed with a ſquadron off the Scilly iſlands, miſtook a fleet of merchant-ſhips for the Breſt fleet, and retired with precipitation to Milford-Haven. In conſequence of this retreat, the privateers took a good number of ſhips from Barbadoes, and five from the Eaſt Indies, valued at a million ſterling. The merchants renewed their clamour againſt the commiſſioners of the admiralty, who produced their orders and inſtructions in their own defence. The marquis of Carmaerthen had been guilty of a flagrant miſconduct on this occaſion; but the chief ſource of thoſe national calamities was the circumſtantial intelligence tranſmitted to France from time to time, by the malcontents of England: for, they were actuated by a ſcandalous principle, which they ſtill retain, namely, that of rejoicing in the diſtreſs of their country.

Toward the end of the year 1696, the nation was again alarmed with the report of an invaſion. It was known that the French were fitting out a ſtrong ſquadron at Breſt; and for what ſervice, the intelligence our ſecretaries had, could not inform them. Sir Cloudeſley Shovel, therefore, was ſent with a conſiderable force to block them up, which however the French avoided; and it was then given out at home, that our vigilance had diſappointed the deſigns of the enemy. In this we only deceived ourſelves; for our merchants quickly came at the knowlege of the true

ſcheme,

scheme, which was the sending a strong squadron into the West Indies, to attack some of the Spanish plantations in those parts. The Sieur Pointis was the person who formed the plan of this undertaking, and who had been no less than three years in bringing it to bear.

The Spaniards were not a little inflamed by the success of Pointis in America, where he took Carthagene, in which he found a booty amounting to eight millions of crowns. Having ruined the fortifications of the place, and received advice that an English squadron, under admiral Nevil, had arrived in the West Indies, with a design to attack him in his return, he bore away for the streights of Bahama. On the 22d day of May, he fell in with the English fleet, and one of his fly-boats was taken; but, such was his dexterity, or good fortune, that he escaped, after having been pursued five days. After some other disappointments, Neville sailed through the gulph of Florida to Virginia, where he died of chagrin; and the command of the fleet devolved to captain Dilkes, who arrived in England on the 24th day of October, with a shattered squadron half manned, to the unspeakable mortification of the people; who flattered themselves with the hopes of wealth and glory from this expedition. Certain it is, the service was greatly obstructed by the faction among the officers, which with respect to the nation had all the effects of treachery and misconduct.

Our limits will not admit our entering into the detail of any naval transactions but those which either in themselves or in their consequences were of importance: and by this time the commerce and maritime strength of the kingdom, were so far advanced, as to render our transactions at sea very numerous and of great influence to our proceedings by land. On so precarious an element, many fleets are fitted out which return without effecting any thing; many such we must occasionally overlook, that we may not omit others that merit special notice. Peace was concluded between England, Spain, and Holland, on the one side, and the crown of France on the other, at Ryswick, on September 10th, 1697, by which the French king acknowleged king William's title, and, as the French historians say, gave up more towns than the confederates could have taken in twenty years: but this was not from any principle either of justice or moderation, but with views of quite another sort, as was foreseen then, and in the space of a few years fully appeared.

We have now brought this long war to a conclusion, and it is but just that we should offer the reader some reflections on the consequences of it, to the naval power and commerce of England. First then, with respect to our navy, we have seen that the war opened with a very bad prospect; for though we had an excellent fleet, a vast number of able seamen, and, perhaps, as good officers as any in the world, yet the French got earlier to sea than we did, appeared with a greater force, and managed it better, though we acted then in conjunction with Holland, and according to the general rule of political reasoning, ought to have had it in our power to have driven the French out of the sea.

All this proceeded from the sudden change in our government, which, perhaps, left many of our officers disaffected, and many more without having any proper degree of credit at court. Want of confidence between the administration and the commanders of our fleets, is always destructive to our maritime power; and therefore, instead of wondering that things went on so ill, we may with more justice be surprised, that they went no worse. Our party-divisions not only enervated our own strength, but created such jealousies between us and the Dutch, as blasted the fruits that must have been otherwise produced by this close and fortunate union of the maritime powers.

But

But when once the government was thoroughly settled, and we acted cordially in conjunction with the States, it soon became evident, that we were much more than a match for France at sea: and on the whole, the French suffered much more in their maritime power than we: consequently, if we consider the situation of both nations, the ease with which it was in our power to repair our losses, and the almost insuperable difficulties the French had to struggle with in this respect, we must conclude, that not only they, but the whole world had full evidence from thence, of their being no way able to struggle against the Dutch and us in a maritime war. To make this still more apparent, king William, in his speech to both houses of parliament, at the conclusion of the war, asserted our naval force to be near double what it was at his accession.

It will now be necessary to take a retrospective view of some past affairs, in order to preserve a connexion with others to come. The revolution brought back to Scotland several worthy patriots, whom the jealousy of former reigns had driven into other countries. These, from the time of their return, thought of nothing so much as the putting of the trade of Scotland, which had been hitherto in a manner totally neglected, on a proper footing. With this view they procured, in 1693, an act of the Scots parliament, for the encouragement of foreign commerce; and in consequence of that law, another in 1695, for setting up an East India company. When this was done, it was found requisite to take in subscriptions: and, as it was not easy to find money enough in Scotland, for the carrying on so expensive a design, the company's agents endeavoured to procure subscriptions abroad, particularly at London, Hamburgh, and Amsterdam, in which they were certainly sufficiently supported both by the royal and legislative authority.

But this scheme, as might be foreseen, gave great umbrage to the East India companies in England and Holland,

OF KING WILLIAM III. 353

Holland, and they took the beft meafures they could to hinder the fuccefs of thefe applications. This, however, had fome very untoward confequences, fince thefe companies could effect nothing but by the interpofition of their refpective governments; and by this means his majefty's name, as king of England and ftadtholder of Holland, came to be made ufe of, to thwart thefe defigns which actually had his fanction as king of Scotland.

In the enfuing feffion of parliament in 1698, the government found itfelf not a little embarraffed with the affairs of the Englifh Eaft India company. A fcheme had been offered for erecting a new company, which was to advance two millions for the public fervice at eight per cent. and were to carry on this trade by a joint ftock. To make way for this, it was propofed to diffolve the old company. The pretence for diffolving it, was a claufe in that very charter, referving fuch a power to the crown. But as it was not fo much as afferted, that fince the granting this new charter, they had done any thing that ought to fubject them to a diffolution, by moderate and impartial people, who knew nothing of ftock-jobbing, this was thought not a little hard.

The Eaft India company in Scotland, finding their defigns fo vigoroufly oppofed, and having, as they conceived, very large powers vefted in them by the late act of parliament, refolved to turn their endeavours another way for the prefent, and to attempt the fettlement of a colony in America, on the Ifthmus of Darien. This is that narrow track of country which unites the two continents of North and South America, and confequently muft be very advantageoufly feated for commerce. As the inhabitants had never been conquered by the Spaniards, and, as the new colony fent thither, actually purchafed their lands from the native proprietors, and fettled there by confent, it was apprehended, that the Spaniards had no right to difpute the eftablifhment; and

VOL. VII.   A a   that

that if they did, the planters might defend themselves without involving the nation in a war. But it was soon found, that great miftakes had been made in relation to the confequences expected from it. For the Spaniards not only confidered it as an invafion on their rights, and began to take our fhips upon it; but the Englifh alfo grew very uneafy, and made warm reprefentations to his majefty on this fubject: this produced private orders to the governors of Jamaica, and other neighbouring plantations, not only to avoid all commerce with the Scots at Darien, but even to deny them provifions. As it was forefeen that thefe meafures would naturally occafion great difturbances in that part of the world, it was found requifite to fend a fquadron thither, under admiral Benbow, to protect our trade, to awe the Spaniards, and to hinder the increafe of pirates, which had been very great ever fince the conclufion of the peace; occafioned chiefly by the multitude of privateers that were then thrown out of employment.

In Scotland difputes ran very high on the ruin of the Darien colony. Things were printed on both fides on purpofe to inflame the minds of the people, and many thought that it would at laft have created a breach between the two nations. The coldnefs of the king's temper prevented this; he could not either be heated by the Englifh reprefentations, or blown into a paffion by the hafty refolutions of the Scots parliament. His moderation toward each of them, if it did not bring them both to a good temper, which was indeed never effected in his reign, yet it gave him an opportunity to keep the wifeft people in England and in Scotland, firm to his government, while in the mean time many unforefeen accidents brought about the ruin of the Scots company; fo that the ends of their Englifh adverfaries were anfwered, without their having recourfe to any harfh means.

The death of the king of Spain now changed all the affairs of Europe, and forced us, who had fo lately

lately made a very neceſſary peace, upon a new, expenſive, and dangerous war. It is certain that the king did all he could to avoid it; and that this was the great, if not the ſole foundation of the two famous partition-treaties, which were ſo much exclaimed againſt by thoſe whoſe ſteady oppoſition to a war, had firſt brought the king and his miniſtry to think of them.

When the reſolution was once taken to have recourſe again to arms, in order to preſerve the balance of power, the firſt care was for the fleet, which his majeſty reſolved ſhould be much ſuperior to that of the enemy. Preparatory to this was the new commiſſion of the admiralty in the ſpring of the year 1701, at the head of which was placed the earl of Pembroke, a man univerſally beloved and eſteemed.

The command of the fleet was very judiciouſly beſtowed upon Sir George Rooke, who, on the 2d of July, went on board the Triumph in the Downs, where he hoiſted the flag. He ſoon after ſailed to Spithead, where he was ſpeedily joined by the reſt of the fleet, conſiſting of 48 ſhips of the line, beſide frigates, fire-ſhips, and ſmall veſſels. He had under him ſome of the greateſt ſeamen of the age, viz. Sir Cloudeſley Shovel, Sir Thomas Hopſon, John Benbow, Eſq; and Sir John Munden: he was not long after reinforced by 15 Dutch men of war of the line, beſide frigates and ſmall veſſels, under the command of lieutenant-admiral Allemonde, vice-admiral Vandergoes, and rear-admiral Waeſſenaar.

Toward the latter end of Auguſt he ſailed from Torbay, and the ſecond of September he detached vice-admiral Benbow with a ſtout ſquadron for the Weſt Indies; and as this was the principal buſineſs of the fleet, and indeed a thing in itſelf of the higheſt importance, the admiral detached a ſtrong ſquadron of Engliſh ſhips under the command of Sir John Munden, and ten ſail of Dutch men of war, beſide frigates, under rear-admiral Waeſſenaar, to ſee the

West India squadron well into the sea. The French expected that this fleet would have actually proceeded to the Mediterranean; and it was to confirm them in this belief, we had demanded the free use of the Spanish harbours: but this was only to conceal things, and to gain an opportunity of sending a squadron early to the West Indies, without putting it in the power of the French to procure any exact account of its strength: the admiral, after performing this, cruised according to his instructions for some time, and then returned with the largest ships into the Downs.

After this fleet was sent to sea, his majesty, on the 18th of January, thought proper to revoke his letters patent to the commissioners of the admiralty, and to appoint Thomas earl of Pembroke and Montgomery, lord high admiral of England and Ireland, and of the foreign plantations. The design of this promotion was, to be rid of the disadvantages attending a board: and this end it answered perfectly.

The war was now the great object of attention, as well here as in France, though hitherto it was not declared; and negotiations were still carried on in Holland, as if both parties had inclined to an amicable determination of these differences; which was, in reality, the intention of neither. In the midst of our preparations, however, care was taken of a point which nearly concerned trade, and that was uniting the two East India companies; which was done under an act of arbitration: and this agreement was the foundation of that company which has subsisted with so great credit to themselves, and benefit to the nation, ever since.

King William's extraordinary attention to business is thought to have hastened his death, which happened on the 8th of March, 1701-2, about eight in the morning. He died, as he lived, with great steadiness of mind; and shewed himself in his last moments, as much a hero as he had ever done in the field. Never any prince better understood the general interest of
Europe,

Europe, or purfued it with greater firmnefs; and whatever unlucky accidents fell out in his reign to the prejudice of our affairs, were not fo much owing to any miftakes in his conduct, as to the circumftances of the times, and our own unfortunate divifions.

Queen Anne afcended the throne on the eighth of March, 1702, in the flower of her age, being then about thirty-eight. She had fhewn a very juft moderation in her conduct from the time of the revolution, and knew how to temper her relation to the ftate, with that which fhe bore to her family; of which fhe gave a remarkable inftance in the latter part of her life, by procuring the ifland of Sicily for her coufin the duke of Savoy: and fhe opened her reign by a very wife and well-confidered fpeech to her privy-council. She expreffed plainly her opinion for carrying on the preparations againft France, and fupporting the allies; and faid, fhe would countenance thofe who concurred with her in maintaining the prefent conftitution and eftablifhment.

The queen, in conformity to this declaration, wrote to the States-general to affure them, that fhe would follow exactly the fteps of her predeceffor, in the fteady maintenance of the common caufe againft the common enemy: and the prudent choice of her fervants, was fufficient to, demonftrate the reality of the queen's intentions.

The firft expedition in this reign, was that of Sir John Munden, rear-admiral of the Red, which was intended for intercepting a fquadron of French fhips, that were to fail from the Groyne, in order to carry the new vice-roy of Mexico to the Spanifh Weft Indies. He failed on the 12th of May, 1702, with eight fhips of the third rate, the Salifbury a fourth rate, and two frigates. On the 28th day of the month, he chafed 14 fail of fhips into Corunna. Then he called a council of war, in which it was agreed, that as the place was ftrongly fortified, and by the intelligence they had received, it appeared that 17 of the enemy's ships of war rode at anchor in the harbour; it would be expedient for them to follow the latter part of their inftructions, by which they were directed to cruife in foundings for the protection of the trade. They returned accordingly; and being diftreffed by want of provifions, came into port, to the general difcontent of the nation. For the fatisfaction of the people, Sir John Munden was tried by a court-martial, and acquitted; but as this mifcarriage had rendered him very unpopular, prince George, who was now created lord high-admiral, difmiffed him from the fervice.

King William had projected a fcheme to reduce Cadiz, with intention to act afterward againft the Spanifh fettlements in the Weft Indies. This defign queen Anne refolved to put in execution. Sir George Rooke commanded the fleet, and the duke of Ormond was appointed general of the land-forces deftined for this expedition. The combined fquadrons amounted to fifty fhips of the line, exclufive of frigates, firefhips, and fmaller veffels; and the number of foldiers embarked was not far fhort of 14,000. In the latter end of June the fleet failed from St. Helen's; and on the 12th of Auguft they anchored at the diftance of two leagues from Cadiz: but the attempt mifcarried. However, captain Hardy, having been fent to water in Lagos-bay, received intelligence, that the galleons from the Weft Indies had put into Vigo, under convoy of a French fquadron. He failed immediately in queft of Sir George Rooke, who was now on his voyage back to England; and falling in with him on the 6th day of October, communicated the fubftance of what he had learned. Rooke immediately called a council of war, in which it was determined to alter their courfe and attack the enemy at Vigo.

He forthwith detached fome fmall veffels for intelligence, and received a confirmation, that the galleons, and the fquadron, commanded by Chateau Renault,

Renault, were actually in the harbour. They failed thither, and appeared before the place on the 11th day of October. The paſſage into the harbour was narrow, ſecured by batteries, forts, and breaſt-works on each ſide; by a ſtrong boom, conſiſting of iron chains, topmaſts, and cables, moored at each end to a ſeventy gun ſhip, and fortified within by five ſhips of the ſame ſtrength, lying athwart the channel, with their broad-ſides to the offing. As the firſt and ſecond rates of the combined fleets were too large to enter, the admirals ſhifted their flags into ſmaller ſhips; and a diviſion of 25 Engliſh and Dutch ſhips of the line, with their frigates, fireſhips and ketches, was deſtined for the ſervice. In order to facilitate the attack, the duke of Ormond landed with 2500 men, at the diſtance of ſix miles from Vigo, and took by aſſault a fort and platform of forty pieces of cannon, at the entrance of the harbour.

The Britiſh enſign was no ſooner ſeen flying at the top of this fort, than the ſhips advanced to the attack. Vice-admiral Hopſon, in the Torbay, crowding all his ſail, ran directly againſt the boom, which was broken by the firſt ſhock; then the whole ſquadron entered the harbour, through a prodigious fire from the enemy's ſhips and batteries. Theſe laſt, however, were ſoon ſtormed and taken by the grenadiers who had been landed. The great ſhips lay againſt the forts at each ſide of the harbour, which in a little time they ſilenced; though vice-admiral Hopſon narrowly eſcaped from a fireſhip by which he was boarded. After a very vigorous engagement, the French finding themſelves unable to cope with ſuch an adverſary, reſolved to deſtroy their ſhips and galleons, that they might not fall into the hands of the victors. They accordingly burned and ran aſhore eight ſhips and as many advice-boats; but the ten ſhips of war were taken, together with eleven galleons. Though they had ſecured the beſt part of their plate and merchandize before the Engliſh fleet arrived, the value of fourteen million of pieces of eight, in plate and rich commodities, was deftroyed in fix galleons that perifhed; but, about half that value was brought off by the conquerors: fo that this was a dreadful blow to the enemy, and a noble acquifition to the allies. Immediately after this exploit Sir George Rooke was joined by Sir Cloudefley Shovel, who had been fent out with a fquadron to intercept the galleons. This officer was left to bring home the prizes and difmantle the fortifications, while Rooke returned in triumph to England.

The glory which the Englifh acquired in this expedition was in fome meafure tarnifhed by the conduct of fome officers in the Weft Indies. Thither admiral Benbow had been detached with a fquadron of ten fail, in the courfe of the preceding year. At Jamaica he received intelligence, that monfieur Du Caffe was in the neighbourhood of Hifpaniola, and refolved to beat up to that ifland. At Leogane he fell in with a French fhip of fifty guns, which her captain ran afhore and blew up. He took feveral other veffels, and having alarmed Petit-Guavas, on the 19th of Auguft, difcovered the enemy's fquadron near St. Martha, confifting of ten fail, fteering along fhore. He formed the line; and an engagement enfued, in which he was very ill feconded by fome of his captains. Neverthelefs, the battle continued till night, and he determined to renew it next morning, when he perceived all his fhips at the diftance of three or four miles aftern, except the Ruby, commanded by captain George Walton, who joined him in plying the enemy with chace-guns. On the 21ft, thefe two fhips engaged the French fquadron; and the Ruby was fo difabled, that the admiral was obliged to fend her back to Jamaica. Next day the Greenwich, commanded by Wade, was five leagues aftern; and the wind changing, the enemy had the advantage of the weather-gage. On the 23d, the admiral renewed the battle with his fingle fhip, unfuftained by the reft of

the

the squadron. On the 24th, his leg was shattered by a chain-shot; notwithstanding which accident, he remained on the quarter-deck in a cradle, and continued the engagement. One of the largest ships of the enemy lying like a wreck upon the water, four sail of the English squadron poured their broad-sides into her, and then ran to leeward, without paying any regard to the signal for battle. Then the French, bearing down upon the admiral with their whole force, shot away his maintopsail-yard, and damaged his rigging in such a manner, that he was obliged to lie by and refit, while they took their disabled ship in tow. During this interval, he called a council of his captains, and expostulated with them on their behaviour. They observed, that the French were very strong, and advised him to desist. He plainly perceived that he was betrayed, and with the utmost reluctance returned to Jamaica, having not only lost a leg, but also received a large wound in his face, and another in his arm, while he in person boarded the French admiral.

Exasperated at the treachery of his captains, he granted a commission to rear-admiral Whetstone and other officers to hold a court-martial, and try them for cowardice. Hudson, of the Pendennis, died before his trial: Kirby and Wade were convicted, and sentenced to be shot: Constable, of the Windsor, was cashiered and imprisoned: Vincent, of the Falmouth, and Fogg, the admiral's own captain of the Breda, were convicted of having signed a paper, that they would not fight under Benbow's command; but, as they behaved gallantly in the action, the court inflicted upon them no other punishment than that of a provisional suspension. Captain Walton had likewise joined in the conspiracy while he was heated with the fumes of intoxication; but he afterward renounced the engagement, and fought with admirable courage until his ship was disabled. The boisterous manners of Benbow had produced this base confederacy. He was a rough seaman; but remarkably

brave,

brave, honeſt, and experienced. He took this miſ-carriage ſo much to heart, that he became melancholy; and his grief co-operating with the fever occaſioned by his wounds, put a period to his life. Wade and Kirby were ſent home in the Briſtol; and, on their arrival at Plymouth, ſhot on board of the ſhip, by virtue of a dead-warrant for their immediate execution, which had lain there for ſome time. The ſame precaution had been taken in all the weſtern ports, in order to prevent applications in their favour. When Du Caſſe arrived at Carthagene, he wrote a letter to Benbow to this effect:—" Sir, I had little hope on Monday laſt, but to have ſupped in your cabin; but it pleaſed God to order it otherwiſe. I am thankful for it. As for thoſe cowardly captains who deſerted you, hang them up; for, by God, they deſerve it. Yours, Du Caſſe."

The grand fleet was commanded in 1703 by Sir Cloudeſley Shovel: it conſiſted at firſt of 27 ſhips of the line, and the admiral had under him rear-admiral Byng, and Sir Stafford Fairborne; and being afterward reinforced with eight ſhips more, theſe were commanded by vice-admiral Leake. His inſtructions were very large; but all of them might be reduced to theſe three heads, viz. annoying the enemy, aſſiſting our allies, and protecting our trade. He purſued his inſtructions as far as he was able; and having ſecured the Turkey fleet, he intended to have ſtaid ſome time upon the coaſt of Italy. But the Dutch admiral, who was with him, informed him, that both his orders and his victuals required his thinking of a ſpeedy return; and it was with much difficulty that Sir Cloudeſley Shovel prevailed upon him to go to Leghorn. In the mean time, the inſtructions he had to ſuccour the Cevennois, who were then in arms againſt the French king, were found impracticable. This admiral having renewed the peace with the piratical ſtates of Barbary, returned to England, without having been able to execute
any

any thing that looked like the refult of a concerted fcheme. The nation naturally murmured at this fruitlefs expedition, by which it had incurred fuch a confiderable expence. The merchants complained that they were ill fupplied with convoys. The fhips of war were victualled with damaged provifion; and every article of the marine being mifmanaged, the blame fell upon thofe who acted as council to the lord high-admiral.

Nor were the arms of England by fea much more fuccefsful in the Weft Indies. Sir George Rooke, in the preceding year, had detached from the Mediterranean captain Hovenden Walker, with fix fhips of the line and tranfports, having on board four regiments of foldiers, for the Leeward iflands. Being joined at Antigua by fome troops under colonel Coddrington, they made a defcent upon the ifland Guadaloupe, where they razed the fort, burned the town, ravaged the country, and reimbarked with precipitation, in confequence of a report that the French had landed 900 men on the back of the ifland. They retired to Nevis, where they muft have perifhed by famine, had not they been providentially relieved by vice-admiral Graydon, in his way to Jamaica. This officer had been fent out with three fhips to fucceed Benbow, and was convoyed about 150 leagues by two other fhips of the line. He had not failed many days, when he fell in with part of the French fquadron, commanded by Du Caffe, on their return from the Weft Indies, very foul and richly laden. Captain Cleland of the Montague engaged the fternmoft; but he was called off by a fignal from the admiral, who proceeded on his voyage without taking farther notice of the enemy.

The only exploit that tended to the diftrefs of the enemy, was performed by rear-admiral Dilkes, who, in the month of July, failed to the coaft of France with a fmall fquadron: and, in the neighbourhood of

Granville,

Granville, took or deftroyed about 40 fhips and their convoy. Yet this damage was inconfiderable when compared to that which the Englifh navy fuftained from the dreadful tempeft that began to blow on the 27th day of November, accompanied with fuch flafhes of lightning, and peals of thunder, as overwhelmed the whole kingdom with confternation. The houfes in London fhook from their foundations, and fome of them falling, buried the inhabitants in their ruins: but the chief national damage fell upon the navy. Thirteen fhips of war were loft, together with 1500 feamen, including rear-admiral Beaumont, who had been employed in obferving the Dunkirk fquadron, and was then at anchor in the Downs, where his fhip foundered. This great lofs, however, was repaired with incredible diligence, to the aftonifhment of all Europe. The queen immediately iffued orders for building a greater number of fhips than that which had been deftroyed; and fhe exercifed her bounty for the relief of the fhipwrecked feamen, and the widows of thofe who were drowned, in fuch a manner as endeared her to all her fubjects.

The emperor having declared his fecond fon Charles, king of Spain, he was conveyed to Portugal by the Englifh fleet, under Sir George Rooke. The admiral having landed king Charles at Lifbon, fent a fquadron to cruife off cape Spartell, under the command of rear-admiral Dilkes, who, on the 12th of March, 1704, engaged and took three Spanifh fhips of war, bound from St. Sebaftian to Cadiz. On the 16th day of June, Sir George Rooke, being joined by Sir Cloudefley Shovel, refolved to proceed up the Mediterranean in queft of the French fleet, which had failed thither from Breft, and which Rooke had actually difcovered in the preceding month, on their voyage to Toulon. On the 17th day of July, the admiral called a council of war in the road of Tetuan, when they refolved to make an attempt upon Gibraltar, which was but flenderly provided with a garrifon.

Thither

Thither they failed, and on the 21ft day of the month the prince of Heffe landed on the ifthmus with eighteen hundred marines: next day the admiral gave orders for cannonading the town; and perceiving that the enemy were driven from their fortifications at the fouth molehead, commanded captain Whitaker to arm all the boats, and affault that quarter. The captains Hicks and Jumper, who happened to be neareft the mole, immediately manned their pinnaces, and entered the fortifications fword in hand. The Spaniards fprung a mine, by which two lieutenants and about 100 men were killed or wounded. Neverthelefs, the two captains took poffeffion of a platform, and kept their ground until they were fuftained by captain Whitaker and the reft of the feamen, who took by ftorm a redoubt between the mole and the town. Then the governor capitulated; and the prince of Heffe entered the place, amazed at the fuccefs of this attempt, confidering the ftrength of the fortifications, which might have been defended by fifty men againft a numerous army.

A fufficient garrifon being left with his highnefs, the admiral returned to Tetuan to take in wood and water; and when he failed, on the 9th day of Auguft, he defcried the French fleet, to which he gave chace with all the fail he could fpread. On the 13th he came up with it, as it lay in a line off Malaga ready to receive him, to the number of 52 great fhips, and 24 gallies, under the command of the count de Tholoufe, high-admiral of France, with the inferior flags of the white and blue divifions. The Englifh fleet confifted of 53 fhips of the line, exclufive of frigates; but they were inferior to the French in number of guns and men, as well as in weight of metal; and altogether unprovided of gallies, from which the enemy reaped great advantage during the engagement. A little after ten in the morning, the battle began with equal fury on both fides, and continued to rage with doubtful fuccefs till two in the after-

afternoon, when the van of the French gave way: neverthelefs the fight was maintained till night, when the enemy bore away to leeward. The wind fhifted before morning, the French gained the weather-gage; but they made no ufe of this advantage: for two fucceffive days, the Englifh admiral endeavoured to renew the engagement, which the count de Tholoufe declined, and at laft he difappeared. The lofs was pretty equal on both fides, though not a fingle fhip was taken or deftroyed by either: but the honour of the day certainly remained with the Englifh.

Philip king of Spain, alarmed at the reduction of Gibraltar, fent the marquis de Villadarias with an army to retake it. The fiege lafted four months; during which the prince of Heffe exhibited many fhining proofs of courage and ability: but the Spaniards were at length forced to abandon the undertaking. A fecond attempt fucceeded no better.

While thefe great things were doing in the Mediterranean, Sir George Byng was fent with a fmall fquadron of cruifers into the Soundings. He failed in the latter end of January, 1705, with a large and rich fleet of outward-bound merchant-fhips. As foon as he had feen thefe fafe into the fea, he difpofed of his fquadron in fuch a manner, as he thought moft proper for fecuring our own trade, and for meeting with the French privateers. Hè was fo fortunate as to take from the enemy a man of war of 44 guns, 12 privateers, and 7 merchant-fhips, moft of which were richly laden from the Weft Indies. The number of men taken on board all thefe prizes was upward of 2,000, and of guns 334. This gave fuch a blow to the French privateers, that they fcarce ventured into the channel all the year after, but chofe rather to fail northward, in hopes of meeting with fome of our fhips homeward-bound from the Baltic.

The firft orders received by the grand fleet, commanded by the famous earl of Peterborough, and Sir Cloudefley Shovel, as joint admirals; were, to proceed

proceed for the Mediterranean, with the force then ready, which amounted to 29 fail of line of battle fhips, befide frigates, firefhips, bombs, and other fmall craft. On the 11th of June they arrived in the river of Lifbon, where they found Sir John Leake, with a fquadron, in great want of provifions. On the 15th of June, a council of war was held, in which it was determined to put to fea with 48 fhips of the line, Englifh and Dutch, and difpofe them in fuch a ftation between cape Spartell and the bay of Cadiz, as might beft prevent the junction of the French fquadrons from Toulon and Breft.

On the 22d of June, Sir Cloudefley Shovel, with the fleet, failed for Lifbon; from thence he failed to Altea-bay, and there took in his catholic majefty, who preffed the earl of Peterborough to make an immediate attempt on the city of Barcelona, and the province of Catalonia; where he was affured the people were well affected to him. This being agreed to, the fleet failed accordingly to Barcelona, and arrived on the 12th of Auguft. The furrender of this capital of Catalonia fo ftrengthened king Charles's party, that the whole principality, Rofes only excepted, fubmitted foon after.

All the world knows, that the reduction of Barcelona has been confidered as one of the moft extraordinary events that fell out in this, or, perhaps, in any modern war; and though we have already many accounts of it, which feem to attribute it, fome to one thing, fome to another; yet nothing but the affiftance given by our fleet could poffibly have reduced it.

In this year our fucceffes had been fo great both by fea and land, and there appeared fo fair a profpect of humbling the houfe of Bourbon in Flanders, and of driving them out of Spain, that when her majefty thought fit to recommend the Spanifh war in a particular manner to parliament, the houfe of commons immediately voted large fupplies for the year 1706:
fo

so that the miniftry had nothing to confider, but how to employ them in fuch a manner, as that thofe, upon whom they were raifed, might be fatisfied that they were laid out for their fervice; and this produced a refolution of equipping a numerous fleet, as early as it was poffible. This, with the fettling the terms of the union, were the matters which principally took up the attention of this feffion of parliament.

Had the iffue of the campaign in Catalonia been fuch as the beginning feemed to prognofticate, the French king might have in fome meafure confoled himfelf for his difgraces in the Netherlands. On the 6th day of April, king Philip, at the head of a numerous army, undertook the fiege of Barcelona, while the count de Thouloufe blocked it up with a powerful fquadron: but the arrival of an Englifh fleet, under Sir John Leake, faved the city: the French fquadron failed away for Toulon, and king Philip abandoned the fiege. The Englifh fleet continued all the fummer in the Mediterranean: they fecured Carthagena, which had declared for Charles: they took the town of Alicant by affault, and the caftle by capitulation. Then failing out of the Streights, one fquadron was detached to the Weft Indies, another ordered to lie at Lifbon, and the reft were fent home to England. But affairs fell into fuch diftraction in the Weft Indies, that we were not either in a condition to hurt the enemy's fettlements, or fo much as able to defend our own. The truth feems to be, that the great fleets we fitted out every year to the Mediterranean, and the cruifers that were neceffary upon our coafts, took up fo many fhips, that it was fcarcely poffible to fupply even the reafonable demands of the Weft Indies.

A fcheme being formed to attempt Toulon, and Sir Cloudefley Shovel having joined Sir George Byng near Alicant, the fleet came to an anchor before Final on the 5th of June, 1707, confifting of 43 men of war and 57 tranfports; where, in a council of war,

at

at which prince Eugene affifted, it was refolved to force a paffage near the van, in which the Englifh admiral promifed to affift. On the laft day of June this enterprife was undertaken, to the great aftonifhment of the French, who believed their works upon that river to be impregnable. Sir John Norris, with fome Britifh, and one Dutch man of war, failed to the mouth of the river, and embarking 600 feamen and marines in open boats, entered it, and advanced within mufket-fhot of the enemy's works, making fuch a terrible fire upon them, that their cavalry and many of their foot began to quit their entrenchments, and could not be prevailed upon by their officers to return. Sir Cloudefly Shovel, who followed Sir John, no fooner faw this confufion, than he ordered the latter to land with the feamen and marines in order to flank the enemy. This was performed with fo much fpirit, and Sir John and his feamen fcampered fo fuddenly over the French works, that the enemy, ftruck with a pannic, threw down their arms and fled with the utmoft precipitation. The duke of Savoy immediately purfued this advantage, and in half an hour paffed that river, which had, without this affiftance, proved the ne plus ultra of his expedition; and marched toward Toulon, with an army of thirty-five thoufand men. The fiege of this place was not formed before the 15th of July, when 100 cannon, with 200 rounds of powder and fhot, and a confiderable number of feamen to ferve as gunners, with all other things wanting for the camp, were fupplied from the fhips: fo that affairs had a very good afpect till the 4th of Auguft, when the enemy, making a vigorous fally, forced the confederate troops out of the works, and drew eight or ten guns into the town. In this action were killed and wounded above 800 men: fo that on the 6th, after embarking the fick and wounded, and withdrawing the cannon, the fiege from that time was turned only to a cannonading and bombardment.

The very day the army began to march, five bomb vessels, supported by the lightest frigates and all the boats of the men of war, under the command of rear-admiral Dilkes, advanced into the creek of fort St. Lewis; and notwithstanding a prodigious fire from the place, bombarded the town and harbour from noon till five next morning with all the success which could be expected, the land army in the mean time quitting their camp at La Villette, which they did in five columns with great safety, the duke of Savoy marching back in two days as far as in his approach to the place he had done in six.

Sir Cloudesly Shovel being not a little chagrined at the miscarriage of an expedition on which he had set his heart, bent his course homeward. Coming into the Soundings on the 23d of October, he struck upon the rocks called the Bishop and his Clerks, and in two minutes nothing more of him or his ship was seen, and three or four more of his fleet also perished with him.

But at the time that our fleets were every where superior to those of the enemy, our trade suffered in almost all parts of the world by their small squadrons of men of war, as well as privateers.

About this time the French played off a project, which they repeated more than once since. This was, the attempt upon Scotland, in favour of the chevalier de St. George; which was the Nomme de Guerre they were pleased to give the person, whom the queen soon after distinguished by the name of the Pretender.

The troops intended for this attempt, were about eleven or twelve battalions, under the command of the marquis de Gace, afterward stiled the marshal de Matignon. The fleet consisted of but eight men of war, which was commanded by the count de Forbin, who is said to have disliked the design, because, very probably, he knew the bottom of it: for it is very certain, the French never intended to land, and refused the chevalier to set him on shore, though he
would

would have gone with his own servants. The true scheme of the French king was, to create a diversion to embarrass the queen and her ministry at home, that they might have the less leisure to prosecute their views abroad: and from these motives, he ordered his ministers in all foreign courts, to talk in very magnificent terms, of the succours he gave to the king of England, as he thought fit to call him; that on the rebound, they might make the louder noise in Britain. Our public securities fell surprisingly, and things would have fallen into downright confusion, if the fright had not been quickly over. This was owing to the care of the admiralty, who, with remarkable diligence, fitted out a fleet of 24 men of war, with which, Sir George Byng, and lord Dursley, sailed for the French coast, on the 27th of February, 1708. On Sir George Byng's anchoring before Gravelin, the French officers laid aside their embarkation; but upon express orders from court, were obliged to resume it; and on the 6th of March, actually sailed out of Dunkirk; but being taken short by contrary winds, came to an anchor till the 8th, and then continued their voyage for Scotland.

Sir George Byng pursued them with a fleet of forty ships of the line, beside frigates and fireships. He afterward detached rear-admiral Baker, with a small squadron, to convoy the troops that were sent from Ostend, and prosecuted his expedition with the rest. He sailed directly to the frith of Edinburgh, where he arrived almost as soon as the enemy, who immediately took the advantage of a land-breeze, and bore away with all the sail they could carry. The English admiral gave chace; and the Salisbury, one of their ships, was boarded and taken. At night monsieur de Fourbin altered his course; so that the next day they were out of reach of the English squadron. The pretender desired they would proceed to the northward, and land him at Invernefs, and Fourbin seemed willing to gratify this request; but the wind changing and blowing in their teeth with great violence, he reprefented the danger of attempting to profecute the voyage ; and, with the confent of the chevalier de St. George and his general, returned to Dunkirk, after having been toffed about a whole month in very tempeftuous weather. In the mean time, Sir George Byng failed up to Leith road, where he received the freedom of the city of Edinburgh in a golden box, as a teftimony of gratitude for his having delivered them from the dreadful apprehenfions under which they laboured.

Certain it is, the pretender could not have chofen a more favourable opportunity for making a defcent upon Scotland. The people in general were difaffected to the government on account of the union ; the regular troops under Leven did not exceed 2500 men ; and even great part of thefe would in all probability have joined the invader : the caftle of Edinburgh was deftitute of ammunition, and would in all appearance have furrendered at the firft fummons ; in which cafe the Jacobites muft have been mafters of the equivalent money lodged in that fortrefs; a good number of Dutch fhips loaded with cannon, fmall arms, ammunition, and a large fum of money, had been driven on fhore in the fhire of Angus : where they would have been feized by the friends of the pretender, had the French troops been landed ; and all the adherents of that houfe were ready to appear in arms.

The campaign in Catalonia, which we cannot enter into, was productive of a great event. Sir John Leake, having taken on board a handful of troops, under the conduct of the marquis D'Alconzel, fet fail for Cagliari, in Sardinia, and fummoned the viceroy to fubmit to King Charles. As he did not fend an immediate anfwer, the admiral began to bombard the city, and the inhabitants compelled him to furrender at difcretion. The greater part of the garrifon enlifted themfelves in the fervice of Charles. Major-
general

general Stanhope having planned the conqueſt of Minorca, and concerted with the admiral the meaſures neceſſary to put it in execution, obtained from count Staremberg a few battalions of Spaniards, Italians, and Portugueſe, embarked at Barcelona, with a fine train of Britiſh artillery, accompanied by brigadier Wade and colonel Petit, an engineer of great reputation. They landed on the iſland about two miles from St. Philip's fort, on the twenty-ſixth of Auguſt, with about eight hundred marines, which augmented their number to about three thouſand. Next day they erected batteries; and general Stanhope ordered a number of arrows to be ſhot into the place, to which papers were affixed, written in the Spaniſh and French languages, containing threats, that all the garriſon ſhould be ſent to the mines, if they would not ſurrender before the batteries were finiſhed. The garriſon conſiſted of a thouſand Spaniards, and ſix hundred French marines, commanded by colonel la Jonquiere, who imagined that the number of the beſiegers amounted to at leaſt ten thouſand; ſo artfully had they been drawn up in ſight of the enemy. The batteries began to play, and in a little time demoliſhed four towers that ſerved as outworks to the fort: then they made a breach in the outward wall, through which brigadier Wade, at the head of the grenadiers, ſtormed a redoubt, with ſuch extraordinary valour as ſtruck the beſieged with conſternation. On the ſecond or third day they thought proper to beat a parley, and capitulate, on condition, That they ſhould march out with the honours of war: That the Spaniards ſhould be tranſported to Murcia, and the French to Toulon. The Spaniſh governor was ſo mortified when he learned the real number of the beſiegers, that on his arrival at Murcia, he threw himſelf out of a window in deſpair, and was killed upon the ſpot. La Jonquiere was confined for life, and all the French officers incurred their maſter's diſpleaſure. Fort St. Philip being thus reduced, to the amazement of all Europe; and the garrison of Port Fornelles having surrendered themselves prisoners to the admirals Leake and Whitaker, the inhabitants gladly submitted to the English government.

During the course of this year the English merchants sustained no considerable losses by sea: the cruisers were judiciously stationed, and the trade was regularly supplied with convoys. In the West Indies Commodore Wager destroyed the admiral of the galleons, and took the rear-admiral on the coast of Carthagene. Had the officers of his squadron done their duty, the greatest part of the fleet would have fallen into his hands. At his return to Jamaica two of his captains were tried by a court-martial, and dismissed from the service.

On the twenty-eighth day of October prince George of Denmark died of an asthma and dropsy, with which he had been long afflicted. He was a prince of an amiable rather than a shining character, brave, good-natured, modest, and humane, but devoid of great talents and ambition. He had always lived in harmony with the queen, who, during the whole term of their union, and especially in his last illness, approved herself a pattern of conjugal truth and tenderness. At his death the earl of Pembroke was created lord high admiral.

As this war was prosecuted chiefly on the continent, where the duke of Marlborough gained such glorious, though unprofitable advantages, over the French; the events of that war rather furnish materials for a general, than for a naval history. Our fleets indeed were respectable where-ever they were sent, and proved of great benefit to King Charles in his contest for Spain: but to follow his fortunes would carry us into too wide a field; and the convoys appointed for every fleet of merchantmen, would prove but tedious details, would our limits allow the mention of them. These therefore we pass over, as well as the unsuccessful attempt on Quebec, under Sir

Hovenden

Hovenden Walker: two wars of a much more interesting nature call for our attention, we therefore pass on to the peace of Utrecht, which was privately signed April 1ft, 1713, at the house of doctor Robinson, bishop of Bristol. In this treaty, though all was not obtained from France that might have been, after so long, and withal, successful a war; yet much was got by it, and greater advantages would certainly have attended it, had it not been for the disturbance given our ministers at home, by the opposition to their measures.

Not to insist on the adequate satisfaction, which was by this treaty stipulated for all our allies, it procured us, as a trading nation, far greater advantages. For Dunkirk having been put into our hands, we shall find what was to become of it from the ninth article of the treaty, by which it was stipulated as follows:—" The most Christian king shall take care that all the fortifications of the city of Dunkirk be razed; that the harbour be filled up; and that the sluices, or moles, which serve to cleanse the harbour, be levelled; and that, at the said king's own expence, within the space of five months, after the conditions of peace are concluded and signed: that is to say, the fortifications toward the sea, within the space of two months; and those toward the land, together with the said banks, within three months; on this express condition also, that the said fortifications, harbour, moles, or sluices, be never repaired again." This demolition was of vast importance, for lying but thirteen leagues from the South Foreland, any easterly wind which carries our ships down the channel, brings out those at Dunkirk to intercept them: the very situation of the place, furnishes the enemy with advantage; for the east end of the channel, which is exposed to Dunkirk, is but seven leagues broad, whence they may see our ships from side to side. So that by this demolition, six parts in nine of our trade from London, is freed from the hazards to which they were

exposed

expofed in time of war, while Dunkirk was open. Befide, this was a heavy blow to the naval power of France, and efpecially their trade to the Weft Indies; and their fubmitting to this article, was not only a clear proof of our fuperior force, but of the great diftrefs they had then been plunged into. They endeavoured indeed to fhift off, and afterward mitigate the execution of this article; but the queen infifting on its demolition, according to the letter, it was done as effectually as could be defired.

To conclude; it may be obferved, that, upon the clofe of the war, the French found themfelves totally deprived of all pretenfions to the dominion of the fea. Moft of our conquefts, indeed all of them that were of any ufe to us, were made by, or at leaft chiefly by, our fleets. Sir George Rooke took Gibraltar, and Sir John Leake reduced Minorca; and it is alfo evident, that it was our fleet alone that fupported king Charles in Catalonia, and kept the king of Portugal fteady to the grand alliance; which, befide the advantages it brought to the common caufe, fecured to us the invaluable profits of our trade to that country: and all this againft the fpirit, genius, and inclination of the king of Portugal, and his minifters, who were all, at that time, in the French intereft in their hearts.

At the fame time, our fleets prevented the French from fo much as failing on the Mediterranean, where they had made a figure in the laft war; and kept many of the Italian ftates in awe. The very Algerines, and other piratical ftates of Barbary, contrary to their natural propenfity toward the French, were now obfequious to us, and entertained no manner of doubt of the fuperiority of our flag. The flacknefs of the Dutch, in lending fhips to this part of the world, had, in this refpect, an effect happy enough for us, fince it occafioned our being confidered as the leading power, by all who had any concerns with us and them.

The

OF KING GEORGE I. 377

The treaty of Utrecht, which put an end to our disputes abroad, proved the cause of high debates, and great distractions at home. The people grew uneasy, the ministry divided, and the heats and violence of party rose to such a height, that her majesty found herself so embarrassed, as not to be able either to depend upon those in power, or to venture to turn them out. The uneasiness of mind, that such a perplexed situation of affairs occasioned, had a very bad effect upon her health, which had been in a declining condition from the time of prince George's death; and a quarrel between two of her principal ministers, in her presence, proved, in some measure, the cause of her death, which happened August 1st, 1714.

ABSTRACT of the ROYAL NAVY, as it stood at the Death of QUEEN ANNE.

Rates.	Number.	Guns.	Men.
I.	7	714	5,312
II.	13	1,170	7,194
III.	39	2,890	16,089
IV.	66	3,490	16,058
V.	32	1,190	4,160
VI.	25	500	1,047
	182	9,954	49,860
Fire-ships, &c. about	50		

We now arrive at another change in our government, brought about by a statute made in the twelfth year of king William III. for limiting the succession of the crown; by which, after the death of the queen, then princess Anne, without issue, it was to pass to the most illustrious house of Hanover, as the next protestant heirs : for the princess Sophia, electress dowager of Hanover, was daughter to the queen of Bohemia, who, before her marriage with the elector Palatine, was stiled the princess Elizabeth of Great Britain,

Britain, daughter to James VI. of Scotland, and I. of England; in whom united all the hereditary claims to the imperial crown of these realms.

But, the princess Sophia dying a very little while before the queen, George-Lewis, elector of Hanover, her son, became heir of this crown, on the demise of queen Anne, and was accordingly called to the succession, in the manner directed by another statute, passed in the fourth year of her majesty's reign.

His majesty arriving from Holland on the 18th of September, and making his public entry on the 20th, took the reins of government into his own hands. A new parliament was summoned, and met at Westminster, March the 17th, 1715, and came to a resolution, to allow ten thousand seamen at four pounds a month; beside other large sums for other naval contingencies. These were thought necessary, because, at this juncture, the fleet of Great Britain was much decayed; and it was foreseen, that, notwithstanding the peace so lately concluded, new disputes were likely to arise.

Amongst these disputes, the most serious was that in which we were engaged with Sweden. This had begun before the queen's death, and was occasioned by the Swedish privateers taking many of our ships, which, with their cargoes, were confiscated; under a pretence that we assisted and supplied the Czar and his subjects, with ships, arms, ammunition, &c. contrary, as was suggested, to our treaties with the crown of Sweden. Several memorials had been presented upon this subject, without receiving any satisfactory answer; and, therefore, it was now thought expedient to send a strong squadron of men of war into the Baltic; the rather, because their high mightinesses the states-general, labouring under the same inconveniencies, found themselves obliged, after all pacific methods had been tried in vain, to have recourse to the same measures.

On

On the 18th of May a squadron of twenty sail was appointed for this service, under Sir John Norris, who arrived in the Sound on the 10th of June following: where, finding the Dutch squadron, it was resolved, that the combined fleet should proceed together, with the English and Dutch merchantmen under their convoy for their respective ports. About the middle of the month of August, the Danish fleet, consisting of twenty ships of the line, with the Russian squadron, resolved to sail up the Baltic, with the English and Dutch.

On the arrival of Sir John Norris in the Baltic, our minister presented a memorial, in which he set forth, the particular damages sustained by our merchants; for which he demanded satisfaction; and, at the same time, insisted on the repeal of an edict, which his Swedish majesty had lately published, and by which the commerce of the Baltic was wholly prohibited to the English. This memorial was presented, June 15, 1715, and in it, the nature of Sir John Norris's commission was explained; but he received a very unsatisfactory answer. Thus far, all this quarrel seems to arise from his majesty's care of the British commerce. But as elector of Hanover, he had also some disputes with his majesty of Sweden, of quite a different nature: for having purchased from the crown of Denmark the duchies of Bremen and Verden, which had been taken from the crown of Sweden, he found himself obliged, in quality of elector, to concur with the first-mentioned power, in declaring war against Sweden; and, even before this was done, some English ships joined the Danish fleet, in order to distress the Swedes. Of this, the Swedish minister here complained, by a memorial, in which he asserted, that the honour of the British flag had been prostituted to serve the interests of another state, and in order to create an intercourse between the king's regal and electoral dominions. The Dutch, though no less injured, no

less

less concerned in their trade than we, did not, however, think it necessary to come to such extremities.

The Swedes had, at this time, a very numerous fleet, and in good condition; but they were too wise to hazard it against such an unequal force as that of the confederates; and, therefore, withdrew it into one of their own ports, till they could receive the king's absolute orders. On the 9th of November, the British men of war, from Dantzick, with the trade, joined Sir John Norris's squadron at Bornholm, and the next day came all with him into the road of Copenhagen. On the 12th, arrived the Dutch trade, with their convoy, which had been obliged to stay after ours at Dantzick, for provisions. A few days after, Sir John sailed from the road of Copenhagen; and, notwithstanding his fleet, as well as the merchantmen under his convoy, were surprized by a violent storm, which dispersed them, and in which the August, of sixty guns, and the Garland of twenty-four, were unfortunately lost; yet the rest, with all the trade, safely arrived at the Trow, on the 29th of November, in the morning. Sir John Norris left seven ships of war under the command of commodore Cleeland, in the Baltic, to act in conjunction with the Danes, and for the further security of the British trade, if necessary.

During the time that this squadron was employed in the Baltic, the rebellion was extinguished in Scotland; but with so little assistance from our naval force, that it scarce deserves to be mentioned. The rebellion broke out under the influence and direction of the earl of Mar, who was soon joined by the clans; and the Duke of Argyll being sent down against him, it quickly appeared how ill their measures had been taken. His grace had, indeed, but a small number of regular troops under his command; but his interest was so extensive, that he not only engaged many powerful families to declare for king George, but, which

perhaps

perhaps was the greater service of the two, engaged many more to remain quiet, who otherwise had joined the rebels. The business was decided by the battle of Sheriff Moore, near Dunblain, fought November 13, 1715, the same day that general Foster and the English, who were in arms, surrendered at Preston. Yet, after this, the Chevalier de St. George ventured over into Scotland, in a very poor vessel; where, soon finding his affairs desperate, and his person in the utmost danger, he contrived to make his escape from the north, with the utmost secrecy; which he effected, by going on board a clean tallow'd French snow, which sailed out of the harbour of Montrose, February the 3d, in sight of some English men of war, but kept so close along shore, that they soon found it was impossible to follow her.

We have already taken notice of what past under Sir John Norris in the Baltic; and have, therefore, only to observe, that this year some of the piratical republics in Barbary having broke the peace, admiral Baker, who had the command of the English squadron in the Mediterranean, received orders to bring them to reason; which he did, without any great difficulty.

In 1718, the king of England had used some endeavours to compromise the difference between his imperial majesty and the Spanish branch of the house of Bourbon. Mr. Stanhope had been sent to Madrid with a plan of pacification, which being rejected by Philip, as partial and iniquitous, the king determined to support his mediation by arms. Sir George Byng sailed from Spithead on the 4th day of June, with twenty ships of the line, two fire-ships, two bomb-vessels, and ample instructions how to act on all emergencies. He arrived off Cape St. Vincent on the 30th day of the month, when he dispatched his secretary to Cadiz with a letter to Colonel Stanhope the British minister at Madrid, desiring him to inform his most catholic majesty of the admiral's arrival in those parts,

parts, and to lay before him his inftructions: which, when cardinal Alberoni perufed, he told colonel Stanhope with fome warmth, that his mafter would run all hazards, and even fuffer himfelf to be driven out of Spain, rather than recal his troops, or confent to a fufpenfion of arms. He faid the Spaniards were not to be frightened; and he was fo well convinced that the fleet would do their duty, that in cafe of their being attacked by admiral Byng, he fhould be in no pain for the fuccefs. This interpofition could not but be very provoking to the Spanifh minifter, who had laid his account with the conqueft of Sicily; and for that purpofe prepared an armament which was altogether furprifing, confidering the late fhattered condition of the Spanifh affairs. He feems to have put too much confidence in the ftrength of the Spanifh fleet. In a few days he fent back the admiral's letter to Mr. Stanhope, with a note under it, importing, that the chevalier Byng might execute the orders he had received from the king his mafter.

The admiral, in paffing by Gibraltar, was joined by vice-admiral Cornwal with two fhips. He proceeded to Minorca, where he relieved the garrifon of Portmahon. Then he failed for Naples, where he arrived on the firft day of Auguft, and was received as a deliverer: for the Neapolitans had been under the utmoft terror of an invafion from the Spaniards. Sir George Byng received intelligence from the viceroy count Daun, who treated him with the moft diftinguifhing marks of refpect, that the Spanifh army, amounting to thirty thoufand men, commanded by the marquis de Lede, had landed in Sicily, reduced Palermo and Meffina, and were then employed in the fiege of the citadel belonging to this laft city: that the Fiedmontefe garrifon would be obliged to furrender, if not fpeedily relieved: that an alliance was upon the carpet between the emperor and the king of Sicily, which laft had defired the affiftance of the imperial troops, and agreed to receive them into the citadel tädel of Meſſina. The admiral immediately refolved to fail thither, and on the 9th of Auguſt was in fight of the Faro of Meſſina. He difpatched his own captain with a polite meſſage to the marquis de Lede, propoſing a ceſſation of arms in Sicily for two months, that the powers of Europe might have time to concert meaſures for reſtoring a laſting peace. The Spaniſh general anſwered, that he had no powers to treat, confequently ſhould obey his orders, which directed him to reduce Sicily for his maſter the king of Spain. The Spaniſh fleet had failed from the harbour of Meſſina on the day before the Engliſh ſquadron appeared. In doubling the point of Faro, he defcried two Spaniſh ſcouts, that led him to their main fléet, which before noon he defcried in line of battle, amounting to 27 fail large and ſmall, befide two fireſhips, four bomb-veſſels, and feven gallies. At fight of the Engliſh ſquadron they ſtood away large, and Byng gave chace all the reſt of the day. In the morning, which was the 11th of Auguſt, the rear-admiral de Mari, with fix ſhips of war, the gallies, fire-ſhips, and bomb-ketches, feparated from the main fleet, and ſtood in for the Sicilian ſhore. The Engliſh admiral detached captain Walton with five ſhips in purſuit of them; and they were foon engaged. He himſelf continued to chace their main fleet; and about ten o'clock the battle began. The Spaniards ſeemed to be diſtracted in their counfels, and acted in confuſion. They made a running fight; and the admirals behaved with courage and activity, in fpite of which they were all taken but Cammock, who made his efcape with three ſhips of war and three frigates. In this engagement, which happened off Cape Paſſaro, captain Haddock of the Grafton fignalized his courage in an extraordinary manner. On the 18th the admiral received a letter from captain Walton, dated off Syracufe, intimating that he had taken four Spaniſh ſhips of war, together with a bomb-ketch, and a veſſel laden with arms; and that he had burned

ed four ships of the line, a fire-ship, and a bomb-vessel. This letter is justly deemed a curious specimen of the laconic style.—" Sir, We have taken and destroyed all the Spanish ships and vessels which were upon the coast, the number as per margin. I am, &c.
G. Walton."

These ships that captain Walton thus thrust into his margin, would have furnished matter for some pages, in a French relation.

Admiral Byng continued to assist the imperialists in Sicily. during the best part of the winter, by scouring the seas of the Spaniards, and keeping the communication open between the German forces and the Calabrian shore, from whence they were supplied with provisions. He acted in this service with equal conduct, resolution, and activity. He conferred with the viceroy of Naples, and the other imperial generals, about the operations of the ensuing campaign; and count Hamilton was dispatched to Vienna, to lay before the emperor the result of their deliberations: then the admiral set sail for Mahon, where his ships might be refitted, and put in a condition to take the sea in the spring.

The destruction of the Spanish fleet was a subject that employed the deliberations and conjectures of all the politicians in Europe. Spain exclaimed against the conduct of England, as inconsistent with the rules of good faith, for the observation of which she had always been so famous. This was the language of disappointed ambition. Nevertheless, it must be owned, that the conduct of England on this occasion was rather irregular; and the Spaniards were not slow in expressing their resentments. On the 1st of September, rear-admiral Guevara, with some ships under his command, entered the port of Cadiz, and made himself master of all the English ships that were there; and, at the same time, all the effects of the English merchants were seized in Malaga, and other ports of Spain; which, as soon as it was known here, produced

duced reprifals on our part. But it is now time to leave the Mediterranean, and the affairs of Spain, in order to give an account of what paffed in the northern feas.

There remains only one tranfaction more of this year, which a work of this kind requires to be mentioned; which is the account of the reduction of the pirates. Captain Woodes Rogers, having been appointed governor of the Bahama iflands, failed for Providence, which was to be the feat of his government, on the 11th of April; and after a fhort and eafy paffage, arriving there, he took poffeffion of the town of Naffau, the fort belonging to it, and of the whole ifland; the people receiving him with all imaginable joy, and many of the pirates fubmitting immediately. Some of them, it is true, rejected, at firft, all terms, and did a great deal of mifchief on the coaft of Carolina; but, when they faw that governor Rogers had thoroughly fettled himfelf at Providence, and that the inhabitants of the Bahama iflands found themfelves obliged, through intereft, to be honeft, they began to doubt of their fituation, and thought proper to go and beg that mercy which at firft they refufed; fo that there were not above three or four veffels of thofe pirates who continued their trade, and two of them being taken, and their crews executed, the reft difperfed out of fear, and became thereby lefs terrible. Thus, in a fhort time, and chiefly through the fteady and prudent conduct of governor Rogers, this herd of villains were in fome meafure difperfed, who for many years had frighted the Weft Indies, and the northern colonies.

On the 17th of December 1718, a declaration of war in form was publifhed againft the crown of Spain; as to the expediency of which, many bold things were faid in the houfe of commons, efpecially with regard to the pretenfions, and the intentions of thofe who made this war. The miniftry, however, continued the purfuit of their own fcheme, in fpite of oppofition, and took fuch vigorous meafures for obliging Spain to accept the terms affigned her by the quadruple alliance, that fhe loft all patience, and refolved to attempt any thing that might either free her from this neceffity, or ferve to exprefs her refentments againft fuch as endeavoured to impofe it upon her: with this view fhe drew together a great number of tranfports at Cadiz and Corunna; but the Spanifh fleet, defigned for this expedition, confifting of five men of war, and about forty tranfports, having on board the late duke of Ormonde, and upward of 5000 men, met with a violent ftorm, which entirely difperfed them. Thus, this defign of the Spaniards, whatever it was, became abortive.

It may be proper, in this place, to take notice, that we acted now in fuch clofe conjunction with France, that the regent declared war againft his coufin the king of Spain; and though many people here fufpected that this war would produce no great effects, it proved quite otherwife; for the marquis de Silly advanced in the month of April as far as Port Paffage, where he found fix men of war juft finifhed, upon the ftocks, all which, prompted thereto by colonel Stanhope, (afterward earl of Harrington) he burned, together with timber, mafts, and naval ftores, to the value of half a million fterling; which was a greater real lofs to the Spaniards, than that they fuftained by our beating their fleet. Soon after, the duke of Berwick befieged Fontarabia; both which actions fhewed, that the French were actually in earneft.

While the Spaniards were pleafing themfelves with chimerical notions of invafions it was impoffible to effect againft us, our admiral in the Mediterranean was diftreffing them effectually; he continued there until he had feen the iflands of Sicily and Sardinia evacuated by the Spaniards, and the mutual ceffions executed between the emperor and the duke of Savoy. In a word, admiral Byng bore fuch a confiderable

derable share in this war of Sicily, that the fate of the island depended wholly upon his courage, vigilance, and conduct.

The king of England, with a view to indemnify himself for the expence of the war, projected the conquest of Corunna in Biscay, and of Peru in South America. Four thousand men, commanded by lord Cobham, were embarked at the Isle of Wight, and sailed on the 21st day of September, under convoy of five ships of war, conducted by admiral Mighels. Instead of making an attempt upon Corunna, they reduced Vigo with very little difficulty. The expedition to the West Indies was prevented by the peace. Spain being oppressed on all sides, and utterly exhausted, Philip saw the necessity of a speedy pacification. He was obliged at last to accede to the quadruple alliance.

The pirates in the West Indies, who had received some check from the vigorous dispositions of governor Rogers, and other commanders in those parts, began to take breath again, and by degrees grew so bold as even to annoy our colonies more than ever; owing to the encouragement they had met with of late from the Spaniards, and to the want of a sufficient force in the North American seas. There was among these pirates one Roberts, a man whose parts deserved a better employment; he was an able seaman, and a good commander, and had with him two very stout ships, to which he soon added a third. With this force, Roberts had done a great deal of mischief in the West Indies, before he sailed for Africa, where he likewise took abundance of prizes, till in the month of April 1722, he was taken by the then captain, afterward Sir Chaloner Ogle.

Captain Ogle was then in the Swallow, and was cruising off Cape Lopez, when he had intelligence of Roberts's being not far from him, and in consequence of this he went immediately in search of him, and soon after discovered the pirates in a very convenient bay, where the biggeſt and the leaſt ſhip were upon the heel, ſcrubbing. Captain Ogle taking in his lower tier of guns, and lying at a diſtance, Roberts took him for a merchantman, and immediately ordered his confort to ſlip his cable, and run out after him. Captain Ogle crouded all the ſail he could to decoy the pirate to ſuch a diſtance, that his conforts might not hear the guns, and then ſuddenly tacked, run out his lower tier, and gave the pirate a broadſide, by which their captain was killed: this ſo diſcouraged the crew, that after a briſk engagement, which laſted about an hour and a half, they ſurrendered. Captain Ogle returned then to the bay, hoiſting the king's colours, under the pirates black flag with a death's head in it. This prudent ſtratagem had the deſired effect; for the pirates, ſeeing the black flag uppermoſt, concluded the king's ſhip had been taken, and came out full of joy to congratulate their confort on the victory. This joy of theirs was, however, of no long continuance, for captain Ogle gave them a very warm reception; and though Roberts fought with the utmoſt bravery, for near two hours, yet being at laſt killed, the courage of his men immediately ſunk, and both ſhips yielded.

Peace affords no events of importance for naval hiſtory; we therefore paſs on to the death of king George I. which happened at his brother's palace, in the city of Oſnaburg, June the 11th, 1727, in the thirteenth year of his reign, and in the ſixty-eighth of his life. He was very well acquainted with the general intereſt of all the princes in Europe, and particularly well verſed in whatever related to German affairs. He was allowed by the beſt judges of military ſkill, to be an excellent officer; was very capable of application, and underſtood buſineſs as well as any prince of his time.

A LIST

A LIST of the ENGLISH NAVY, as it stood at the Accession of GEORGE II.

Rates.	N° of Ships.	Men.	Guns.	Swivels.
I.	7	5,460	700	
II.	13	8,840	1,170	
III.	16	8,320	1,280	
	24	10,568	1,680	
IV.	24	37,600	1,440	
	40	17,200	2,000	
V.	24	4,800	960	
	1	155	30	
VI.	1	140	22	
	28	3,580	560	
Fire-ships	3	155	24	
Bombs	3	120	16	16
Store-ship	1	90	20	
Sloops	15	990	78	78
Yachts	7	260	64	
Ditto, small	5	29	26	6
Hoys	11	87	12	2
Smacks	2	4		
Total	225	98,398	10,082	

After the accession of king George II. notwithstanding the seeming pacific disposition of the court of Spain in Europe, and their engagements lately entered into, there was great reason to suspect, that their governors in the West Indies had secret instructions to carry on a depredatory war : for no sooner were our men of war called off from action in those seas, than our merchants severely felt the effects of a perfidious treaty ; and every ship from our colonies and islands, brought fresh subject of complaint, concerning their depredations on our trade, and their cruelties to our sailors. Also in Europe, from the lessening of our naval force in the Mediterranean, the Sallee rovers were encouraged to infest our navigation in the Streights

Streights and Western ocean. Upon all this the parliament, which met on the 22d of January, agreed to employ 15,000 seamen, at four pounds a man per month, for thirteen months, for the current year; and also voted 206,025 pounds, for the ordinary of the navy during the same time.

The house of commons having examined the accounts of the Spanish depredations, came to the following resolution; That ever since the peace of Utrecht, concluded in 1713, to this time, the British trade and navigation to and from the several colonies in America, had been greatly interrupted by the continual depredations of the Spaniards; in manifest violation of the treaties subsisting between the two crowns. In consequence of which resolution, it was further unanimously resolved, that an humble address be presented to his majesty, to desire he would be graciously pleased to use his utmost endeavours to prevent such depredations, to procure just and reasonable satisfaction for the losses sustained; and to secure to his subjects the free exercise of commerce and navigation, to and from the British colonies in America. The consequence was, an order for putting 27 ships in commission; which joined to a Dutch squadron, were intended to act in conjunction under Sir Charles Wager.

This confederate fleet of the English and Dutch at Spithead, raised expectations in the public, who now imagined that some bold stroke was intended in favour of our merchants. But after spending above three months in a pompous parade, the Dutch sailed homeward; and twelve of our largest ships were ordered to be laid up. This fleet, however, it is generally thought, accelerated the signing of the convention, and also the dispatching those orders which were carried to Cuba, by the new governor of that island; by virtue of which, he imprisoned his predecessor, and even laid him in irons; at the same time declaring, that his instructions were to live in amity with the English. But all this, as appeared by the
conse-

consequences, proved no more than grimace; for the guarda costas continued their former depredations.

After the conclusion of the peace with Spain, Great Britain was drawn into an agreement, to carry Don Carlos, infant of Spain, and with the consent of the court of Vienna, to place him on the throne of Naples: notwithstanding which, every ship from the W. Indies brought an account of a continued series of Spanish depredations and cruelties; a shocking instance of the latter, not to mention others, was the inhuman treatment of Robert Jenkins, master of the Rebecca, whose ear they cut off, and, at the same time, delivered it into his hands, insolently telling him to carry that present home to his master. Notwithstanding the pacific disposition of the British ministry at that time, the popular clamours rose very high on these and other acts of violence committed by the Spaniards; which year after year grew so violent, that the British ministry was no longer able to stem the current of national resentment shewn by the daily petitions brought up from all parts of the kingdom, calling aloud for satisfaction from Spain. His majesty issued a proclamation on the 10th of July, 1739, setting forth the Spanish depredations, the expiration of the term limited for the payment of 95,000 pounds compensation, and on the non-payment of it, thereby authorizing general reprisals and letters of marque against the ships, goods, and subjects of the king of Spain.

These orders, under his majesty's sign manual, dated June the 15th, had been dispatched above a month before their publication in London, to commodore Brown, who then commanded a squadron at Jamaica; in order to have an opportunity of making the best use of them, before the Spaniards had notice of our designs, and consequently prepared against them. The commodore published these orders on the 8th of August. In the mean time the British ministry now foreseeing that a war with Spain could no longer be avoided, the first thing they did, was to form a
resolution

resolution of endeavouring to preclude the Spaniards from the resources of their wealth in the West Indies and the South Seas.

With this view two squadrons were immediately ordered to be got ready with all expedition, the one to be put under the command of George Anson, Esq; who was then captain of his majesty's ship the Centurion, and the other under that of captain Cornwall. The particulars of Anson's voyage to the South Seas, are to be found in the third volume of this collection.

Notwithstanding these preparations of war, Mr. Keene, the British minister at Madrid, declared to the court of Spain, that his master, although he had permitted his subjects to make reprisals, would not be understood to have broken the peace; and, that this permission would be recalled as soon as his catholic majesty should be disposed to make the satisfaction which had been so justly demanded. He was given to understand, that the king of Spain looked upon those reprisals as acts of hostility; and that he hoped, with the assistance of heaven and his allies, he should be able to support a good cause against his adversaries. He published a manifesto in justification of his own conduct. The French ambassador at the Hague declared, that the king his master was obliged by treaties to assist his catholic majesty by sea and land, in case he should be attacked? he dissuaded the states-general from espousing the quarrel of Great Britain; and they assured him they would observe a strict neutrality, though they could not avoid furnishing his Britannic majesty with such succours as he could demand, by virtue of the treaties subsisting between the two powers. The people of England were inspired with uncommon alacrity at the near prospect of war, for which they had so long clamoured; and the ministry seeing it unavoidable, began to be earnest and effectual in their preparations.

The great view of the nation now being to distress the Spaniards, another squadron was ordered to be

fitted

OF KING GEORGE II. 393

fitted out for the Weft Indies, and the command of it given to Edward Vernon, Efq; then juft made vice admiral of the blue, who, on account of the eminent fervices he had formerly done his king and country in that part of the world, was looked on by all as the moft proper perfon to be intrufted with fo important an enterprize. He had withdrawn from employment, and on feveral accounts, had been difgufted at the conduct of the miniftry; yet upon the firft application made to him to undertake the command of a fquadron for the fervice of his country, he immediately laid afide all private animofity, and facrificing all other confiderations to the welfare of the public, very chearfully obeyed the fummons, defiring only a few days to fettle his family affairs. He was counted a good officer, and his boifterous manner feemed to enhance his character. As he had once commanded a fquadron in Jamaica, he was perfectly well acquainted with thofe feas; and in a debate upon the Spanifh depredations, he chanced to affirm, that Porto Bello on the Spanifh main might be eafily taken: nay, he even undertook to reduce it with fix fhips only. This offer was echoed from the mouths of all the members in the oppofition. Vernon was extolled as another Drake or Raleigh: he became the idol of a party, and his praife refounded from all corners of the kingdom. The minifter, in order to appeafe the clamours of the people on this fubject, fent him as commander in chief to the Weft Indies. He was pleafed with an opportunity to remove fuch a troublefome cenfurer from the houfe of commons; and perhaps, he was not without hope, that Vernon would difgrace himfelf and his party, by failing in the exploit he had undertaken. His catholic majefty having ordered all the Britifh fhips in his harbours to be feized and detained, the king of England would keep meafures with him no longer, but denounced war againft him on the 23d day of October, 1739. Many Englifh merchants began to equip privateers,

and

and arm their trading veffels, to protect their own commerce as well as to diftrefs that of the enemy.

On the 13th of March, 1740, a fhip arrived from the Weft Indies, difpatched by admiral Vernon, with an account of his having taken Porto Bello, on the ifthmus of Darien, and demolifhed all the fortifications of the place. The Spaniards acted with fuch pufillanimity on this occafion, that their forts were taken almoft without bloodfhed. And though the admiral was not able to pufh his conquefts further up the country, yet the national advantage arifing from what he had already done was very confiderable: particularly as the traders of Jamaica had now a fair opportunity of opening an extenfive commerce with the Spaniards, who were fond of clandeftinely conveying their money from Panama over the ifthmus.

Sir Chaloner Ogle arrived at Jamaica on the 9th day of Jan. 1741; and admiral Vernon did not fail on his intended expedition to Carthagena, till toward the end of the month. He refolved to beat up againft the wind to Hifpaniola, in order to obferve the motion of the French fquadron, commanded by the marquis d' Antin: but the French admiral had failed for Europe in great diftrefs, for want of men and provifions, which he could not procure in the Weft Indies. Admiral Vernon, thus difappointed, fet fail for the continent of New Spain, and on the 4th of March anchored in Playa Grande, to the windward of Carthagena. There they lay inactive till the 9th, when the troops were landed on the ifland of Tierra Bomba, near the mouth of the harbour, known by the name of Boca chica, or Little mouth, which was furprifingly fortified with caftles, batteries, bombs, chains, cables, and fhips of war. The Britifh forces erected a battery on fhore, with which they made a breach in the principal fort, while the admiral fent in a number of fhips to divide the fire of the enemy, and cooperate with the endeavours of the army. Lord Aubrey Beauclerc, a gallant officer, who commanded

one

one of thefe fhips, was flain on this occafion. The breach being deemed practicable, the forces advanced to the attack: but the forts and batteries were abandoned; the Spanifh fhips that lay athwart the harbour's mouth were deftroyed or taken; the paffage was opened, and the fleet entered without further oppofition. Then the forces were reimbarked with the artillery, and landed within a mile of Carthagena, where they were oppofed by about 700 Spaniards, whom they obliged to retire. The admiral and general had contracted a hearty contempt for each other, and took all opportunities of expreffing their mutual diflike: far from acting vigoroufly in concert, each appeared more eager for the difgrace of his rival, than zealous for the honour of the nation: and this contributed in great meafure to the ruin of the enterprize.

The forces miftook their rout, and advanced to the ftrongeft part of the fortification, where they were moreover expofed to the fire of the town. Their number was fo much reduced, that they could no longer maintain their footing on fhore: befide, the rainy feafon had begun with fuch violence, as rendered it impoffible for them to live in camp. They were therefore reimbarked; and all hope of further fuccefs immediately vanifhed.

The mifcarriage of 'this expedition, which had coft the nation an immenfe fum of money, was no fooner known in England, than the kingdom was filled with murmurs and difcontent; and the people were depreffed, in proportion to that fanguine hope by which they had been elevated. Admiral Vernon, inftead of undertaking any enterprize which might have retrieved the honour of the Britifh arms, fet fail from Jamaica with the forces in July, and anchored at the fouth-eaft part of Cuba, in a bay, on which he beftowed the appellation of Cumberland harbour. The troops were landed, and encamped at the diftance of twenty miles farther up the river, where

where they remained totally inactive, and subsisted chiefly on salt and damaged provisions, till the month of November; when, being considerably diminished by sickness, they were put on board again, and reconveyed to Jamaica. He was afterward reinforced from England by four ships of war, and about 3000 soldiers; but he performed nothing worthy of the reputation he had acquired.

While admiral Haddock, with twelve ships of the line, lay at anchor in the bay of Gibraltar, the Spanish fleet passed the Streights in the night, and was joined by the French squadron from Toulon. The British admiral sailing from Gibraltar, fell in with them in a few days, and found both squadrons drawn up in line of battle. As he bore down upon the Spanish fleet, the French admiral sent a flag of truce to inform him, that as the French and Spaniards were engaged in a joint expedition, he should be obliged to act in concert with his master's allies. This interposition prevented an engagement, the combined fleets amounting to double the number of the English squadron. Admiral Haddock was obliged to desist; and proceeded to Portmahon, leaving the enemy to prosecute their voyage without molestation. The people of England were incensed at this transaction, and did not scruple to affirm, that the hands of the British admiral were tied up by the neutrality of Hanover.

The court of Madrid seemed to have shaken off that indolence and phlegm which had formerly disgraced the councils of Spain. They no sooner learned the destination of commodore Anson, who had sailed from Spithead in the course of the preceding year, than they sent Don Pizarro, with a more powerful squadron upon the same voyage to defeat his design. Their privateers were so industrious and successful, that in the beginning of this year, they had taken, since the commencement of the war, 407 ships, belonging to the subjects of Great Britain, and valued

at

at near four millions of piasters. The traders had therefore too much cause to complain, considering the formidable fleets which were maintained for the protection of commerce. In the course of the summer, Sir John Norris had twice sailed toward the coast of Spain, at the head of a powerful squadron, without taking any effectual step for annoying the enemy; as if the sole intention of the ministry had been to expose the nation to the ridicule and contempt of its enemies. The inactivity of the British arms appears the more inexcusable, when we consider the great armaments which had been prepared. The landforces of Great Britain, exclusive of Danish and Hessian auxiliaries, amounted to 60,000 men; and the fleet consisted of above 100 ships of war, manned by 54,000 sailors.

The new ministry in England (1742) had sent out admiral Matthews to assume the command of this squadron, which had been for some time conducted by Lestock, an inferior officer, as Haddock had been obliged to resign his commission on account of his ill state of health. Matthews was likewise invested with the character of minister plenipotentiary to the king of Sardinia and the states of Italy. Immediately after he had taken possession of his command, he ordered captain Norris to destroy five Spanish gallies which had put into the bay of St. Tropez; and this service was effectually performed. In May he detached commodore Rowley with eight sail, to cruise off the harbour of Toulon; and a great number of merchantships belonging to the enemy fell into his hands. In August he sent commodore Martin with another squadron into the bay of Naples, to bombard that city, unless his Sicilian majesty would immediately recal his troops which had joined the Spanish army, and promise to remain neuter during the continuance of the war. Naples was immediately filled with consternation: the king subscribed to these conditions; and the English squadron rejoined the admiral in the road of Hieres, which he had chosen for his winter-station. But before this period he had landed some men at St. Remo, in the territories of Genoa, and destroyed the magazines that were erected for the use of the Spanish army. He had likewise ordered two of his cruisers to attack a Spanish ship of the line, which lay at anchor in the port of Ajaccio, in the island of Corsica; but, the Spanish captain set his men on shore, and blew up his ship, rather than she should fall into the hands of the English.

In the course of this year admiral Vernon and general Wentworth made another effort in the West Indies. They had received, in January, a reinforcement from England, and planned a new expedition. Their design was to disembark the troops at Porto-Bello, and march across the isthmus of Darien, to attack the rich town of Panama. They sailed from Jamaica on the 9th day of March, and on the 28th arrived at Porto-Bello. There they held a council of war, in which it was resolved, that as the troops were sickly, the rainy season begun, and several transports not yet arrived, the intended expedition was become impracticable. In pursuance of this determination, the armament immediately returned to Jamaica, exhibiting a ridiculous spectacle of folly and irresolution. Vernon and Wentworth received orders to return to England, with such troops as remained alive; and these did not amount to a tenth part of the number which had been sent abroad in that inglorious service.

In England the merchants still complained, that their commerce was not properly protected; and the people clamoured against the conduct of the war. They said, their burdens were increased to maintain quarrels with which they had no concern; to defray the enormous expence of inactive fleets and pacific armies. The lord C. had now insinuated himself into the confidence of his sovereign, and engrossed the whole direction of public affairs. The war with Spain was now become a secondary consideration, and neglected accordingly;

while

while the chief attention of the new minister was turned upon the affairs of the continent.

The British fleet commanded by admiral Matthews overawed all the states that bordered on the Mediterranean. About the end of June, 1743, understanding that 14 xebecks, loaded with artillery and ammunition for the Spanish army, had arrived at Genoa, he sailed thither from the road of Hieres, and demanded of the republic, that they would either oblige these vessels with the stores to quit their harbour, or sequester their ladings until a general peace should be established. After some dispute, it was agreed, that the cannon and stores should be deposited in the castle of Bonifacio, situated on a rock at the south end of Corsica: and, that the xebecks should have leave to retire without molestation. Admiral Matthews, though he did not undertake any expedition of importance against the maritime towns of Spain, continued to assert the British empire at sea through the whole extent of the Mediterranean. The Spanish army under Don Philip was no sooner in motion, than the English admiral ordered some troops and cannon to be disembarked for the security of Villa-Franca; stores having been landed at Civita-Vecchia for the use of the Spanish forces under count Gages, Matthews interpreted this transaction into a violation of the neutrality which the pope had professed, and sent thither a squadron to bombard the place. The city of Rome was filled with consternation; and the pope had recourse to the good offices of his Sardinian majesty, in consequence of which the English squadron was ordered to withdraw. The captains of single cruising ships, by their activity and vigilance, wholly interrupted the commerce of Spain; cannonaded and burnt some towns on the sea-side, and kept the whole coast in continual alarm.

In the West Indies some unsuccessful efforts were made by an English squadron, commanded by commodore Knowles. He attacked La Gueira, on the coast of Carraccas, in the month of February; but met with such a warm reception, that he was obliged to desist, and make the best of his way for the Dutch island Curaçoa, where he repaired the damage he had sustained. His ships being refitted, he made another attempt upon Porto-Cavallo in April, which, like the former, miscarried.

By the parliamentary disputes, the loud clamours, and general dissatisfaction of the people of Great Britain, the French ministry were persuaded, that the nation was ripe for revolt. This belief was corroborated by the assertions of their emissaries in different parts of Great Britain and Ireland. They gave the court of Versailles to understand, that if the chevalier de St. George, or his eldest son Charles-Edward, should appear at the head of a French army in Great Britain, a revolution would instantly follow in his favour. This intimation was agreeable to cardinal de Tencin, who had succeeded Fleury, as prime minister of France. He was of a violent interprising temper. He had been recommended to the purple, by the chevalier de St. George, and was warmly attached to the Stuart family. His ambition was flattered with a prospect of giving a king to Great Britain; of and performing such eminent service to his benefactor, in restoring him to the throne of his ancestors. He foresaw, that even if his aim should miscarry, a descent upon Great Britain would make a considerable diversion from the continent in favour of France, and embroil and embarrass his Britannic majesty, who was the chief support of the house of Austria and all its allies. Actuated by these motives, he concerted measures with the chevalier de St. George at Rome; who being too much advanced in years to engage personally in such an expedition, agreed to delegate his pretensions and authority to his son Charles. Count Saxe was appointed by the French king commander of the troops designed for this expedition, which amounted to 15,000. Charles departed from
Rome

Rome about the end of December, in the difguife of a Spanifh courier, attended by one fervant only : and profecuting his journey to Paris, was indulged with a private audience of the French king. The Britifh miniftry being apprifed of his arrival in France, at once comprehended the deftination of the armaments prepared at Breft and Boulogne. Mr. Thomfon, the Englifh refident at Paris, received orders to make a remonftrance to the French miniftry, on the violation of thofe treaties by which the pretender to the crown of Great Britain was excluded from the territories of France. But he was given to underftand, that his moft chriftian majefty would not explain himfelf on that fubject, until the king of England fhould have given fatisfaction on the repeated complaints which had been made to him, touching the infractions of thofe treaties which had been fo often violated by his orders.

In the month of January, M. de Roquefeuille failed from Breft, directing his courfe up the Englifh channel, with twenty fhips of war. Sir John Norris was forthwith ordered to take the command of the fquadron at Spithead, with which he failed round to the Downs, where he was joined by fome fhips of the line from Chatham, and then he found himfelf at the head of a fquadron confiderably ftronger than that of the enemy.

Several regiments marched to the fouthern coaft of England: all governors and commanders were ordered to repair immediately to their refpective pofts: the forts at the mouth of the Thames and the Medway were put in a pofture of defence. A proclamation was iffued for putting the laws in execution againft papifts and nonjurors, who were commanded to retire ten miles from London; and every precaution taken which feemed neceffary for the prefervation of the public tranquillity.

Mean while the French court proceeded with their preparations, at Boulogne and Dunkirk, under the eye

eye of the younger pretender; and 7000 men were actually embarked. M. de Roquefeuille failed up the channel as far as Dungenefs, a promontory on the coaft of Kent, after having detached M. de Barreil with five fhips, to haften the embarkation at Dunkirk. While the French admiral anchored off Dungenefs, he perceived, on the 24th day of February, the Britifh fleet under Sir John Norris, doubling the South-Foreland from the Downs; and, though the wind was againft him, taking the opportunity of the tide to come up and engage the French fquadron. Roquefeuille, who little expected fuch a vifit, could not be altogether compofed, confidering the great fuperiority of his enemies; but the tide failing, the Englifh admiral was obliged to anchor two leagues fhort of the enemy. In this interval, M. Roquefeuille called a council of war; in which it was determined to avoid an engagement, to weigh anchor at funfet, and make the beft of their way to the place from whence they had fet fail. This refolution was favoured by a very hard gale of wind, which began to blow from the north-eaft, and carried them down the channel with incredible expedition. But the fame ftorm which, in all probability, faved their fleet from deftruction, utterly difconcerted the defign of invading England. A great number of their tranfports was driven afhore and deftroyed, and the reft fo much damaged that they could not be fpeedily repaired.

The Englifh were now mafters at fea, and their coaft was fo well guarded, that the enterprife could not be profecuted with any probability of fuccefs. The French generals nominated to ferve in this expedition returned to Paris, and the pretender refolved to wait a more favourable opportunity. The French king no longer preferved any meafures with the court of London: the Britifh refident at Paris was given to underftand, that a declaration of war muft enfue; and this was actually publifhed on the 20th day of March,

March, 1744. The king of Great Britain was taxed with having diffuaded the court of Vienna from entertaining any thoughts of an accommodation; with having infringed the convention of Hanover; with having exercifed piracy upon the fubjects of France, and even with blocking up the harbour of Toulon. On the 31ft of March, a like denunciation of war againft France was publifhed at London, amidft the acclamations of the people.

An action happened in the Mediterranean between the Britifh fleet, commanded by admiral Matthews, and the combined fquadrons of France and Spain, which had been for fome time blocked up in the harbour of Toulon. On the 9th day of February, 1744, they were perceived ftanding out of the road, to the number of 34 fail: the Englifh admiral immediately weighed from Hieres-bay; and on the 11th, part of the fleets engaged. Matthews attacked the Spanifh admiral, Don Navarro, whofe fhip, the Real, was a firft rate, mounted with above 100 guns. The rear-admiral Rowley fingled out M. de Court, who commanded the French fquadron; and a very few captains followed the example of their commanders: but vice-admiral Leftock, with his whole divifion, remained at a great diftance aftern; and feveral captains, that were immediately under the eye of Matthews, behaved in fuch a manner as reflected difgrace upon their country.

The whole tranfaction was conducted without order or deliberation. The French and Spaniards would have willingly avoided an engagement, as the Britifh fquadron was fuperior to them in ftrength and number. M. de Court therefore made the beft of his way toward the Streights mouth, probably with intention to join the Breft fquadron: but he had orders to protect the Spanifh fleet; and as they failed heavily, he was obliged to wait for them, at the hazard of maintaining a battle with the Englifh. Thus circum-ftanced, he made fail and lay to by turns; fo that the British admiral could not engage them in proper order; and as they out-sailed his ships, he began to fear they would escape him altogether should he wait for vice-admiral Lestock, who was so far astern. Under this apprehension, he made the signal for engaging, while that for the line of battle was still displayed; and this inconsistency naturally introduced confusion. The fight was maintained by the few who engaged, with great vivacity. The Real being quite disabled, and lying like a wreck upon the water, Mr. Matthews sent a fireship to destroy her; but the expedient did not take effect. The ship ordered to cover this machine, did not obey the signal; so that the captain of the fireship was exposed to the whole fire of the enemy. Nevertheless, he continued to advance until he found the vessel sinking; and being within a few yards of the Real, he set fire to the fusees. The ship was immediately in flames, in the midst of which, he and his lieutenant, with twelve men, perished. This was likewise the fate of a Spanish launch, which had been manned with fifty sailors to prevent the fireship from running on board the Real. One ship of the line, belonging to the Spanish squadron, struck to captain Hawke, who sent a lieutenant to take possession of her; she was afterward retaken by the French squadron; but was found so disabled, that they left her deserted; and she was next day burned by order of admiral Matthews.

At night, the action ceased; and the admiral found his own ship so much damaged, that he moved his flag into another. Captain Cornwall fell in the engagement, after having exhibited a remarkable proof of courage and intrepidity: but, the loss of men was very inconsiderable. Next day the enemy appeared to leeward, and the admiral gave chace till night, when he brought to, that he might be joined by the ships a-stern. They were perceived again on the 13th at a considerable distance, and pursued till the evening. In the morning of the 14th, 20 sail of them

them were seen diftinctly, and Leftock with his divifion had gained ground of them confiderably, by noon; but admiral Matthews difplayed the fignal for leaving off chace, and bore away for Port-mahon, to repair the damage he had fuftained. Mean while, the combined fquadrons continued their courfe toward the coaft of Spain.

Admiral Matthews, on his arrival at Minorca, accufed Leftock of having mifbehaved on the day of action; fufpended him from his office, and fent him prifoner to England; where, in his turn, he accufed his accufer. Long before the engagement, thefe two officers had expreffed the moft virulent refentment againft each other. Matthews was brave, open, and undifguifed; but proud, imperious, and precipitate. Leftock had fignalized his courage on many occafions, and perfectly underftood the whole difcipline of the navy; but he was cool, and vindictive. He had been treated fuperciliously by Matthews, and in revenge took advantage of his errors and precipitation. To gratify this paffion, he betrayed the intereft and glory of his country; for, it is not to be doubted, but that he might have come up in time to engage; and in that cafe, the fleets of France and Spain would in all likelihood have been deftroyed: but he intrenched himfelf within the punctilios of difcipline, and faw with pleafure his antagonift expofe himfelf to the hazard of death, ruin, and difgrace. Matthews himfelf, in the fequel, facrificed his duty to his refentment, in reftraining Leftock from purfuing and attacking the combined fquadrons on the third day after the engagement, when they appeared difabled and in manifeft diforder, and would have fallen an eafy prey, had they been vigoroufly attacked. One can hardly, without indignation, reflect upon thofe inftances, in which a community has fo feverely fuffered from the perfonal animofity of individuals. The mifcarriage off Toulon became the fubject of a parliamentary enquiry in England.

A court-martial was conſtituted, and proceeded to trial. Several commanders of ſhips were caſhiered: vice-admiral Leſtock was honourably acquitted, and admiral Matthews rendered incapable of ſerving for the future in his majeſty's navy. All the world knew that Leſtock kept aloof, and that Matthews ruſhed into the hotteſt part of the engagement: yet, the former triumphed on his trial, and the latter narrowly eſcaped ſentence of death for cowardice and miſconduct. Such deciſions are not to be accounted for, except from prejudice and faction.

After the action at Toulon, nothing of conſequence was atchieved by the Britiſh ſquadron in the Mediterranean; and indeed the naval power of Great Britain was, during the ſummer, quite inactive. In the month of June, commodore Anſon returned from his voyage of three years and nine months, in which he had ſurrounded the terraqueous globe. Though this fortunate commander enriched himſelf by an occurrence that may be termed almoſt accidental, the Britiſh nation was not indemnified for the expence of the expedition, and the original deſign was entirely defeated. Had the Manilla ſhip eſcaped the vigilance of the Engliſh commodore, he might have been, at his return to England, laid aſide as a ſuperannuated captain, and died in obſcurity: but his great wealth inveſted him with conſiderable influence, and added luſtre to his talents. He ſoon became the oracle which was conſulted in all naval deliberations: and the king raiſed him to the dignity of a peerage.

In July, Sir John Balchen, an admiral of approved valour and great experience, ſailed from Spithead with a ſtrong ſquadron, in queſt of an opportunity to attack the French fleet at Breſt, under the command of M. de Rochambault. In the bay of Biſcay, he was overtaken by a violent ſtorm, that diſperſed the ſhips, and drove them up the Engliſh channel. Admiral Stewart, with the greater part of them, arrived at Plymouth; but Sir John Balchen's own ſhip, the Victory, which was counted the moſt beautiful firſt rate in the world, foundered at ſea; and this brave commander periſhed with all his officers, volunteers, and crew, amounting to 1100 choice ſeamen.

The naval tranſactions of Great Britain were in the year 1745 remarkably ſpirited. In the Mediterranean, admiral Rowley had ſucceeded Matthews in the command; and Savona, Genoa, Final, St. Remo, with Baſtia the capital of Corſica, were bombarded: ſeveral Spaniſh ſhips were taken; but he could not prevent the ſafe arrival of their rich Havannah ſquadron at Corunna. Commodore Barnet in the Weſt Indies made prize of ſeveral French ſhips richly laden; and commodore Townſhend, in the latitude of Martinico, took about 30 merchant-ſhips belonging to the enemy, under convoy of four ſhips of war, two of which were deſtroyed. The Engliſh privateers likewiſe met with uncommon ſucceſs. But the moſt important atchievement was the conqueſt of Louiſburgh, on the iſland of Cape-Breton, in North America; a place of great conſequence, which the French had fortified at a prodigious expence. The ſcheme of reducing this fortreſs was planned in Boſton, recommended by their general-aſſembly, and approved by his majeſty; who ſent inſtructions to commodore Warren, ſtationed off the Leeward Iſlands, to ſail for the northern parts of America, and to co-operate with the forces of New England in this expedition. A body of 6000 men was formed under the conduct of Mr. Pepperel, a trader of Piſcataway, whoſe influence was extenſive in that country; though he was a man of little or no education, and utterly unacquainted with military operations. In April, Mr. Warren arrived at Canſo with ten ſhips of war; and the troops of New England being embarked in tranſports, ſailed immediately for the iſle of Cape-Breton, where they landed without oppoſition. The enemy abandoned their grand battery, which was detached from the town; and the immediate ſeizure of it contributed

tributed in a good meafure to the fuccefs of the enterprize. While the American troops, reinforced by 800 marines, carried on their approaches by land, the fquadron blocked up the place by fea in fuch a manner, that no fuccours could be introduced. A French fhip of the line, with fome fmaller veffels, deftined for the relief of the garrifon, were intercepted and taken by the Britifh cruifers; and indeed, the reduction of Louifburgh was chiefly owing to the vigilance and activity of Mr. Warren, one of the braveft and beft officers in the fervice of England. The operations of the fiege were wholly conducted by the engineers and officers who commanded the Britifh marines; and the Americans, being ignorant of war, were contented to act under their directions. The town being confiderably damaged by the bombs and bullets of the befiegers, and the governor defpairing of relief, capitulated on the 17th day of June. The garrifon and inhabitants engaged, that they would not bear arms for twelve months againft Great Britain or her allies; and were tranfported to Rochfort. In a few days after the furrender of Louifburgh, two French Eaft India fhips, and another from Peru laden with treafure, failed into the harbour, on the fuppofition that it ftill belonged to France; and were taken by the Englifh fquadron*.

The poffeffion of Cape-Breton was, doubtlefs, a valuable acquifition to Great Britain. It not only diftreffed the French in their fifhery and navigation, but removed all fears of encroachment and rivalfhip from the Englifh fifhers on the banks of Newfoundland. It freed New England from the terrors of a dangerous neighbour; over-awed the Indians of that country; and fecured the poffeffion of Acadia to the crown of Great Britain. The natives of New England acquired great glory from the fuccefs of this enterprife. Britain, which had in fome inftances behaved like a ftepmother to her own colonies, was now convinced

* See Ulloa's Voyage, in our firft volume, p. 484.

of their importance; and treated thofe as brethren whom fhe had too long confidered as aliens and rivals. Circumftanced as the nation is, the legiflature cannot too tenderly cherifh the interefts of the Britifh plantations in America. They are inhabited by a brave, hardy, induftrious people, animated with an active fpirit of commerce; infpired with a noble zeal for liberty and independence.

While the continent of Europe and the ifles of America were expofed to the ravages of war, Great Britain underwent a dangerous convulfion in her own bowels. The fon of the chevalier de St. George refolved to make another effort, which, though it might not be crowned with fuccefs, fhould at leaft aftonifh all Chriftendom. He was amufed with the promife of powerful fuccours from France, though the miniftry of that kingdom were never hearty in his caufe: neverthelefs they forefaw, that his appearance in England would embarrafs the government, and make a confiderable diverfion in their favour. Certain it is, that if he had been properly fupported, he could not have found a more favourable opportunity of exciting an inteftine commotion in Great Britain; for Scotland was quite unfurnifhed with troops, and the king was in Germany.

The young pretender accordingly embarked on board a frigate at Port Lazare in Brittany, and failed for Scotland on the 14th of July, 1745. The frigate was joined off Belleifle by the Elizabeth, a French man of war of fixty guns, which the miniftry had fitted out to convoy him in this expedition. As his defign was to fail round Ireland, and land in the north-weft of Scotland, the fhips fteered for the foutherm coaft of the former; but in their paffage were met by the Lion man of war, commanded by captain Brett, which, after a long engagement, fo effectually difabled the Elizabeth, that fhe was obliged to return to Breft. The frigate efcaped, and continued her courfe with fuch expedition, that on the 23d of July, the

the young pretender found himfelf in the weftern ifles of Scotland, where he continued cruifing till the 26th between the iflands of Bara and South Vift; but finding there was no hopes of being joined by the Elizabeth, the frigate ftood in for the coaft of Lochaber, one of the maritime counties on the north-weft of Scotland, inhabited principally by papifts; and on the 27th of July, landed the young pretender and his companions at Moidart, between the iflands of Sky and Mull.

We fhall not follow this young adventurer, as the fubject is very foreign to a naval hiftory; it being fufficient to obferve, that his party was totally defeated by his royal highnefs the duke of Cumberland at Culloden, on the 16th of April, 1746, which put an end to this rebellion.

During thefe tranfactions, our miniftry feemed determined to make an attempt on Quebec; and a large fquadron was accordingly affembled at Portfmouth, and feveral regiments, under the command of lieutenant-general Sinclair, embarked: but after many delays, the expedition to Quebec was laid afide, and the fleet failed to the coaft of Brittany, and landed the troops in Quimperlay-bay, near Port l'Orient, which they befieged: but when the city was juft going to furrender, they retreated in the night with the greateft precipitation, leaving behind them a mortar, and a confiderable quantity of ammunition and ftores. The Exeter man of war however engaged the Ardente, a 64 gun fhip, forced her afhore and burnt her.

The French king, baffled in his projects upon Italy, in 1747, was not more fortunate in his naval operations. He had, in the preceding year, equipped an expenfive armament, under the command of the duke d'Anville, for the recovery of Cape-Breton; but it was rendered ineffectual by ftorms, diftempers, and the death of the commander. Not yet difcouraged by thefe difafters, he refolved to renew his efforts againft

the

the British colonies in North America, and their settlements in the East Indies. For these purposes two squadrons were prepared at Brest; one to be commanded by the commodore de la Jonquiere, and the other, destined for India, by monsieur de St. George. The ministry of Great Britain, being apprized of these measures, resolved to intercept both squadrons, which were to set sail together. For this purpose vice-admiral Anson and rear-admiral Warren took their departure from Plymouth with a formidable fleet, and steered their course to Cape Finisterre on the coast of Gallicia.

On the 3d day of May, they fell in with the French squadrons, commanded by la Jonquiere and St. George, consisting of six large ships of war, as many frigates, and four armed vessels equipped by their East India company, having under their convoy about thirty ships laden with merchandize. Those prepared for war immediately shortened sail, and formed a line of battle; while the rest, under the protection of the six frigates, proceeded on their voyage with all the sail they could carry. The British squadron was likewise drawn up in a line of battle: but Mr. Warren perceiving that the enemy began to sheer off, now their convoy was at a considerable distance, advised admiral Anson to haul in the signal for the line, and hoist another for giving chace and engaging, otherwise the French would in all probability escape by favour of the night. The proposal was embraced: and in a little time the engagement began with great fury, about four o'clock in the afternoon. The enemy sustained the battle with equal conduct and valour, until they were overpowered by numbers, and then they struck their colours. The admiral detached three ships in pursuit of the convoy, nine sail of which were taken; but the rest were saved by the intervening darkness. About seven hundred of the French were killed and wounded in this action. The English lost about five hundred; and among these,

captain

captain Grenville, commander of the ſhip Defiance. The ſucceſs of the Britiſh arms, in this engagement, was chiefly owing to the conduct, activity, and courage of the rear-admiral. A conſiderable quantity of bullion was found in the prizes, which were brought to Spithead in triumph; and the treaſure being landed, was conveyed in twenty waggons to the bank of London. Admiral Anſon was ennobled, and Mr. Warren honoured with the order of the Bath.

About the middle of June, commodore Fox, with ſix ſhips of war, cruiſing in the latitude of Cape Ortegal in Gallicia, took about forty French ſhips, richly laden from St. Domingo, after they had been abandoned by their convoy. But the French king ſuſtained another more important loſs at ſea, in the month of October. Rear-admiral Hawke ſailed from Plymouth in the beginning of Auguſt, with 14 ſhips of the line, to intercept a fleet of French merchant-ſhips bound for the Weſt Indies. He cruiſed for ſome time on the coaſt of Bretagne; and at length, the French fleet ſailed from the iſle of Aix, under convoy of nine ſhips of the line, beſide frigates, commanded by monſieur de Letenduer. On the 14th day of October, the two ſquadrons were in ſight of each other, in the latitude of Belleiſle. The French commodore immediately ordered one of his great ſhips and the frigates to proceed with the trading ſhips, while he formed the line of battle, and waited the attack. At eleven in the forenoon, admiral Hawke diſplayed the ſignal to chace, and in half an hour both fleets were engaged. The battle laſted till night, when all the French ſquadron, except the Intrepid and Tónant, had ſtruck to the Engliſh flag. Theſe two capital ſhips eſcaped in the dark, and returned to Breſt in a ſhattered condition. The French captains ſuſtained the unequal fight with uncommon bravery and reſolution, and did not yield until their ſhips were diſabled. Their loſs in men amounted to 800: the number of Engliſh killed in this engagement did not exceed 200, including captain Saumarez, a gallant officer, who had ſerved under lord Anſon in his expedition to the Pacific Ocean. Indeed, it muſt be owned, for the honour of that nobleman, that all the officers formed under his example, and raiſed by his influence, approved themſelves in all reſpects worthy of the commands to which they were preferred. Immediately after the action, admiral Hawke diſpatched a ſloop to commodore Legge, whoſe ſquadron was ſtationed at the Leeward Iſlands, with intelligence of the French fleet of merchantſhips, outward-bound, that he might take the proper meaſures for intercepting them in their paſſage to Martinique, and the other French iſlands. In conſequence of this advice, he redoubled his vigilance, and a good number of them fell into his hands.

In the Mediterranean, vice-admiral Medley blocked up the Spaniſh ſquadron in Carthagena; aſſiſted the Auſtrian general on the coaſt of Villa Franca; and intercepted ſome of the ſuccours ſent from France to the aſſiſtance of the Genoeſe. At his death, which happened in the beginning of Auguſt, the command of that ſquadron devolved upon rear-admiral Byng, who proceeded on the ſame plan of operation. Commodore Griffin had been ſent with a reinforcement of ſhips, to aſſume the command of the ſquadron in the Eaſt Indies; and although his arrival ſecured Fort St. David's, and the other Britiſh ſettlements in that country, from the inſults of monſieur de la Bourdonnais, his ſtrength was not ſufficient to enable him to undertake any enterpriſe of importance againſt the enemy: the miniſtry of England therefore reſolved to equip a freſh armament, that, when joined by the ſhips in India, ſhould be in a condition to beſiege Pondicherry, the principal ſettlement belonging to the French on the coaſt of Coromandel. For this ſervice, a ſtrong ſquadron was ſent, under the conduct of rear-admiral Boſcawen, an officer of unqueſtioned

tioned valour and capacity. In the courfe of this year, the Britifh cruifers were fo alert and fuccefsful, that they took 644 prizes from the French and Spaniards; whereas the lofs of Great Britain, in the fame time, did not exceed 550.

All the belligerant powers were, by this time, heartily tired of a war which had confumed an immenfity of treafure, had been productive of fo much mifchief, and in the events of which, all, in their turns, had found themfelves difappointed. Immediately after the battle of Laffeldt, the king of France had, in a perfonal converfation with Sir John Ligonier, expreffed his defire of a pacification; and afterward his minifter at the Hague prefented a declaration on the fame fubject, to the deputies of the ftates-general. The fignal fuccefs of the Britifh arms at fea, confirmed him in thefe fentiments, which were likewife reinforced by a variety of other confiderations. His finances were almoft exhaufted, and his fupplies from the Spanifh Weft Indies rendered fo precarious, by the vigilance of the Britifh cruifers, that he could no longer depend on their arrival. The trading part of his fubjects had fuftained fuch loffes, that his kingdom was filled with bankruptcies; and the beft part of his navy now contributed to ftrengthen the fleets of his enemies. The election of a ftadtholder had united the whole power of the ftates-general againft him, in taking the moft refolute meafures for their own fafety: his views in Germany were entirely fruftrated; the fuccefs of his arms in Italy had not at all anfwered his expectation: and Genoa was become an expenfive ally. He had the mortification to fee the commerce of Britain flourifh in the midft of war, while his own people were utterly impoverifhed. The parliament of England granted, and the nation payed, fuch incredible fums as enabled their fovereign, not only to maintain invincible navies and formidable armies, but likewife to give fubfidies to all the powers of Europe. His moft
chriftian

Christian majesty, moved by thefe confiderations, made farther advances toward an accommodation, both at the Hague and in London; and the contending powers agreed to a congrefs, which was opened in March, 1748, at Aix-la-Chapelle, where peace was figned the 7th of October following.

The Britifh fleet in the Eaft Indies, under the command of admiral Bofcawen, undertook the fiege of Pondicherry; but after the moft vigorous attempts to take the place, the admiral was obliged to raife the fiege, and return to Fort St. David.

Thus have we brought this war to a conclufion; and fhall conclude with obferving, that the number of prizes taken by the Englifh, from the beginning to the figning the preliminaries of peace, was 3434; namely, 1249 from the Spaniards, and 2185 from the French: and that they loft, during the war, 3238; 1360 being taken by the Spaniards, and 1878 by the French. Several of the fhips taken from the Spaniards were immenfely rich; fo that the balance upon the whole amounted to almoft two millions, in favour of the Englifh.

Notwithftanding a general peace was figned, yet the French gave continual proofs of their intention to obferve it no longer than was confiftent with their intereft; and that they intended to make themfelves mafters of fome parts of our fettlements in America. In order to which, they built a chain of forts on the back of our colonies, from the Miffifippi to Canada, and gained over great part of the Indians to their intereft.

Every method of negotiation was tried to put an end to thefe difputes; but the repeated and undoubted intelligence received from France, Holland, Italy, &c. of the great naval preparations making in every port of France, and of a great number of veteran troops drawn out of their feveral corps, and deftined for America, convinced the Britifh miniftry, that nothing was to be hoped for from a negotiation.

Accord-

Accordingly a strong fleet was fitted out in 1754, to frustrate the designs of the enemy, and protect the British colonies in America.

Whilst all Europe was in suspence about the fate of the English and the French squadrons, preparations for a vigorous sea-war were going forward in England with an unparalleled spirit and success. Other branches of the public service went on with equal alacrity; and such was the eagerness of the people to lend their money to the government, that instead of one million, which was to be raised by way of lottery, three millions eight hundred and eighty thousand pounds were subscribed immediately.

Admiral Boscawen, with eleven ships of the line and a frigate, having taken on board two regiments at Plymouth, sailed in April for the banks of Newfoundland: and, in a few days after his arrival there, the French fleet from Brest came to the same station, under the command of M. Bois de la Mothe. But the thick fogs, which prevail upon these coasts, especially at that time of the year, kept the two armaments from seeing each other; and part of the French squadron escaped up the river St. Lawrence, whilst another part of them went round, and got into the same river through the streights of Belleisle, by a way which was never known to be attempted before by ships of the line. However, whilst the English fleet lay off Cape Race, which is the southernmost point of Newfoundland, two French ships, the Alcide, of 64 guns and 480 men, and the Lys, pierced for 64 guns, but mounting only 22, being separated from the rest of their fleet in a fog, were both taken, with several considerable officers and engineers, and about eight thousand pounds in money.

Though the taking of these ships, from which the commencement of the war may in fact be dated, fell greatly short of what was hoped for from this expedition; yet, when the news of it reached England, it was of infinite service to the public credit of every kind,

and

and animated the whole nation, who now faw plainly that the government was determined to keep no farther meafures with the French; but juftly to repel force by force, and put a ftop to their fending more men and arms to invade the property of the Englifh in America, as they had hitherto done with impunity. The French, who, for fome time, did not even attempt to make reprifals on our fhipping, would gladly have chofen to avoid a war at that time; and to have continued extending their encroachments on our fettlements, till they had executed their grand plan of fecuring a communication from the Miffifippi to Canada by a line of forts: many of thefe they had already erected, and had alfo deftroyed one of ours on the Ohio; whilft they endeavoured to amufe us with fruitlefs negotiations about the boundaries of Nova Scotia.

The vaft increafe of the French marine of late years, which in all probability would foon be employed againft Britain, very properly occafioned an order for making reprifals general in Europe as well as in America; and that all the French fhips, whether outward or homeward bound, fhould be ftopt and brought into Britifh ports. To give the greater weight to thefe orders, it was refolved to fend out thofe admirals who had diftinguifhed themfelves moft, toward the end of the laft war. Accordingly, Sir Edward Hawke failed on a cruife to the weftward, with 18 fhips of the line, a frigate and a floop; but, not meeting with the French fleet, thefe fhips returned to England. Another fleet, confifting of 22 fhips of the line, two frigates, and two floops, failed again on a cruife to the weftward, under admiral Byng, in hopes of intercepting the French fquadron under Duguay, and likewife that commanded by La Mothe, in cafe of its return from America. But this fleet likewife returned to Spithead, without having been able to effect any thing; though it was allowed, that the admiral had acted judiciously in the choice of his stations.

In the mean time, the French trade was so annoyed by the English cruisers, that, before the end of this year, 300 of their merchant-ships, many of which, from St. Domingo and Martinico, were extreamly rich; and 8000 of their sailors were brought into English ports. By these captures the British ministry answered many purposes: they deprived the French of a great body of seamen, and withheld from them a very large property, the want of which greatly distressed their people, and ruined many of their traders. The outward-bound merchant-ships were insured at the rate of 30 per cent. whilst the English paid no more than the common insurance. This intolerable burden was felt by all degrees of people amongst them: their ministry was publicly reviled, even by their parliaments; and the French name, from being the terror, began to be the contempt of Europe.

Though the English continued to make reprisals upon the French, not only in the seas of America, but also in those of Europe, by taking every ship they could meet with; yet the French, whether from a consciousness of their want of power by sea, or that they might have a more plausible plea to represent England as the aggressor, were so far from returning these hostilities, that their fleet, which escaped Sir Edward Hawke, having taken the Blandford man of war, with governor Lyttelton on board, going to Carolina, they set the governor at liberty, as soon as the court was informed of the ship's being brought into Nantes, and shortly after released both the ship and the crew. However, at the same time, their preparations for a land-war still went on with great diligence; and their utmost arts and efforts were fruitlesly exerted to persuade the Spaniards and Dutch to join with them against Great Britain.

The

The English navy, so early as in the month of September, 1755, consisted of one ship of 110 guns, five of 100 guns each, thirteen of 90, eight of 80, five of 74, twenty-nine of 70, four of 66; one of 64, thirty-three of 60, three of 54, twenty-eight of 50, four of 44, thirty-five of 40, and forty-two of 20; four sloops of war of 18 guns each, two of 16, eleven of 14, thirteen of 12, and one of 10; beside a great number of bomb-ketches, fireships, and tenders: a force sufficient to oppose the united maritime strength of all the powers in Europe. Whilst that of the French, even at the end of this year, and including the ships then upon the stocks, amounted to no more than six ships of 80, twenty-one of 74, one of 72, four of 70, thirty-one of 64, two of 60, six of 50, and thirty-two frigates.

Under the cloak of an invading armament, which engrossed the attention of the British nation, the French were actually employed in preparations for an expedition, which succeeded according to their wish. In the beginning of the year 1756, advice was received that a French squadron would soon be in a condition to sail from Toulon, consisting of 12 or 15 ships of the line, with a great number of transports; that they were supplied with provision for two months only, consequently could not be intended for America. Notwithstanding these particulars of information, which plainly pointed out Minorca as the object of their expedition; notwithstanding the extensive and important commerce carried on by the subjects of Great Britain in the Mediterranean; no proper care was taken to send thither a squadron of ships capable to protect the trade, and frustrate the designs of the enemy. Nay, the ministry seemed to pay little or no regard to the remonstrance of general Blakeney, deputy-governor of Minorca, who, in repeated advices, represented the weakness of the garrison which he commanded in St. Philip's castle, the chief fortrefs on the ifland. Far from ftrengthening the garrifon with a proper reinforcement, they did not even fend thither the officers belonging to it, who were in England upon leave of abfence; nor gave direction for any veffel to tranfport them, until the French armament was ready to make a defcent upon that ifland. At laft their defign was fo univerfally known, that the miniftry could not any longer defer fending fuccours to a place of fo much importance to the trade of Great Britain. Accordingly vice-admiral Byng was fent with ten fhips of the line to the Mediterranean in April; and war was declared in May.

When admiral Byng arrived at Gibraltar, he found captain Edgecumbe with the Princefs Louifa fhip of war, and a floop; who informed him, that the French armament, commanded by Mr. de la Galifioniere, confifting of 13 fhips of the line, with a great number of tranfports, having on board a body of 15,000 land-forces, had made a defcent upon the ifland of Minorca; from whence he (captain Edgecumbe) had been obliged to retire at their approach.

This admiral, being ftrengthened by Mr. Edgecumbe, and reinforced by a detachment from the garrifon, fet fail from Gibraltar on the 8th day of May, and was joined off Majorca by his majefty's fhip the Phœnix, captain Hervey, who confirmed the intelligence he had already received. When he approached Minorca, he defcried the Britifh colours ftill flying at the caftle of St. Philip's, and feveral bomb-batteries playing upon it from different quarters, where the French banners were difplayed. The French fleet appeared foon after, to the fouth-eaft, and the wind blowing ftrong off fhore, he formed the line of battle. About fix o'clock in the evening, the enemy, to the number of 17 fhips, 13 of which appeared to be very large, advanced in order; but about feven tacked, with a view to gain the weather-gage. Mr. Byng, in order to preferve that advantage, as well as to make fure of the land-wind in the morning,

ing, followed their example, being then about five leagues from Cape Mola.

At day-light the enemy could not be defcried; but foon re-appearing, the line of battle was formed on each fide; and, about two o'clock, admiral Byng threw out a fignal to bear away two points from the wind, and engage. At this time his diftance from the enemy was fo great, that rear-admiral Weft, perceiving it impoffible to comply with both orders, bore away with his divifion feven points from the wind; and, clofing down upon the enemy, attacked them with fuch impetuofity, that the fhips which oppofed him were in a little time driven out of the line. Had he been properly fuftained by the van, in all probability the Britifh fleet would have obtained a compleat victory: but the other divifion did not bear down, and the enemy's center keeping their ftation, rear-admiral Weft could not purfue his advantage without running the rifque of feeing his communication with the reft of the line entirely cut off.

In the beginning of the action, the Intrepid, of Mr. Byng's divifion, was fo difabled in her rigging, that fhe could not be managed, and drove on the fhip that was next in pofition: a circumftance which obliged feveral others to throw all a-back, in order to avoid confufion; and for fome time retarded the action. Certain it is, that Mr. Byng, though accommodated with a noble fhip of 90 guns, made little or no ufe of his artillery; but kept aloof, either from an over-ftrained obfervance of difcipline, or timidity. When his captain exhorted him to bear down upon the enemy, he very coolly replied, That he would avoid the error of admiral Matthews, who, in his engagement with the French and Spanifh fquadrons off Toulon, during the preceding war, had broke the line by his own precipitation, and expofed himfelf fingly to a fire that he could not fuftain. Mr. Byng, on the contrary, was determined againft acting, except with the line entire; and, on pretence of rectifying the diforder which had happened among fome of the fhips, hefitated fo long, and kept at fuch a wary diftance, that he never was properly engaged, though he received fome few fhots in his hull. Mr. de la Galiffoniere feemed equally averfe to the continuance of the battle: part of his fquadron had been fairly obliged to quit the line; and though he was rather fuperior to the Englifh in number of men and weight of metal, he did not chufe to abide the confequence of a clofer fight: he therefore took advantage of Mr. Byng's hefitation, and edged away with an eafy fail to join his van, which had been difcomfited. The Englifh admiral gave chace; but the French fhips being clean, he could not come up and clofe with them again, fo they retired at their leifure. Then he put his fquadron on the other tack, in order to keep the wind of the enemy; and next morning they were altogether out of fight.

While, with the reft of his fleet he lay to, at the diftance of ten leagues from Mahon, he detached cruifers to look for fome miffing fhips, which joined him accordingly, and made an enquiry into the condition of the fquadron. Three of the capital fhips were fo damaged in their mafts, that they could not keep the fea, with any regard to their fafety: a great number of the feamen were ill, and there was no veffel which could be converted into an hofpital for the fick and wounded. In this fituation, Mr. Byng called a council of war, at which the land-officers were prefent. He reprefented to them, that he was much inferior to the enemy in weight of metal and numbers of men; that they had the advantage of fending their wounded to Minorca, from whence at the fame time they were refrefhed and reinforced occafionally; that, in his opinion, it was impracticable to relieve St. Philip's fort, and therefore they ought to make the beft of their way back to Gibraltar, which might require immediate protection. They unanimoufly concurred with his fentiments, and thither he directed

his

his courfe accordingly. How he came to be fo well acquainted with the impracticability of relieving general Blakeney, is not eafy to determine, inafmuch as no experiment was made for that purpofe. Indeed, the neglect of fuch a trial feems to have been the leaft excufable part of his conduct; for it afterward appeared, that the officers and foldiers belonging to the garrifon might have been landed at the Sally-port, without running any great rifk; and a gentleman, then in the fort, actually paffed and repaffed in a boat, unhurt by any of the enemy's batteries.

Mr. Byng's letter to the admiralty, containing a detail of this action, is faid to have arrived fome days before it was made public; and when it appeared, was curtailed of divers expreffions and whole paragraphs, which either tended to his own juftification, or implied a cenfure on the conduct of his fuperiors. Whatever ufe might have been made of this letter, while it remained a fecret to the public, we fhall not pretend to explain: but fure it is, that on the 16th day of June, Sir Edward Hawke and admiral Saunders failed from Spithead to Gibraltar, to fuperfede the admirals Byng and Weft, in their commands of the Mediterranean fquadron; and Mr. Byng's letter was not publifhed till the twenty-fixth day of the fame month: when it appeared, it produced all the effect which that gentleman's bittereft enemies' could have defired. The populace took fire like a train of combuftibles, and broke out in fuch a clamour of rage againft the devoted admiral, as could not have been exceeded, if he had loft the whole navy of England, and left the coafts of the kingdom naked to invafion. In a word, he was devoted as the fcape-goat of the m———y, to whofe mifconduct the lofs of that important fortrefs was undoubtedly owing. Byng's mifcarriage was thrown out like a barrel to the whale, in order to engage the attention of the people, that it might not be attracted by the real caufe of the national misfortune. In order to keep up the flame which had been kindled againſt the admiral, recourſe was had to the loweſt artifices. Agents were employed to vilify his perſon in all public places of vulgar reſort; and mobs were hired at different parts of the capital to hang and burn him in effigy.

The two officers who ſucceeded to his command in the Mediterranean were accompanied by the lord Tyrawley, whom his majeſty had appointed to ſuperſede general Fowke in the government of Gibraltar; that gentleman having incurred the diſpleaſure of the miniſtry for not having underſtood an order which was unintelligible. Directions were diſpatched to Sir Edward Hawke, that Byng ſhould be ſent home under arreſt: and an order to the ſame purpoſe was lodged at every port in the kingdom. He was accompanied by Mr. Weſt, general Fowke, and ſeveral other officers, who were alſo recalled in conſequence of having ſubſcribed to the council of war, which we have mentioned above. When they arrived in England, Mr. Weſt met with ſuch a reception from his majeſty as was thought due to his extraordinary merit; but Mr. Byng was committed cloſe priſoner in an apartment of Greenwich hoſpital.

From thence Mr. Byng was ſent to Portſmouth, where he was tried by a court-martial; the ſum of whoſe opinion was, that he did not do his utmoſt to relieve Minorca; and that during the engagement he did not do his utmoſt to take, ſeize, and deſtroy the ſhips of the French king, and aſſiſt ſuch of his own ſhips as were engaged. That he therefore fell under part of the twelfth article of war, and the court adjudged him to be ſhot: but as it appeared to the court that it was neither through cowardice or diſaffection, they unanimouſly recommended him to mercy. However, notwithſtanding this recommendation of the court-martial to his majeſty's mercy, and notwithſtanding the interceſſion made for him, an order was ſent down for the execution of the ſentence; and he

was

was shot on board the Monarque at Portsmouth, pitied by all the dispassionate part of the nation.

The loss of Minorca was severely felt in England, as a national disgrace; but, instead of producing dejection and despondence, it excited an univerfal resentment, not only against Mr. Byng, who had retreated from the French squadron, but also in reproach of the administration.

Sir Edward Hawke, being disappointed in his hope of encountering la Galissoniere, and relieving the English garrison of St. Philip's, at least afferted the empire of Great Britain in the Mediterranean, by annoying the commerce of the enemy, and blocking up their squadron in the harbour of Toulon. Understanding that the Austrian government at Leghorn had detained an English privateer, and imprisoned the captain, on pretence that he had violated the neutrality of the port; he detached two ships of war to insist, in a peremptory manner, on the release of the ship, effects, crew, and captain: and they thought proper to comply with his demand, even without waiting for orders from Vienna. The person in whose behalf the admiral thus interposed, was one Fortunatus Wright, a native of Liverpool; who, though a stranger to a sea-life, had, in the last war, equipped a privateer, and distinguished himself in such a manner, by his uncommon vigilance and valour, that, if he had been indulged with a command suitable to his genius, he would have deserved an honourable place in the annals of the navy. An uncommon exertion of spirit was the occasion of his being detained at this juncture. While he lay at anchor in the harbour of Leghorn, commander of the St. George privateer of Liverpool, a small ship of twelve guns and eighty men; a large French xebeque, mounted with sixteen cannon, and nearly three times the number of his complement, chose her station in view of the harbour, in order to interrupt the British commerce. The gallant Wright could not endure this insult:

notwith-

notwithstanding the enemy's superiority in metal and number of men, he weighed anchor, hoisted his sails, engaged him within sight of the shore, and after a very obstinate dispute, in which the captain, lieutenant, and above threescore of the men belonging to the xebeque were killed on the spot, he obliged them to sheer off, and returned to the harbour in triumph. This brave corsair would, no doubt, have signalized himself by many other exploits, had not he, in the sequel, been overtaken by a dreadful storm, in which the ship foundering, he and all his crew perished.

Sir Edward Hawke, having scoured the Mediterranean, and insulted the enemy's ports, returned with the homeward-bound trade to Gibraltar; from whence, about the latter end of the year, he set sail for England with part of his squadron, leaving the rest in that bay for the protection of our commerce.

No action of great importance distinguished the naval transactions of this year on the side of America. In the beginning of June, captain Spry, who commanded a small squadron, cruising off Louisbourg, in the island of Cape Breton, took the Arc en Ciel, a French ship of 50 guns, having on board near 600 men, with a large quantity of stores and provisions for the garrison. He likewise made prize of another French ship, with stores of the like destination. On the 27th day of July, commodore Holmes, being in the same latitude, with two large ships and a couple of sloops, engaged two French ships of the line and four frigates, and obliged them to sheer off, after an obstinate dispute.

A great number of privateers were equipped in this country, as well as in the West India islands belonging to the crown of Great Britain; and as these seas swarmed with French vessels, their cruizes proved very advantageous to the adventurers.

Scenes of still higher import were this year acted by the British arms in the East Indies. The English and French companies on the peninsula of Indus,

profe-

profecuted their operations, no longer as auxiliaries to the princes of the country, but as principals and rivals, both in arms and commerce. Major Laurence, who now enjoyed the chief command of the Englifh forces, obtained divers advantages over the enemy; when the progrefs of his arms was interrupted by an unfortunate event at Calcutta, the caufe of which is not eafily explained. Surajah Doula, viceroy of Bengal, Bakar, and Orixa, taking umbrage at the refufal of certain duties, to which he had laid claim, being particularly incenfed at the Englifh governor of Calcutta, for having granted protection to one of his fubjects, whom he had outlawed; and, moreover, irritated by other practices of the company, which we cannot pretend to unfold, levied a numerous army, and marching to Calcutta, invefted the place, which was then in no pofture of defence. The governor, intimidated by the number and power of the enemy, abandoned the fort; and the defence of the place devolved to Mr. Holwell the fecond in command, who, with the affiftance of a few gallant officers, and a very feeble garrifon, maintained it with uncommon courage and refolution, againft feveral attacks, until he was over-powered by numbers, and the enemy had forced their way into the caftle. He was then obliged to fubmit; and the fuba, or viceroy, promifed, on the word of a foldier, that no injury fhould be done to him or his garrifon. Neverthelefs, they were all driven, to the number of 146 perfons of both fexes, into a place, called the Black-hole prifon, a cube of about 18 feet, walled up to the eaftward and fouthward, the only quarters from which they could expect the leaft refrefhing air, and open to the weftward by two windows ftrongly barred with iron, through which there was no perceptible circulation.

The humane reader will conceive with horror the miferable fituation to which they muft have been reduced, when thus ftewed up in a clofe fultry night,

under

under such a climate as that of Bengal. In the morning, the suba being informed that the greater part of the prisoners were suffocated, enquired if the chief was alive; and being answered in the affirmative, sent an order for their immediate release, when no more than 23 survived of 146 who had entered alive.

By the reduction of Calcutta, the English East India company's affairs were so much embroiled in that part of the world, that perhaps nothing could have retrieved them but the interposition of a national force, and the good fortune of a Clive; whose enterprizes were always crowned with success. In consequence of the company's representations to the government, a small squadron of large ships was sent to the East Indies, under the command of admiral Watson; and in the course of this year arrived at Fort St. David's. The governor of that fortress having received intelligence, that Tullagee Angria, a piratical prince in the neighbourhood of Bombay, was on the eve of concluding a treaty with the nation of the Marahattas, which might prove prejudicial to the interests of the English company; a resolution was taken to drive him from his residence at Geriah, which was well fortified, and formidable to all the trading ships of Europe. He maintained a considerable number of armed gallies, called Grabs, with which he often attacked the largest ships, when they happened to be becalmed on that part of the coast of Malabar. He was in the fourth generation from the first freebooter, who rendered himself independent, and lived like a sovereign prince. The undertaking against Angria was originally concerted with the Marahattas, who likewise equipped an armament both by sea and land against Geriah; but they acted entirely on their own score: and in the reduction of the place gave no manner of assistance to the English.

Admiral Watson sailed from the coast of Coromandel to Bombay, where his squadron was cleaned and refitted; and having on board a body of troops commanded

manded by colonel Clive, he failed on the 7th day of February, and found in the neighbourhood of Geriah the Marahatta fleet, lying to the northward of the place, in a creek called Rajipore; and a land-army of horfe and foot, amounting to 7 or 8000 men, commanded by Rhamagee Punt, who had already taken one fmall fort, and was actually treating about the furrender of Geriah. Angria himfelf had quitted the place; but his wife and family remained under the protection of his brother-in-law; who, being fummoned to furrender by a meffage from the admiral, replied, that he would defend the place to the laft extremity. In confequence of this refufal, the whole Englifh fleet, in two divifions, failed into the harbour; and a fhell being thrown into one of Angria's armed veffels, fet her on fire, and the flames communicating to the reft, they were all deftroyed: the fort was fet on fire by another fhell; and as the magazine of the fort afterward blew up, the governor was at length obliged to fubmit. In this place, which was reduced with a very inconfiderable lofs, the conquerors found above 200 cannon, fix brafs mortars, a large quantity of ammunition; with money and effects to the value of 130,000 pounds. The fleet which was deftroyed, confifted of eight grabs, one fhip finifhed, two upon the ftocks, and a good number of gallivats. Among the prifoners, the admiral found Angria's wife, children, and mother, toward whom he demeaned himfelf with great humanity.

The admiral and Mr. Clive failed back to Madrafs in triumph, and there another plan was formed for reftoring the company's affairs upon the Ganges; for recovering Calcutta, and taking vengeance on the cruel viceroy of Bengal: all which was happily executed.

In the courfe of the year 1756, the clamorous voice of diffatisfaction had been raifed by a feries of difappointments and mifcarriages, which were imputed to want of intelligence, fagacity, and vigour in the adminiftration:

tion: and the prospect of their acquiescing in a continental war brought them still farther in contempt and detestation with the body of the people. In order to conciliate the good-will of those whom their conduct had disobliged, to acquire a fresh stock of credit with their fellow subjects, and remove from their own shoulders part of what future censure might ensue; they, in 1757, admitted into a share of the administration a certain set of gentlemen, remarkable for their talents and popularity, headed by Mr. Pitt and Mr. Legge, the two most illustrious patriots of Great Britain, alike distinguished and admired for their unconquerable spirit and untainted integrity. But the old junto found their new associates very unfit for their purposes. They could neither persuade, cajole, nor intimidate them into measures which they thought repugnant to the true interest of their country: they were accordingly soon after displaced.

What was intended as a disgrace to Mr. Pitt and Mr. Legge, turned out one of the most shining circumstances of their character. The whole nation seemed to rise up, as one man, in the vindication of their fame; every mouth was opened in their praise; and a great number of respectable cities and corporations presented them with the freedom of their respective societies, inclosed in golden boxes, as testimonials of their peculiar veneration. Nothing could be more expressive of that reverence which ever waits on superior virtue, than the manner in which the nation displayed its respect and affection for those two fellow citizens; whose names will always be dear to Britain, while her sons are warmed with the flame of honesty and freedom.

A great number of addresses, dutifully and loyally expressed, sollicited the king to restore Mr. Pitt and Mr. Legge to their former employments. Upon this they rested the security and honour of the nation, as well as the public expectation of the speedy and successful issue of a war, hitherto attended with disgraces and

and misfortunes. Accordingly his majesty was graciously pleased to redeliver the seals to Mr. Pitt, appointing him secretary of state for the southern department, on the 29th day of June; and five days after, the office of chancellor of the exchequer was restored to Mr. Legge: promotions that afforded universal satisfaction.

The accumulated losses and disappointments of the preceding year, made it absolutely necessary to retrieve the credit of the British arms and councils, by some vigorous and spirited enterprize. A powerful fleet was ordered to be got in readiness to put to sea on the shortest notice, and ten regiments of foot were marched to the Isle of Wight. The naval armament, consisting of 18 ships of the line, beside frigates, fireships, bomb-ketches, and transports, was put under the command of Sir Edward Hawke, an officer, whose faithful services recommended him, above all others, to this command. Sir John Mordaunt was preferred to take the command of the land-forces; and both strictly enjoined to act with the utmost unanimity and harmony.

Europe beheld with astonishment these mighty preparations. The destination of the armament was wrapped in the most profound secrecy: it exercised the penetration of politicians, and filled France with very serious alarms. Various were the impediments which obstructed the embarkation of the troops for several weeks, while they expressed an eager impatience to signalize themselves against the enemies of the liberties of Europe: but the superstitious drew unfavourable presages from the dilatoriness of the embarkation.

At last the transports arrived, the troops were put on board with all expedition, and the fleet got under sail on the 8th day of September, attended with the prayers of every man warmed with the love of his country, and solicitous for her honour. The public, big with expectation, dubious where the stroke would fall, but confident of its success, were impatient for tidings

tidings from the fleet; but it was not till the 14th, that even the troops on board began to conjecture that a defcent was meditated on the coaft of France near Rochfort, or Rochelle. But though fome difpofitions were made toward a difembarkation, no troops were landed, except on the little ifland of Aix, fituated in the mouth of the river Charente, leading up to Rochfort. After a parade of deftroying the fortifications here, this grand fleet returned to England. Such was the iffue of an expedition that raifed the expectation of all Europe, threw the coafts of France into the utmoft confufion, and coft the people of England little lefs than a million of money.

The fleet was no fooner returned than the whole nation was in a ferment. Certain it was, that blame muft fall fomewhere, and the m——y refolved to acquit themfelves, and fix the accufation, by requefting his majefty to appoint a board of officers of character and ability. to enquire into the caufes of the late mifcarriage. This alone was what could appeafe the public clamours, and afford general fatisfaction. Sir John Mordaunt was alfo tried, by his own defire, and acquitted.

Befide the diverfion intended by a defcent on the coaft of France, feveral other methods were employed to amufe the enemy, as well as to protect the trade of the kingdom, fecure our colonies in the Weft Indies, and infure the continuance of the extraordinary fuccefs which had lately bleffed his majefty's arms in the Eaft Indies: but thefe we could not mention before, without breaking the thread of our narration.

In February, admiral Weft failed with a fquadron of men of war to the weftward; as did admiral Coates with the fleet under his convoy to the Weft Indies: and commodore Stevens with the trade to the Eaft Indies, in the month of March. Admiral Holbourn, and commodore Holmes, with eleven fhips of the line, a firefhip, a bomb-ketch, and fifty tranfports, failed from St. Helen's for America in April. The

admiral

admiral had on board 6200 effective men, exclusive of officers, under the command of general Hopson, assisted by lord Charles Hay. In May, admiral Osborne, forced back to Plymouth with his squadron by stress of weather, set sail to the Mediterranean; as did two ships of war sent to convoy the American trade.

In the mean time the privateers fitted out by private merchants, and societies, greatly annoyed the French commerce. The Antigallican, a private ship of war, equipped by a society of gentlemen who assumed that name, took the Duke de Penthievre Indiaman off the port of Corunna, and carried her into Cadiz. The prize was estimated worth 200,000 pounds; and immediate application was made by France to the court of Spain for restitution, as the French East India company asserted, it was taken within shot of a neutral port. The Penthievre was wrested out of the hands of the captors, detained as a deposit, with sealed hatches, and a Spanish guard on board, till the claims of both parties could be examined; and at last was adjudged to be an illegal capture, and restored to the French. Beside the success which attended a great number of other privateers, the lords of the admiralty published a list of above thirty ships of war and privateers taken from the enemy, in the space of four months, by the English sloops and men of war; exclusive of the Duke de Aquitaine Indiaman, now fitted out as a ship of war; the Pondicherry Indiaman, valued at 160,000 pounds; and above six privateers, which last were brought into port by the diligent and brave captain Lockhart, and for which he was honoured with a variety of presents of plate by several corporations. This turn of good fortune was not, however, without some retribution on the side of the enemy, who, out of 21 ships, homeward-bound from Carolina, made prize of 19; whence the merchants sustained considerable damage, and a great quantity of valuable commodities, indigo in particular, was loft to this country.

The operations at sea, during the course of the year 1757, either in Europe or America, were far from being decisive or important. The commerce of Great Britain sustained considerable damage from the activity and success of French privateers. The Greenwich ship of war of 50 guns, and a frigate of 20, fell into the hands of the enemy, together with a very considerable number of trading vessels. On the other hand, the English cruisers and privateers acquitted themselves with equal vigilance and valour. The Duc d'Aquitaine, of 50 guns, was taken; the Aquilon, of nearly the same force, was driven on shore and destroyed. A French frigate, of 26 guns, called the Emeraude, was taken by a ship of inferior force under the command of captain Gilchrift, a gallant officer. All the sea-officers seemed to be animated with a noble emulation, to distinguish themselves in the service of their country; and the spirit descended even to the captains of privateers, who, instead of imitating the former commanders of that class, in avoiding ships of force, and centering their whole attention in advantageous prizes, now encountered the armed ships of the enemy, and fought with the most obstinate valour in the pursuit of national glory.

Perhaps history cannot afford a more remarkable instance of desperate courage, than that which was exerted in December of the preceding year, by the officers and crew of an English privateer, of 26 guns and 200 men, called the Terrible, under the command of captain William Death. He engaged, and made prize of, a large French ship from St. Domingo, with the loss of his own brother and 16 seamen: he then directed his course to England; but in a few days he had the misfortune to fall in with the Vengeance, a privateer of St. Malo, carrying 36 large cannon,

cannon, with 360 men. Their firſt ſtep was to attack the prize, which was eaſily retaken; then the two ſhips bore down upon the Terrible, which maintained ſuch a furious engagement againſt both, as can hardly be paralleled in the annals of Britain. The French commander and his ſecond were killed, with two-thirds of his company; but the gallant captain Death, with the greater part of his officers, and almoſt his whole crew, having met with the ſame fate, his ſhip was boarded by the enemy, who found no more than 26 perſons alive, 16 of whom were mutilated by the loſs of legs or arms, and the other 10 grievouſly wounded. The ſhip itſelf was ſo ſhattered that it could ſcarcely be kept above water; and the whole exhibited a ſcene of blood, horror, and deſolation. The victor itſelf lay like a wreck on the ſurface; and in this condition made ſhift, with great difficulty, to tow the Terrible into St. Malo, where ſhe was not beheld without aſtoniſhment and terror. This adventure was no ſooner known in England, than a liberal ſubſcription was raiſed for the ſupport of Death's * widow, and that part of the crew which ſurvived the engagement.

In this, and every ſea-rencounter that happened within the preſent year, the ſuperiority in ſkill and reſolution, was aſcertained to the Britiſh mariners: for even when they fought againſt great odds, their courage was generally crowned with ſucceſs. In the month of November, captain Lockhart, a young gentleman, who had already rendered himſelf a terror to the enemy, as commander of a ſmall frigate, now added conſiderably to his reputation, by reducing the Melampe, a French privateer of Bayonne, greatly ſuperior to his ſhip, in men and metal; and

---

* There was a ſtrange combination of names belonging to this privateer: the *Terrible*, equipped at *Execution-Dock*, commanded by captain *Death*, whoſe lieutenant was called *Devil*, and he had one *Ghoſt* for his ſurgeon. It may be added, that it was taken by the *Vengeance*.

also another French adventurer, called the Countefs of Gramont. A third large privateer of Bayonne was taken by captain Saumarez, of the Antelope. In a word, the narrow feas were fo well guarded, that in a little time fcarce a French fhip durft appear in the Englifh channel, which the Britifh traders navigated without moleftation. The Britifh cruifers kept the fea during all the feverity of the winter, in order to protect the commerce of the kingdom, and annoy that of the enemy. They exerted themfelves with fuch activity, and their vigilance was attended with fuch fuccefs, that the trade of France was almoft totally extinguifhed. A very gallant exploit was atchieved by one captain Bray, commander of the Adventurer, a fmall armed veffel in the government's fervice: falling in with the Machault, a large privateer of Dunkirk, near Dungenefs, he ran her aboard, faftened her boltfprit to his capftan, and after a warm engagement, compelled her commander to fubmit. A French frigate, of 36 guns, was taken by captain Parker, in a new firefhip of inferior force. Divers privateers of the enemy were funk, burned, or taken; and a great number of merchant-fhips fell into the hands of the Englifh.

Nor was the fuccefs of the Britifh fhips of war confined to the Englifh channel. An action happened off the ifland of Hifpaniola, between three Englifh fhips of war and a French fquadron. Captain Forreft had, in the fhip Augufta, failed from Port Royal in Jamaica, accompanied by the Dreadnought and Edinburgh, under the command of the captains Suckling and Langdon, to cruize off Cape François: and this fervice he literally performed, in the face of a French fquadron lately arrived at that place from the coaft of Africa. The commander, piqued at feeing himfelf thus infulted by an inferior armament, refolved to come forth and give them battle; and that he might either take them, or at leaft drive them out of thefe feas, fo as to afford a free paffage to a

great

great number of merchant-ſhips then lying at the Cape, bound for Europe; he took every precaution which he thought neceſſary to inſure ſucceſs. He weighed anchor and ſtood out to ſea, having under his command four large ſhips of the line, and three ſtout frigates. They were no ſooner perceived advancing, than capain Forreſt held a ſhort council with his two captains. "Gentlemen, (ſaid he) you know our own ſtrength, and ſee that of the enemy: ſhall we give them battle?" They replying in the affirmative, he added, "Then fight them we will; there is no time to be loſt: return to your ſhips, and get them ready for engaging." After this laconic conſultation among theſe three gallant officers, they bore down upon the French ſquadron without further heſitation, and between three and four in the afternoon the action began with great impetuoſity. The enemy exerted themſelves with uncommon ſpirit, conſcious that their honour was peculiarly at ſtake, and that they fought in ſight, as it were, of their own coaſt, which was lined with people expecting to ſee them return in triumph. But notwithſtanding all their endeavours, their commodore, after having ſuſtained a ſevere engagement that laſted two hours and a half, found his ſhip in ſuch a ſhattered condition, that he made ſignal for one of his frigates to come and tow him out of the line. His example was followed by the reſt of his ſquadron, which, with the favour of the land-breeze and the approach of night, made ſhift to accompliſh their eſcape from the three Britiſh ſhips, that were too much diſabled in their maſts and rigging to proſecute their victory. They were ſo much damaged, that, being unable to keep the ſea, they returned to Jamaica; and the French commodore ſeized the opportunity of ſailing with a convoy for Europe.

The courage of captain Forreſt was not more conſpicuous in his engagement with the French ſquadron near Cape François, than his conduct and ſagacity in
a ſub-

a subsequent adventure near Port au Prince, a French harbour, situated at the bottom of a bay on the western part of Hispaniola. After Mr. de Kerfin had taken his departure from Cape François for Europe, captain Forrest was commanded by admiral Cotes to cruize off the island of Gonave for two days only, enjoining him to return at the expiration of the time, and rejoin the squadron at Cape Nicholas. Accordingly, captain Forrest, in the Augusta, proceeded up the bay, between the island Gonave and Hispaniola, with a view to execute a plan which he had himself projected. Next day in the afternoon, though he perceived two sloops, he forbore chasing, that he might not risque a discovery: for the same purpose he hoisted Dutch colours, and disguised his ship with tarpaulins. At five in the afternoon, he discovered seven sail of ships steering to the westward, and hauled from them to avoid suspicion; but at the approach of night gave chace with all the sail he could carry. About ten, he perceived two sail, one of which fired a gun, and the other made the best of her way for Leoganne, another harbour in the bay. At this period, captain Forrest reckoned eight sail to leeward, near another fort called Petit Goave: coming up with the ship which had fired the gun, she submitted without opposition, after he had hailed and told her captain what he was, produced two of his largest cannon, and threatened to sink her if she should give the least alarm. He forthwith shifted the prisoners from this prize, and placed on board of her 35 of his own crew, with orders to stand for Petit Goave, and intercept any of the fleet that might attempt to reach that harbour. Then he made sail after the rest, and in the dawn of the morning, finding himself in the middle of their fleet, he began to fire at them all in their turns, as he could bring his guns to bear: they returned the fire for some time; at length three of them struck their colours. These, being secured, were afterward used in taking the other five. Thus, by by a well-conducted ftratagem, a whole fleet of nine fail were taken by a fingle fhip in the neighbourhood of four or five harbours, in any one of which they would have found immediate fhelter and fecurity.

The miniftry having determined, in 1758, to make vigorous efforts againft the enemy in North America, admiral Bofcawen was vefted with the command of the fleet deftined for that fervice, and failed from St. Helen's on February, when the Invincible of 74 guns, one of his beft fhips, run aground and perifhed.

In the courfe of the fucceeding month, Sir Edward Hawke fteered into the bay of Bifcay with another fquadron, in order to intercept any fupplies from France defigned for Cape-Breton or Canada; and about the fame time, the town of Emden, belonging to his Pruffian majefty, which had fallen into the hands of the enemy, was fuddenly retrieved by the conduct of commodore Holmes, ftationed on that coaft. Admiral Ofborne, while he cruifed between Cape de Gatt and Carthagena, on the coaft of Spain, fell in with a French fquadron, commanded by the marquis du Quefne, confifting of four fhips; namely, the Foudroyant of 80 guns, the Orphée of 64, the Oriflamme of 50, and the Pleiade frigate of 24, in their paffage from Toulon to reinforce M. de la Clue, who had for fome time ,been blocked up by admiral Ofborne in the harbour of Carthagena. The enemy no fooner perceived the Englifh fquadron than they difperfed, and fteered different courfes: Mr. Ofborne detached divers fhips in purfuit of each, while he himfelf, with the body of his fleet, ftood off for the bay of Carthagena, to watch the motions of the French fquadron which there lay at anchor. About feven in the evening, the Orphée ftruck to captain Storr in the Revenge. The Monmouth of 64 guns, commanded by captain Gardener, engaged the Foudroyant, one of the largeft fhips in the French navy, under the command of the marquis du Quefne. The action

action was maintained with great fury on both sides; and the gallant captain Gardener loft his life: nevertheless the fight was continued with unabating vigour by his lieutenant Mr. Carkett, and the Foudroyant disabled in such a manner, that her commander struck as soon as the other English ships, the Swiftsure and the Hampton-court, appeared. This mortifying step, however, he did not take until he saw his ship lie like a wreck upon the water, and the decks covered with carnage. The Oriflamme was driven on shore under the castle of Aiglos, by the ships Montague and Monarque, commanded by the captains Rowley and Montague, who could not compleat their destruction without violating the neutrality of Spain. As for the Pleiade frigate, she made her escape.

This was a severe stroke upon the enemy, who not only lost two of their capital ships, but saw them added to the navy of Great Britain; and the disaster was close followed by another, which they could not help feeling with equal sensibility of mortification and chagrin. In the beginning of April, Sir Edward Hawke discovered off the isle of Aix a French fleet at anchor, consisting of five ships of the line, with six frigates, and forty transports, having on board 3000 troops, and a large quantity of stores and provision, intended as a supply for their settlements in North America. They no sooner saw the English admiral advancing, than they began to slip their cables and fly in the utmost confusion. Some of them escaped to sea, but the greater number ran into shoal water, where they could not be pursued; and next morning they appeared aground, lying on their broadsides. Sir Edward Hawke, who had rode all that night at anchor abreast of the isle of Aix, furnished the ships Intrepid and Medway, with trusty pilots, and sent them farther in when the flood began to make, with orders to sound a-head, that he might know whether there was any possibility of attacking the enemy; but the want of a sufficient depth of

water.

water rendered this scheme impracticable. In the mean time, the French threw overboard their cannon, stores, and ballast; and the boats and launches from Rochefort, were employed in carrying out warps to drag their ships through the soft mud, as soon as they should be waterborne by the flowing tide. By these means, their large ships of war, and many of their transports, escaped into the river Charente; but their loading was lost, and the end of their equipment totally defeated. Another convoy of merchant-ships, under the protection of three frigates, Sir Edward Hawke, a few days before, had chaced into the harbour of St. Martin's, on the isle of Rhé, where they still remained, waiting an opportunity for hazarding a second departure: a third, consisting of twelve sail, bound from Bourdeaux to Quebec, under convoy of a frigate and armed vessel, was encountered at sea by one British ship of the line and two fireships, which took the frigate and armed vessel; and two of the convoy afterward met with the same fate: but this advantage was over-balanced by the loss of captain James Hume, commander of the Pluto fireship, a brave accomplished officer, in an unequal combat with the enemy: and by the unfortunate burning of admiral Broderick's ship, the Prince George of 80 guns, which happened in his passage to the Mediterranean.

On the 29th day of May, the Raisonable, a French ship of the line, mounted with 64 cannon, having on board 630 men, commanded by the prince de Mombazon chevalier de Rohan, was, in her passage from Port l'Orient to Brest, attacked by captain Dennis in the Dorsetshire of 70 guns; and taken after an obstinate engagement, in which 160 men of the prince's complement were killed or wounded, and he sustained great damage in his hull, sails and rigging.

The king of Great Britain, being determined to renew his attempt upon the coast of France, ordered a formidable armament to be equipped for that purpose,

pose. Two powerful squadrons by sea were destined for the services of this expedition: the first, consisting of eleven great ships, was commanded by Lord Anson and Sir Edward Hawke; the other, composed of four ships of the line, seven frigates, six sloops, two fireships, two bombs, ten cutters, twenty tenders, ten store-ships, and one hundred transports, under the direction of commodore Howe. A body of troops, consisting of sixteen regiments, nine troops of lighthorse, and six thousand marines, was assembled for the execution of this design, and embarked under the command of the duke of Marlborough, assisted by lord George Sackville. The troops, having for some time been encamped upon the Isle of Wight, were embarked in the latter end of May, and the two fleets sailed in the beginning of June for the coast of Bretagne, leaving the people of England flushed with the gayest hopes of victory and conquest.

The two fleets parted at sea: lord Anson with his squadron proceeded to the bay of Biscay, in order to watch the motions of the enemy's ships, and harrass their navigation; while commodore Howe, with the land forces, steered directly toward St. Malo, on the coast of Bretagne, against which the purposed invasion seemed to be chiefly intended. The town, however, was found too well fortified to admit of any attempt with prospect of success; and therefore it was resolved to make a descent in the neighbourhood. After the fleet had been, by contrary winds, detained several days in sight of the French coast, it arrived in the bay of Cancalle, about two leagues to the eastward of St. Malo; where the troops were landed without much opposition. The duke of Marlborough immediately began his march toward St. Servan, with a view to destroy such shipping and magazines as might be in any accessible parts of the river; and this scheme was executed with success. A great quantity of naval stores, two ships of war, several privateers, and about fourscore vessels of different sorts, were set on fire, and reduced to ashes, almost

under

under the cannon of the place; which, however, they could not pretend to befiege in form. His grace, having received repeated advices that the enemy were bufily employed in affembling forces to march againft him, returned to Cancalle; where Mr. Howe had made fuch a mafterly difpofition of the boats and tranfports, that the reimbarkation of the troops was performed with furprifing eafe and expedition.

The Britifh forces being reimbarked, the fleet was detained by contrary winds in the bay of Cancalle for feveral days; during which a defign feems to have been formed for attacking Granville, and afterward for landing at Havre de Grace, and at Cherbourg: neither of which took effect, from the tempeftuoufnefs of the weather. The fleet therefore fteered for the Ifle of Wight, and anchored at St. Helen's.

Such was the iffue of an enterprize atchieved with confiderable fuccefs, if we confider the damage done to the enemy's fhipping, and the other objects which the miniftry had in view; namely, to fecure the navigation of the channel, and make a diverfion in favour of our German allies, by alarming the French king, and obliging him to employ a great number of troops to defend his coaft from infult and invafion: but whether fuch a mighty armament was neceffary for the accomplifhment of thefe petty aims, is left to the reader's own reflection.

The defigns upon the coaft of France, though interrupted by tempeftuous weather, were not as yet laid afide for the whole feafon: but, in the mean time, the troops were difembarked on the Ifle of Wight. The duke of Marlborough and lord George Sackville being appointed to conduct this Britifh corps upon the continent, the command of the marine expeditions devolved to lieutenant-general Bligh, an old experienced officer, who had ferved with reputation; and his royal highnefs prince Edward, afterward created Duke of York, entered as a volunteer
with

with commodore Howe, in order to learn the rudiments of the sea-service.

Every thing being prepared for the second expedition, the fleet sailed from St. Helen's on the first of August; and after a tedious passage, anchored on the 7th in the bay of Cherbourg. Here, though they met with opposition, the troops made good their landing, two miles from the town; the French retired, and the English forces marching to Cherbourg, found it abandoned; and the gates being open, entered it without opposition. The next morning, the place being reconnoitred, the general determined to destroy, without delay, all the forts and the bason; and the execution of this design was left to the engineers, assisted by the officers of the fleet and artillery. Great sums of money had been expended upon the harbour and bason of Cherbourg, which at one time was considered by the French court as an object of great importance, from its situation respecting the river Seine, as well as the opposite coast of England; but as the works were left unfinished, in all appearance the plan had grown into disreputation. While the engineers were employed in demolishing the works, the light horse scoured the country. About twenty pieces of brass cannon were secured on board the English ships; a contribution was exacted upon the town; and a plan of reimbarkation concerted: as it appeared from the reports of peasants and deserters, that the enemy, who encamped about four leagues off, were already increased to a formidable number. The forces marched from Cherbourg down to the beach, and reimbarked without the least disturbance from the enemy.

This service being happily performed, the fleet anchored in the bay of St. Lunaire, two leagues to the westward of St. Malo, against which it was determined to make another attempt. The troops landed on a fair open beach, and a detachment of grenadiers was sent to the harbour of St. Briac, above the

town

town of St. Malo, where they deftroyed above 15 fmall veffels. But St. Malo being properly furveyed, appeared to be above infult, either from the land-forces or the fhipping. The defign againft St. Malo was therefore dropped; but the general being unwilling to reimbark without having taken fome ftep for the further annoyance of the enemy, refolved to penetrate into the country; conducting his motions, however, fo as to be near the fleet, which had, by this time, quitted the bay of St. Lunaire, where it could not ride with any fafety, and anchored in the bay of St. Cas, about three leagues to the weftward.

General Bligh, with his little army, marched to Guildo, at the diftance of nine miles, which he reached in the evening. Next morning he proceeded to the village of Matignon, where, after fome fmart fkirmifhing, the French piquets appeared, drawn up in order, to the number of two battalions; but having fuftained a few fhot from the Englifh field-pieces, and feeing the grenadiers advance, they fuddenly difperfed. General Bligh continuing his route through the village, encamped in the open ground about three miles from the bay of St. Cas, which was this day reconnoitred for reimbarkation: for he now received undoubted intelligence, that the duke d'Aiguillon had advanced from Breft to Lambale, within fix miles of the Englifh camp, at the head of twelve regular battalions, fix fquadrons, two regiments of militia, eight mortars, and ten pieces of cannon. The bay of St. Cas was covered by an intrenchment which the enemy had thrown up, to prevent or oppofe any difembarkation; and on the outfide of this work, there was a range of fand-hills extending along fhore, which could have ferved as a cover to the enemy, from whence they might have annoyed the troops in reimbarking: for this reafon, a propofal was made to the general, that the forces fhould be reimbarked from a fair open beach on the left, be-

tween

tween St. Cas and Guildo; but this advice was rejected; and, indeed, the subsequent operations of the army favoured strongly of blind security and rash presumption.

Had the troops decamped in the night without noise, in all probability they would have arrived at the beach before the French had received the least intelligence of their motion: but instead of this cautious manner of proceeding, the drums were beaten at two o'clock in the morning, as if with intention to give notice to the enemy, who forthwith repeated the same signal. The troops were in motion before three, and though the length of the march did not exceed three miles, the halts and interruptions were so numerous and frequent, that they did not arrive on the beach of St. Cas till nine. Then the embarkation was begun, and might have been happily finished, had the transports lain near the shore, and received the men as fast as the boats could have conveyed them on board without distinction; but many ships rode at a considerable distance, and every boat carried the men on board the respective transports to which they belonged; a punctilio of disposition, by which a great deal of time was unnecessarily consumed.

The British forces had skirmished a little on the march, but no considerable body of the enemy appeared until the embarkation was begun; then they took possession of an eminence by a wind-mill, and forthwith opened a battery of ten cannon and eight mortars, from whence they fired with considerable effect upon the soldiers on the beach, and on the boats in their passage. Many swam toward the boats and vessels, which were ordered to give them all manner of assistance; but by far the greater number were either butchered on the beach, or drowned in the water. About 1000 chosen men of the English army were killed and taken prisoners on this occasion: nor was the advantage cheaply purchased by the

the French troops, among whom the fhot and fhells from the frigates and ketches had done great execution.

The whole ftrength of Great Britain, during the campaign of 1758, was not exhaufted in petty defcents on the coaft of France. The continent of America was the great theatre on which her chief vigour was difplayed; nor did fhe fail to exert herfelf in fuccefsful efforts againft the French fettlements on the coaft of Africa: there, a fmall fquadron without much trouble, took poffeffion of Fort Louis and the town of Senegal. But the attempt on Goree mifcarried; though the failure was not attended with any great lofs. This fettlement was however taken afterward by a fmall fquadron under commodore Keppel, after a warm but fhort difpute.

Scenes of ftill greater importance were acted in North America, where, exclufive of the fleet and marines, the government had affembled about 50,000 men, including 22,000 regular troops. About 12,000 of thefe were deftined to undertake the fiege of Louifbourg, on the ifland of Cape Breton. The reduction of Louifbourg, being on object of immediate confideration, was undertaken with all poffible difpatch. Major-general Amherft, being joined by admiral Bofcawen, with the fleet and forces from England, the whole armament, confifting of 157 fail, took their departure from the harbour of Halifax, in Nova Scotia; and on the 2d of June part of the tranfports anchored in the bay of Gabarus, about 7 miles to the weftward of Louifbourg. The garrifon of this place, commanded by the chevalier Drucour, confifted of 2500 regular troops, 300 militia, formed of the burghers; and toward the end of the fiege, they were reinforced by 350 Canadians, including 60 Indians. The harbour was fecured by fix fhips of the line, and five frigates, three of which the enemy funk acrofs the harbour's mouth, in order to render it inacceffible to the Englifh fhipping. The governor

nor had taken all the precautions in his power to prevent a landing, by eftablifhing a chain of pofts along the moft acceffible parts of the beach: but there were fome intermediate places which could not be properly fecured, and in one of thefe the Englifh troops were difembarked; on which occafion brigadier Wolfe diftinguifhed himfelf greatly.

The landing was not effected, however, without an obftinate oppofition: and the ftores, with the artillery, being brought on fhore, the town of Louifbourg was formally invefted. The difficulty of landing ftores and implements in boifterous weather, and the nature of the ground, which, being marfhy, was unfit for the conveyance of heavy cannon, retarded the operations of the fiege; and Mr. Amherft made his approaches with great circumfpection. A very fevere fire, well directed, was maintained againft the befiegers and their work, from the town, the ifland battery, and the fhips in the harbour; and divers fallies were made, though without much effect. Befide the regular approaches to the town, conducted by the engineers, under the immediate command and infpection of general Amherft, divers batteries were raifed by the detached corps under brigadier Wolfe, who exerted himfelf with amazing activity. The three great fhips, the Entreprenant, Capricieux, and Celebre, were fet on fire by the bomb-fhells, and burned to afhes; fo that none remained but the Prudent and Bienfaifant, which the admiral undertook to deftroy. For this purpofe, the boats of the fquadron were detached into the harbour in the night time, through a terrible fire. The Prudent, being aground, was fet on fire, and deftroyed; but the Bienfaifant was towed out of the harbour in triumph.

In the profecution of the fiege, the admiral and general co-operated with remarkable harmony: the fire of the town was alfo managed with equal fkill and activity, and kept up with great perfeverance; until, at length, their fhipping being all taken or
deftroyed,

destroyed, and divers practicable breaches effected, the governor was constrained to submit.

Thus, at the expence of about 400 men killed or wounded, the English obtained possession of the important island of Cape Breton, and the strong town of Louisbourg; in which the victors found 221 pieces of cannon, 18 mortars, and a considerable quantity of stores and ammunition. The loss of Louisbourg was the more severely felt by the French king, as it had been attended with the destruction of so many considerable ships.

In the East Indies the transactions of the war were chequered with a variety of success; but, on the whole, the designs of the enemy were entirely defeated. The French king had sent a considerable reinforcement to the East Indies, under the command of general Lally, with such a number of ships as rendered the squadron of Mr. d'Apché superior to that of admiral Pocock; who succeeded after the death of admiral Watson, to the command of the English squadron, stationed on the coast of Coromandel; which, in the beginning of this year, was reinforced from England with several ships, under the direction of commodore Stevens. Immediately after this junction, admiral Pocock, who had already signalized himself by his courage and conduct, sailed to intercept the French squadron, of which he had received intelligence. In two days he descried in the road of Fort St. David the enemy's fleet, consisting of nine ships; which immediately stood out to sea, and formed the line of battle a-head. The admiral took the same precaution, and, bearing down upon Mr. d'Apché, the engagement began about three in the afternoon. The French commodore, having sustained a warm action for about four hours, bore away with his whole fleet; and being joined by two ships, formed a line of battle again to leeward. Admiral Pocock's own ship, and some others, being greatly damaged in their masts and rigging, two of his captains

tains having mifbehaved in the action, and night coming on, he did not think it advifeable to purfue them clofely; neverthelefs, he followed them at a proper diftance, and maintained the weather gage, in cafe he fhould be able to renew the action in the morning. However, in the morning, not the leaft veftige of them appeared. Such was the iffue of the firft action between the Englifh and French fquadrons in the Eaft Indies, which, over and above the lofs of a capital fhip, difabled and run afhore, is faid to have coft the enemy about 500 men, whereas the Britifh admiral did not lofe one fifth part of that number.

In the mean time, Mr. Lally had difembarked his troops at Pondicherry, and, taking the field, immediately invefted the fort of St. David, while the fquadron blocked it up by fea; two Englifh fhips being at anchor in the road when the enemy arrived, their captains, feeing no poffibility of efcaping, ran them on fhore, fet them on fire, and retired with their men into the fortrefs, which, however, was in a few days furrendered. Admiral Pocock having, to the beft of his power, repaired his fhips, fet fail again, in order to attempt the relief of Fort St. David's; but notwithftanding his utmoft endeavours, could not reach it in time to be of any fervice. On the 30th day of May he came in fight of Pondicherry, from whence the French fquadron ftood away early next morning; nor was it in his power to come up with them, though he made all poffible efforts for that purpofe. He failed a third time in queft of Mr. Apché, and in two days perceived his fquadron, confifting of eight fhips of the line and a frigate, at anchor in the road of Pondicherry. They no fooner defcried him advancing, than they ftood out to fea as before, and he continued to chace, in hope of bringing them to an engagement; but all his endeavours proved fruitlefs, till the 3d day of Auguft, when, having obtained the weather-gage, he bore down upon them in order of battle. The engagement began

gan with great impetuofity on both fides, but in little more than ten minutes Mr. d'Apché fet his fore-fail and bore away, his whole fquadron following his example, and maintaining a running fight in a very irregular line. The Britifh admiral then hoifted the fignal for a general chace, which the enemy perceiving, thought proper to cut away their boats, and croud with all the fail they could carry. They efcaped by favour of the night into the road of Pondicherry, and Mr. Pocock anchored with his fquadron off Carical, a French fettlement; having thus obtained an undifputed victory, with the lofs of 30 men killed. The French fleet was fo much damaged, that their commodore failed for the ifland of Bourbon, in the fame latitude with Madagafcar, in order to refit; thus leaving the command and fovereignty of the Indian feas to the Englifh admiral.

Previous to the more capital operations by fea, we fhall fpecify the moft remarkable captures that were made upon the enemy by fingle fhips of war, during the courfe of the fummer and autumn, 1759. A French privateer, belonging to Granville, called the Marquis de Marigny, of 20 guns and 200 men, was taken by captain Parker, of the Montague; who likewife made prize of a fmaller armed veffel, from Dunkirk, of 8 cannon and 60 men. About the fame period, captain Gravès, of the Unicorn, brought in the Moras privateer of St. Malo, of 22 guns and 200 men. Two large merchant-fhips, loaded on the French king's account, for Martinique, with ftores for the troops on that ifland, were taken by captain Lendrick, of the Brilliant. Captain Hood, of the Veftal, belonging to a fmall fquadron commanded by admiral Holmes, who had failed for the Weft Indies in January, being advanced a confiderable way a-head of the fleet, defcried and gave chace to the Bellona, of 32 guns and 220 men. Captain Hood, having made a fignal to the admiral, continued the chace until he advanced within half mufket-fhot of the enemy, and then poured in a broadside, which was immediately retorted. The engagement was maintained with great vigour on both sides, for the space of four hours; at the expiration of which, the Bellona struck, after having lost all her masts and rigging, with about 40 men killed in the action: nor was the victor in a much better condition. The Bellona had sailed in January from the island of Martinique, along with the Florissant, and another French frigate, from which she had been separated in the passage.

Immediately after this exploit, captain Elliot, of the Æolus frigate, accompanied by the Isis, made prize of French ship, the Mignonne, of 20 guns and 140 men; one of four frigates employed as a convoy to a large fleet of merchant-ships, near the island of Rhée.

In the month of March, the English frigates the Southampton and Melampe, commanded by the captains Gilchrist and Hotham, being at sea to the northward on a cruise, fell in with the Danae, of 40 cannon, and 330 men, which was engaged by captain Hotham in a ship of half the force, who maintained the battle a considerable time with admirable gallantry, before his consort could come to his assistance. As they fought in the dark, captain Gilchrist was obliged to lie by for some time, because he could not distinguish the one from the other; but no sooner did the day appear than he bore down upon the Danae, and soon compelled her to surrender.

Another remarkable exploit was about the same juncture atchieved by captain Barrington, of the Achilles, of 60 cannon, who, to the westward of Cape Finisterre, encountered a French ship of equal force, called the Count de St. Florentin; who was obliged to strike after a close and obstinate engagement. Captain Falkner, in the Windsor, of 60 guns, cruising to the westward, discovered four large ships to leeward; which formed the line of battle a-head,

in

in order to give him a warm reception. He closed with the sternmost ship, which sustained his fire about an hour: then the other three bearing away, she struck her colours, and was conducted to Lisbon. She proved to be the Duc de Chartres, pierced for 60 cannon, though at that time carrying no more than 24, with 300 men. She belonged, with the other three that escaped, to the French East India company, was loaded with gunpowder and naval stores, and bound for Pondicherry.

In the month of May, a French frigate, called the Arethusa, of 32 guns, and well manned, submitted to two British frigates, the Venus and the Thames, commanded by the captains Harrison and Colby.

Several armed ships of the enemy, and rich prizes, were taken in the West Indies; particularly two French frigates, and two Dutch ships with French commodities, all richly laden, by some of the ships of the squadron which vice-admiral Cotes commanded in the Jamaica station. But notwithstanding the vigilance and courage of the English cruizers in those seas, the French privateers swarmed to such a degree, that, in the course of this year, they took above 200 sail of British ships, valued at 600,000 pounds sterling. This their success is the more remarkable, as by this time the island of Guadalupe was in possession of the English, and commodore Moore commanded a numerous squadron in those very latitudes.

Having taken notice of some remarkable captures that were made by single ships, we shall now proceed to describe the actions that were performed in this period by the different squadrons of Great Britain. Intelligence having been received, that the enemy meditated an invasion upon some of the British territories, and that a number of flat-bottomed boats were prepared at Havre de Grace, for the purpose of disembarking troops; rear-admiral Rodney was detached with a small squadron of ships and bombs, to overawe that part of the coaft of France. He accordingly anchored in the road of Havre, and made a difpofition to execute the inftructions he had received. The bomb veffels being placed in the narrow channel of the river leading to Honfleur, began to throw their fhells, and continued the bombardment for 52 hours, without intermiffion; during which, a numerous body of French troops was employed in throwing up entrenchments, erecting new batteries, and firing both fhot and fhells upon the affailants. The town was fet on fire in feveral places, and burned with great fury; fome of the boats were overturned, and a few of them reduced to afhes, while the inhabitants forfook the place in the utmoft confternation: neverthelefs, the damage done to the enemy was too inconfiderable to make amends for the expence of the armament, and the lofs of 1900 fhells and 1100 carcaffes, which were expended on this expedition. Bombardments of this kind are at beft but expenfive and unprofitable operations, and may be deemed a barbarous method of profecuting war; inafmuch as the damage falls rather upon the innocent inhabitants, than on the government.

The honour of the Britifh flag was much more effectually afferted by the gallant admiral Bofcawen, who was entrufted with the conduct of a fquadron in the Mediterranean. It muft be owned, however, that his firft attempt favoured of temerity. Having in vain difplayed the Britifh flag in fight of Toulon, by way of defiance to the French fleet that there lay at anchor; he ordered three fhips of the line, commanded by the captains Smith, Harland, and Barker, to advance and burn two fhips that lay clofe to the mouth of the harbour. They accordingly approached with great intrepidity, and met with a very warm reception from divers batteries which they had not before perceived: fo that they were towed off with great difficulty, in a very fhattered condition. The admiral feeing three of his beft fhips fo roughly handled

handled in this enterprize, returned to Gibraltar in order to refit; and M. de la Clue, commander of the squadron at Toulon, seized this opportunity of sailing, in hope of passing the Streights mouth unobserved; his fleet consisting of 12 large ships and 3 frigates. Admiral Boscawen, who commanded 14 sail of the line, with 2 frigates, and as many fireships, having refitted his squadron, detached 2 frigates to keep a good look-out, and give timely notice in case the enemy should approach. On the 17th of August, in the evening, the Gibraltar frigate made a signal that 14 sail appeared on the Barbary shore. Upon which the English admiral immediately went to sea: at day-light he descried seven large ships lying to; but when the English squadron did not answer their signal, they discovered their mistake, set all their sails, and made the best of their way. Even now perhaps he might have escaped, had he not been obliged to wait for the Souveraine, which was a heavy sailer. At noon the wind, which had blown a fresh gale, died away; and it was some time before his headmost ships could close with the rear of the enemy; which, though greatly out-numbered, fought with uncommon bravery. The English admiral, without waiting to return the fire of the sternmost, used all his endeavours to come with the Ocean, which Mr. de la Clue commanded in person; and about four o'clock in the afternoon, running athwart her hawse, poured into her a furious broadside: thus the engagement began with equal vigour on both sides. This dispute, however, was of short duration; in about half an hour admiral Boscawen's mizen-mast and topsail-yards were shot away; and the enemy hoisted all the sail they could carry. Mr. Boscawen, having shifted his flag from the Namur to the Newark, joined some other ships in attacking the Centaur of 74 guns, which, being thus overpowered, was obliged to surrender. The British admiral pursued them all night, during which the Souveraine and Guerrier altered their courfe, and deferted their commander. At day-break, Mr. de la Clue, whofe left leg had been broke in the engagement, perceived the Englifh fquadron crowding all their fails to come up with him, and finding himfelf on the coaft of Portugal, determined to burn his fhips rather than they fhould fall into the hands of the victors. The Ocean was run afhore two leagues from Lagos, near the fort of Almadana, the commander of which fired three fhots at the Englifh: another captain of the French fquadron followed the example of his commander; and both endeavoured to difembark their men: but the fea being rough, this proved a very tedious and difficult attempt. The captains of the Temeraire and Modefte, inftead of deftroying their fhips, anchored as near as they could to the forts Exavier and Lagres, in hope of enjoying their protection; but in this hope they were difappointed. Mr. de la Clue had been landed, and the command of the Ocean was left to the count de Carne; who having received one broadfide from the America, ftruck his colours, and the Englifh took poffeffion of this noble prize, the beft fhip in the French navy, mounted with 80 cannon. Captain Bentley of the Warfpight, who had remarkably fignalized himfelf by his courage during the action of the preceding day, attacked the Temeraire of 74 guns, and brought her off with little damage. Vice-admiral Broderick, the fecond in command, advancing with his divifion, burned the Redoubtable of 74 guns, which was bulged and abandoned by her men and officers; but they made prize of the Modefte, carrying 64 guns, which had not been much injured in the engagement. This victory was obtained by the Englifh admiral at a very fmall expence of men; the whole number of the killed and wounded not exceeding 250 on board of the Britifh fquadron; though the carnage among the enemy muft have been much more confiderable: but the moft fevere circumftance of this difafter was the

lofs

loss of four capital ships, two of which were destroyed, and the other two brought in triumph to England, to be numbered among the best bottoms of the British navy. What augmented the good fortune of the victors, was, that not one officer lost his life in the engagement.

The court of Versailles, in order to embarrass the British ministry, and divert their attention from all external expeditions, had, in the winter, projected a plan for invading some part of the British dominions; and, in the beginning of the year, had actually begun to make preparations on different parts of their coast, for carrying this design into execution. Every precautionary step was, however, taken to frustrate their intentions; but the administration wisely placed their chief dependence upon the strength of the navy; part of which was so divided and stationed, as to block up all the harbours of France, in which the enemy were known to make any naval armament of consequence. Notwithstanding the disaster of Mr. de la Clue, the French ministry persisted in their design: toward the execution of which, they had prepared another considerable fleet, at the harbours of Rochfort, Brest, and Port-Louis, to be commanded by Mr. de Conflans, and reinforced by a considerable body of troops. Flat-bottomed boats, and transports to be used in this expedition, were prepared in different ports on the coast of France; and a small squadron was equipped at Dunkirk, under the command of an enterprising adventurer called Thurot, who had, in the course of the preceding year, signalized his courage and conduct in a large privateer called the Belleisle.

This man's name became a terror to the merchants of Great Britain; for his valour was not more remarkable in battle than his conduct in eluding the pursuit of the British cruisers, who were successively detached in quest of him. The court of Versailles was not insensible to his merit. He obtained a commission

mission from the French king, and was vested with the command of the small armament now fitting out in the harbour of Dunkirk.

The British government, apprised of all these particulars, took such measures to defeat the proposed invasion, as must have conveyed a very high idea of the power of Great Britain to those who considered, that, exclusive of the force opposed to this design, they at the same time carried on the most vigorous and important operations of war in Germany, America, the East and West Indies. Thurot's armament at Dunkirk was watched by an English squadron in the Downs, commanded by commodore Boys; the port of Havre was guarded by rear-admiral Rodney; Mr. Boscawen had been stationed off Toulon; and the coast of Vannes was scoured by a small squadron detached from Sir Edward Hawke, who had, during the whole summer, blocked up the harbour of Brest, where Conflans lay with his fleet, in order to be joined by the other divisions of the armament. These different squadrons of the British navy were connected by a chain of separate cruisers; so that the whole coast of France, from Dunkirk to the extremity of Bretagne, were distressed by an actual blockade.

The French ministry being thus hampered, forbore their attempt upon Britain; and the projected invasion seemed to hang in suspence, till the month of August, in the beginning of which their army in Germany was defeated at Minden. Their designs in that country being baffled by this disaster, they seemed to convert their chief attention to their sea-armament; the preparations were resumed with redoubled vigour: even after the defeat of La Clue, they resolved to try their fortune in a descent upon Ireland: and the young pretender remained in the neighbourhood of Vannes incognito, in order once more to hazard his person, and countenance a revolt in the dominions of Great Britain.

The

The execution of this fcheme was, however, prevented by the vigilance of Sir Edward Hawke, who blocked up the harbour of Breft, with a fleet of 23 capital fhips; while another fquadron of fmaller fhips and frigates, under the command of captain Duff, continued to cruife along the French coaft from Port L'Orient in Bretagne to the point of St. Gilles in Poitou. At length, however, in the beginning of November, the Britifh fquadron were driven from the coaft of France by ftrefs of weather, and on the 9th day of the month anchored in Torbay. Admiral Conflans fnatched this opportunity of failing from Breft, with 21 fail of the line and 4 frigates, in hope of being able to deftroy the Englifh fquadron commanded by captain Duff, before the larger fleet could return from the coaft of England. Sir Edward Hawke, having received intelligence that the French fleet had failed from Breft, immediately ftood to fea, in order to purfue them ; and, in the mean time, the government iffued orders for guarding all thofe parts of the coaft that were thought the moft expofed to a defcent.

While thefe meafures were taken with equal vigour and deliberation, Sir Edward Hawke fteered his courfe directly for Quiberon, on the coaft of Bretagne, which he fuppofed would be the rendezvous of the French fquadron. On the 20th of November, he fell in with them, as they were giving chace to captain Duff's fquadron, which now joined the large fleet, after having run fome rifque of being taken. Sir Edward Hawke, who had formed the line a-breaft, now perceiving that the French admiral endeavoured to efcape, threw out a fignal for feven of his fhips that were neareft the enemy to chace, and endeavour to detain them, until they could be reinforced by the reft of the fquadron. Confidering the roughnefs of the weather, the nature of the coaft, which is in this place very hazardous, and entirely unknown to the Britifh failors, it required extraordinary refolution in

the

the Englifh admiral to attempt hoftilities on this occafion. With refpect to his fhips of the line, he had but the advantage of one in point of number, and no fuperiority in men or metal; confequently Mr. de Conflans might have hazarded a fair battle in the open fea, without any imputation of temerity: but he thought proper to play a more artful game, and retired clofe in fhore, with a view to draw the Englifh fquadron among the fhoals and iflands, while he and his officers, who were perfectly acquainted with the navigation, could either ftay, and take advantage of their difafter, or, if hard preffed, retire through channels unknown to the Britifh pilots.

At half an hour after two, the van of the Englifh fleet began the engagement with the rear of the enemy, in the neighbourhood of Belleifle. Every fhip as fhe advanced poured in a broadfide on the fternmoft of the French, and bore down upon their van, leaving the rear to thofe that came after. Sir Edward Hawke, in the Royal George of 110 guns, referved his fire in paffing through the rear of the enemy, and ordered his mafter to bring him along-fide of the French admiral, who commanded in perfon on board of the Soleil Royal, of 80 guns and 1200 men. When the pilot remonftrated that he could not obey his command, without the moft imminent rifque of running upon a fhoal, the brave 'veteran replied, " You have done your duty in fhewing the danger; now you are to comply with my order, and lay me along-fide the Soleil Royal." His wifh was gratified: the Royal George ranged up with the French admiral. The Thefée, another large fhip of the enemy, running up between the two commanders, fuftained the fire referved for the Soleil Royal; but in returning the firft broadfide foundered, in confequence of the high fea that entered her lower deck-ports, and filled her with water. Notwithftanding the boifterous weather, a good number of fhips on both fides fought with equal fury and dubious fuccefs, till about

four

four in the afternoon, when the Formidable ſtruck her colours. The Superbe ſhared the fate of the Theſée in going to the bottom. The Heros hauled down her colours in token of ſubmiſſion, and dropped anchor; but the wind was ſo high, that no boat could be ſent to take poſſeſſion. By this time day-light began to fail, and the greater part of the French fleet eſcaped under colour of the darkneſs.

Night approaching, the wind blowing with augmented violence on a lee-ſhore, and the Britiſh ſquadron being intangled among unknown ſhoals and iſlands, Sir Edward Hawke made the ſignal for anchoring to the weſtward of the ſmall iſland Dumet; and here the fleet remained all night in a very dangerous riding, alarmed by the fury of the ſtorm, and inceſſant firing of guns of diſtreſs, without their knowing whether it proceeded from friend or enemy. The Soleil Royal had, under favour of the night, anchored alſo in the midſt of the Britiſh ſquadron; but at day-break, Mr. de Conflans ordered her cable to be cut, and ſhe drove aſhore to the weſtward of Crozie. The Engliſh admiral immediately made ſignal to the Eſſex to ſlip her cable and purſue her; but in obeying this order, ſhe ran unfortunately on a ſandbank, called Lefour, where the Reſolution, another ſhip of the Engliſh ſquadron, was already grounded. Here they were both irrecoverably loſt, in ſpite of all the aſſiſtance that could be given: but all their men, and part of their ſtores, were ſaved, and the wrecks burnt. He likewiſe detached the Portland, Chatham, and Vengeance, to deſtroy the Soleil Royal, which was burned by her own people, before the Engliſh ſhips could approach; but they arrived time enough to reduce the Heros to aſhes on Lefour, where ſhe had been alſo ſtranded: and the Juſte, another of their great ſhips, periſhed in the mouth of the Loire.

The admiral perceiving ſeven large ſhips of the enemy riding at anchor between Point Penvas and
the

the mouth of the river Vilaine, made the fignal to weigh, in order to attack them; but the fury of the ftorm increafed to fuch a degree, that he was obliged to remain at anchor, and even ordered the top-gallant-mafts to be ftruck.

In the mean time, the French fhips being lightened of their cannon, their officers took advantage of the flood, and a more moderate gale under the land, to enter the Vilaine; where they lay within half a mile of the entrance, protected by fome occafional *batteries erected on the fhore, and by two large frigates, moored acrofs the mouth of the harbour. Thus they were effectually fecured from any attempts of fmall veffels; and as for large fhips, there was not water fufficient to float them within fighting diftance of the enemy.

On the whole, this battle, in which a very inconfiderable number of lives were loft, may be confidered as one of the moft perilous and important actions that ever happened in any war between the two nations: for it not only defeated the projected invafion, which had hung menacing fo long over the apprehenfions of Great Britain; but it gave the finifhing blow to the naval power of France, which was totally difabled from undertaking any thing of confequence in the fequel.

By this time, indeed, Thurot had efcaped from Dunkirk, and directed his courfe to the North Sea, whither he was followed by commodore Boys, who neverthelefs was difappointed in his purfuit; but the fate of that adventurer falls under the occurrences of the enfuing year.

As for Sir Edward Hawke, he continued cruifing off the coaft of Bretagne for a confiderable time after the victory he had obtained, taking particular care to block up the mouth of the river Vilaine, that the feven French fhips might not efcape, and join Mr. Conflans, who made fhift to reach Rochfort with the fhattered remains of his fquadron. Indeed, this fervice

vice became such a considerable object in the eyes of the British ministry, that a large fleet was maintained upon this coast, apparently for no other purpose, during a whole year; and, after all, the enemy eluded their vigilance.

A plan had been formed for improving the success of the preceding year in North America, by carrying the British arms up the river St. Laurence, and besieging Quebec, the capital of Canada. The armament employed against the French islands of Martinique and Guadalupe, constituted part of this design; inasmuch as the troops embarked on that expedition were, in case of a miscarriage at Martinique, intended to reinforce the British army in North America, which was justly considered as the chief seat of the war. Martinique was reduced to great distress by the ruin of its trade, and by want of all, even necessary provisions, when the inhabitants every day expected a visit from the British armament, whose progress we are now to relate. In November of the preceding year, captain Hugh's sailed from St. Helen's, with eight sail of the line, one frigate, four bomb-ketches, and a fleet of transports, containing land forces, under the command of major-general Hopson. At Barbadoes they joined commodore Moore, who now assumed the command of the united squadrons, amounting to ten ships of the line, beside frigates and bomb-ketches.

After an unsuccessful attempt on Martinique, the failure of which it is not easy to account for, the whole armament directed their course to Guadalupe, another of the French Carribbee islands, lying 30 leagues to the westward. Having arrived at Basseterre, a council of war was held on board the commodore's ship; where it was resolved to make a general attack by sea, upon the citadel, the town, and other batteries by which it was defended. A disposition being made for this purpose, the large ships took their

their respective stations next morning, being the 23d of January.

In this present attack, all the sea commanders behaved with extraordinary spirit and resolution, particularly the captains Leslie, Burnet, Gayton, Jekyl, Trelawney, and Shuldam; who, in the hottest tumult of the action, distinguished themselves equally by their courage, impetuosity, and deliberation. The four bombs being anchored near the shore, began to ply the town with shells and carcasses; so that in a little time the houses were in flames, the magazines of gunpowder blew up with the most terrible explosion, and about ten o'clock the whole place blazed out one general conflagration.

Next day at two in the afternoon, the fleet come to an anchor in the road of Basseterre, where they found the hulls of divers ships which the enemy had set on fire at their approach: several ships turned out and endeavoured to escape, but were intercepted and taken by the English squadron. At five, the troops landed without opposition, and took possession of the town and citadel, which they found entirely abandoned. They learned from a Genoese deserter, that the regular troops of the island consisted of five companies only, the number of the whole not exceeding 100 men; and that they had laid a train to blow up the powder-magazine in the citadel: but had been obliged to retreat with such precipitation, as did not permit them to execute this design. The train was immediately cut off, and the magazine secured. The nails with which they had spiked up their cannon were drilled out by the matrosses; and in the mean time, the British colours were hoisted on the parapet. Part of the troops took possession of an advantageous post on an eminence, and part entered the town, which still continued burning with great violence.

In the morning, at day-break, the enemy appeared, to the number of 2000, about four miles from
the

the town, and began to throw up intrenchments in the neighbourhood of a houſe where the governor had fixed his head-quarters, declaring he would maintain his ground to the laſt extremity. In the mean time, the reduction of the iſlanders on the ſide of Guadalupe appearing more and more impracticable, the general reſolved to transfer the ſeat of war to the eaſtern and more fertile part of the iſland, called Grand-Terre; which, as we have already obſerved, was defended by a ſtrong battery, called Fort Louis. In purſuance of this determination, the great ſhips were ſent round to Grand-terre, in order to reduce this fortification, which they accordingly effected on the 13th of February. After a ſevere cannonading, which laſted ſix hours, a body of marines being landed, with the highlanders, they drove the enemy from their intrenchments ſword in hand, and, taking poſſeſſion of the fort, hoiſted the Engliſh colours.

In a few days after this exploit, general Hopſon dying at Baſſe-terre, the chief command devolved to general Barrington, who reſolved to proſecute the final reduction of the iſland with vigour and diſpatch.

In the mean time, commodore Moore having received certain intelligence that Monſ. de Bompart had arrived at Martinique with a ſquadron, conſiſting of eight ſail of the line and three frigates, having on board a whole battalion of Swiſs, and ſome other troops, to reinforce the garriſons of the iſlands; he called in his cruiſers, and ſailed immediately to the bay of Dominique, an iſland to the windward, at the diſtance of nine leagues from Guadalupe; whence he could always ſail to oppoſe any deſigns which the French commander might form againſt the operations of the Britiſh armaments.

Without entering into a detail of the proceedings of the land-forces, toward a reduction of the internal parts of the iſland, which was a work of ſome time; it is ſufficient to obſerve, that the inhabitants capitulated on May 1ſt, 1759, at the very time that a confiderable reinforcement from Martinique had landed on another part of the ifland; which on knowlege of this event, returned directly.

The town of Baffe-terre being reduced to a heap of afhes, the inhabitants began to clear away the rubbifh, and erected occafional fheds, where they refumed their feveral occupations with that good humour fo peculiar to the French nation; and general Barrington humanely indulged them with all the affiftance in his power.

Immediately after the capitulation of Guadalupe, he fummoned the iflands called Santos and Defeada to furrender; and they, together with Petit-terre, fubmitted on the fame terms which he had granted to the great ifland: but his propofal was rejected by the inhabitants of Marigalante, which lies about three leagues to the fouth-eaft of Grand-terre, extending 20 miles in length, 15 in breadth, flat and fertile, but poorly watered, and ill-fortified. The general, refolving to reduce it by force, embarked a body of troops on board of tranfports, which failed thither under convoy of three fhips of war and two bomb veffels from prince Rupert's Bay; and at their appearance the iflanders fubmitting, received an Englifh garrifon.

Three regiments were allotted as a fufficient guard for the whole ifland, and the other three were embarked for England. General Barrington himfelf went on board the Roebuck in the latter end of June, and with the tranfports, under convoy of captain Hughes, and a fmall fquadron, fet fail for Great Britain; while commodore Moore, with his large fleet, directed his courfe to Antigua.

The reduction of Niagara, and the poffeffion of Crown-point, were exploits much more eafily atchieved than the conqueft of Quebec, the great object to which all thefe operations were fubordinate. Of that we now come to give the detail, fraught with fingular events; in the courfe of which a noble fpirit

of

of enterprize was difplayed. It was about the middle of February that a confiderable fquadron failed from England for Cape Breton, under the command of the admirals Saunders and Holmes: but the harbour was blocked up with ice in fuch a manner, that they were obliged to bear away for Halifax in Nova Scotia. From hence admiral Saunders arrived at Louifbourg; and the troops being embarked, to the number of 8000, proceeded up the river without further delay. The operations at land were intrufted to the conduct of major-general James Wolfe, whofe talents had fhone with fuch fuperior luftre at the fiege of Louifbourg; and his fubordinates in command were the brigadiers Monckton, Townfhend, and Murray.

The armament intended for Quebec failed up the river St. Laurence, without having met with any interruption, or having perceived any of thofe difficulties and perils with which it had been reported that the navigation of it was attended. Their good fortune in this particular, indeed, was owing to fome excellent charts of the river, which had been found in veffels taken from the enemy. About the latter end of June the land-forces were difembarked in two divifions upon the ifle of Orleans, fituated a little below Quebec. General Wolfe no fooner landed on the ifland of Orleans than he diftributed a manifefto among the French colonifts, explaining the nature of the undertaking; that the hoftilities were intended againft the fettlements and forces of the king of France, but not againft the innocent inhabitants; affuring them of his protection while they gave him no difturbance, which he fhewed them muft be ineffectual, and would only expofe them to his refentment. This declaration produced no immediate effect; nor, indeed, did the Canadians depend upon the fincerity and promifed faith of a nation, whom their priefts had induftrioufly reprefented as the moft favage and cruel enemy on earth. Poffeffed of thofe notions, which prevailed even among the better fort, they chofe to abandon

abandon their habitations, and expofe themfelves and families to certain ruin, in provoking the Englifh by the moft cruel hoftilities, rather than to be quiet, and confide in the general's promife of protection: fo that Mr. Wolfe, in order to intimidate the enemy into a ceffation of thefe outrages, found it neceffary to connive at fome irregularities in the way of retaliation.

Mr. de Montcalm, who commanded the French troops, though fuperior in number to the invaders, very wifely refolved to depend upon the natural ftrength of the country, which appeared almoft infurmountable, and had carefully taken all his precautions of defence. The city of Quebec was fkilfully fortified, fecured with a numerous garrifon, and plentifully fupplied with provifion and ammunition. Montcalm had reinforced the troops of the colony, and had taken the field, in a very advantageous fituation, encamped along the fhore of Beaufort, from the river St. Charles to the falls of Montmorenci; every acceffible part being deeply intrenched. To undertake the fiege of Quebec againft fuch odds and advantages, was not only a deviation from the eftablifhed maxims of war, but feemingly a rafh enterprize: Mr. Wolfe was well acquainted with the difficulties of the undertaking; but he knew at the fame time he fhould always have it in his power to retreat, in cafe of emergency, while the Britifh fquadron maintained its ftation in the river; and he was not without hope of being joined by general Amherft. Underftanding that there was a body of the enemy pofted, with cannon, at the Point of Levi, on the fouth fhore, oppofite to the city of Quebec, he detached againft them brigadier Monckton, at the head of four battalions, who paffed the river at night; and next morning, having fkirmifhed with fome of the enemy's irregulars, obliged them to retire from that poft, which the Englifh immediately occupied. At the fame time colonel Carlton, with another detachment,

tachment, took poffeffion of the weftern point of the ifland of Orleans; and both thefe pofts were fortified, in order to anticipate the enemy, who, had they kept poffeffion of either, might have rendered it impoffible for any fhip to lie at anchor within two miles of Quebec. Befide, the Point of Levi was within cannon-fhot of the city, againft which a battery of mortars and artillery was immediately erected. Montcalm, forefeeing the effect of this expedient, detached a body of fixteen hundred men acrofs the river, to attack and deftroy the works before they were completed: but this detachment fell into diforder, fired upon each other, and retired in confufion. The battery being finifhed, without further interruption, the cannon and mortars began to play with fuch fuccefs, that in a little time the upper town was confiderably damaged, and the lower town reduced to a heap of rubbifh.

In the mean time the fleet was expofed to the moft imminent danger. Immediately after the troops had been landed on the ifland of Orleans, the wind increafed to a furious ftorm, which blew with fuch violence, that many tranfports ran foul of one another, and were difabled; a number of boats and fmall craft foundered, and divers large fhips loft their anchors. The enemy refolving to take advantage of the confufion which they imagined this difafter muft have produced, prepared feven firefhips, and at midnight fent them down from Quebec among the tranfports, which lay fo thick as to cover the whole furface of the river. The fcheme, though well contrived, and feafonably executed, was entirely defeated by the deliberation of the Britifh admiral, and the dexterity of his marines, who refolutely boarded the firefhips, and towed them faft a-ground; where they lay burning to the water's edge, without having done the leaft prejudice to the Englifh fquadron. On the very fame day of the fucceeding month, they fent
down

down a raft of firefhips, or radeaus, which were likewife confumed, without producing any effect.

The works for the fecurity of the hofpital, and the ftores on the ifland of Orleans, being finifhed, the Britifh forces croffed the north channel in boats, and landing under the cover of two floops, encamped on the fide of the river Montmorenci, which divided them from the left of the enemy; and next morning a company of rangers, pofted in a wood to cover fome workmen, were attacked by the French Indians, and totally defeated: however, the neareft troops advancing, repulfed the Indians in their turn with confiderable lofs. On the 18th day of July, the admiral, at general Wolfe's requeft, fent two fhips of war, two armed floops, and fome tranfports, having troops on board, up the river; and they paffed the city of Quebec, without having fuftained any damage. The general, being on board of this little armament, carefully obferved the banks on the fide of the enemy, which were extreamly difficult from the nature of the ground; and thefe difficulties were redoubled by the forefight and precaution of the French commander. Though a defcent feemed impracticable between the city and Cape Rouge, where it was intended, general Wolfe, in order to divide the enemy's force, and procure intelligence, ordered a detachment, under the command of colonel Carlton, to land higher up at the Point Au Tremble; to which place he was informed, a good number of the inhabitants of Quebec had retired with their moft valuable effects. This fervice was performed with little lofs, and fome prifoners were brought away; but no magazine was difcovered.

The general, thus difappointed in his expectation, returned to Montmorenci, where brigadier Townfhend had, by maintaining a fuperior fire acrofs that river, prevented the enemy from erecting a battery, which would have commanded the Englifh camp: and now he refolved to attack them, though pofted to great advantage, and every where prepared to give him a warm reception. His defign was, firft to reduce a detached redoubt clofe to the water's edge; feemingly fituated without gun-fhot of the intrenchment on the hill. Should this fortification be fupported by the enemy, he forefaw that he fhould be able to bring on a general engagement: on the contrary, fhould they remain tame fpectators of its reduction, he could afterward examine their fituation at leifure, and determine the place at which they could be moft eafily attacked. Preparations were accordingly made for ftorming the redoubt: which was undertaken with great bravery, but the fire of the French was fo hotly maintained, that the Englifh were for that time obliged to give up the conteft. Had the attack fucceeded, the lofs of the Englifh muft have been very heavy, and that of the French inconfiderable; becaufe the neighbouring woods afforded them immediate fhelter: finally, the river St. Charles ftill remained to be paffed, before the town could be invefted.

Immediately after this mortifying check, in which above five hundred men, and many brave officers were loft, the general detached brigadier Murray, with twelve hundred men, in tranfports above the town, to co-operate with rear-admiral Holmes, whom the admiral had fent up with fome force againft the French fhipping, which he hoped to deftroy. The brigadier was likewife inftructed to feize every opportunity of fighting the enemy's detachments, and even of provoking them to battle. In purfuance of thefe directions, he twice attempted to land on the north fhore; but thefe attempts were unfuccefsful; the third effort was more fortunate; he made a fudden defcent at Chambaud, and burned a confiderable magazine, filled with arms, cloathing, provifion, and ammunition.

The difafter at the falls of Montmorenci made a deep impreffion on the mind of general Wolfe; he knew

knew the character of the English people, rash, impatient, and capricious; elevated to exultation by the least gleam of success, dejected even to despondency by the most inconsiderable frown of adverse fortune. Among those who shared his confidence, he was often seen to sigh, he was often heard to complain, and even in the transports of his chagrin, declare, that he would never return without success, to be exposed, as other unfortunate commanders had been, to the censure and reproach of an ignorant populace. This tumult of the mind, added to the fatigues of body he had undergone, produced a fever and dysentery; by which, for some time, he was totally disabled.

When we consider the situation of this place, and the fortifications with which it was secured; the natural strength of the country; the great number of vessels and floating batteries they had provided for the defence of the river; the skill, valour, superior force, and uncommon vigilance of the enemy; their numerous bodies of savages continually hovering about the posts of the English, to surprize parties and harrass detachments; we must own that there was such a combination of difficulties, as might have discouraged and perplexed the most resolute and intelligent commander.

As no possibility appeared of annoying the enemy above the town, the scheme of operations was totally changed. The three brigadiers formed, and presented a plan for conveying the troops farther down in boats, and landing them in the night within a league of Cape Diamond, in hope of ascending the heights of Abraham, which rise abruptly, with a steep ascent from the banks of the river; that they might take possession of the ground on the back of the city, where it was but indifferently fortified. The dangers and difficulties attending the execution of this design were so peculiarly discouraging, that one would imagine it could not have been embraced but by a spirit

of

of enterprize that bordered on desperation. The stream was rapid; the shore shelving; the bank of the river lined with centinels; the landing place so narrow as to be easily missed in the dark; and the ground so difficult as hardly to be surmounted in the day-time, had no opposition been expected.

The previous steps being taken, and the time fixed for this hazardous attempt, admiral Holmes moved with his squadron farther up the river, about three leagues above the place appointed for the disembarkation; that he might deceive the enemy, and amuse Mr. de Bougainville, whom Montcalm had detached with 1500 men to watch the motions of that squadron: but the English admiral was directed to sail down the river in the night, so as to protect the landing of the forces; and these orders he punctually fulfilled. On the 12th of September, an hour after midnight, the first embarkation, consisting of four compleat regiments, the light infantry, commanded by colonel Howe, a detachment of Highlanders, and the American grenadiers, was made in flat-bottomed boats, under the immediate command of the brigadiers Monckton and Murray. Without any disorder the boats glided gently along; but, by the rapidity of the tide, and darkness of the night, they overshot the mark, and the troops landed a little below the place at which the disembarkation was intended.

How far the success of this attempt depended upon accident, may be conceived from the following particulars.—In the twilight two French deserters were carried on board a ship of war, commanded by captain Smith, and laying at anchor near the North shore. They told him, that the garrison of Quebec expected that night to receive a convoy of provisions, sent down the river in boats, from the detachment above, commanded by Mr. de Bougainville. These deserters standing upon deck, and perceiving the English boats, with the troops, gliding down the river in the dark, began to shout, and make a noise; declaring

claring they were part of the expected convoy. Captain Smith, who was ignorant of general Wolfe's defign, believing their affirmation, had actually given orders to point the guns at the British troops; when the general perceiving a commotion on board, rowed along-fide in perfon, and prevented the difcharge, which would have alarmed the town, and entirely fruftrated the attempt.

The French had pofted fentinels along-fhore, to challenge boats and veffels, and give the alarm occafionally. The firft boat that contained the Englifh troops, being queftioned accordingly, a captain of Frafer's regiment, who had ferved in Holland, and who was perfectly well acquainted with the French language and cuftoms, anfwered, without hefitation, to *Qui vit?* which is their challenging word, *la France:* nor was he at a lofs to anfwer the fecond queftion, which was much more particular and difficult. When the fentinel demanded *a quel regiment?* of what regiment? the captain replied, *de la Reine,* which he knew, by accident, to be one of thofe that compofed the body commanded by Bougainville. The foldier took it for granted, this was the expected convoy; and faying *paffe,* allowed all the boats to proceed without further queftion. In the fame manner the other fentinels were deceived; though one more wary than the reft, came running down to the water's edge, and called, *pourquoy eft que vous ne parlez plus haut?* "Why don't you fpeak aloud?" To this interrogation, which implied doubt, the captain anfwered with admirable prefence of mind, in a foft tone of voice, *Tai tei, nous ferons entendues!* "Hufh! we fhall be overheard and difcovered." Thus cautioned, the fentinel retired without farther altercation. The midfhipman who piloted the firft boat, paffing by the landing-place in the dark, the fame captain, who knew from his having been pofted formerly with his company on the other fide of the river, infifted upon the pilot's being miftaken, and commanded the rowers

rowers to put ashore in the proper place, or at least very near it.

As the troops landed, the boats were sent back for the second embarkation, which was superintended by brigadier Townshend. In the mean time colonel Howe, with the light infantry and the Highlanders, ascended the woody precipices with admirable courage and activity; and dislodged a captain's guard, which defended a small intrenched narrow path, by which alone the rest of the forces could reach the summit. Then they mounted, without further molestation from the enemy, and the general drew them up in order, as they arrived. Monsieur de Montcalm no sooner understood that the English had gained the heights of Abraham, which in a manner commanded the town on its weakest part, than he resolved to hazard a battle, and began his march without delay; after having collected his whole force from the side of Beauport.

General Wolfe, perceiving the enemy crossing the river St. Charles, began to form his own line; the French had lined the bushes and corn-fields in their front with 1500 of their best marksmen, who kept up an irregular galling fire, which proved fatal to many brave officers, thus singled out for destruction. This fire, indeed, was in some measure checked by the advanced posts of the British line; who piqueered with the enemy for some hours before the battle began. Both armies were destitute of artillery, except two small pieces on the side of the French, and a single gun, which the English seamen had made shift to draw up from the landing-place. This was very well served, and galled their column severely. General Wolfe was stationed on the right, at the head of Bragg's regiment, and the Louisbourg grenadiers, where the attack was most warm. As he stood conspicuous in the front of the line, he had been aimed at by the enemy's marksmen; and received a shot in the wrist, which, however, did not oblige him to

quit

quit the field. Having wrapped a handkerchief round his hand, he continued giving orders without the least emotion; and advanced at the head of the grenadiers, with their bayonets fixed, when another ball unfortunately pierced the breast of this young hero, who fell in the arms of victory, just as the enemy gave way! For, at this very instant, every separate regiment of the British army seemed to exert itself for the honour of its own peculiar character. General Wolfe being slain, and, at the same time, Mr. Monckton dangerously wounded at the head of Lascelles's regiment, where he distinguished himself with remarkable gallantry, the command devolved to brigadier Townshend, who hastened to the centre; and finding the troops disordered in the pursuit, formed them again with all possible expedition. This necessary task was scarce performed, when M. de Bougainville, with a body of 2000 fresh men, appeared in the rear of the English. He had begun his march from Cape Rouge, as soon as he received intelligence that the British troops had gained the heights of Abraham; but did not come up in time to have any share in the battle.

Mr. Townshend immediately ordered two battalions, with two pieces of artillery, to advance against this officer, who retired, at their approach. The French general Mr. de Montcalm was mortally wounded in the battle, and conveyed into Quebec; from whence, before he died, he wrote a letter to general Townshend, recommending the prisoners to that generous humanity by which the British nation is distinguished. His second in command was left wounded on the field, and next day expired on board an English ship, to which he had been conveyed. About one thousand of the enemy were made prisoners, including a great number of officers; and about five hundred were slain on the field of battle. The wreck of their army, after they had reinforced the garrifon of Quebec, retired to Trois Rivieres and Montreal.

This important victory was obtained at the expence of fifty men killed, including nine officers; and of about 500 men wounded; but the death of general Wolfe was a national lofs, and univerfally lamented.

Immediately after the battle of Quebec, admiral Saunders fent up all the boats of the fleet, with artillery and ammunition; and failed up, with all the fhips of war, in a difpofition to attack the lower town; while the upper part fhould be affaulted by general Townfhend. But on the 17th of September, before any battery could be finifhed, a flag of truce was fent from the town, with propofals of capitulation; which, being maturely confidered by the general and admiral, were accepted and figned at eight next morning.

They granted the more favourable terms, as the enemy continued to affemble in the rear of the Britifh army; as the feafon was become wet, ftormy, and cold; threatening the troops with ficknefs, and the fleet with accident; and as a confiderable advantage would refult from taking poffeffion of the town while the walls were in a ftate of defence.

The capitulation was no fooner ratified, than the Britifh forces took poffeffion of Quebec, and guards were pofted in different parts of the town, to preferve order and difcipline. The death of Montcalm, which was indeed an irreparable lofs to France, in all probability, overwhelmed the enemy with confternation; and confounded all their councils: otherwife we cannot account for the tame furrender of Quebec to a handful of troops, even after the victory they had obtained: for the feafon was fo far advanced, that the Britifh forces in a little time muft have been forced to defift, by the feverity of the weather, and even retire with their fleet before the approach of winter, which never fails to freeze up the river St. Laurence.

The

The city of Quebec being reduced, together with great part of the circumjacent country, brigadier Townshend, who had accepted his commission with the express proviso, that he should return to England at the end of the campaign, left a garrison of 5000 effective men, victualled from the fleet, under the command of brigadier Murray; and embarking with admiral Saunders, arrived in Great Britain about the beginning of winter. As for brigadier Monckton, he was conveyed to New York, where he happily recovered of his wounds.

While the arms of Great Britain triumphed in Europe and America, her interest was not suffered to languish in other parts of the world. This was the season of ambition and activity, in which every separate armament seemed to exert themselves with the most eager appetite of glory. The East Indies, which, in the course of the preceding year, had been the theatre of operations carried on with various success, exhibited nothing now but a succession of trophies to the English commanders. During the operations by land, the superiority at sea was still disputed between the English and French admirals. On the 1st day of September, vice-admiral Pocock sailed from Madrass to the southward, in quest of the enemy; and next day descried the French fleet, consisting of fifteen sail, standing to the northward. He used his utmost endeavours to bring them to a battle, which they still declined, and at last they disappeared. He then directed his course to Pondicherry, on the supposition that they were bound to that harbour; and on the 8th day of the month, perceived them standing to the southward: but he could not bring them to an engagement till the 10th, when Mr. d'Apche, about two in the afternoon, made the signal for battle, and the cannonading began without further delay. The British squadron did not exceed nine ships of the line; the enemy's fleet consisted of eleven;

eleven; but they had still a greater advantage in number of men and artillery. Both squadrons fought with great impetuosity, till about ten minutes after four, when the enemy's rear began to give way: this example was soon followed by their centre: and finally the van, with the whole squadron, bore to the south south-east, with all the canvas they could spread. The British squadron was so much damaged in their masts and rigging, that they could not pursue; so that M. d'Apche retreated at his leisure unmolested. On the 15th, admiral Pocock returned to Madrafs, where his squadron being prepared by the 26th, he sailed again to Pondicherry, and in the road saw the enemy lying at anchor in line of battle. The wind being off shore, he made the line of battle a-head, and for some time continued in this situation. At length the French admiral weighed anchor, and came forth; but instead of bearing down upon the English squadron, which had fallen to leeward, he kept close to the wind, and stretched away to the southward. Admiral Pocock finding him averse to another engagement, and his own squadron being in no condition to pursue, he, with the advice of his captains, desisted, and measured back his course to Madrafs; while the French squadron made the best of their way to the island of Mauritius, in order to be refitted, having on board general Lally, and some other officers. Thus they left the English masters of the Indian coast; a superiority still more confirmed by the arrival of rear-admiral Cornish with four ships of the line, who had set sail from England in the beginning of the year, and joined admiral Pocock at Madrafs on the 18th day of October.

The French were not the only enemies with whom the English had to cope in the East Indies. The great extension of their trade in the kingdom of Bengal, had excited the envy and avarice of the Dutch factory, who possessed a strong fort at Chinchura in the river of Bengal; and resolved, if possible, to engross the whole salt-petre branch of commerce. Their scheme was approved by the governor of Batavia, who charged himself with the execution of it; and for that purpose, chose the opportunity when the British squadron had retired to the coast of Malabar. On pretence of reinforcing the Dutch garrisons in Bengal, he equipped an armament of seven ships, having on board 500 European troops, and 600 Malayese, under the command of colonel Russel. This armament having touched at Negapatam, proceeded up the bay, and arrived in the river of Bengal about the beginning of October. Colonel Clive, who then resided at Calcutta, had received information of their design, which he was resolved, at all events, to defeat. He complained to the Subah, who, upon such application, could not decently refuse an order to the director and council of Hughley, implying, that this armament should not proceed up the river. The colonel at the same time sent a letter to the Dutch commodore, that as he had received information of their design, he could not allow them to land forces, and march to Chinchura. In answer to this declaration, the Dutch commodore, whose whole fleet had not yet arrived, assured the English commander that he had no intention to send any forces to Chinchura; and begged liberty to land some of his troops for refreshment; a favour that was granted, on condition that they should not advance. Notwithstanding the Subah's order, and his own engagement to this effect, the rest of the ships were no sooner arrived, than he proceeded up the river to the neighbourhood of Tannah-fort, where his forces being disembarked, began their march to Chinchura. In the mean time, by way of retaliating the affront he pretended to have sustained, in being denied a passage to their own factory, he took several small vessels on the river belonging to the English company: and the Calcutta Indiaman, commanded by captain Wilson, homeward-bound, sailing down the river, the Dutchman

gave

gave him to underſtand, that if he preſumed to paſs, he would ſink him without further ceremony. The Engliſh captain ſeeing them run out their guns, as if really reſolved to put the threats in execution, returned to Calcutta, where two other India ſhips lay at an anchor; and reported his adventure to colonel Clive, who forthwith ordered the three ſhips to prepare for battle, and attack the Dutch armament. The ſhips being properly manned, and their quarters lined with ſalt-petre, they fell down the river, and found the Dutch ſquadron drawn up in line of battle, in order to give them a warm reception; for which indeed they ſeemed well prepared: for three of them were mounted with 36 guns each; three of them with 26; and the ſeventh carried 16. The duke of Dorſet, commanded by captain Forreſter, being the firſt that approached them, dropped anchor cloſe to their line, and began the engagement with a broadſide, which was immediately returned. A dead calm unfortunately intervening, this ſingle ſhip was for a conſiderable time expoſed to the whole fire of the enemy; but a ſmall breeze ſpringing up, the Calcutta and the Hardwick advanced to her aſſiſtance, and a ſevere fire was maintained on both ſides, till two of the Dutch ſhips ſlipping their cables, bore away, and a third was driven aſhore. Their commodore thus weakened, after a few broadſides, ſtruck his flag to captain Wilſon; and the other three followed his example. The victory being thus obtained, without the loſs of one man on the ſide of the Engliſh, captain Wilſon took poſſeſſion of the prizes, the decks of which were ſtrewed with carnage, and ſent the priſoners to colonel Clive at Calcutta. The detachment of troops, which they had landed to the number of 1100 men, was not more fortunate in their progreſs. Colonel Clive no ſooner received intelligence that they were in full march to Chinchura, than he detached colonel Forde, with 500 men from Calcutta, in order to put a ſtop to their march. The Dutch advanced to the charge with great resolution and activity; but found the fire of the English artillery and battalion so intolerably hot, that they soon gave way, and were totally defeated.

In the mean time, proposals of accommodation being sent to him by the directors and council of the Dutch factory at Chinchura, a negotiation ensued, and a treaty was concluded to the satisfaction of all parties. Above 300 of the prisoners entered into the service of Great Britain: the rest embarked on board their ships, which were restored as soon as the peace was ratified, and set out on their return for Batavia.

The navy in 1760 amounted to 120 ships of the line, beside frigates, fireships, sloops, bombs, and tenders. Of these ships 17 were stationed in the East Indies, 20 for the defence of the West Indian islands, 12 in North America, 10 in the Mediterranean, and 61 either on the coast of France, in the harbours of England, or cruising in the English seas for the protection of the British commerce. Notwithstanding these numerous and powerful armaments, the enemy, who had not a ship of the line at sea, were so alert with their small privateers and armed vessels, that, in the beginning of this year, from the 1st of March to the 10th of June, they had made prize of 200 vessels belonging to Great Britain and Ireland. The prodigious number of British vessels, taken by their petty coasting privateers, in the face of such mighty armaments, numerous cruisers, and convoys, seems to argue, that either the English ships of war were inactive or improperly disposed; or that the merchants hazarded their ships without convoy. Certain it is, in the course of this year we find fewer prizes taken from the enemy, and fewer exploits atchieved at sea, than we had occasion to record in the annals of the past.

Not that the present year is altogether barren of events, which redound to the honour of our marine commanders. We have, in recounting the transactions

actions of the preceding year, mentioned a small armament equipped at Dunkirk, under the command of Mr. de Thurot; who, in spight of all the vigilance of the British commander stationed in the Downs, found means to escape from the harbour in the month of October, and arrived at Gottenburgh in Sweden, from whence he proceeded to Bergen in Norway. His instructions were to make occasional descents upon the coast of Ireland; and, by dividing the troops, and distracting the attention of the government in that kingdom, to facilitate the enterprize of Mr. de Conflans, the fate of which we have already narrated. The original armament of Thurot consisted of five ships, one of which, called the Marefchal de Belleisle, was mounted with 44 guns; the Begon, the Blond, the Terpsichore, had 30 guns each; and the Marante carried 24. The number of soldiers put on board this little fleet, did not exceed 1270, exclusive of mariners to the number of 700: but in their voyage between Gottenburgh and Bergen they lost company of the Begon, during a violent storm. The intention of Thurot was to make a descent about Derry; but before this design could be executed, the weather growing tempestuous, they were driven out to sea, and, in the night, lost sight of the Marante, which never joined them in the sequel. After having been tempest-beaten for some time, the officers requested of Thurot, that he would return to France, lest they should all perish by famine; but he lent a deaf ear to this proposal, and frankly told them, he could not return to France, without having struck some stroke for the service of his country. Nevertheless, in hope of meeting with some refreshment, he steered to the island of Isla, where the troops were landed; and here they found black cattle, and a small supply of oatmeal, for which they payed a reasonable price; and it must be owned, Thurot himself behaved with great moderation and generosity.

While

While this spirited adventurer struggled with these wants and difficulties, his arrival in those seas filled the whole kingdom with alarm. Bodies of regular troops and militia were posted along the coasts of Ireland and Scotland; and beside the squadron of commodore Boys, who sailed to the northward on purpose to pursue the enemy, other ships of war were ordered to scour the British channel, and cruize between Scotland and Ireland. The weather no sooner permitted Thurot to pursue his destination, than he sailed from Isla to the bay of Carrickfergus in Ireland, and made all the necessary preparations for a descent; which was accordingly effected, with 600 men, on the 21st day of February. Lieutenant colonel Jennings commanded four companies of raw undisciplined men at Carrickfergus. A regular attack was carried on, and a spirited defence made, until the ammunition of the English failed: then colonel Jennings retired in order to the castle; which, however, was in all respects untenable. Nevertheless, they repulsed the assailants in their first attack, even after the gate was burst open; and supplied the want of shot with stones and rubbish. At length, the colonel and his troops were obliged to surrender, on condition that they should not be sent prisoners to France, but be ransomed. The enemy, after this exploit, did not presume to advance farther into the country; a step which indeed they could not have taken, with any regard to their own safety: and the defeat of Conflans, which they had also learned, obliged them to reimbark with some precipitation, after having laid Carrickfergus under moderate contribution.

The fate they escaped on shore, they soon met with at sea. Captain John Elliot, who commanded three frigates at Kinsale, was informed by a dispatch, that three of the enemy's ships lay at anchor in the bay of Carrickfergus; and thither he immediately shaped his course in the ship Æolus, accompanied by the Pallas

and

and Brilliant, under the command of the captains Clements and Logie. On February the 28th they descried the enemy, and gave chace, in fight of the Isle of Man; and about nine in the morning captain Elliot, in his own ship, engaged the Belleisle, commanded by Thurot, although considerably his superior in strength of men, number of guns, and weight of metal. In a few minutes his consorts were also engaged with the other two ships of the enemy. After a warm action maintained with great spirit on all sides for an hour and a half, in which Thurot was killed; captain Elliot's lieutenant boarded the Belleisle, and, striking her colours with his own hand, the commander submitted: his example was immediately followed by the other French captains; and the English commodore, taking possession of his prizes, conveyed them into the bay of Ramsay in the Isle of Man, that their damage might be repaired. The name of Thurot was become terrible to all the trading sea-ports of Britain and Ireland; and therefore the defeat and capture of his squadron were celebrated with as hearty rejoicings, as the most important victory could have produced.

The incidents of the war were much more important and decisive in America. Brigadier-general Murray had been left to command the garrison of Quebec, amounting to about 6000 men; a strong squadron of ships was stationed at Halifax in Nova Scotia, under the direction of lord Colvil, an able and experienced officer, who had instructions to revisit Quebec in the beginning of summer, as soon as the river St. Laurence should be navigable: and general Amherst, the commander in chief of the forces in America, wintered in New York, that he might be at hand to assemble his troops in the spring, and recommence his operations for the entire reduction of Canada. The garrison, however, within the walls of Quebec, suffered greatly from the excessive cold in the winter, and the want of vegetables and fresh provision, infomuch that, before the end of April, 1000 foldiers were dead of the fcurvy, and twice that number rendered unfit for fervice. Such was the situation of the garrifon, when Mr. Murray received undoubted intelligence, that the French commander, the chevalier de Levis, was employed in affembling his army, which had been cantoned in the neighbourhood of Montreal; and determined to undertake the fiege of Quebec, whenever the river St. Laurence fhould be fo clear of ice, that he might ufe his four frigates, and other veffels, by means of which he was entirely mafter of the river.

The French accordingly landed, and Mr. Murray was defeated in an engagement with them. The French therefore formed the fiege of the place.

Lord Colvil had failed from Halifax, with the fleet under his command, but was retarded in his paffage by thick fogs, contrary winds, and great fhoals of ice floating down the river. Commodore Swanton, who had failed from England with a fmall reinforcement, arrived about the beginning of May at the Ifle of Bec, in the river St. Laurence; where, with two fhips, he purpofed to wait for the reft of his fquadron, which had feparated from him in the paffage: but one of thefe, the Loweftoffe, commanded by captain Deane, had entered the harbour of Quebec on the 9th day of May, and communicated to the governor the joyful news that the fquadron was arrived in the river. Commodore Swanton no fooner received intimation that Quebec was befieged, than he failed up the river with all poffible expedition, and anchored above Point Levi. The brigadier expreffing an earneft defire, that the French fquadron above the town might be removed, the commodore ordered captain Schomberg of the Diana, and captain Deane of the Loweftoffe, to flip their cables early next morning, and attack the enemy's fleet, confifting of two frigates, two armed fhips, and a good number of fmaller veffels. They were no fooner in motion than the
French

French ships fled in the utmost disorder. One of their frigates was driven on the rocks above Cape Diamond; the other ran ashore, and was burned at Point au Tremble, about ten leagues above the town; and all the other vessels were taken or destroyed.

The enemy were so confounded and dispirited by this disaster, and the certain information that a strong English fleet was already in the river of St. Laurence, that in the following night they raised the siege of Quebec, and retreated with great precipitation. The reduction of Montreal followed soon after.

The French ministry had attempted to succour Montreal, by equipping a considerable number of storeships, and sending them out in the spring under convoy of a frigate; but as their officers understood that the British squadron had sailed up the river St. Laurence before their arrival, they took shelter in the bay of Chaleurs on the coast of Acadia, where they did not long remain unmolested. Captain Byron, who commanded the ships of war that were left at Louisbourg, having received intelligence of them, sailed thither with his squadron, and found them at anchor. The whole fleet consisted of one frigate, two large store-ships, and nineteen sail of smaller vessels, the greater part of which had been taken from the merchants of Great Britain: all these were destroyed, together with two batteries which had been raised for their protection. The French town, consisting of 200 houses, was demolished, and the settlement totally ruined.

The conquest of Canada being atchieved, nothing now remained to be done in North America, except the demolition of the fortifications of Louisbourg on the island of Cape Breton; for which purpose, some able engineers had been sent from England with the ships commanded by captain Byron. By means of mines artfully disposed and well constructed, the fortifications were reduced to a heap of rubbish; the glacis was levelled, and the ditches were filled. All the artillery, ammunition, and implements of war, were conveyed to Halifax; but the barracks were repaired so as to accommodate 300 men occasionally; and the hospital, with the private houses, were left standing.

Rear-admiral Holmes, who commanded at sea, in the West Indies, took every precaution to secure the island of Jamaica from insult or invasion, and also contrived schemes for annoying the enemy. Having, in the month of October, received intelligence that five French frigates were equipped at Cape Francois on the island of Hispaniola, in order to convoy a fleet of merchant-ships to Europe, he stationed the ships under his command in such a manner as was most likely to intercept this fleet: and by the prudent disposition of the admiral, supported by the gallantry of his captains, two large frigates of the enemy were taken, viz. the Sirenne and the Valeur; and three destroyed.

The spirit of the officers was happily supported by an uncommon exertion of courage in the men, who chearfully engaged in the most dangerous enterprizes. Immediately after the capture of the French frigates, eight of the enemy's privateers were destroyed or brought into Jamaica.

The same activity and resolution distinguished the captains and officers belonging to the squadron commanded by Sir James Douglas off the Leeward islands. In the month of September, the captains Obrien and Taylor, of the ships Temple and Griffin, being on a joint cruise off the islands Granadas, received intelligence that the Virgin, formerly a British sloop of war, which had been taken by the enemy, then lay at anchor, together with three privateers, under protection of three forts on the island; he sailed thither in order to attack them; and the enterprize was crowned with success. After a warm engagement, that lasted several hours, the enemy's batteries were demolished,

and

and the English captains took possession of the four prizes. They afterward entered another harbour of that island, having first demolished another fort; and carried off three more prizes. In their return to Antigua, they fell in with thirteen ships bound to Martinique with provisions, and took them all without resistance. About the same time, eight or nine privateers were taken by the ships which commodore Douglas employed in cruising round the island of Guadaloupe; so that the British commerce in those seas flourished under his care and protection.

No action of importance was in the course of this year atchieved by the naval forces of Great Britain in the seas of Europe. A powerful squadron still remained in the bay of Quiberon, in order to amuse and employ a body of French forces on that part of the coast; and interrupt the navigation of the enemy: though the principal aim of this armament seems to have been to watch and detain the few French ships, which had run into the river Villaine, after the defeat of Conflans; an object the importance of which will doubtless astonish posterity.

Admiral Rodney still maintained his former station off the coast of Havre de Grace, to observe what should pass at the mouth of the Seine. In the month of July, while he hovered in this neighbourhood, five large flat-bottomed boats loaded with cannon and shot, set sail from Harfleur in the middle of the day, with their colours flying, as if they had set the English squadron at defiance; for the walls of Havre de Grace, and even the adjacent hills were covered with spectators, assembled to behold the issue of this adventure. Having reached the river of Caen, they stood backward and forward upon the shoals, intending to amuse Mr. Rodney till night, and then proceed under cover of the darkness. He perceived their drift, and gave directions to his small vessels as soon as day-light failed, to make all the sail they could to cut off the enemy's retreat; while he himself

stood

stood with the larger ships to the steep coast of Port Baffin. The scheme succeeded to his wish. The enemy, seeing their retreat cut off, ran ashore at Port Baffin, where the admiral destroyed them, together with the small fort which had been erected for the defence of this harbour. Each of those vessels was 100 feet in length, capable of containing 400 men for a short passage. What their destination was, we cannot pretend to determine: but the French had provided a great number of these transports; for ten escaped into the river Orne leading to Caen; and in consequence of this disaster 100 were unloaded and sent up again to Rouen. The cutters belonging to Mr. Rodney's squadron scoured the coast toward Dieppe, where a considerable fishery was carried on, and where they took or destroyed near 40 vessels of considerable burden.

Of the domestic transactions relating to the war, the most considerable was the equipment of a powerful armament destined for some secret expedition. The troops were actually embarked with a great train of artillery; and the eyes of the whole nation were attentively fixed upon this armament, which could not have been prepared without incurring a prodigious expence. Notwithstanding these preparations, the whole summer was spent in idleness and inaction; and at the end of the season the undertaking was laid aside.

We shall now turn our attention to the progress of the British arms in the East Indies. Colonel Coote, after having defeated the French general Lally in the field, and reduced divers of the enemy's settlements on the coast of Coromandel, at length cooped them up within the walls of Pondicherry, the principal seat of the French East India company. In the month of October admiral Stevens sailed from Trincamaley with all his squadron, in order to its being refitted, except five sail of the line, which he left under the command of captain Haldane, to block up Pondicherry by sea, while Mr. Coote should carry on his operations by land. By this disposition, and the vigilance of the British officers, the place was so hampered as to be greatly distressed for want of provisions, even before the siege could be undertaken in form; for the rainy season rendered all regular approaches impracticable. Lally made a gallant defence, and had he been properly supplied with provision, the conquest of the place would not have been so easily atchieved. He was obliged, however, to surrender the place at discretion,

By the reduction of Pondicherry the French interest was annihilated on the coast of Coromandel, and therefore it was of the utmost importance to the British nation. It may be doubted, however, whether colonel Coote, with all his spirit, vigilance, and military talents, could have succeeded in this enterprize, without the assistance of the squadron, which co-operated with him by sea, and effectually excluded all succours from the besieged. It must be owned, for the honour of the service, that no incident interrupted the good understanding which was maintained between the land and sea-officers; who vied with each other in contributing their utmost efforts toward the success of the expedition.

While the arms of great Britain still prospered in every effort tending to the real interest of the nation, an event happened which, for a moment, obscured the splendour of her triumphs. On the 25th day of October, 1760, George II. king of Great Britain, without any previous disorder, died suddenly in his palace at Kensington; at the age of seventy-seven, after a long reign of thirty-three years, distinguished by a variety of important events, and chequered with a vicissitude of character and fortune. He loved war as a soldier; he studied it as a science; and corresponded on the subject with some of the greatest officers whom Germany had produced. The extent of his understanding, and the splendour of his virtue, we shall

shall not presume to ascertain, nor attempt to display. With respect to his government, it very seldom deviated from the institutions of law; encroached upon private property; or interfered with the common administration of justice. The circumstances that chiefly mark his public character, were a predilection for his native country, and a close attention to the political interests of the Germanic body: points and principles to which he adhered invincibly.

We postpone giving the state of the navy at this period; proposing to give a particular list of the British navy as it stood at the ensuing peace.

The demise of the crown was no sooner signified to the secretaries of state, than Mr. Pitt repaired to Kew, and communicated these tidings to his new sovereign George III. grandson to the late king, who thus ascended the throne in the 23d year of his age. How much soever the new king might have disapproved of those measures which had involved the nation in such an expensive war on the continent of Europe, affairs were so situated, that he could not abruptly renounce that system of politics, with any regard to the dignity of his crown, or to the honour of the public faith, which was in some measure engaged to support the German allies of Great Britain. With the crown he inherited a war, which he thought it his duty to prosecute with vigour, until it could be terminated by a general peace; in which the honour and advantage of the nation might be equally consulted. It was therefore agreed, that the armament then preparing at Portsmouth should proceed on the expedition for which it was originally intended; but it was countermanded in the sequel.

The chief command of the army in Great Britain rested in the person of lord Ligonier. The German army in Westphalia, payed by England, remained under the auspices of prince Ferdinand of Brunswick: the marquis of Granby commanded the British forces on that service; and the direction of the troops in
Ame-

America was still retained by Sir Jeffery Amherst. Neither was any material change produced in the disposition of the different squadrons which constituted the navy of Great Britain. Admiral Holborne's flag continued flying at Spithead. Sir Edward Hawke and Sir Charles Hardy were stationed in the bay of Quiberon. Sir Charles Saunders kept the sea in the Mediterranean. The rear-admirals Stevens and Cornish commanded one squadron in the East Indies; rear-admiral Holmes another at Jamaica; Sir James Douglas a third at the Leeward Islands; Lord Colvil a fourth at Halifax in Nova Scotia. These were stationary; but other squadrons were equipped occasionally, under different commanders; beside the single ships that cruised in and about the Channel, and those that were stationed to protect the trade of Great Britain in different parts of the world.

Even from the beginning of winter, the single ships that cruised in the Channel were conducted with such care and dexterity, that they made prize of a great number of French privateers; a circumstance that evinced their own vigilance and the enemy's activity. In the month of January, captain Elphinston, of the Richmond, of 32 guns, fell in with the Felicite, a French frigate, of the same force, off the coast of Holland: a severe engagement began about ten in the morning, near Gravesande, about eight miles from the Hague, to which place the prince of Orange, general Yorke the British envoy, and the count d'Affry the French ambassador, repaired, with a great multitude of people, to behold the conflict. About noon both ships ran ashore; nevertheless the action was still maintained, until the enemy deserted their quarters: they afterward abandoned the ship, which was entirely destroyed, after having lost their captain and about 100 men, who fell in the dispute. The Richmond soon floated, without any damage; and the victory cost but three men killed, and thirteen wounded. The French court

court loudly exclaimed againſt this attack as a violation of the Dutch neutrality, and demanded ſignal ſatisfaction for the inſult and damage they had ſuſtained. Accordingly the States General made ſome remonſtrances to the court of London, which found means to remove all cauſe of miſunderſtanding on this ſubject. The Felicite was bound for Martinique, with a valuable cargo, in company with another frigate of the ſame force, which ſuffered ſhipwreck on the coaſt of Dunkirk.

In the courſe of the ſame month, captain Hood, in the Minerva frigate, cruiſing in the chops of the channel, deſcried a great ſhip of two decks ſteering to the weſtward, and found it to be the Warwick, an Engliſh ſhip, which had carried ſixty cannon, and been taken by the enemy. She was now mounted with thirty-five guns, and commanded by Mr. le Verger de Belair, with a commiſſion from the French king. Her crew amounted to about 300 men, including a detachment of ſoldiers; and he was bound to Pondicherry in the Eaſt Indies. Captain Hood, notwithſtanding her ſuperior ſize, attacked her without heſitation, and was very warmly received. In the iſſue the captain of the Warwick ſtruck his colours, having loſt about 14 men killed outright, beſide 35 wounded. The loſs in number of men was equal on board the Minerva, and all her maſts went by the board: nevertheleſs the prize was brought in triumph to Spithead. In the progreſs of the ſame cruize, captain Hood had alſo taken the Ecurneil privateer from Bayonne, of 14 guns, and 122 men.

In March, another French ſhip, called the Entreprenant, pierced for 44 guns, but mounted with 26 only, having 200 men on board, and a rich cargo, bound for St. Domingo, was encountered near the Land's-end by the Vengeance frigate of 26 guns, commanded by captain Nightingale. The action was maintained on both ſides with uncommon fury, until the Vengeance being ſet on fire by the enemy's wadding;

ding; the French resolved to take advantage of the confusion produced by this accident, and, running their boltsprit upon the taffaril of the English frigate, attempted to board her. In this design, however, they miscarried, through the courage and activity of captain Nightingale; who found means to disengage himself, and sheered off to repair his rigging, which had greatly suffered in the engagement. The ship was no sooner in proper condition, than he ranged up again close to the enemy, and renewed the contest, which lasted a full hour: then the Entreprenant bore away. Captain Nightingale, though a second time disabled in his masts and rigging, wore ship, ran within pistol-shot, and began a third vigorous attack, which lasted an hour and a half before the enemy called for quarter. Fifteen of their men were killed, and about twice that number wounded. The victors lost about half as many. The issue of all these engagements between single ships, proves, to demonstration, that the French mariners neither work their ships nor manage their artillery with that skill and dexterity which appear in the English navy: a circumstance the more remarkable, as all the French seamen are regularly taught the practical part of gunnery; whereas no such pains are taken with the sailors of Great Britain.

In April, another French frigate, called the Comete, of 32 guns, and 250 men, just sailed from Brest, was taken to the westward of Ushant by the Bedford, captain Deane. About the same period, and near the same place, a fourth frigate of the enemy, called the Pheasant, manned with 125 mariners, was taken by captain Brograve, of the Albany sloop; whose victory was the cheaper, as the crew of the Pheasant had thrown 14 of her guns over-board during the chace. In the course of the same month, a large East India ship, fitted out from France, with 28 guns, and 350 men, fell in with the Hero and the

Venus,

Venus, commanded by the captains Fortefcue and Harrifon, and were taken without oppofition.

The cruizers belonging to the fquadron commanded by vice-admiral Saunders in the Mediterranean, were diftinguifhed by the fame fpirit of enterprize and activity. In the beginning of this very month, the Oriflamme, a French fhip of 40 guns, being off Cape Tres Foreas, was taken by the Ifis, captain Wheeler, who being unfortunately killed in the beginning of the action, the command devolved to lieutenant Cunningham: fhe was brought into the bay of Gibraltar. In July another exploit was performed by a fmall detachment from the fquadron commanded by the fame admiral. Captain Proby, in the Thunderer, together with the Modefte, Thetis and Favourite floop, being ordered to cruife upon the coaft of Spain with a view to intercept the Achilles and Bouffon, two French fhips of war, which lay in the harbour of Cadiz; they at length ventured to come forth, and were defcried by the Britifh cruizers. About midnight, the Thunderer came up with the Achilles, which ftruck, after a warm engagement of half an hour. The Thetis engaged the Bouffon, and the fire was maintained on both fides with great vivacity for half an hour, when the Modefte ranging up, and firing a few guns, the French captain fubmitted. His fhip and her confort fuffered confiderably, both in their crews and rigging; neverthelefs, the victors carried them fafely into the bay of Gibraltar.

One of the moft remarkable and fhining actions that diftinguifhed this war, and proved, beyond all contradiction, the fuperiority which the Englifh claimed over the French in point of naval difcipline, was an incident which we fhall now relate. Auguft 10th, captain Faulkner of the Bellona, a fhip of the line, and captain Logie of the Brilliant, a frigate, failed from the Tagus for England, having on board a confiderable fum of money for the merchants of London.

In the afternoon, being then off Vigo, they difcovered three fail of fhips ftanding in for the land, one of the line of battle, and two frigates. They no fooner defcried captain Faulkner, than they bore down upon him, until within the diftance of feven miles, when, feeing the Bellona and a frigate through the magnifying medium of a hazy atmofphere, they miftook them both for two-decked fhips, and dreading the iffue of an engagement, refolved to avoid the encounter. For this purpofe, they fuddenly wore round, filled their fails, and crouded away. Captain Faulkner, being by this time convinced of their fize, and conjecturing, from the intelligence he had received, that the large fhip was the Courageux (in which particular he was not miftaken) he hoifted all the canvas he could carry, and gave chace until funfet; when one of the French frigates hauling out in the offing, he difplayed a fignal to the Brilliant to purfue in that direction, and his order was immediately obeyed. They kept fight of the enemy during the whole night, and at fun-rife had gained but about two miles upon them in a chace of fourteen hours; fo that the French commodore might have ftill avoided an engagement for the whole day, and enjoyed the chance of efcaping in the darknefs of the fucceeding night; but he no longer declined the action. The air being perfectly ferene, he now perceived that one of the Englifh fhips was a frigate; and the Bellona herfelf which was one of the beft conftituted fhips in the Englifh navy, lay fo flufh in the water as to appear at a diftance confiderably fmaller than fhe really was. The French commodore, therefore, hoifted a fignal for his two frigates to clofe with and engage the Brilliant. At the fame time he wore round, and ftood for the Bellona under his topfails; while captain Faulkner advanced toward her with an eafy fail, and ordered his quarters to be manned. The fea was undulated by a gentle breeze, which facilitated the working of the fhips, and at the fame time permitted the full ufe of their heavy artillery. The two fhips were equal in burden, in number of guns, and in weight of metal. The crew on board the Courageux amounted to 700 men, able to ftand to their quarters; and they were commanded by M. du Guy Lambert, an officer of approved valour and ability. The Bellona's compliment confifted of 550 chofen men, accuftomed to difcipline, and inured to fervice. All the officers were gentlemen of known merit, and the commander had on many occafions diftinguifhed himfelf by his bravery and conduct. The fire on both fides was fufpended till they were within mufket-fhot of each other, and then the engagement began with a dreadful difcharge of fire-arms and artillery. In lefs than nine minutes, all the Bellona's braces, bowlings, fhrowds, and rigging, were cut and fhattered by the fhot, and the mizen-maft fell over the ftern, with all the men on the round-top; who, neverthelefs, faved their lives, by clambering into the port-holes of the gun-room. Captain Faulkner, apprehenfive that the enemy would feize the opportunity of his being difabled, and endeavour to efcape, gave orders for immediate boarding; an attempt which the pofition of the two fhips foon rendered altogether impracticable. The Courageux was now falling athwart the fore-foot, or bows of the Bellona, in which cafe the Englifh fhip muft have been raked fore and aft with great execution. The haul-yards, and moft of the other ropes by which the Bellona could be worked, were already fhot away. Captain Faulkner, however, with the affiftance of his mafter, made ufe of the ftudding fails with fuch dexterity, as to ware the fhip quite round, and fall upon the oppofite quarter of the Courageux. His prefence of mind and activity in this delicate fituation, were not more admirable than the difcipline and difpatch of his officers and men, who, perceiving this change of their fituation, flew to the guns on the other fide, now oppofed to the enemy, from whence

whence they poured in a moſt terrible diſcharge, and maintained it without intermiſſion or abatement. Every ſhot took place, and bore deſtruction along with it. The ſides of the Courageux were ſhattered and torn by every ſucceſſive broadſide, and her decks were ſtrewed with carnage. About twenty minutes did the enemy ſuſtain the havock made by this battery, ſo inceſſantly plied and ſo fatally directed. At length it became ſo intolerable, that the French enſign was hauled down: the rage of battle ceaſed; the Engliſh mariners had left their quarters, and the officers congratulated each other on the ſucceſs of the day. At this juncture, a ſhot being unexpectedly fired from the lower tire of the Courageux, the Britiſh ſeamen ran to their quarters; and, without orders, poured in two broadſides upon the enemy, who now called for quarter, and an end was put to the engagement. The damage done to the rigging of the Bellona was conſiderable; but ſhe ſuffered very little in the hull, and the number of the killed and wounded did not exceed forty. The caſe was very different with the Courageux, which now appeared like a wreck upon the water. Nothing was ſeen ſtanding but her foremaſt and boltſprit; large breaches were made in her ſides; her decks were torn up in ſeveral parts; many of her guns were diſmounted; and her quarters filled with the mangled bodies of the dying and the dead. Above 220 were killed outright, and half that number was brought aſhore wounded to Liſbon, to which place the prize was conveyed. Captain Faulkner was not more commendable for his gallantry in the action, than for the humanity and politeneſs with which he treated his priſoners; whoſe grateful acknowlegment, and unſolicited applauſe, conſtitute the faireſt teſtimony that a man of honour can enjoy. Nor ought captain Logie of the Brilliant to be forgotten, whoſe valour and dexterity, in a great meaſure, contributed to the ſucceſs of his commodore. The two Engliſh captains joined

joined in a liberal subscription with the British factory at Lisbon, for the relief of the wounded French prisoners, who, without this generous interposition, must have starved, as no provision was made by their sovereign.

In the West Indies, rear-admiral Holmes, commander of the squadron at Jamaica, planned his cruizes with equal judgment and success. Having received intelligence in the beginning of June, that several ships of war belonging to the enemy had sailed from Port Louis, and in particular, that the St. Anne had just quitted Port au Prince; he forthwith made such a disposition of his squadron as was most likely to intercept them. . He fell in with and took the St. Anne, a beautiful new ship, pierced for 64 cannon, but mounting only 40, manned with near 400 mariners and soldiers; and loaded with a rich cargo of coffee, indigo, and sugar. Nor was the squadron stationed off the Leeward Islands, under the direction of Sir James Douglas, less alert and effectual in protecting the British traders, and scouring those seas of the Martinico privateers, of which he took a great number.

The island of Dominique, which the French had settled and put in a posture of defence, was attacked and reduced by a small body of troops, commanded by lord Rollo, and conveyed thither from Guadalupe by Sir James Douglas, with four ships of the line, and some frigates.

According to the laudable custom of these latter times, a powerful squadron had been stationed all the winter in the bay of Quiberon, under the command of Sir Edward Hawke and Sir Charles Hardy. In January, they took two small French frigates, bound to the coast of Guinea, and a few merchant-ships of little value; and in March, the two admirals returned to Spithead: but another squadron was afterward sent to occupy the same station. In July, while the English were employed in demolishing the fortifications on the isle of Aix, the great ships that protected this service were attacked by a French armament from the Charante, consisting of six prames*, a few row-gallies, and a great number of launches crouded with men. They dropped down with the ebb, and placing themselves between the isle of d'Enet and Fort Fouras, played upon the English ships in Aix road, with 12 mortars, and 70 large cannon: but they met with such a warm reception from the British squadron, that in a few hours they retreated to their former station, where the water was too shallow for the English ships to return the attack.

These were part of that armament which had loitered in the preceding year at Spithead, until the season for action was elapsed. It had been a favourite scheme of the minister, to reduce the island of Belleisle on the coast of Brittany, and this was the aim of the expedition. Belleisle lies about four leagues from the point of Quiberon, about half way between Port Louis and the mouth of the Loire. It extends about six leagues in length, and little more than two in breadth; contains a pretty large town, called Palais, fortified with a citadel, beside a good number of villages: and the whole number of inhabitants, exclusive of the garrison, may amount to 6000, chiefly maintained by the fishery of pilchards. It was supposed the reduction of this island would be easily atchieved, and the conquest attended with manifold advantages.

The squadron equipped for this enterprize consisted of ten ships of the line, several frigates, two fireships, and two bomb-ketches, commanded by commodore Kepple, brother to the earl of Albemarle, a gallant officer, who had signalized himself on several occasions, in the course of this and the last

---

* A prame is a long broad vessel of two decks, mounted with 26 large cannon below, and 3 mortars above. They are rigged like ketches, and draw very little water.

war. The whole armament came to anchor in the
great road of Belleifle April 7th, where a difpofition
was made for landing the forces. This attempt failed,
with the lofs of near 500 men, and about 50 mariners. Notwithftanding this unfavourable beginning,
another fcheme was laid, and the execution of it
crowned with fuccefs. On the 22d day of the month
in the morning, the troops were difpofed in the flat-bottomed boats, and rowed to different parts of the
ifland, as if they intended to land in different places:
thus the attention of the enemy was diftracted in fuch a
manner, that they knew not where to expect the defcent, and were obliged to divide their forces at random. Mean while brigadier Lambert pitched upon
the rocky point of Lomaria, where captain Paterfon,
at the head of Beauclerk's grenadiers, and captain
Murray, with a detachment of marines, climbed the
precipice with aftonifhing intrepidity, and fuftained
the fire of a ftrong body of the enemy, until they
were fupported by the reft of the Englifh troops.
Then the French abandoned their batteries, and retired with precipitation: but this advantage was not
gained without bloodfhed. The landing was followed
by the reduction of the citadel. A conqueft which
could in no refpect be confidered as a compenfation
for the expence of the armament, and the lives of
about 2000 men, who might have been much better
employed.

A negociation was now entered into toward a peace,
but the intervention of fome Spanifh claims, which
led to the difcovery of a private family-compact entered into between France and Spain, fruftrated it;
and Mr. Pitt, difgufted that his advice for rigorous
meafures with Spain was difapproved, refigned his
pofts.

A plan for the conqueft of Martinique was already
formed. In the month of October, rear-admiral
Rodney failed from England with a fquadron of fhips,
having under convoy a number of tranfports, with
four

four battalions from Belleifle, to join at Barbadoes a ftrong body of forces from North America, together with fome regiments and volunteers from Guadalupe and the Leeward Iflands; thence to proceed, in conjunction with the fleet already on that ftation, to the execution of the projected invafion. This was doubtlefs an object of great importance, and might have been eafily accomplifhed in the firft attempt under the conduct of general Hopfon; but now the enterprize was encumbered by many difficulties. The ifland was ftrengthened with new fortifications, a ftrong body of troops, a numerous regulated militia, experienced officers, and plenty of provifion, artillery, and ammunition.

War againft Spain was declared January 4th, 1762.

The armament from North America and England, under the command of major-general Monckton and rear-admiral Rodney, amounting to 18 battalions, and as many fhips of the line, befide frigates, bombs, and firefhips; which having rendezvoufed at Barbadoes in the month of December, proceeded from thence and anchored in St. Anne's Bay, in the eaftern part of Martinique, after the fhips of war had filenced fome batteries which the enemy had erected on that part of the coaft. In the courfe of this fervice, the Raifonable, a fhip of the line, was, by the ignorance of the pilot, run upon a reef of rocks, from whence fhe could not be difengaged, though the men were faved, together with her ftores and artillery.

The troops being landed at Cas des Navires, and reinforced with two battalions of marines, which were fpared from the fquadron, the general refolved to befiege the town of Fort-Royal; which was profecuted with great bravery. The governor of the citadel, perceiving the Englifh employed in erecting batteries on the different heights by which he was commanded, ordered the chamade to be beat, and furrendered the place by capitulation, on the 4th of February. The most remarkable circumstance of this enterprize was the surprising boldness and alacrity of the seamen, who, by force of arm, drew a number of heavy mortars and ships cannon up the steepest mountains to a considerable distance from the sea, and across the enemy's line of fire, to which they exposed themselves with amazing indifference. Fourteen French privateers were found in the harbour of Port Royal; and a much greater number, from other parts of the island, were delivered up to admiral Rodney, in consequence of the capitulation with the inhabitants, who, in all other respects, were very favourably treated.

The French were now expelled from all their settlements in North America, except that of Louisiana, which was deemed an object of little or no importance: the seat of war was transferred from that continent to the French islands, the conquest of which we have already described; and it was now resolved to make a vigorous impression upon Spain, not only by attempting the reduction of the Havanna, which may be considered as the key of the bay of Mexico; but also by making a descent on the island of Manilla, in the East Indies, a country in which the French had now nothing left to be conquered.

The first of these expeditions was entrusted to the conduct of the earl of Albemarle, commander of the land-forces, recommended for this service by the duke of Cumberland, under whose auspices he had been formed to war; and the ships of war, destined to co-operate in the attack, were commanded by admiral Sir George Pocock, who had already distinguished himself by his gallantry in the East Indies: his second was Mr. Keppel, brother to the earl, an able officer, who had reduced the Isle of Goree, on the coast of Africa. They sailed from Portsmouth in the beginning of March; and reached the place of their destination without accident or obstruction. Their proceedings shall be particularized in their proper place.

The

The design against Manilla was executed by rear-admiral Cornish, which we shall recount.

For the defence of the British coast, and in order to answer the emergencies of war, a powerful squadron was kept in readiness at Spithead, under the direction of Sir Edward Hawke; another rode at anchor in the Downs, under the command of rear-admiral Moore; and from these two were occasionally detached into the channel, and all around the coasts of the island, a number of light cruizers, which acted with such vigilance and activity, that not a ship could venture from any of the French sea-ports, without running the most imminent risque of being taken.

Sir Charles Saunders was reinforced in such a manner, as enabled him to give law in the Mediterranean, and either to prevent a junction of the French and Spanish fleets, or, if that should be found impracticable, to give them battle when joined. Lord Colville was continued in the command of the squadron at Halifax in Nova Scotia, in order to protect the coast of North America, and the new conquests, in the gulph and river of St. Laurence. Sir James Douglas still commanded the ships of war appointed for the defence of the Leeward Islands; and captain Forrest, since the death of admiral Holmes, directed the small squadron at Jamaica. Such was the general disposition for the offensive as well as the defensive measures of the campaign; and the greatest enemies of the ministry must allow it was planned with sagacity, and maintained with resolution.

A fruitless attempt had been made by the enemy to burn the British ships of war at anchor in the road of Basque. They prepared three fire-vessels, which being chained together, were towed out of the port, and set on fire with a strong breeze that blew directly on the English squadron. This attempt, however, was made with hurry and trepidation; and the wind luckily shifting, drove them clear of the ships

ships they were intended to destroy. They continued burning for some time, after having blown up with a terrible explosion, and every person on board perished.

Captain Gambier, of the Burford, arrived at Plymouth in April with a large French East India ship from the Isle of Bourbon, laden with coffee and pepper, which had been taken by one of Sir George Pococke's squadron. In May, two British frigates, cruising off Cape St. Vincent, made prize of the Hermione, a Spanish register ship, bound from Lima to Cadiz, loaded with treasure and valuable effects, by which all the captors were enriched. Her cargo amounted to about one million sterling, which was considerably more than had ever before been taken in any one bottom: and the loss of so much treasure, in the beginning of such an expensive war, must have been a severe stroke on the court of Madrid. The prize was brought from Gibraltar to England, and the gold and silver being conveyed in covered waggons to London, was carried in procession to the bank; happening to arrive the same morning the prince of Wales was born, which was the 12th of August.

About the latter end of May, a French squadron, under the command of Mr. de Ternay, escaped from Brest in a fog. The French commander steered his course to Newfoundland, and entered the bay of Bulls, where he landed some troops without opposition. Having taken possession of an inconsiderable English settlement in that bay, they advanced to the town of St. John's, which being in no condition of defence, was surrendered upon capitulation. They also took the officers and crew of the Gramont sloop which was in the harbour, with several other vessels; and did considerable damage to the English fishers and settlers on different parts of the coast. The ministry were no sooner informed of this small check, which it was impossible either to foresee or prevent, than they

they took meafures for retrieving the lofs; and this petty triumph of the enemy was of very fhort duration. The armament fitted out in England for retaking Newfoundland, was rendered unneceffary by the vigilance and activity of Sir Jeffery Amherft and lord Colville, who commanded by land and fea in North America.

In September, the Hunter floop of war, one of admiral Moore's cruizers, falling in with four Dutch merchant fhips in the Channel, under convoy of a frigate of 36 guns, the Englifh captain prepared to examine the lading of the Dutch veffels, when the commander of the frigate interpofing, declared he would not fuffer any fuch fearch to be made. The other infifted upon the examination, but being prevented by fuperior force, made a fignal to the Diana and Chefter fhips of war, which happened to be in fight, and they advanced accordingly. After fome expoftulation, the Dutch captain continuing obftinate, the Diana fired a gun to bring him to, and he returned a whole broadfide. An engagement immediately enfued, and was maintained with great vivacity for about fifteen minutes, when the Dutchman thought proper to ftrike his colours, having loft his own nofe, and nine or ten men in the action. He was brought into the Downs, together with his convoy, which were found laden with contraband merchandize from Havre to Breft. The Zephyr, a French frigate of 32 guns, bound to Newfoundland, with troops, artillery, ftores, and ammunition, was alfo taken in the channel, by the Lion fhip of war. In the beginning of November, a French fhip of 20 guns, was taken by captain Ruthven, of the Terpfichore, after a fharp action, in which he himfelf was wounded. The enemy loft likewife the Oifeau, another frigate of 26 guns, which fell in with captain Tonyn of the king's fhip the Brune. A third French frigate, called the Minerve, was wrecked in the harbour of Villa Franca, through the pride, precipitation,

tion, and ignorance of her commander. She had, in company with four French ſhips of war, given chace to the Sheerneſs frigate, captain Clarke, from Gibraltar, who took refuge in the harbour of Villa Franca, and there anchored, the wind blowing freſh. He was immediately followed by the enemy, when the captain of the Minerve, actuated by an idle ſpirit of vanity and infolence, refolved to lie between him and the ſhore, and ran his ſhip upon the rocks that bound the eaſtern ſide of the harbour. On this melancholy occaſion, captain Clarke, forgetting they were enemies, obeyed the dictates of humanity, by exerting himſelf for their relief. He ſent his boats manned to their affiſtance, and actually ſaved the lives of the greater part of their company : an act of generous benevolence, for which he was thanked in perſon by the French commodore.

About the end of Auguſt, captain Hotham of the Æolus, chaced two Spaniſh ſhips into the bay of Aviles, in the neighbourhood of Cape Pinas; and ſtanding into the bay, came to an anchor in ſuch a ſituation, as to bring his guns to bear, not only upon one of the ſhips, but alſo upon a ſmall battery ſituated upon an eminence. After a ſhort conteſt, both the battery and the ſhip were abandoned : but before captain Hotham could take poffeffion of his prize, ſhe ran aground, and bulging, was burned by the captors : the other eſcaped in the night. Captain Hotham afterward fell in with a French ſquadron, confiſting of ſeven ſail, between St. Andero and Bilboa, and kept company with them till the 16th, as far to the weſtward as Cape Finiſterre, when he returned to his ſtation. By a ſloop from Bourdeaux, which he took, he underſtood that this ſquadron had a body of troops on board for St. Domingo.

The navy of France was by this time reduced to ſuch a ſmall number, that their miniſtry was obliged to ſend reinforcements to their ſettlements abroad in ſingle ſhips; ſome of which were intercepted by the Britiſh

British cruisers, particularly one transport, containing the best part of a regiment, designed to reinforce their colony of Louisiana, which had engaged a good share of their attention since the reduction of Canada.

The cruizers of Great Britain were not less alert in the seas of America. Captain Ourry of the Actæon, in the latitude of Tobago, took a large Spanish register ship, bound to Lagueira, laden with artillery, stores, and ammunition. A fleet of 25 sail of French merchant-ships, richly laden with sugar, coffee and indigo, took their departure from Cape François for Europe, under convoy of four frigates. Five of these vessels were surprised and taken in the night by some privateers of New York and Jamaica. Next day it was their misfortune to fall in with commodore Keppel, who made prize of their whole fleet and convoy, which were carried into the harbour of Port-Royal in Jamaica.

In the course of this war the French nation lost 37 ships of the line, and 55 frigates; of these the English took 18 capital ships of war, and 36 frigates; and destroyed 14 of the line, and 13 frigates; five large ships and six frigates they lost by accidents. On the other hand, the French took two, and destroyed three English frigates; and 13 capital British ships, and 14 frigates, were lost by accident. Of merchant ships belonging to Great Britain, the enemy took 812, from the commencement of the war to the cessation of arms.

In September, the honourable Augustus Hervey and captain Nugent, arrived in London with dispatches from the earl of Albermarle and sir George Pococke. We have already observed that the armament under the conduct of those two commanders had sailed from Portsmouth in March; and, according to the general opinion, was destined to act against the island of Cuba. They were joined by a detachment of the fleet from Martinique, under Sir James Douglas; and, in consequence of this junction, their whole

whole force confifted of 19 fail of the line, 18 fmaller fhips of war, and about 150 tranfports, having on board about 10,000 land forces and marines. Without accident or danger, on July 6th, the admiral lay to, about five leagues to the eaftward of the Havanna, after having taken a Spanifh frigate and a ftore-fhip in the paffage. Having iffued directions to the mafters of the tranfports, with refpect to the difembarkation of the army, and left commodore Keppel to fuperintend this fervice, with fix fail of the line and fome frigates, he bore away with the reft of the fleet, and ran down off the harbour, where he defcried 12 Spanifh fhips of the line, with feveral trading veffels. Next morning he embarked his marines in boats, and made a fhew of landing about four miles to the weftward of the Havanna; while the earl of Albemarle landed with the whole army, between the rivers Bocanao and Coxemar, about fix miles to the eaftward of the Moro Caftle, which was the enemy's chief fortrefs for the defence of the town and harbour. Three bomb-veffels being anchored in fhore, began to throw fhells into the town. Though this invafion of the Englifh was altogether unexpected, the place being ftrongly fortified and well fupplied, preparations were inftantly made for a vigorous defence, by Don Juan de Prado, governor of the city, and the marquis del Real, commodore of the fhipping; affifted by the counfels and experience of the viceroy of Peru and the governor of Carthagena, who happened to be at the Havanna, in the way to or from their refpective governments. The attack of the Moro was commanded by major-general Keppel, brother to the earl of Albemarle; and the chief engineer was Mr. Mackellar, who difplayed uncommon abilities at the fiege of Louifbourg, and on many other occafions both in this and the laft war.

Fafcines, ftores, and artillery, being landed from the fhips with great expedition by the feamen, the engineers began to erect batteries of bombs and cannon,

non, while a body of pioneers were employed to cut parallels in the wood, and form a line with fascines to secure the guards from the fire of the enemy, which began to be very troublesome. About 1000 chosen men of the enemy, with a detachment of armed negroes and mulattoes, landed on two divisions to the right and left of the Moro, in order to destroy the works of the besiegers: but they were repulsed by the piquets and advanced posts, and retreated in great confusion, with the loss of 200 men, killed and taken.

The admiral's cruizers, who scoured the sea round the whole island, brought in the Venganza frigate of 26 guns, the Marté of 18, and a schooner, laden with coffee. Sir James Douglas, who had parted from the admiral immediately after their junction, and steered his course to Jamaica, in a single ship, now arrived off the Havanna, having under his convoy a fleet of merchant ships bound for England.

The parapet of Fort Moro was all of masonry; the ditch of the front attacked, was seventy feet deep from the edge of the counterscarp, and more than forty feet of that depth sunk in the rock. The soil of the country in the neighbourhood, being very thin, afforded little earth; and as it was thought necessary to carry on the approaches by sap, this method might have been found altogether impracticable, had not Sir James supplied the engineers with cotton bags, from some ships of his convoy, which were partly loaded with this commodity. Mean while, the enemy made such a vigorous defence, that the siege was protracted beyond expectation; a considerable delay was likewise occasioned by an unlucky accident. On July 3d, the principal battery of the besiegers, chiefly constructed of timber and fascines, being dried by the heat of the weather and the continual cannonade, took fire, and the flames raged with such violence, that almost the whole work was consumed. The besiegers were subjected to various other

other discouragements. Epidemical distempers, such as never fail to attack the natives of Britain who visit those countries, began to make great havock, both in the army and the navy. These were rendered more fatal by the want of necessaries and refreshments. The provision was bad; and the troops were ill supplied with water. The great number of the sick rendered the duty more fatiguing to those that were well. In those warm climates, the human body being in a state of relaxation, is incapable of such a degree of labour as it can bear in more northern latitudes; and the men are subject to a species of dejection, which always augments the general mortality: this was now increased by the delay of the troops from North America, which they had long expected to no purpose.

On the 2d of August, the second division of the transports, with the troops from North America, arrived; and this reinforcement added fresh vigour to the operations of the siege. In a few days, the seamen and soldiers belonging to four of the American transports, which had been wrecked in the straights of Bahama, were brought off in five sloops, detached by the admiral on this service: but, at the same time, he received information that five other transports, having on board 350 soldiers of Anstruther's regiment, and 150 provincial troops, were taken by a French squadron, near the passage between Maya Guanna, and the North Caicos. All the rest of the troops, however, arrived in perfect health.

July 19th the besiegers took possession of the covered-way, before the point of the right bastion, and a new sap was begun at this lodgment. The only place by which the foot of the wall was accessible, happened to be a thin ridge of rock, left at the point of the bastion, to cover the extremity of the ditch, which would otherwise have been open to the sea. Along this ridge the miners passed, without cover, to the foot of the wall, where they made a lodgment with little loſs. Mean while, they ſunk a ſhaft without the covered-way, in order to form a mine for throwing the counterſcarp into the ditch, ſhould it be found neceſſary to fill it; and continued their former ſap along the glacis. In the night of the 21ſt a ſergeant and 12 men ſcaled the walls by ſurprize; but, the garriſon being alarmed before they could be ſuſtained, they were obliged to retreat with precipitation. Next day, at four in the morning, a ſally was made from the town, by 1500 men, divided into three detachments, who attacked the beſiegers in three different places, while a warm fire was kept up in their favour from the forts and their ſhipping in the harbour. After a warm diſpute, which coſt the Engliſh about fifty men killed or wounded, all their three parties were repulſed, and fled with ſuch precipitation, that a conſiderable number was drowned in the hurry of their retreat. On the 30th day of the month, about two in the morning, a floating battery was towed out into the harbour, and fired with grapeſhot and ſmall-arms into the ditch, though without any great interruption to the miners; and the cloſe fire of the covering party ſoon compelled the enemy to retire.

In the afternoon, two mines were ſprung by the beſiegers, with ſuch effect, that a practicable breach was made in the baſtion; and orders were immediately given for the aſſault. The troops mounted with great intrepidity, and, forming on the top of the breach, drove the enemy from every part of the ramparts, after a ſhort, though very warm, diſpute; in which about 130 Spaniards were killed, including ſeveral officers of diſtinction. Don Louis de Velaſco, governor of the fort, had diſtinguiſhed himſelf from the beginning of the ſiege, by ſuch activity and courage, as attracted the admiration and eſteem even of his enemies. In this laſt action, he did all that could be expected from the moſt romantic gallantry; and fell by a ſhot he received in defending the colours of Spain.

Spain. The marquis Gonzales, who was second in command, likewise lost his life on this occasion. About 400 of the garrison threw down their arms, and were made prisoners: the rest were either killed or drowned, in attempting to escape to the Havanna. Lieutenant-colonel Stuart, who commanded the attack, lost but 2 lieutenants, and 12 men.

The reduction of the Moro was not immediately attended with the surrender of the Havanna; on the contrary, the governor of the place now directed his chief fire against the fortress which they had lost. On the 11th of August, at day-break, about 45 cannon and 8 mortars began to play against the town and the Punta, which last was silenced before ten; in another hour the north bastion was almost disabled. About two in the afternoon, white flags were hung out all round the place, as well as on board the admiral's ship in the harbour; and, in a little time, a flag of truce arrived at the head quarters, with proposals of capitulation. The governor stickled hard to obtain permission to send the ships to Spain, and to have the harbour declared neutral: but neither of these points could be given up, and hostilities were ordered to be renewed; when the enemy thought proper to recede from their demands. By the capitulation, which was signed on the 13th, the inhabitants were secured in their private property, in the enjoyment of their own laws and religion; and next day the English troops took possession of this important conquest. As for the Spanish garrison, which amounted to about 900, including officers, they were indulged with the honours of war; and it was stipulated, that they and the sailors should be conveyed to Old Spain. In the progress of the siege, about 500 of the British troops, including 15 officers, were killed out-right or died of their wounds; and about 700, comprehending 39 officers, were cut off by distemper, which raged with redoubled violence after the reduction of the place.

So

So much treasure intercepted by the English, first in the ship Hermione, and now in the island of Cuba, must have been a severe stroke upon the king of Spain: but the ruin of his navy was of much greater importance, and even that but a trifle in comparison to the loss of the Havanna; the port at which all their galleons and flota, loaded with the riches of Mexico and Peru, rendezvoused in their return to Old Spain; the port which absolutely commanded the only passage by which their ships could sail from the bay of Mexico to Europe. The reduction of the Havannah, therefore, was an acquisition, that not only distressed the Spaniards in the most essential manner, by stopping the sources of their wealth, but likewise opened to the conquerors an easy avenue to the centre of their American treasures. In no former war had Great Britain acquired such large sums at the expence of her enemies. Her success in the East Indies is said to have brought into England near six millions in treasure and jewels, since the commencement of hostilities: but every million thus acquired, she expended tenfold in the course of her subsidies and expeditions.

The loss of the Havanna, with the ships and treasure there taken, was not the only disaster sustained by Spain in the short course of the war, which she had so imprudently declared against Great Britain. She received another dangerous wound in the East Indies by the loss of Manilla, a considerable settlement on Luconia, the largest of the Philippine islands. This city is the centre of the Spanish trade, from whence two large ships are sent annually across the vast Pacific ocean to Acapulco, on the coast of Mexico, laden with the spices, stuffs, jewels, and other rich merchandize of India. (See our account of the Spanish American trade, in vol. 1. and Anson's voyage in vol. 3.)

Against this settlement, a plan of attack was formed at Madrass, to be executed by part of the squadron of vice-admiral Cornish, and a few battalions under the command of brigadier-general Draper, who had signalized himself in the defence of Madrass, when it was besieged by the enemy. Vice-admiral Cornish, supplied a strong battalion of seamen and marines; so that the whole force amounted to 2300 effective men.

The forces, with the stores and artillery, being embarked, the admiral sailed in two divisions about the beginning of August, and on the 23d of September anchored in the bay of Manilla, where they found the enemy but ill prepared for a siege, and much alarmed at this unexpected visit. The governor was the archbishop, who stiles himself captain-general of the Philippine islands: but the garrison, amounting to 800 men of the royal regiment, was commanded by the marquis de Villa-Medina, a brigadier-general, who now reinforced it with a body of 10,000 Indians, from the province of Pampanga, a fierce and savage nation.

The admiral, having sounded the coast, discovered a convenient place for landing the troops, about two miles to the southward of Manilla. The proper dispositions being made, and the three frigates, Argo, Sea-horse, and Seaford, moored very near the shore, to cover the descent; three divisions of the forces were put on board the boats of the fleet, and landed at the church and village of Malata, not without some difficulty from a great surf that rolled on the beach. The enemy began to assemble in great numbers, both horse and infantry, to oppose the descent; but the frigates maintained such a warm fire of cannon, to the right and left, that they soon dispersed; and the general disembarked his troops without the loss of one man; while the Spanish garrison were employed in burning the suburbs of Manilla.

The governor had been already twice summoned to surrender, but returned a resolute refusal; and, indeed, if the valour of his troops had corresponded with the vigour of his declaration, he had but little to apprehend from an handful of enemies, who, far

from

from being in a condition to invest the city on all sides, were obliged to confine their operations to one corner, leaving two thirds of it open to all manner of supplies. The front, which the general resolved to attack, was defended by the bastions of St. Diego, and St. Andrew; a ravelin, which covered the royal gate, a wet ditch, a covered way, and a glacis. The bastions were in good order, mounted with a great number of fine brass cannon: but the ravelin was not armed; nor the covered way in good repair: the glacis was too low, and the ditch was not carried round the capital of the bastion of St. Diego. The breadth of the ditch was about thirty yards, but the depth of water did not exceed five feet. It was sounded by a detachment, headed by captain Fletcher, who begged leave to undertake this dangerous enterprize, which he atchieved in the midst of the enemy's fire, with the loss of three men. Some straggling seamen having been murdered by the savages, the governor sent out a flag of truce on the 27th, to apologize for these barbarities, and request the release of his own nephew, who had been lately taken in the bay, by the boats of the fleet. Next day, while lieutenant Fryar, with a flag of truce, conducted this prisoner to the town, a detachment of the garrison, intermixed with Indians, sallied out to attack one of the posts of the besiegers: when the savages, without respecting the law of nations, or the sacred character of an officer, under the protection of a flag of truce, fell upon Mr. Fryar, with the most inhuman fury, murdered him on the spot, and mortally wounded the Spanish gentleman who endeavoured to protect his conductor. In their attack, they were soon repulsed by the British party that defended the post, who were so exasperated by their barbarity, that they gave them no quarter.

Meanwhile several mortars bombarded the town day and night, without ceasing; and the engineers were employed in erecting batteries to play upon their works.

works. At length the greater part of their Indians, discouraged by repeated defeats, returned to their own habitations. The fire from the garrison grew faint; and all their defences appeared to be in a ruinous condition. On the 5th of October, the fire of the besiegers was so well directed, that the breach became practicable; and it was hoped the garrison would demand a capitulation: but they seemed to be obstinate and sullen, without courage or activity: they had not exerted themselves in repairing their works; and now they neglected all means of obtaining favourable terms, without having taken the resolution to defend the breach; so that the English general made a disposition for storming the town.

On the 6th, at four o'clock in the morning, the troops destined for this service, filed off from their quarters, in small bodies, to avoid suspicion, and gradually assembling at the church of St. Jago, concealed themselves in the place of arms, and the parallel between the church and the battery. Meanwhile, major Barker maintained a close fire upon the works of the enemy, and those places where they might be lodged or intrenched; the mortars co-operating in the same service. At day-break, a large body of Spaniards was seen formed on the bastion of St. Andrew, as if they had received intimation of the intended assault, and had resolved to annoy the assailants with musquetry and grape-shot from the retired flank of the bastion, where they had still two cannon fit for service; but a few shells falling among them, they retired in confusion. The British troops seized this opportunity, and, directed by the signal of a general discharge from the artillery and mortars, rushed on to the assault, under cover of the thick smoke which blew directly on the town. According to colonel Draper's own account, the total of the troops with which he entered Manilla amounted to little more than 2000, a motley composition of seamen, soldiers, Sepoys, Cafres, Lascars, Topasses, with French and German

man deserters. These assailants mounted the breach with incredible courage and rapidity; while the Spaniards, on the bastion, retired so suddenly, that it was imagined they depended entirely on their mines. Captain Stephenson was immediately ordered to examine the ground; but this precaution was needless. The English troops penetrated into the town with very little opposition, the governor, with the principal magistrates, retiring into the citadel. This retreat was in itself imprudent, because they did not so much as attempt either to defend themselves or to make their escape; and it was accordingly attended with the most disagreeable consequences. Colonel Draper, having no offer of capitulation or surrender made him, could not prevent his troops, for some hours, from making the city feel all the rapaciousness to which a city taken by storm is subjected from the common men; and those he commanded, we may easily suppose, excepting the few regulars among them, were of the most unruly kind. At last, the citadel being in no condition of defence, the archbishop and the magistrates surrendered themselves prisoners at discretion. The marquis de Villa-Medina, with the rest of the Spanish officers, were admitted as prisoners of war, on their parole of honour; and all the Indians were dismissed in safety. The success of the victors was the more agreeable, as it was obtained with very little bloodshed; their loss in the action not exceeding 20 men.

Manilla was no sooner possessed by the British forces, than the admiral went on shore to consult with general Draper on this great event; and to settle a capitulation, that might save so fine a city from destruction: but a draught of terms, in the name of the archbishop, the royal audience, and the city and commerce of Manilla, was presented, which were so unsuitable to their desperate situation, that they were rejected as unsatisfactory and inadmissible. The English commanders then took the pen, and dictated the conditions

conditions on which the city of Manilla should be preserved from plunder, and the inhabitants maintained in their religion, liberties, and properties; to which the Spaniards consented. In consequence of this capitulation, the town and port of Cavite, with the islands and forts depending upon Manilla, were to be surrendered to his Britannic majesty; and four millions of dollars paid as a ransom for the city of Manilla, and the effects of the inhabitants. All the British forces employed in this expedition were but barely sufficient to garrison these important conquests, which were atchieved with so little loss, that not above one hundred men were killed in the whole service.

The acquisition of Luconia, with its towns, treasures, artillery, stores, islands, and dependencies, was rendered compleat by another fortunate event. Admiral Cornish no sooner understood by letters taken in the galley with the Spanish governor's nephew, that the galleon Philippina was arrived from Acapulco at Cajayagan, than he sent the Panther and Argo in quest of her. On the 30th of October, being off the island Capul, near the entrance of the Embocadero, they descried a sail standing to the northward; they came up with, and engaged her: after having been cannonaded two hours at a very small distance, she struck their colours and surrendered. But they were not a little surprised, when the Spanish general came on board, to learn, that, instead of the St. Philippina, they had taken the Santissima Trinidad, which had departed from Manilla on the 1st day of August, bound for Acapulco. She was a very large ship, so thick in the sides, that the shot of the Panther did not penetrate any part of her, except the upper works. She had 800 men on board; was pierced for sixty cannon, but no more than 13 were mounted. The merchandize on board was registered to the amount of one million and a half of dollars, and the whole cargo supposed to be worth double that sum; so that this capture

capture was a valuable addition to the conqueft, and a frefh wound to the enemy.

At no period of time had the Spanifh monarchy fuffered fuch grievous and mortifying difafters, as thofe fhe fuftained in the courfe of this year, from a war into which fhe was precipitately plunged, againft all the dictates of found policy and caution, meerly to gratify the private inclinations of her fovereign.

The recovery of St. John's, in Newfoundland, was likewife numbered among the fucceffes which gave a luftre to the Britifh arms in the courfe of this autumn; and was regained without much trouble or lofs.

Thus the operations of war were profecuted with unremitting ardour in the Eaft and Weft Indies; while the king ftill perfifted in his refolution to embrace the firft opportunity of re-eftablifhing peace, which, exclufive of motives of humanity, he thought abfolutely neceffary for the advantage of his own people. He faw them exhaufting their blood and treafure in quarrels, not their own, upon the continent of Germany; and that this fatal drain could not be effectually ftopped, but by a general pacification. The national debt was encreafed to fuch an enormous burden, as feemed to threaten the immediate ruin of public credit, which a peace alone could prevent. The original fcope of the war, namely, the fecurity of the Britifh colonies in America, was fully accomplifhed; forty fhips of the line were rendered ufelefs by hard fervice: 30,000 recruits were wanted for the army; and the war had occafioned fuch a fcarcity of men, that, during the preceding year, it had been found impracticable to raife above 1500 recruits for the eftablifhed regiments, though great premiums had been offered to engage men in the fervice. Thefe confiderations reinforced the other reafons which induced his majefty to wifh for peace; and his fentiments were warmly efpoufed by all the members of his council.

The

The king of Sardinia is said to have offered his best offices for reviving the negotiation between the courts of London and Versailles; and, in all probability, his mediation was cordially embraced by both. Certain it is, they agreed to treat in good earnest, and to send mutually to each other, a person of the first rank, vested with the powers and character of ambassador and plenipotentiary. The duke of Bedford being chosen for this purpose, by the king of Great Britain, set out for France in the beginning of September; and, at the same time, the duke de Nivernois arrived in England with the same character from his most christian majesty. Many difficulties were levelled by the hearty desire of peace, which animated both monarchs. The humours and interests of their German allies no longer obstructed the progress of the negotiation, which now turned only upon the re-establishment of peace between England and the houses of Bourbon. The king of Prussia delivered from two formidable enemies, in consequence of his late accommodation with Russia and Sweden, was now in a condition to take care of himself: beside, that system was changed, by which his interests had been so warmly espoused at the court of London. In settling the preliminaries, which were discussed in concert with the kings of Spain and Portugal, the belligerant powers made allowances for what might have happened in the East and West Indies, and regulated the concessions to be made in proportion to the success or miscarriage that might attend the British armaments.

We have now nothing remaining unnoticed, but an unfortunate affair which was the last transaction of the war; and which stands in a manner unconnected with any other. Upon the dispute with Spain, some private merchants and adventurers had fitted out two ships called the Lord Clive and the Ambuscade privateers. The former, being equal in force to a ship of 50 guns, was commanded by one captain M'Namara, who was esteemed as a brave experienced officer,

officer, and he was to be joined by other ships, particularly a Portuguese frigate, to proceed on an expedition to the South Seas. In December 1762, the whole squadron arrived in the river Plata; which they found much better prepared to receive them than they had imagined. The expedition was originally planned for getting possession of Buenos Ayres; but finding the navigation of the river very difficult, they resolved, before they proceeded farther, to attack Nova Colonia; a colony on the north side of the river Plate, which the Spaniards had some time before taken from the Portuguese: an English pilot, whom they found on board a Portuguese ship, undertaking to bring the commodore within pistol-shot of the chief battery on shore. On the 6th of January 1763, the Lord Clive made the signal for engaging, and soon after anchored under the fire of the eastmost battery of the place, while the Ambuscade was severely handled by the fire of the middle and westmost batteries, and from some Spanish frigates. A most fierce cannonading began on both sides, which lasted from eleven in the forenoon till three in the afternoon; when the enemy's fire, that had been before kept up very steadily, began to flag, and they themselves to retire to the eastmost battery, as the place of greatest safety. In this state of the engagement, when the English expected every moment to see the Spanish colours struck, the Lord Clive was found to be on fire. No sooner did the flames appear, than it was easy to perceive that it was impossible to extinguish them. In an instant the attack was discontinued: the Ambuscade, with vast difficulty, got clear of the other ship's flames, but was little better than a wreck, having received a great number of shot between wind and water. As to the crew of the Lord Clive, some perished in the water, some in the flames, and many by the enemy's fire, which recommenced on the occasion: so that no more than 78 of 340, the complement of the ship when the engagement began, escaped with their lives, the ship blowing

blowing up about eight in the evening. The fate of the unhappy fufferers was the more affecting, as it would have been certain deftruction for any of the other fhips to have moved to their relief. The Ambufcade, in danger of finking every moment, found means to ftop her leaks in the river Plate, and to efcape to the Portuguefe fettlement of Rio de Janeiro, with the lofs of 24 killed. It ought however to be confeffed, that fuch of the Lord Clive's crew as reached the fhore, were humaneiy received, treated, and cloathed, by the Spaniards, whofe refentment feemed to be extinguifhed in the calamity of their enemies.

The definitive treaty of peace was figned at Paris on February 10th, 1763; and the terms of it were more advantageous to Great Britain and her allies, than thofe which were agreed to by the late minifter. It muft be acknowleged that Great Britain, by extending the frontiers of Canada, to the middle of the Miffifippi, gained a large tract of fertile country lying on the banks of that river, befide the advantage of a free navigation upon it, and the poffeffion of the port of Mobile: but, in order to fecure the Englifh American colonies from all poffibility of difturbance from the French, that reftlefs nation ought to have been expelled from the whole country of Louifiana.

England, by this peace, likewife gained an acceffion, in France's ceding to her the ifland of Grenada; which, when fully cultivated and peopled, may be of fome confequence. She moreover acquired the unfettled iflands of Dominica, Tobago, and St. Vincent; but yielded to France the ifland of St. Lucie, faid to be worth all the reft. She retains the fettlement of Senegal on the coaft of Africa, by which fhe engroffes the whole gum trade of that country; as for the rock of Goree, which fhe reftored, it was no great facrifice. The article that relates to the Eaft Indies, was dictated by the directors of the Englifh company; and furely the French

have

have no reason to complain of its severity, as it restores them to the possession of all the places they had at the beginning of the war, on condition that they shall maintain neither forts nor forces in the kingdom of Bengal: thus they will enjoy all their former advantages in trade, without the temptation and expence of forming schemes of conquest and dominion.

The demolition of the works belonging to the harbour of Dunkirk, is no doubt a sensible mortification to France, though of little consequence to England, while a squadron of ships is kept at anchor in the Downs. It became an object of some consideration in the war of queen Anne, as a nest of privateers that infested the channel; and was afterward used as an inflammatory term of faction. The danger that may threaten England from Dunkirk, does not depend upon vessels which could be received into the harbour; but must arise from a strong squadron of ships of the line, which may always lie at anchor in the road.

The liberty of cutting logwood in the bay of Honduras, granted to the subjects of Great Britain, was undoubtedly a great point gained in their favour; but their obliging themselves to demolish their fortifications on that coast, was a tacit acknowlegement that the privilege was not founded upon right, but derived from favour. The cession of Florida, with the forts of St. Augustine and Pensacola, to Great Britain, was an object of much greater importance. It extended the British dominions along the coast to the mouth of the Missisippi. It removed an asylum for the slaves of the English colonies, who were continually making their escape to St. Augustine. It deprived the Spaniards of an easy avenue, through which they had it in their power to invade Georgia and Carolina; it afforded a large extent of improveable territory, a strong frontier, and a good port in the bay of Mexico, both for the convenience of trade, and the annoyance of the Spaniards in any future conteft. But neither the ceffion of Florida, nor the renunciation of the right to the fifhery, nor the permiffion granted to the Englifh logwood cutters, nor the evacuation of Portugal; nor all thefe articles together, can ever be efteemed equivalent to the reftitution of the Havanna; for which, indeed, the Spanifh monarch had no fuitable compenfation to make, without difmembring his kingdom; unlefs he had thrown into the fcale with his other conceffions, that of a free navigation, without fearch, to the Britifh traders on the coaft of New Spain. The crown of Spain was much favoured by the article which ftipulates, that the conquefts, not included in the treaty either as ceffions or reftitutions, fhould be reftored without compenfation. Neither France nor Spain had any armament on foot, from which they could expect the leaft acquifition or fuccefs; whereas the miniftry of England had great reafon to believe that the ifland of Luconia was already reduced.

On the whole, the treaty, though it might have been more favourable in fome articles, certainly confirmed great and folid advantages to Great Britain; and will remain as an eternal monument of that moderation which forms the moft amiable flower in the wreath of conqueft.

Such was the iffue of a war, fanguinary beyond example, which had raged with uncommon fury in the four quarters of the globe; which had ruined many fair provinces; and, in the fpace of feven years, deftroyed above a million of lives; which had coft Great Britain, in particular, above two hundred and eighty thoufand men, including a great number of brave and able officers, with an incredible quantity of treafure; and increafed the burthen of her national debt, from fourfcore, to one hundred and thirty millions fterling.

The

The Royal Navy of GREAT BRITAIN as it stood at the close of the Year 1762.

N. B. Those in *Italics* were taken from the French or Spaniards.

FIRST RATES.

Guns
- 100 Britannia
- 100 Royal George
- 100 R. *Sovereign*

SECOND RATES.

- 90 Blenheim
- 90 Duke
- 90 St. George
- 90 Namur
- 90 *Neptune*
- 90 Ocean
- 90 Prince
- 90 Princess Royal
- 84 Royal William
- 90 Sandwich
- 90 Union

THIRD RATES.

- 64 Africa
- 64 *Alcide*
- 74 Arrogant
- 64 Bedford
- 64 *Belliqueux*
- 74 Bellona
- 64 Belleisle
- 64 *Bienfaisant*
- 70 Buckingham
- 70 Burford
- 80 Cambridge
- 64 Captain
- 74 *Centaur*
- 70 Chichester
- 74 Cornwall
- 74 *Culloden*
- 64 Defiance
- 66 Devonshire
- 70 Dorsetshire
- 74 Dragon
- 74 Dublin
- 64 Elizabeth
- 64 Essex
- 74 Fame
- 80 *Foudroyant*
- 70 Grafton
- 64 Hampton-Court
- 74 Hercules
- 74 Hero
- 74 Kent
- 74 Lenox
- 74 *Magnanime*

Guns
- 68 Marlborough
- 74 Mars
- 64 *Modeste*
- 64 Monmouth
- 64 Nassau
- 80 Newark
- 74 Norfolk
- 70 Northumberland
- 70 Orford
- 64 Pr. Frederick
- 80 Princess Amelia
- 60 Princess Mary
- 64 Revenge
- 74 Shrewsbury
- 70 Somerset
- 74 Sterling-Castle
- 74 *Superb*
- 70 Swiftsure
- 74 *Temeraire*
- 70 Temple
- 74 Terrible
- 74 Thunderer
- 74 Torbay
- 64 *Trident*
- 74 Valiant
- 70 Vanguard
- 74 Warspight

FOURTH RATES.

- 60 Achilles
- 60 America
- 60 Anson
- 50 Antelope
- 50 Assistance
- 50 Centurion
- 50 Chatham
- 50 Chester
  Dreadnought
- 50 Deptford
- 60 Dunkirk
- 60 Edgar
- 50 Falkland
- 50 Falmouth
- 60 *Firme*
- 60 *Florentine*
- 50 Guernsey
- 50 Hampshire
- 60 *Intrepide*
- 50 *Isis*
- 60 Lion
- 60 Medway
- 60 Montague

Guns
- 50 Norwich
- 60 Nottingham
- 50 *Oriflame*
- 60 Panther
- 60 Pembroke
- 50 Portland
- 50 Preston
- 60 Prince of Orange
- 60 Rippon
- 50 Romney
- 50 Rochester
- 50 Salisbury
- 50 Sutherland
- 60 Weymouth
- 50 Winchester
- 60 Windsor
- 60 York

FIFTH RATES.

- 32 Adventure
- 32 Alarm
- 32 *Arethusa*
- 32 Æolus
- 32 *Bologne*
- 32 Boston
- 32 *Blonde*
- 36 Brilliant
- 32 *Crescent*
- 38 *Danae*
- 32 Diana
- 44 Dover
- 32 Emerald
- 44 Enterprize
- 32 *Flora*
- 44 Gosport
- 32 Juno
- 32 Lark
- 44 Launceston
- 30 Looe
- 44 Lynn
- 36 *Melampe*
- 32 Minerva
- 32 Montreal
- 32 *Niger*
- 36 Pallas
- 44 Penzance
- 44 Phœnix
- 44 Prince Edw.
- 32 Quebec
- 44 *Rainbow*
- 36 Renown
- 32 *Repulse*
- 32 Richmond
- 32 Saphire

Guns
- 32 Southampton
- 32 Stagg
- 32 Thames
- 32 *Thetis*
- 30 Torrington
- 32 Tweed
- 36 Venus
- 32 *Vestal*
- 44 Woolwich

SIXTH RATES.

- 28 Actæon
- 28 *Active*
- 20 Aldborough
- 24 *Amazon*
- 28 *Aquilon*
- 28 Argo
- 24 Arundel
- 28 Boreas
- 28 Cerberus
- 24 Coventry
- 20 Deal-Castle
- 24 Dolphin
- 24 Echo
- 20 Flamborough
- 24 Fowey
- 24 Garland
- 20 Gibraltar
- 20 Glasgow
- 20 Greyhound
- 24 Hind
- 24 Kennington
- 28 Levant
- 24 Lively
- 28 Liverpool
- 28 Lizard
- 24 Ludlow Castle
- 28 Maidstone
- 24 Mercury
- 28 Milford
- 24 Nightingale
- 24 Portmahon
- 20 Rose
- 24 Rye
- 20 Scarborough
- 20 Seaford
- 20 Seahorse
- 28 Shannon
- 24 Sheerness
- 24 Solebay
- 0 Syren
- 24 Surprize
- 28 Tartar
- 4 *Terpsichore*
- 28 Trent

NAVAL HISTORY.

Guns		Guns.		Guns.			
28	Trent	14	Grampus	8	Savage	Infernal	
28	*Valeur*	10	Granado	14	Senegal	Fire-Sh. no Guns	
28	Unicorn	8	Goree	14	Sardome	Ætna	
24	Wager	8	Happy	8	Speedwell	Cormorant	
	SLOOPS.	8	Hazard	10	Spy	Grampus	
		14	Hornet	14	Swallow	Lightning	
14	Albany	14	Hound	14	Swift	Pluto	
10	Alderney	10	Hunter	14	Swan	Raven	
10	Antigua	14	Jamaica	16	Tamer	Roman Emperor	
12	Badger	10	King's Fisher		Terror	Proserpine	
16	Baltimore	8	Laurel	10	Thunder	Salamander	
10	Barbados	6	Lurcher	14	Trial	Stromboli	
10	Bonetta	18	Merlin	14	Vulture	Vesuvius	
8	Cruzier	16	Mortar	8	Wasp	YACHTS.	
18	Cygnet	18	Nautilus	16	Weazle	10 Dorset	
10	Diligence	8	Peggy	8	Wolf	8 Fubbs	
14	Dispatch	10	Pomona	10	Zephir	8 Katherine	
10	Druid	10	Otter		BOMB Vessels.	Augusta	
14	Escorte	14	Pelican				
16	Favourite	14	Porcupine		Basilisk	STORESHIPS.	
18	Ferret	18	Postillion		Blast	20 Crown	
8	*Flambre's Prize*	8	Ranger		Carcass	24 South-Sea Castle	
8	Fly		Racehorse		Firedrake		
14	Fortune	14	Saltash		Furnace		

Ships out of Commission and building.

Rates.	Guns.	Names.	Rates.	Guns.	Names.	Rates.	Guns.	Names.
3	74	Albion	5	44	Eltham	3	84	Ramillies
3	64	Asia	5	44	Expedition	3	64	Royal Oak
4	60	Augusta	3	80	*Formidable*	4	60	Rupert
5	44	Anglesea	4	50	Gloucester	4	50	Ruby
5	32	Aurora	5	44	Glory			R. Charlotte Yacht
2	90	*Barfleur*	6	28	Guadalupe			
		Ditto, a new ship	5	44	Hastings	3	64	Suffolk
3	80	Boyne	5	44	Hector	4	60	St. Albans
4	50	Bristol	5	30	Jason	6	24	Sphinx
6	24	Blandford	2	90	London	•3	74	Triumph
	90	Blenheim	5	44	Mary Galley		28	Vengeance
		Hospital-ship			Martin Sloop		10	Viper
3	74	Canada			Mary Yacht	1	100	Victory
4	60	Canterbury	3	74	Monarch			Vulture Sloop
3	74	*Courageux*	4	50	Nonsuch	4		Warwick
4	50	Colchester	3	80	Pr. Caroline	5		Winchelsea
3	74	Defiance	4	60	Pr. Louisa	4	60	Worcester
6	24	Experiment	4	60	Plymouth			William and
4	60	Eagle	5	44	Poole			Mary Yacht
3	64	Edinburgh	1	90	Queen	3	64	Yarmouth
4	60	Exeter	1	100	Royal Anne			

Complement of Men, and Weight of Metal, in the Royal Navy.

Ships of three Decks.				Guns.	Men.	Metal.		
Guns.	Men.	Metal.			60	420	24	12 6
100	850	42	24 12 6		60	400	24	9 6
90	750	32	18 12 6		50	350	24	12 6
80	600	32	18 9 6		50	300	18	9 6
Ships of two Decks.					44 40	250	18	9 6
80 74	650	32	18 9		Frigates of one Deck.			
70	520	32	18 9		36	240	12	6
63	Ditto				32	220	12	6
66	Ditto				28	200	9	4
64	480	24	12 6		20	160	9	4

The End of the SEVENTH VOLUME.

www.ingramcontent.com/pod-product-compliance
Lightning Source LLC
Chambersburg PA
CBHW051843300426
44117CB00006B/250